Hindu Rashtra

Political analyst, author and columinst in both English and Hindi, Ashutosh is one of the most recognised and credible figures in Indian televion and digital journalism today. He began his three decades long career in print before drifting to television. He was part of the original team of AAJTAK and went on to be Managing Editor, IBN7 for eight years before he quit to join the Aam Aadmi Party. In 2018, disillusioned with politics, he returned to journalism to start a hugely popular YouTube channel called SatyaHindi, along with a few journalist friends.

He has authored three books, *Anna: 13 Days that Awakened India*, *The Crown Prince, the Gladiator and the Hope: Battle for Change* and *Mukhaute ka Rajdharma*.

Hindu Rashtra

ASHUTOSH

First published by Context, an imprint of Westland Publications Private Limited, in 2019

Published by Context, an imprint of Westland Books, a division of Nasadiya Technologies Private Limited, in 2023

No. 269/2B, First Floor, 'Irai Arul', Vimalraj Street, Nethaji Nagar, Alapakkam Main Road, Maduravoyal, Chennai 600095

Westland, the Westland logo, Context and the Context logo are the trademarks of Nasadiya Technologies Private Limited, or its affiliates.

Copyright © Ashutosh, 2019

The excerpt on pp. 92 – 93 is taken from *Being the Other: The Muslim in India* by Saeed Naqvi, first published by Aleph Book Company in 2016.

ISBN: 9789360452896

10 9 8 7 6 5 4 3 2 1

The views and opinions expressed in this work are the author's own and the facts are as reported by him, and the publisher is in no way liable for the same.

All rights reserved

Typeset by Jojy Philip, New Delhi 110 015
Printed at

No part of this book may be reproduced, or stored in a retrieval system, or transmitted in any form or by any means, electronic, mechanical, photocopying, recording, or otherwise, without express written permission of the publisher.

Contents

Preface to the Second Edition   vii

Introduction   xi

1. Making Sense of Saffronisation   1
2. The Politics of Gau Raksha   14
3. Victimhood No More: Dalits versus Hindutva   37
4. Hindutva at War with History   60
5. The Kashmir Question   88
6. The Line between Nationalism and Terrorism   115
7. Matters of Statecraft   131
8. Wheels of Justice Squeaking and Squealing   161
9. Hindutva and the Caucus Race   185
10. The Money Trick   209
11. Hindutva, Media and Propaganda   228

Epilogue   261

Endnotes   282

Acknowledgements   327

Preface to the Second Edition

What is a Hindu Rashtra? Is the Narendra Modi government hellbent on making India a Hindu Rashtra? Will minorities be treated as second-class citizens and have no civil or religious rights? Will the constitution of India be changed to make India a Hindu Rashtra, and will India be officially declared as a Hindu Rashtra, like Pakistan and Iran have become Islamic republics? And in this Hindu Rashtra, will parliamentary democracy survive or will it be a theocratic state? These are troubling questions which are staring us in the face. As of now, there are no definite answers. But there is speculation that if Modi comes back with a bigger majority in 2024 than he did in 2019, it is very likely that the Hindu Rashtra will become a constitutional reality.

There is no denying the fact that since 2014, when Modi formed the government at the Centre with a majority—the last time a single party won majority in Parliament was in 1984—a cataclysmic change has been ushered in through the use of state power. Forces of Hindutva that were mostly dormant during the Congress regimes suddenly woke up, and the aggressive manifestation of Hindutva has shaken the basic foundation of our liberal democracy. Today, the nature of the political discourse has changed, the relationship between state and citizens has acquired a different connotation, minority rights have shrunk. Secularism, once considered crucial to the basic structure of the constitution, has become a cuss word; the Hindu religion has become the defining creed and social equilibrium has been disrupted, with all things leaning right.

The surround sound is the demand for a Hindu Rashtra. In the garb of Hindutva, there is a call for genocide of Muslims while state machineries look the other way. The Supreme Court is concerned, but the train of radicalisation is running unhindered. Leaders of the RSS and the BJP are unapologetic while asserting that the so-called mistakes of the past have to be corrected and in the words of Sunil Ambekar, a high-ranking pracharak of the RSS, 'India has to be reclaimed'. To assume that Narendra Modi becoming the prime minister was a routine transfer of power, as stated by a few prominent intellectuals of the country in 2014, is a mistake. In my opinion, it could only be equated with the transfer of power which took place on 15 August 1947. Modi is the mascot of that 'reclamation project' whose ultimate goal is to make India a Hindu Rashtra. He is no ordinary leader; he is a product of a belief-system that insists that Hindus were wronged by Muslims and Christians in the past and 'Hindu-united' is the only way forward.

Surprisingly, the phrase 'Hindu Rashtra' has not been defined as a thought structure. It's a vague idea. Its advocates claim that unlike the Islamic state, the Hindu Rashtra is not a theocratic state, it's not a religious concept, it does not believe in discrimination between different faiths. In the words of M.S. Golwalkar, the second chief of the RSS, '...it is amazing that some people should harbour fear that the "minorities" will live in mortal peril if Hindu Rashtra comes into its own. The fear, if at all genuine, can only be due to their misconception that "Hindu Rashtra" would treat other religious groups in much the same way as Semitic religions did.' He further claimed, 'Here in this land, there can be no objection to God being called by any name whatsoever. Ingrained in this soil is love and respect for all faiths and religious beliefs. He cannot be a son of soil at all who is intolerant of other faiths.'

Decades later, Mohan Bhagwat, the present chief of the RSS, when faced with the serious charge of increasing attacks on Muslims in India, said, 'Ours is a Hindu Rashtra. This in no way means that Muslims are excluded. The day it is said that Muslims are not wanted, Hindutva will cease to exist.' In the RSS fold, the Sar-Sanghchalak's words are taken very seriously. Why, then, have attacks on Muslims continued? Can it be construed that due to Modi's ascendence, Bhagwat's authority has weakened to the extent that his words go unheeded? Or is this a classic case of doublespeak?

The same Golwalkar who talked about 'love and respect for all faiths' sings a different tune in his book *We or Our Nationhood Defined*. He is no longer a reconciler. He spews venom against Muslims and Christians. He writes, 'the foreign races in Hindusthan must either adopt the Hindu culture and language, must learn to respect and hold in reverence Hindu religion, must entertain no idea but those of the glorification of the Hindu race and culture, i.e., of the Hindu nation and must lose their separate existence to merge in the Hindu race, or may stay in the country, wholly subordinated to the Hindu nation, claiming nothing, deserving no privileges, far less preferential treatment, not even citizens' rights.'

It is rather interesting that the RSS has since disowned Golwalkar's statement, which could be interpreted as an attack on minorities. To dispel its anti-Muslim image, Sunil Ambekar opined that 'Hindu Rashtra is not anti-Muslim. It never was.' He writes, 'Sangh ... always propounded the idea that Bharat belongs to all who were born here and continue to live here, irrespective of religion, faith or the school of thought they may belong to.'

The reality, of course, is different. His assertion is not supported by actions on the ground. For example, in the assembly elections in Karnataka in May 2023, every effort was made to whip up anti-Muslim hysteria. The imaginary issues of love jihad and land jihad were declared core issues. In the last few years, the consumption of halal meat, a ban on hijab in schools, an economic boycott of Muslims and other such subjects were foregrounded by Hindutva forces and the BJP was seen supporting them vigorously. The state machinery appeared to be favouring Hindus at the cost of Muslims.

Mob lynching continues still, in the name of cow slaughter, in various parts of the country. A recent example is from Rajasthan, where two Muslim boys were burnt alive, allegedly by Bajrang Dal members. In Uttar Pradesh, bulldozers seem to have become symbols of state sponsored atrocities against minorities. Assam, under its chief minister Himanta Biswa Sarma, is turning into a new laboratory for Hindutva. A former leader of the Congress party, Sarma seems to be out to prove that he is more Hindutvavadi than the original pracharaks of the RSS. Leaders like Anurag Thakur, who allegedly exhorted people to violence during the Delhi assembly elections, when the movement against the NRC and Citizen Amendment Act was ongoing, was promoted to Cabinet rank in the Modi government. Yet, the Modi government talks about Sabka Sath, Sabka Vikas (all together, progress for all). After the 2019 victory, this slogan was further improved to Sabka Sath, Sabka Vikas aur Sabka Vishwas (all together, progress for all and the confidence of all).

Modi is the most powerful prime minister India has had since Indira Gandhi. He has total control not only over his government but also over his party. No other leader dares challenge or defy his authority. He has emerged as a cult figure for those who profess their allegiance to Hindutva and aspire to make India a Hindu Rashtra. Despite his public posturing that he believes in harmony between different faiths, the anti-Muslim rhetoric is loud and unabashed, and government agencies have been accused of being partisan in the execution of rule of law while dealing with Hindu-Muslim conflict. Why and how has this become the reality of India? My book tries to answer this question in some detail.

Hindu Rashtra deals with the first five years of the Modi government. It examines the transformation that Indian society underwent between 2014 and 2019 and the role of the state under Modi. The process which began in 2014 got a further boost with the BJP's victory in 2019. As I have argued in the book, the installation of the Modi government in 2014 was the starting point of the march of the ideological state in India; that process was further strengthened with the victory of the BJP in 2019. Today, Hindutva is even more entrenched in society. The state is more ideologically inspired. Democratic institutions that were once vibrant have meekly surrendered.

In the first five years, the Modi government was busy creating an ecosystem for the exaltation of Hindutva as an idea. In its second term, it is more focused on making structural changes to subvert the secular-democratic edifice of the country, which was based on Nehruvian consensus, to make way for the construction of the Hindu Rashtra. The removal of Article 370, the legislation on Triple Talaq, the Citizenship Amendment Act 2019 were not stray steps. They were intended to pave the way for the construction of the utopia called Hindu Rashtra.

Introduction

'Hitler was a great leader.'

'What did you say?' I was shocked.

'Yes, he was a great leader. He was demonised because he suffered defeat; because he lost.'

This was my younger brother, who I was meeting after many years. Unlike me, he had studied in an English medium school. He had spent most of his life in metropolitan cities. I had reacted rather sharply after seeing Modi on TV and that is where our conversation had begun. I had some inkling about his political preferences and I wanted to delve further into his mind. I told him, 'Do you have any idea how many people were killed by Hitler in concentration camps? 11 million in total including 6 million Jews.'

He told me that he in no way condoned what Hitler had done to the Jews and many others. Then he said, 'Let me ask you, which ruler of those times did not kill people? Have you forgotten Stalin and other communist leaders? But you all call them great! Why?' He had a point.

I knew he was a Modi supporter like my father and my other brother. But what stunned me was his ideological conviction. With intent to provoke him I said, 'Look at the mandate Modi had when he started, but he squandered it all. He made a mess of India's foreign policy. He has no idea about international politics. India's relationship with almost every neighbouring country has deteriorated. The relationship with Pakistan was always tense, but now it has gone from bad to worse due to which Kashmir is burning. China has swooped in and developed close ties with Pakistan and Sri Lanka. There has been no improvement in relations with Bangladesh and the only Hindu state in the world, Nepal, too, is no longer India's friend.'

His answer was caustic. 'Modi has done everything to improve our foreign policy. But there is an international conspiracy hatched by Muslim and Christian countries that do not want him to succeed. They all want him to fail, just so that Hindus don't regain their past glory.'

To be fair, he did not utter a word against Muslims or Christians. He was focussed on the words 'Hindu' and 'Hindutva'. I don't know if he deliberately avoided that topic or if his views about different religions diverged from that of the Hindutva warriors. I only knew I was talking to a man who had been converted to Hindutva. I decided to change the topic and move on. But his words kept ringing in my ears. I wondered if he had joined the RSS. I avoided asking him that.

This conversation reminded me of another conversation I had had with my father more than a quarter of a century ago. I was then studying in JNU, which had not yet been declared the bastion of 'anti-nationals' or of 'terrorists'. It was in many ways a radical university dominated by the Left ideology. The student wing of The Communist Party of India, Marxist, called the Student Federation of India had an overwhelming presence and used to dominate the public and academic space in the campus. This was also the time when the Ayodhya movement was on the rise. I had just joined *Saptahik Hindustan*, the prestigious Hindi weekly of the Hindustan Times group. A Hindu–Muslim riot had broken out in the Madanpura area of Banaras, the holy city in Uttar Pradesh (UP), which in 2014 would be PM Modi's parliamentary constituency. My father was posted there at the time. He used to live near Orderly Bazar. I was very upset with the kind of campaign being run by the volunteers of the Vishwa Hindu Parishad (VHP), Bajrang Dal (the youth wing of the VHP), the Bharatiya Janata Party (BJP) and the propaganda they were spreading in the streets of Banaras. Since I had mostly been away in JNU, I had no idea about the degree of vitriol and the level of hatred spread in the public domain. It was common in those days to hear the provocative slogan—'Jab katuwe kate jayenge to Ram Ram chillayenge. (If Muslims are cut into pieces, then they will chant Lord Ram's name.)'

I was sent to cover the riots in Banaras. One morning I got back home after visiting Nazeer Benarsi, the famous Urdu poet of the city. He was ill and bed-ridden. His son had allegedly been killed by the UP police. Everyone seemed to know about the incident but it was not reported by the mainline newspapers of the city. I was extremely upset and as I reached home I narrated the whole incident to my father and brother. They seemed to know about it. I don't remember which one of them said, 'Agar danga karenge to maare hi jaayenge. (If they indulge in rioting, then they will be killed.)' It was the most simplistic sentence I had ever heard. I was stunned. I did not know what to say.

My father had been a Congress party supporter all his life. He had great admiration for Jawaharlal Nehru, Indira Gandhi and, up to a certain extent, Rajiv Gandhi. I don't remember him voting for any party other than the Congress, except in 1977. But the Ram mandir movement led by the Rashtriya Swayamsewak Sangh (RSS) and its affiliate organisation VHP, and politically supported by the BJP, changed it all. He became a mute supporter of Hindutva politics. We were a middle class family and politics was rarely discussed, and my father did not speak much anyway. But one day, when we got into a bit of an argument, he did not have good words for the Congress. My brother was then in his early twenties and he was more vocal. 'Ye Musalman isi layak hai, khate yahan hain aur gaate Pakistan ka hai. (These Muslims deserve this. They eat in India but sing praises of Pakistan).' My angry retort was drowned in their chorus. They were angst ridden and wanted to share it with me. 'Why? Why should the Ram temple not be built in Ayodhya?' they questioned. I argued, 'How do you know Ram was born there? How can you take revenge on Muslims for a crime committed more than five hundred years ago by some bigot?' To this, I was told point-blank, 'Keep your gyaan (knowledge) to yourself and don't teach us. If Ram temple is not built in Ayodhya then where will it be made?' I had no answer. My views had no takers. I was in the minority and kept quiet.

As a young student, my father had migrated to Faizabad from a small village in Gonda district. Ayodhya was part of the Faizabad district. In its zeal to erase every symbol of Islam, the Yogi Adityanath government in UP, changed the name Faizabad to Ayodhya in 2018. So, now the whole district is called Ayodhya, including Ayodhya itself. My father spent many years there before he moved out and got a government job. He is a devout Hindu and a religious person. He regularly visits temples and other places of worship. When he visits me in Noida, he gets up early in the morning, bathes and goes to the temple in our apartment complex. He has had many Muslim friends. And my Muslim friends were always welcome in my house.

Neither he nor my mother had ever objected to their presence. He loves his non-vegetarian food. I have never heard him say anything objectionable about Muslims or Islam. But that day he was livid. He was upset—Why had the Ram temple not been built? Why was it demolished in the first place?

As a child I did try to be religious. I was a regular visitor to Satya Narain Bhagwan's katha recitations and used to read the Ram Charit Manas (the story of Lord Ram, which is considered to be a religious book by the Hindus) for a whole day at a stretch, and sometimes the whole night, whenever the reading was organised in my neighbourhood in Mirzapur, UP. Many a times, I tried to ape my older cousin who used to live with us and read the Hanuman Chalisa (the story of Lord Hanuman, which is also considered a religious text) after a morning shower. I did it for months. Like other Hindus, I used to bow my head at every temple I passed by and every Tuesday I used to visit the Hanuman temple. But later in my life, and much before coming to JNU, I turned into a non-believer. My father and other family members never insisted that I should continue reading religious books; it never bothered them that I stopped being religious. My father was more worried about my education and employment. Over a period of time I turned more radical in my views while he continued to be an orthodox Hindu. But that was never a bone of contention between us; we never fought on religious matters. Yes, we did have our little skirmishes on political issues, especially when he used to praise the BJP.

My father is in his eighties now—fit and energetic. And still the same. He still supports the BJP and Modi but I know that he does not subscribe to their ultra aggressive politics. A few years ago when I was in the Aam Aadmi Party, he heard Modi launching a personal attack on Arvind Kejriwal in a TV programme and told me, 'Ye theek nahi hai. (This is not right.)' When on TV in my capacity as party spokesperson, if I got aggressive with fellow panellists in TV debates, he would gently say, 'Shant raha karo. Apni baat shanti se kahni chahiye. (You should not lose your cool; you should put forth your arguments gently.)' For me, he is an ideal Hindu who loves his Hindu identity. He might be called a conservative but he never placed any restrictions, of any kind, on his children, be it on matters of religion or our daily lives, on what to wear or with whom to mingle or not. He is no hate monger. He wants to live in peace and harmony with every one—Hindu, Muslim, Sikh or Christian.

One must give credit to the RSS that in the last ninety-four years it has succeeded in making people like my father more aware of their Hindu identity. It has succeeded in luring a section of such Hindus away from the Congress and other secular parties to the BJP. Its clever rhetoric and perseverance has made Hindutva attractive to a section of young Hindus like my younger brother, who has imbibed their interpretation of history and politics.

But pause for a minute and remember that despite its best performance, the BJP could garner only 31 per cent votes in the 2014 parliamentary elections. It did, of course, manage to install its government in more than twenty states, but one cannot overlook the fact that as recently as 11 December 2018, the BJP lost three of its powerful citadels in north India—Rajasthan, Madhya Pradesh and Chhattisgarh—to a party which it thought was on its deathbed, to a party it had promised to eradicate from the country's consciousness, to a party headed by a man the BJP had pejoratively called Pappu. Yes, Rahul Gandhi, the fifth generation leader of the Nehru–Gandhi family, who has always been viewed as the weakest in the dynasty, has emerged as a very strong challenger to Modi for the 2019 elections. Since the Gujarat elections in December 2017, Gandhi has metamorphosed himself into a Hindu leader. He is hopping from one temple to another, flaunting his Hindu identity, proclaiming that he wears the janeyu (sacred thread), and not hiding his gotra (which traces the ancestry of a person according to Hinduism). The election manifesto of the Congress party in these three states is no different from that of the BJP's, with programmes and promises to make Hindus happy. It has readily accepted the cow in its fold as a divine animal, and is ready to make every effort to make its life comfortable.

When I asked a very senior RSS leader how he would counter the newly acquired Hindutva of the Congress party, his reply was interesting. He said, 'This is what the RSS wanted. Despite 80 per cent people living in India being Hindu, they never used to flaunt their religious identity. They used to feel ashamed of being called Hindu. If Rahul Gandhi and the Congress are forced to claim themselves as Hindu, it is a positive development for us.'

Since the rise of Hindutva in the late 1980s, the RSS, the BJP and the Hindutva warriors have been attacking the Congress on the issue of secularism, calling it pseudo-secular. They have accused the Congress and other secular parties of pursuing the policy of Muslim appeasement. The allegation is not entirely untrue. Some of these secular parties shamelessly catered to the vested interests of Muslim clergies and danced to their tunes. It is also a fact that since independence, the socio-economic condition of Muslims has deteriorated drastically. The Sachar Committee report is a revelation.[1] It said that as a community, the condition of Muslims was worse than that of the scheduled castes. And though Muslims constituted 14 per cent of the population, only 2.5 per cent of them were employed in the bureaucracy at the time of the report.

But two events turned the tide. The reversal of the judgment passed by the supreme court (SC) on the Shah Bano case in parliament by the Congress government in 1986 and the Ram mandir movement led by the RSS in the late 1980s and early 1990s. If the former convinced the majority community that the Indian state led by the Congress went out of its way to bend backwards and pamper Muslims then the latter helped Hindus discover their 'Hindu-ness'. Both the events in my opinion are complimentary, organically interconnected and clearly establish the causal connection between the two communal streams. This also proves that majority communalism feeds on minority communalism. In the absence of the Shah Bano case, I doubt if the Ram mandir movement would have been a success.

But in this maze of ideological beliefs the distinction has to be made between 'Hindu assertion' and 'Hindutva'. My father's assertion of his Hindu identity can't be mistaken as being communal or sectarian. At best, it can be called the expression of a suppressed feeling that had been dormant for long. On the other hand, the demand for the establishment of a Hindu Rashtra is a political thesis. This is a programme to turn Hindu civilisation upside down and change India's democracy into an ideological state where the distinction between religion and politics will blur, and this is a disturbing development.

The two recent assertions of Hindutva are another indication in that direction. The RSS has been critical of the highest court's verdict on the Sabarimala temple. The court has pronounced that women between the ages of ten and fifty be allowed to visit the Lord Ayyappa temple and offer their prayers. The RSS's second in command, Bhaiyaji Joshi, said, 'While the Sangh supports the court verdict, the sentiments of millions of devotees, including women, could not be ignored.'[2]

But their statement took a different turn on the ground. Foot soldiers of Hindutva resorted to violent protests. Women devotees who wished to visit the temple were physically attacked. It is also true that the Congress too opposed the SC verdict, but this can only be viewed as a strategic move to not lose out in competitive politics, though even that can't be condoned.

The other assertion is the sudden outburst of the RSS on the issue of the construction of the Ram mandir in Ayodhya (about which I have talked in detail later in the book). What is common in both the matters is the defiance of the constitution and the refusal to follow the verdict of the court.

Democracy can't survive if the rule of law is challenged in the name of faith. The courts are accorded the privilege of being the final arbiter in the matter of dispute. The refusal to accept an SC judgment or even the intent to not accept the SC as the final arbiter, will lead to chaos and anarchy. The very premise of a democratic state is based on the negation of religion in the public sphere. It is not the faith of an individual or of a community, but the collective wisdom of the people that is supreme in a constitutional democracy. Hindutva has been using religion to further its political interest. The intermixing of religion and politics has created mayhem since Mr Modi became the prime minister. This cocktail has pushed India a few steps towards the construction of an ideological state, whose final destination is the utopia called Hindu Rashtra. It's a dream. It's a fantasy world. It is on such constructs that Milan Kundera had said, 'Political movements rest not so much on rational attitudes as on fantasies, images, words and archetypes that come together to make up this or that political kitsch.'[3]

Hindu Rashtra in its stated purpose does not espouse making Hindu dharma the national religion. Neither does it argue for a theocratic state. In that it is theoretically different from radical Islam, which is a war to establish an Islamic state. But Hindutva ideologues do interpret history as an eternal war between Islam and Hinduism and believe that this war will continue till Hinduism finally defeats Islam. Though they aspire to unite Hindus as one being, they abhor the essential features of the Hindu religion. They believe that the values that define Hinduism per se—compassion, tolerance, non-violence and truth—are 'feminine' in nature and have termed these 'perverted virtues' that have made Hindus weak and cowardly. These values, they believe, are the reason for the foreign rule over Hindus for more than 1,200 years. The basic dream of Hindutvavadis is to make Hindus ruthless and masculine, as they assume Islam did to its followers. They are convinced that Islam could, in such a short span of time, establish itself as a global power and occupy vast territories across the world, because it effectively used state power to spread religion—the combination of the ethical values of the holy book and the might of the sword was deadly.

It is not surprising that since 26 May 2014 the Indian state has been a mute spectator to crimes perpetrated in the name of Hindutva. The killing of Muslims on the pretext of cow protection has increased phenomenally in these past few years. What is more baffling and scary is the role of the state. Be it the mob lynching of Mohammad Akhlaq in Dadri as early as in September 2015, or the daylight murder of police inspector Subodh Kumar Singh in Bulandshahr district as late as in December 2018 by the so-called cow vigilantes, the government machinery did not move with the pace required to nail the culprits. Instead leaders belonging to the RSS and its affiliates built an alternate narrative in each case, indirectly weaving justifications for these crimes. Moral and legal support was extended to the perpetrators of these heinous acts. Ministers of the central government felicitated such men; and, above all, the chief minister of UP, Yogi Adityanath, instead of ensuring an impartial inquiry, presupposed the nature and motive of the crime.

The mob violence in the district of Bulandshahr, where a rampaging mob killed a police officer on duty, is a classic example of the government's criminal apathy towards such incidents. The violence was allegedly provoked by a Hindutva activist named Yogesh Raj, the district convener of the Bajrang Dal. On the day of the incident he presented himself before the police as an eyewitness to cows being slaughtered. He filed an FIR against six persons, out of which two were ten- to eleven-years-old kids. Later, the other four accused were also found to be innocent. Raj had vouched in the FIR that he had seen all of them slaughtering a cow. Police found no evidence against the accused. Raj's eyewitness account proved to be untrue.

This raises the suspicion that violence in the name of cow slaughter was engineered with an ulterior motive. If no cow had been seen slaughtered then what was the reason for the violence? What was more astonishing was the response of the state government. The chief minister termed the murder of the inspector 'a mere accident'.[4]

He later pronounced the whole episode a political conspiracy.[5] The main accused, Yogesh Raj, was not traced for long. Although he had been releasing video statements regularly, the police remained clueless about his whereabouts. He was later arrested.

Incidents like these that occur and are defended by the party and the organisations that are in the government, have vitiated the atmosphere. The society is highly polarised on communal lines. No sane debate is possible without generating hostility towards each other. It has become almost impossible to be neutral. A new twist, in the name of nationalism, is being given to any and all discussions. Those who don't subscribe to the idea of Hindutva are easily labelled anti-national. Criminal charges like treason and sedition are freely slapped on people, and government-controlled media can easily paint any individual as the enemy of the nation. Bright students like Kanhaiya Kumar and Umar Khalid, against whom cases of sedition have been lodged for allegedly shouting anti-India slogans in a programme on the JNU campus, are overnight turned into villains who should be lynched, killed, physically harmed or taught a lesson. Alternate viewpoints have no place. Kashmir, Pakistan and Islam are the new phantoms that have become the duty of every Indian to fight. Everybody has become an armed knight fighting for a cause without knowing exactly what that cause is.

Long before Modi became the prime minister, I had told my friends and colleagues in IBN7, the news channel where I was the managing editor for eight years, that things would not be the same once he assumed charge. What I had not foreseen was how dramatic the change would be. It's not that I had underestimated the power of his personality, but I had been unaware of the power of the Hindutva ideology. The years that have followed 2014 have seen catastrophic changes in the body of Indian politics. What is more unnerving is the change it has infused in the collective psyche of the people. To be Indian has become the stick used to exclude anyone from the general discourse essential for public life, to paint someone as criminal and anti-national, to traumatise an entire community, to build walls between societies, to sharpen the religious divides, to make Muslims feel that they are no longer wanted in this country, to create monsters who are roaming the streets to devour anyone or anything they feel is 'un-Indian' in their narrow and bigoted world view, to kill the idea of India, which we all cherished while growing up, and finally, to mutilate the collective memory that India is the land of shastrarth with a great civilisational heritage and eternal values in which every idea has a place and where every thought process has an organic connect with the spiritual being called India.⁶

This book is not an attempt to chronicle Modi's years in power. It is an attempt to understand why things happened the way they did. It is not an attempt to narrate incidents but to find reasons for their occurrence. It is not an attempt to criticise the government but to explore the ideological foundation, the rationale behind the logic of the regime. It is not an attempt to find loopholes in the system but to pinpoint holes in the larger narrative to which we had shut our eyes for years. It is an attempt to highlight the fact that it was not randomness that dictated the painful events that shocked the nation and tore into its secular fabric, but rather a definite design. In the understanding of the followers of Hindutva, Hindu Rashtra is not a chimera but a reality that must be transposed over the existing idea of Hinduism, which they believe to be the reason for the age-old mental slavery of Hindus. The Hindu Rashtra, in their view, is not a mere solution but will be the final salvation of Hindus.

It is in this context that I have contested in this book the theoretical understanding of scholars like Christophe Jaffrelot about the RSS. Jaffrelot has written, 'Collusion between the police and Hindu nationalist movements is indeed evidence of the start of a transition from a state-building process, in which the administrative and coercive apparatus is supposed to treat all citizens equally, to a state-formation process wherein majoritarian non-state actors impose a social and cultural order.'⁷ Jaffrelot is absolutely accurate in his diagnosis about the process that has been unleashed by Hindutva since 2014 but he errs in his inference when he says, 'What adds a layer of complexity to Berman and Lonsdale's model is that in India, these non-state actors enjoy state protection. Though the authority they exercise is illegal, it is nevertheless seen as legitimate by the state in that it is inspired by the values and interests of the dominant community to which the government is accountable.'⁸

I disagree with his formulation of non-state actors. What Jaffrelot dubs non-state actors are in reality the informal extensions of actors-in-power. Many intellectuals and scholars in India and abroad have concluded that the RSS and its affiliates and the BJP are different entities. In reality, they are one, like a big joint Hindu family. It is no wonder they are called the Sangh Parivar. The RSS is like a mega corporate house, which has many branches with different verticals headed by individuals but all ultimately reporting to one person—the sarsanghchalak—the father figure of the Hindutva movement, who, for practical purposes, is called the RSS chief.

To keep itself away from any unnecessary controversy or any unforeseen casualty, the RSS leadership maintains the facade that it is a separate entity from the BJP and that it has no role to play in the functioning of the government. That it has only an advisory role and offers guidance or consultations only when asked. But in reality the Modi government is the RSS government. To buttress my argument, let me ask a simple question. Who is Narendra Modi, the prime minister? He is a lifelong swayamsevak of the RSS. Who is Rajnath Singh, the home minister in the cabinet, the second most powerful man in the pecking order? He is also a swayamsevak. Who is Nitin Gadkari, supposedly the most efficient minister in the central cabinet, the former president of the BJP and perhaps the future face of the BJP? He is also a swayamsevak, as are more than two-thirds of the ministers in the central cabinet. Let me also ask, who is Amit Shah, the most powerful man in the country after Prime Minister Modi? He is also a swayamsevak.

The RSS chief is like the chairperson of a corporation who formulates policies according to the vision of the ideology, with the help of his advisers; the rest of the individuals, departments, verticals and organisations are there to execute his vision. It is not possible for the leaders of the different organisations to disagree with the chief and survive in the saddle. The different state governments and various ministries at the centre are regularly reviewed and performances are routinely evaluated. Even the prime minister is not exempt from this process, though he may be more autonomous because of the exalted status of his office.

Let me cite one example, which I have discussed in detail in the book. L.K. Advani was the mascot of Hindutva and the tallest leader of the BJP after Atal Bihari Vajpayee. He committed a mistake by tangentially calling Mohammad Ali Jinnah, the man responsible for the creation of Pakistan, secular. The RSS was so miffed by his statement that Advani was asked to resign from the post of party president. He was left with no option but to vacate the seat for Rajnath Singh in 2005. Again in 2009, when the RSS decided to make a generational shift in the BJP, Nitin Gadkari, a small provincial leader of Maharashtra, was foisted upon the BJP as party president, ignoring relatively senior leaders like Arun Jaitley, Sushma Swaraj, Venkaiah Naidu and Anant

Kumar. Gadkari, till then, had no working experience in Delhi and had not played any substantial role at the national level. Even as recently as 2017, after the massive victory in UP, Modi and Shah wanted their man Manoj Sinha, the minister of state for railways, to take over the reins of the UP government but the RSS prevailed upon them and Yogi Adityanath was appointed the chief minister. Therefore Jaffrelot's thesis that 'the Sangh Parivar is more of India's deep state than a parallel government' is erroneous.[9] It is far from the reality. The RSS has deliberately created different nomenclatures and structures; one, for reasons of functional necessity and two, to free itself from any untoward eventuality. Let's not forget that the RSS has been banned three times in the past. The divide between the RSS and the BJP is artificial, in fact they all live under one roof. In Hindu philosophy, aatma (soul) and brahma (ultimate reality) are two separate entities, when in reality they are one. The aatma has no existence without the brahma and the difference between them is maya, or illusion. Similarly, RSS is the brahma and BJP is the aatma. The division between the two is maya.

The BJP's defeat in December 2018 in Rajasthan, Madhya Pradesh and Chhatisgarh has jolted the whole ideological edifice of Hindutva. A meeting took place between the leaders of the RSS and the BJP, led by Bhaiyyaji Joshi and Shah, on 19 December 2018 at the temporary RSS headquarters, Udaseen Akhara in Delhi. Their dilemma was whether to pursue the issue of the Ram mandir vigorously or put it on the back burner.

The RSS has realised that Modi has lost his Midas touch and is not as popular with the voters as he once was. The RSS can't afford to lose the government at the centre. For Modi the target might be to save his seat but for Mohan Bhagwat it is the construction of the Hindu Rashtra, the ideological state, whose ultimate aim is to fundamentally transform the Sanatan Hindu. For the larger goal of the Hindu Rashtra the personal agenda of individuals can be sacrificed. But there is a question that is bigger than the goal of Hindutva and the idea of Hindu Rashtra. The question that lies at the core of the spiritual being of this nation we love to call Hindustan, a nation that has successfully withstood several onslaughts, is: Will this nation succeed in withstanding the onslaught this time too? The book tries to answer this question. Only time will tell if the conviction of my brother will succeed or the assertion of my father.

ONE

Making Sense of Saffronisation

'I feel betrayed, stabbed in the back,' he said.

I was stunned into silence. I could see he was trying not to cry.

The man was a veteran of Indian journalism, one of the most respected names in the field since India's Independence, his fearless spirit legendary. An icon from before my time. He had invited me to lunch at the India International Centre. Conversation flowed as we ate. He was curious to know what was happening with the Aam Aadmi Party (AAP), whether I was going to be the AAP's candidate for the Rajya Sabha. He had a lot of good words for the AAP and Arvind Kejriwal. Then the conversation veered to the Modi government. Suddenly this chirpy gentleman's face clouded over with worry.

Ever since Narendra Modi had become the prime minister, attacks on Muslims were far more frequent, he noted. He was especially shaken after the mob lynching of Mohammad Akhlaq in Dadri, Uttar Pradesh. Then more such incidents had followed. And now, he said, a perception had been created that Muslims living in India were anti-nationals, that there was no place for them in this country and that they should all go to Pakistan.

He had seen many governments since Independence, he continued, but none so anti-Muslim. Riots did happen before, Muslims did get killed in large numbers, but the state apparatus had not been so indifferent to the plight of the minorities. The police, he added, was now openly siding with the perpetrators. 'In 1947,' he continued, 'when the country was divided and Pakistan came into existence, we had the option of going to Pakistan, but we decided to stay back in Lucknow, the city I was born and brought up in and still carry in my breath, despite having lived in Delhi for decades.'

He was speaking haltingly now, in a typical Lucknawi accent: 'My parents made a mistake. They should have gone to Pakistan.' I knew he did not mean it.

'We stayed back because we loved this country. We stayed back because we had faith in this country. We stayed back because we knew this country was secular. We stayed back because we knew our neighbours were more than brothers and sisters. We had differences, but they were minor ones. We never felt threatened. We never felt scared. We never felt orphaned. It was one big happy family with all its traumas and turbulence, with all its pains and pleasures. But in the last three-and-a-half years, everything has changed. Now we, the sons of the soil, are made to believe that we are interlopers and that we don't belong to this land. We are perceived as foreigners.'

'हमारे साथ धोखा हो गया। हमें पता होता कि हमारे साथ ये होगा तो हम कभी न रुकते। चले जाते इस्लाम के नाम पर जो भी होता हमारे साथ वहाँ कोई गिला तो नहीं होता। हमें तो इस मुल्क से मुहब्बत की सज़ा दी जा रही है। 'हम तो दोनो तरफ से गये।'

(We have been deceived. If we knew this was to become of us, we would never have stayed. Whatever would've happened to us in the name of Islam, we would not have complained. We are being punished for loving this country. We don't belong to any side now.)

This was a very uncharacteristic statement for him, and shook me up. This gentleman is Muslim but has never worn his religion on his sleeve. He has always been a bitter critic of fundamentalist Islam and opposed the radicalisation of a section of Muslims, and naturally, its adherents have no love for him. He has only disgust for the mullahs and the maulanas, and he blames them for the backwardness of the Muslim community in India. To say that he is an enlightened Muslim is to insult him and his breed of citizens. He firmly believes in the Indian state. He firmly believes in Indian secularism. He cherishes the freedom granted by the Indian constitution.

Given what I knew of him, I could hardly imagine his pain. Now, after seventy years as a citizen of India, he felt distrusted by the Hindus and discarded by the Muslims. He considers himself a rare beast, one who belongs nowhere, standing in a no-man's-land with nowhere to go. Such is his predicament. Such is his tragedy. His eyes were still shimmering with the unshed tears of a brave man who did not want to be seen as vulnerable. I was still speechless. And then it was time to leave.

I have known Amitabh and Pammi for more than two decades. They are like family to me. Amitabh is a seasoned journalist. Pammi had a short sojourn in journalism, and then drifted to astrology, which she is quite good at. One evening, after dinner at my place we got talking about politics and the media. Modi was an obvious point of reference. Amitabh admitted that the man was very popular and his control over the media was absolute. No channel could write against him. We agreed that during the Manmohan Singh regime, anyone could question the prime minister; in fact, during the latter part of his tenure, it was routine to criticise his government. Today, the scenario is diametrically different. A few channels have become government mouthpieces—instead of playing watchdog to the government, they are targeting the opposition, fomenting communal strife over Hindu–Muslim issues and discussing events in Kashmir and Pakistan in a bid to hit out at Muslims at home.

Amitabh is active on Facebook. He is often trolled and abused, pilloried and threatened. Obviously, neither of them is a follower of Modi, nor do they support the BJP or the RSS. They did not support the Congress either, but now they feel that the Congress was far better than the present regime. At least it was more democratic, accommodative and tolerant of dissent.

Pammi interjected, 'The atmosphere is so bad that one has to think ten times before writing anything.' This was at the time when several writers and creative artists had been returning prestigious national awards in protest against a climate of intolerance. Nationalism and patriotism had become easy excuses to condemn foes as 'anti-national' and condone friends. I readily agreed with Pammi, but I had not expected what Amitabh went on to say: 'We were lucky that we lived in a time when India was free and did not have to worry about what we said or wrote; those days will not come back in our lifetime. We have lived longer than we ought to have lived.'

I met Sajid at a social gathering recently. We used to play cricket together in your youth, and go back more than thirty years. Though he is older than I am, we are good friends. Eid has always meant a meal at his place. Sajid's brother-in-law, Arshad, is a lawyer and lives in Okhla. I have known him ever since he was a young lad as well. Both are practising Muslims. I don't remember Sajid ever having mentioned eating beef but I knew Arshad did. When we met he said, 'Now I won't even touch beef with a bargepole. I don't want to risk my life.' Many of his friends too have given up beef out of fear. He told me that no one he knows carries even goat meat or chicken any more when they travel by train or bus. They used to have no such inhibitions earlier; now, they don't want to take any chances—aloo-puri and paratha-sabzi have become their regular companions. Only half-jokingly, he said, 'I have also become a Hindu, a vegetarian.'

My friend, Aniruddha, is still a non-vegetarian. He loves chicken and goat meat. He hails from a small town, but has done well for himself after moving to Delhi. He is definitely not a Leftist, just a liberal at heart. Overall, he has no strong affinity with any ideology. Yet, even he once got rather agitated during a phone call: 'We are bloody idiots. How can we Hindus let our gods be stolen from us? The Hindutva brigade can't have exclusive rights over Hindu gods. We have to snatch our gods (back) from them.' At the time, this was a new perspective for me.

THE BEGINNINGS OF AN IDEOLOGICAL STATE

Certainly things have drastically changed since Modi became the prime minister. I had written in my book *The Crown Prince, the Gladiator and the Hope* that '(The) BJP's victory in May was not an accident in history—in fact, history has taken a decisive turn and the BJP is here to stay. The pendulum has swung from the Left of centre to the Right ... and a new epoch has begun which will be defined by the ideological predilections of RSS's Hindutva.'[1] That the change would be so radical and rapid, I had not imagined. There is no denying the fact that the RSS is an ideological organisation, but what I did not comprehend at the time was the fact that the Indian state would also be converted into an ideological state.

Despite some of the leaders of the freedom movement having flirted with socialist thinking, despite the nostalgic appeal of the communist revolution in the Soviet Union and in Eastern Europe, despite the intellectual dominance of the Left in academia and in civil society, India did not employ communism in its statecraft and decided to be a democracy, a liberal state. It was a hybrid of capitalism and socialism—a mixed economy. The one thing it was not was an ideological state. Based on the separation of powers, federalism defined the centre-state relationship. Freedom of expression was a cardinal principle, so that like communism and socialism, Hindutva was also free to preach, profess and propagate itself within the constitutional limits. Dissent, debate and disagreement underlined the larger persona of India and Indianness. Yet the last four years have witnessed a sea change. The Indian state has surrendered to ideological pressures. Institutions are undergoing a change, a new persona is asserting itself and a new voice is challenging the basic premise of what it means to be Indian. This is new, this is explosive, this is unprecedented and this is transformative.

THE MODI WAVE

There is no doubt that Modi belonged to the core group within the RSS, that he was a swayamsevak and that he was groomed in the Hindutva ideology.[2] He grew from within the ranks, a pracharak who left home at a young age, never to go back, living for years in a single room with nothing but a cot and a suitcase.[3] Even as general secretary of the party, he had been little known. However, L.K. Advani and M.M. Joshi recognised his talent and entrusted him with bigger responsibilities. Eventually, he was given the charge of Gujarat by Atal Bihari Vajpayee and Advani. He became the first swayamsevak to don the hat of chief minister, without any prior legislative experience—until then, he had never contested elections. Yet the fact that Modi became the chief minister of Gujarat in 2001 came as a shock only to a few. What no one realised, however, was what he hid in him … That would come to the fore only when he assumed power in Gandhinagar.

The man who had no experience of running a government turned out to be a control freak. The way he exercised power over the administration and the party in Gujarat will be a subject for research in the future. Nothing happened without his knowledge; if it did, the person concerned did not survive long. After the departure of his predecessor Keshubhai Patel, the BJP had been in a shambles, faction-ridden and directionless. Modi's Midas touch turned it into an organic machine which won three consecutive elections. Only one man mattered in the organisation—Narendra Modi.

The 2002 Gujarat riots catapulted him into the spotlight on the national stage—suddenly he was the most talked-about leader, seen as polarising, communal and ruthless, with a streak of authoritarianism. One could love him or hate him but no one could ignore him. Suspicions were raised about his exact role in the 2002 Gujarat riots, but he never betrayed either guilt or remorse. Indeed, he was cleared of all charges by the supreme court. After the demise of the National Democratic Alliance (NDA) government in 2004, Atal Bihari Vajpayee faded away and Advani unsuccessfully tried to fill the vacuum left by the popular leader. Modi, meanwhile, watched from the sidelines, biding his time.

The BJP's loss in the 2009 elections opened up a window of opportunity for him. The most credible mascot of masculine Hindutva, Modi meticulously planned his march to victory. After winning Gujarat for the third time in a row, it was established that no one could challenge him in the state. For the 2014 parliamentary elections, he was the natural choice to lead the party. Surprisingly, during the campaign, the poster boy of masculine Hindutva, did not flaunt his Hinduness; instead, 'development' was his catchword. He was projected as a messiah who had the power to cure all ills and solve all problems. As I noted in my earlier book:

> He promised everything to everybody. He promised that the sluggishness of the economy would evaporate overnight; that the GDP would race up to 9% in no time; that the unemployment would be a thing of the past; that inflation, the bane of the Manmohan Singh government would melt and that the prices of essential commodities would come down and return to normal; law and order would improve and women all over the country would no longer feel unsafe; terrorists and Naxals would shrink away into their den; Pakistan would mend its ways and stop sponsoring cross-border terrorism; Kashmir would be peaceful; China would retreat to its original position and not dare to intrude on our territory; and so on. In this utopian vision, everybody would be happy and India would very soon realise its potential as a global superpower, the king of all nations, a *Vishwa Guru*.[4]

In contrast, Manmohan Singh was a mild-mannered person, a man of few words who triggered transformative changes in the economy as finance minister and later as prime minister. Unfortunately, by his second term, he seemed to have no control over his cabinet and will go down in history as having presided over an extremely corrupt regime. In the latter part of his second term, his government was riddled by policy paralysis, indecisiveness, red-tapism, multiple power-centres and weak leadership. The economy was slowing down; inflation was high; disappointment, despondency and despair were writ large on people's faces. The country was waiting for him to depart. We, the people, were waiting to welcome the new leader. Modi made sure to be in the right place at the right time. His genius lay in grabbing an opportunity with both hands. His positioning was perfect. And the rest, as they say, is history.

But there was a problem. Modi raised expectations so high that it was impossible for any leader to fulfil them and meet the demands of the people. However, what perplexed most people was not his non-delivery but the unfolding of a new agenda instead—dismantling the establishment, superimposing an ideology, restructuring the aspirations of the people, espousing a vitriolic political message, reconstructing the nation's consciousness and finally creating an illusion. He had risen to power promising a new India; but the route and the ideal he chose now harked back to the past. The past is always open to interpretation, and Modi's regime took advantage of just that. History was dissected, conflicts and contradictions highlighted, old wounds reopened and a new thesis, championing Hindutva, written. 'Villains' were carefully chosen based on this thesis, and then they were systematically destroyed. A new project was launched that had many dimensions but just one goal—to construct an ideological Hindu state.

Santosh Desai is a fiercely independent journalist with a sharp mind. His columns in the *Times of India* are eloquent. While comparing the discourse between the Left liberals and the Hindutva Right, Desai tries to sketch two contrasting personalities and reaches a conclusion: '[The]Right has the tendency to live in an imagined past, and to use it as a truth that can't be challenged or argued with ... with the fixed notions of good and bad it can work visibly and vociferously to limit freedom and tell us how to behave. It can abuse and intimidate and exploit social fault lines to deepen divides.'[5]

Hindutva has an infinite appetite to quarrel with the past. History is a sore point for its adherents, as the imagined past pricks their pride and attacks their self-defined identity as members of a great civilisation. In the pursuit of justice for their forefathers, they attempt to heal the wounds of their great culture. To this end, they invent victimhood, propagate a false religious consciousness that vilifies other religions, resurrect forgotten icons and excavate artificial enemies.

Vinayak Damodar Savarkar (popularly known as Veer Savarkar), the greatest Hindutva icon, was in search of civilisational justice when he wrote

Six Glorious Epochs of Indian History and rubbished traditional history writing. His venom for historians was legendary. He wrote (italics mine):

> Many English writers had so much perverted the Indian history and obliged two or three generations of Indian students in their schools and colleges to learn it in such a way, that not only the rest of the world but even our people were misled. Absurd and *malicious statements* implying that *India as a nation* has always been under some *foreign rule* or the other or that Indian history is an unbroken chain of *defeat of the Hindu*, have been used like currency and are accepted by our people *without affront or remonstrance or even a formal protest*.[6]

The highlighted words and phrases quite clearly denote his opinion that a great injustice had been done to India as a nation and to Hindus in particular, by foreign forces and that this needed to be redressed.

In his quest to find reasons for the civilisational conflict, Savarkar, who was opposed to the mainstream historical wisdom, blamed Muslims for the discord and opined that, unlike pre-Islamic invaders such as the Greeks, Sakas and Huns, Muslims had a religious agenda. He said:

> These new Islamic enemies not only aspired to crush the Hindu political power and establish in its place Muslim sovereignty over the whole of India, but they also had seething in their brain another fierce religious ambition ... many times more diabolical than their political one, these millions of Muslims invaders from all over Asia fell over India century after century with all the ferocity at their command to destroy the Hindu religion which was the life blood of the nation.[7]

Madhav Sadashiv Golwalkar, the second chief of RSS, the ideological fountainhead of the organisation, echoed similar sentiments. He devoted a whole chapter of his book *Bunch of Thoughts* to identifying the enemies of India. He concluded that Muslims, Christians and communists were the three greatest internal threats to the Indian nation. For him, the last 1,200 years of Indian history were one long religious war to dominate and decimate the native Hindus, as was done by the Christian invaders in the Americas, Australia and Africa. Golwalkar was especially harsh on Muslims. For him, the Partition was not a division of land but part of a bigger religious design. In his book, Gowalker says:

From the day the so-called Pakistan came into being, we in the Sangh have been declaring that it is a clear case of continued Muslim aggression. The Muslim desire, growing ever since they stepped on this land some twelve hundred years ago, to convert and enslave the entire country could not bear fruit, in spite of their political domination for several centuries, because the conquering spirit of the nation rose in the form of great and valiant men from time to time who sounded the death knell of their kingdoms here. But even though their kingdoms lay shattered, their desire for domination did not break up. In the coming of the British they found an opportunity to fulfil their desire. They played their cards shrewdly, sometimes creating terror and havoc, and ultimately succeeded in browbeating our leadership into panicky surrender to their sinful demand of Pakistan.[8]

Golwalkar minced no words. In his opinion—one shared by the RSS—the Muslim aggression continued even after the creation of Pakistan. The invasion of Kashmir and its partial occupation just after the declaration of India's Independence is part of that narrative, which still continues. To buttress his argument, he used the example of Assam: 'It is a potent fact that Muslims from Pakistan had poured into Assam in truckloads to carry out their design.'[9] According to Golwalkar, all Muslims harbour the same ambition, they have no love for India and they collude with the arch-enemy, Pakistan. Thus, all Muslims in India are traitors; wherever they live, they treat it as an independent territory, creating mini Pakistans where they indulge in anti-national activities:

> There are sure signs that an explosive situation similar to that of 1946–47 is fast brewing and there is no knowing when it will blow up. Right from Delhi to Rampur and Lucknow, the Muslims are busy hatching a dangerous plot, piling up arms and mobilising their men and probably biding their time to strike from within when Pakistan decides upon an armed conflict with our country.[10]

Golwalkar remained the chief of the RSS until 1973. He and Savarkar were the most influential thinkers within the Hindutva fold and inspired many generations. Nathuram Godse, who killed Mohandas Karamchand Gandhi, was one such acolyte. Godse had worked in the RSS by his own admission, but he claimed that he had left the organisation long before he pulled the trigger. In his testimony to the court after the assassination of

Gandhi, Godse said, 'I have worked for several years in the RSS and … subsequently joined the Hindu Mahasabha and volunteered myself to fight as (a) soldier under its Pan-Hindu flag.'[11] However, he was contradicted by his brother and co-accused Gopal Godse, who said that he and Nathuram had never severed their relationship with the RSS. As recently as August 2016, Satyaki Savarkar, great-nephew of Nathuram Godse and V.D. Savarkar, admitted in an interview to the *Economic Times* that 'Nathuram joined the RSS when he was in Sangli in 1932 and he remained a boudhik karyawah till his death.[12] He was never expelled nor did he ever leave the organisation. I am definitely upset with the RSS for denying the fact that he was a swayamsewak.'[13]

Godse hated Gandhi as he believed that the Mahatma's love for Muslims was the reason for the Partition of the country: 'Gandhiji himself was the greatest supporter and advocate of Pakistan … In these circumstances the only effective remedy to relieve the Hindus from the Muslim atrocities was to my mind, to remove Gandhiji from this world.'[14] Godse was not naïve. He was well-read and the editor of the daily, *Hindu Rashtra*. When he was asked by Devdas Gandhi, the Mahatma's son and editor of the *Hindustan Times*, 'Why did you do it?', Godse replied without any remorse or bitterness, 'The reason is purely political and political alone.'[15]

The RSS's involvement in Gandhi's assassination remains a mystery. Very recently, Rahul Gandhi blamed the RSS for Gandhi's death and was taken to court over it. Before the supreme court, he opted to face trial rather than apologise for 'defaming' the RSS.

Sardar Vallabhbhai Patel, who is revered by the RSS and other Hindutva warriors, was the home minister at the time of Gandhi's assassination. Rahul Gandhi's claim recalls the disagreement between Patel and Jawaharlal Nehru about the nature of the RSS. In Patel's biography, Rajmohan Gandhi writes,

> The RSS was banned early in February. Patel and Jawahar have differed in their assessment of the body with Nehru thinking it fascist and Vallabhbhai believing it to be patriotic but misguided. After receiving reports that in some places RSS men had celebrated Gandhiji's assassination Patel concluded that it was indulging in dangerous activities and agreed that it should be banned.[16]

Nehru was of the opinion that the RSS had a role in Gandhi's killing; Patel did not share his estimation. Patel wrote to Nehru on 27 February 1948,

I have kept myself almost in daily touch with the progress of the investigation regarding Bapu's assassination case ... it emerges clearly from these statements (of the accused) that RSS was not involved in it at all. It was the fanatical wing of the Hindu Mahasabha that (hatched) the conspiracy and saw it through.[17]

This should not be construed to mean that Patel gave a clean chit to the RSS. Patel's letter to Golwalkar dated 11 September 1948, highlights the fact that Patel was pained to see the communal face of the RSS and its hatred towards Muslims:

There can be no doubt that RSS did service to the Hindu Society ... But the objectionable part arose when they, burning with revenge, began attacking Mussalmans. Organising Hindus and helping them is one thing but going in for revenge for its sufferings on innocent and helpless men, women and children is quite another thing,' wrote Patel. He added, 'All (RSS men) their speeches were full of communal poison. It was not necessary to spread communal poison and enthuse the Hindus and organise for their protection ... As a result of the poison, the country has to suffer the sacrifice of the valuable life of Gandhiji.[18]

The RSS's and Hindutva forces' antipathy to Nehru is well known, but Sardar Patel is one of their icons. Indeed, some in the Hindutva circle believe that instead of Nehru, Patel should have been the prime minister. Thus, it behoves us to take Patel's words seriously when even he has underlined the RSS's vengeful attitude towards Muslims. Since then, much water has flowed down the Yamuna and one might imagine that in the twenty-first century, the RSS might have moved on from its adversarial thesis on Muslims and Islam. Alas, the narrative in these circles remains the same, their historical perspective is the same and they still carry the ideological legacy of Savarkar and Golwalkar. The demolition of the Babri Masjid in 1992 was the culmination of their quest for reparation. Over time, many top leaders have become more circumspect and subtle, but the middle- and lower-rung leaders' campaign on the ground is so regressive, and uses terms so abusive that it is unprintable.

Their aggression and stridency vary, depending upon the nature of the government at the Centre and in the states. Yogi Adityanath, the chief minister of Uttar Pradesh, had this to say about Muslims before he was elected to the post: 'In places where there are 10–20% minority populations, stray communal incidents take place. Where there are 20–35% of them, serious communal riots take place and where they are more than 35%, there is no place for non-Muslims.'[19] He was arrested for making anti-Muslim speeches in Gorakhpur in 2007, though the case did not reach its logical conclusion since his government refused to grant permission for his prosecution. Meanwhile, Vinay Katiyar, the firebrand leader of the BJP, active member of the RSS and a Rajya Sabha member, had this to say very recently: 'Muslims should not stay in this country. They have partitioned the country on the basis of population. So why are they here? Muslims have been given their share. They should go to Bangladesh or Pakistan … they have no business being in India.'[20]

Does this prove that in almost a hundred years, from Savarkar to Katiyar, nothing has changed? The understanding with which Keshav Baliram Hedgewar had founded the RSS in 1925 still remains the guiding principle of the organisation. Debate around the role of Muslims in Indian history and the distortion caused by them is the central focal point of the Hindutva ideology. Now this ideology is in power at the Centre. Yet, to assume that the Modi government, which on paper is run by the BJP but in my opinion is a RSS government, will behave in the same fashion as the earlier governments did would be a grave mistake.

Before the Modi government, when Manmohan Singh was the prime minister, the guiding principles of his government were enshrined in the Left liberal philosophy. However, the Left liberals were not as organised as the RSS is. Their sentiment was, at least, well-accepted and did not suffer the credibility crisis that Hindutva contends with. Therefore, when in power, Hindutva adherents will certainly try to attain credibility and to that purpose, will use all the tools they can command. Other than the state apparatus, violence and intimidation can also play a crucial role. Let's not forget that when communism attained power in the Soviet Union in 1917, it used violence at a much larger scale. Communism was new as a statecraft, and not palatable to many, and therefore it was incumbent on the communist party to make it all-pervasive and acceptable, alongside annihilating its enemies by purges, murders and mass slaughter.

India has not confronted the play of an organised ideology before. It is no coincidence that post 2014, the debates on love jihad, cow protection, beef eating, vegetarianism, triple talaq and nikah halala have occupied a larger space.²¹ Mob lynching, brutal beatings, intimidation, threats and abuses are the reflections of that process. It is in this context that the killing of Akhlaq and others in the name of beef eating has to be understood. In the theatre of ideology, these are the scenes staged to consolidate the gains and perpetuate it to the last mile, with targeted persons as mere props.

TWO

The Politics of Gau Raksha

It was a dark and silent night. There was no electricity. Dim light shone in some of the houses thanks to an inverter. Suddenly, near the village temple, three figures emerged from the shadows. One of them was in police uniform. The other two were in regular clothes. The priest, Sukhdas Mahatma, was winding up for the day. As he got up to close the door to the temple, the uniformed person confronted the priest. Mahatma was new to the village, having moved here two-and-a-half months ago. He wondered what the matter could be. It was around 10 p.m. and half the village was fast asleep.

The uniformed person, in his late twenties, was Vinay. He was a constable in the Uttar Pradesh Home Guard. On that particular day, he was supposed to be on leave from his duties. However, he told the priest that an announcement had to be made immediately. The priest was curious. Vinay explained that Mohammad Akhlaq, a local resident, had killed a cow during the day and cooked its meat to eat. Vinay insisted the villagers should assemble to teach Akhlaq a lesson. The priest hesitated. The other two men also pressed him to do as Vinay demanded. The priest refused to make any announcement. Vinay grew furious and threatened the priest. Since he was in uniform, the priest felt he had no option but to comply.

The announcement was made. In no time, a crowd had assembled at the temple. Vinay took the mic and addressed the gathering. He told people that something sinful had happened—Akhlaq had killed a cow and he had to be taught a lesson. The crowd was furious. The other two men, named Vishal Rana and Shivam, twenty-year-old cousins, joined Vinay in leading the mob towards Akhlaq's house. It was around 10.30 p.m. Vishal was a class XII dropout, working at a factory in the Okhla area of Delhi.

Shivam was a B.Pharm student at Santosh Medical College in Ghaziabad, Uttar Pradesh.

Akhlaq, fifty-eight years old, and his son Danish were about to go to bed. There were hardly any lights on at home. The mob had reached the gate. Akhlaq's daughter Shaista heard the commotion. By then, the house was surrounded and she could sense danger—the crowd was exceptionally aggressive; abuses were being hurled at the family from every side. The mob tried to break down the gate and when they did not succeed, scaled the walls and entered the house. Before Shaista and the family realised what was happening, a few boys had entered the kitchen. They were frantically searching for something. One of them opened the fridge and shouted, 'We have found the evidence!' He held some meat in his hands.

The family immediately realised that their lives were in danger. They tried to explain to the crowd that it was not beef but goat meat, but their pleas fell upon deaf ears. Mohammad Akhlaq called up his childhood friend Manoj Sisodia, who ran a grocery shop in the village and lived nearby. Manoj was surprised to receive a call at that hour. He picked up the phone to find a hysterical Akhlaq on the other end. Akhlaq was saying, 'Manoj bhai, hum khatre me hain, kisi tarah phone karke force bulwa lo (Manoj, our lives are in danger, please call the police somehow).' After that, Akhlaq's voice was not heard again and Manoj only heard shouting and abuses. The Akhlaq family members were running hither and thither to save themselves. The crowd ran to the first floor. They caught Mohammad Akhlaq there and hit him on the head. Danish, who tried to intervene, was also beaten mercilessly.

By the time the police reached the spot, Mohammad Akhlaq had been dragged out of the house, bleeding profusely; Danish was also in bad shape, unconscious. According to some reports, Mohammad Akhlaq's mother had locked herself in the washroom. The police had arrived too late to save Akhlaq; he was already dead. However, they took charge of the house while one team took both father and the son to the hospital.

The village Bisada, in Dadri, Uttar Pradesh, approximately fifty kilometres from the national capital of Delhi, has been much in the news due to the Akhlaq case in recent years. In this village of nearly 6,000 people, around forty families are Muslims. There are no past records of any communal clashes in Bisada. The village had seemingly been a byword for communal harmony for generations. Hindus and Muslims had lived peacefully together. Social tension of any kind had never been witnessed. Festivals were celebrated together. Everybody enjoyed each other's company. Yet now Bisada is notorious in India's annals of communal violence.

It remains a mystery why the village suddenly erupted in anger and killed Akhlaq. What was the real provocation for such a ghastly act? Akhlaq's family seemed numb with incomprehension. The police ruled out personal enmities. Akhlaq's eldest son Mohammad Sartaj works in the Indian Air Force. At the time of the incident, he was posted in Chennai. Sartaj had spoken to his father half an hour before the attack. Everything had been normal then. Sartaj has been quoted as saying that he failed to understand how his father could have been beaten to death, and his brother seriously injured, over a rumour that they had killed a cow, that they had eaten beef and that they had stocked the rest for further consumption. As such, the Akhlaq family no longer lives in Bisada; they have moved to Delhi.

Surprisingly, the police later denied the role of the Home Guard constable in the lynching. Senior police officers changed their tune while the case was sub judice, saying that Vinay's participation was just a rumour, though he had been detained by the police for questioning; that he was later let off as no evidence was found against him in the matter. Therefore, his name did not figure in the first information report (FIR), nor was he arrested. In all, ten people featured in the FIR, of which six were arrested within six hours and another four over the next twenty days. To everyone's surprise, the priest, who was supposed to be the prime witness and accused, disappeared most mysteriously. Sukhdas Mahatma hailed from Saharanpur but could not be traced.

On the surface it appeared that some young men instigated the mob with reports about a cow-killing. But was it as simple as that? The initial investigation unearthed a planned conspiracy to stoke unrest in the area. If intelligence agencies are to be believed, the plan was to create a situation similar to Muzaffarnagar in western Uttar Pradesh.[1] Other than Akhlaq's killing, a mosque was also to be demolished in a nearby village. The Bisada incident could have blown up in a bigger way, the area being surrounded by the Rajput villages known as the Satha Chaurasi, and the adjacent villages of Dasna and Masuri, which have large minority populations.[2] Some miscreants had been seen in the area earlier, spreading rumours and misguiding people in the name of religion.

A report released by a group of academics, journalists and students who visited Bisada and spoke to a large section of the people in the area says, 'This incident showed the sophistication of forces behind such communal violence. It's all about low-intensity, high impact communal violence that targets better-off Muslims and puts a general sense of fear in the minds of others.'[3] A lot of small but identity-based organisations have mushroomed in the area in the recent past. Organisations such as the Rashtravadi Pratap Sena, the Samadhan Sena and the Ram Sena have sprung up there recently, with posters and banners displayed around the villages. These organisations keep tabs on the educated but unemployed youth and try to engage with them. According to Alok Sharma, Inspector General of Police (IGP), Meerut, the police keeps an eye on these outfits that protest at the drop of a hat. Some of these organisations were vociferous supporters of a ban on cow slaughter.[4] A person named Yashpal Singh, belonging to the Rashtravadi Pratap Sena, was arrested for Akhlaq's murder too.

Common sense dictates that any conspiracy requires more than one person to plan and execute. Despite holding that the Dadri incident was pre-planned to stoke unrest in the area, the police has been unable to unearth the details of the conspiracy—it has no clue who planned it or how many people were involved. What was the motive and was the motive linked to any political party, large organisation or any fringe groups active in the area? The police report only offers conjectures, which don't tell a complete story. Three aspects of this incident look particularly suspicious and raise serious doubts about the police investigation:

1. Role of the home guard constable
Why was a clean chit given to the Home Guard constable even before the investigation reached its logical end? It was puzzling that the same police force that had spoken to the *Indian Express*, citing his involvement, went back on its words. A senior police officer had stated, that Vinay had a personal dispute with Akhlaq and had been instigating a group of youngsters to attack Akhlaq's family, alleging that they were involved in cow slaughter. 'According to the police, on September 28, Vinay, accompanied by Vishal and Shivam arrived at the village temple at night, just as the priest, Sukhdas Mahatma, was closing the door. Vinay allegedly asked the priest to announce that a cow had been slaughtered in the village and everyone

should assemble at the temple.'⁵ The police at first offered up very specific information that put the Home Guard constable on the spot. Yet later, the police denied the entire story, gave the constable a clean chit and called the newspaper report a concoction. Why would a reputed paper concoct such a story? Was some political pressure being brought to bear upon the police? We may never know.

2. The disappearance of the priest

The disappearance of Sukhdas Mahatma (also called Sukhbar Das in some reports) raises serious questions about the nature of the police investigation. Subodh Kumar Singh, station in-charge at the Jarcha village police station informed the media of the priest's disappearance under mysterious circumstances. 'The priest… in Saharanpur has gone missing under mysterious circumstances. Two and half months back he had come to Bisada village. On the day of the incident, one of his disciples had come to the village. We have sent a team to Saharanpur to track him down because he is an important link in the case.'⁶ Surprisingly, the priest's name was missing from the first chargesheet, which was filed in the third week of December 2015. His name neither figured as a witness nor as an accused. The circle officer for Dadri, Anurag Singh, offered an explanation that convinces no one: 'For us, there are only two most important witnesses, Akhlaq's injured son Danish and his daughter. We did not need to record the pujari's statement as a witness.'⁷ The police had earlier admitted while making him the main witness that the priest was forced to make the announcement about a cow slaughter and call on people to assemble. Subsequently, and bizarrely, they argued, 'Our investigation is limited to whatever is mentioned in the FIR and the statements given by Danish and his sister. We can't rely on the statement of the accused; they can name anyone as conspirators.'⁸

There is a contradiction in these statements. Subodh Kumar Singh admitted in October that the priest was an important link and a team had been sent to track him down, but two-and-a-half months later, the Dadri police did not find him important enough to even mention. Danish and his sister were present inside the house. They can only speak of the people involved in the violence within. They would not have had any clue as to what had happened earlier or how the mob reached their house. They would not know who instigated the mob, when or how.

The disappearance of the priest and the denial of the Home Guard constable's involvement considerably limited the sphere of the investigation. Since the police were not relying on the statements of Vishal and Shivam, because according to them, they were the accused, the possibility of investigating for a conspiracy was ruled out. In that case, why did the police earlier say that the lynching planned to stoke unrest to create a bigger communal strife than Muzaffarnagar riots?[9]

3. Lab reports on the meat sample seized
A major dispute arose over the nature of the meat found at the spot. There were two reports, one filed by the State Veterinary Hospital, Dadri, and another by a forensic lab based in Mathura. The Dadri report, prepared on 29 September, indicates that the meat was from a goat whereas the Mathura lab said that the meat was beef per its examination on 8 October.

While the Dadri lab had not carried out any chemical examination but suggested after a prima facie physical examination that it could be goat, the Mathura lab's report was supposedly based on a chemical examination, and claimed it was the meat of 'a cow or its progeny'.[10] This report, which was made public many months later, turned Akhlaq's family from victims to the accused, as cow slaughter is banned in UP. Akhlaq's family contested this report and said that the investigating officer of the case, senior sub inspector, Subodh Kumar Singh, had prepared a seizure report that mentioned around 2 kg of meat apart from portions of four legs and skin of the chest and head. Akhlaq's son Sartaj added, 'The local lab in Dadri in its report dated September 2, 2015 stated that the sample comprises pieces of meat weighing around 4 to 5 kg. How can 2 kg meat collected at the site turn into 4 to 5 kg by the time it reached the lab?'[11] Sartaj in his petition to the Additional Director General of Police (Law and Order), cited another anomaly per newspaper reports: 'Samples were sent to Mathura lab after being sealed in two plastic containers. However, the samples that reached Mathura lab were sealed inside a single jar'. The petition also questions the disappearance of skin pieces and legs seized by the police from the spot.'[12]

The two differing reports again raise serious questions. Was there an attempt to deliberately derail the investigation? How can goat meat turn into cow meat? Was the meat sample switched at some point during the investigation? Were there external influences on the investigation? As the events unfolded, it seemed obvious that every attempt was being made to save the accused, while an entire army of individuals insisted upon framing Akhlaq's family for cow slaughter.

It must also be noted that the meat seized by the police and sent for examination for investigation was not seized from Akhlaq's house but from outside his house. 'No meat was found at Mohammad Akhlaq's house, this is what the official seizure report prepared by the Gautama Budh Nagar police after the lynching, states.'[13] This implies that the mob's claim that the meat was found in Akhlaq's fridge may not have been true. How could Akhlaq's family be held responsible for meat found at a distance from their house? Unfortunately this perspective seems to have gotten lost in the din.

Ideally, the BJP government holding power at the Centre should have demanded action against the culprits, but they gave a different twist to the matter. The local Member of Parliament (MP) and Union Minister of Culture Mahesh Sharma did not condemn the incident. Instead, he said it was the result of some misunderstanding. Another BJP leader and one of the accused in the Muzaffarnagar riots, Sangeet Som visited Bisada village on 4 October. He preferred to meet the families of those suspected of the lynching; he refused to meet Mohammad Akhlaq's family. He said, 'In UP, no one has the legal right to slaughter a cow or eat its meat. So a case should be registered under the relevant sections against Mohammad Akhlaq's family. It is true that Akhlaq died so you arrested people and sent them to jail. But now the people who slaughtered a cow, which is Akhlaq's family, should also be sent to jail.'[14] On 1 October 2015, 'in the midst of the communal tension following the lynching of Akhlaq, the local unit of BJP held a meeting in a school in Dhoom Manikpur village under Dadri and passed a resolution to demand the arrest of cow slaughterers (meaning the Akhlaq family) and release of six persons accused of lynching.'[15]

It is noteworthy that one of the accused, Vishal Rana, was the son of Sanjay Rana, who happens to be a member of the BJP's district organising committee. He himself had admitted that he had been associated with the BJP since 1995.[16] Even the state BJP president, Laxmikant Bajpai, instead of sympathising with the victim's family, hinted that Akhlaq's family should be arrested: 'Whatever has happened in Dadri village is highly unfortunate. Cow slaughter is illegal in Uttar Pradesh and law should have taken its course if the slaughtered animal is indeed a cow.'[17] It was only later that Bajpai dissociated himself from Rana. The VHP is an organisation floated by the RSS to work among Hindu religious gurus. Its leader Sadhvi Prachi said that 'she (would) try her best to deliver justice to those arrested for the murder'.[18] Yogi Adityanath, who later became the chief minister of UP, was as insistent as Som on registering a case against the Akhlaq family: 'The innocent Hindus arrested in the matter should be released and a case of cow slaughter should be registered against Akhlaq's family.'[19]

Finally, the pressure tactics worked and a case was registered against Mohammad Akhlaq and six members of his family to comply with the order of Surajpur court which instructed Jarcha Police to file an FIR on 14 July 2016. The Jarcha police station registered the case under Section 3/8 of the Uttar Pradesh Prevention of Cow Slaughter Act and Section 3/11 of the Prevention of Cruelty to Animals Act. The VHP welcomed the FIR. Its spokesperson Surendra Jain said, 'Unfortunately, in the din of the secular mafia of the country, truth was buried and instead the Hindu society was shown as if they were the perpetrators of the crime of killing Akhlaq.'[20]

What has been most baffling in the entire episode was the silence of the prime minister. Prime Minister Modi, who reacts even to trivial issues on social media, waited for ten days and spoke only after President Pranab Mukherjee had condemned the incident. Even then, Modi was very mild. Instead of an outright condemnation, he only said that people should follow the president's call for tolerance and unity, ignoring all other voices. It was too little and too late. Swaminathan S. Anklesaria Aiyar wrote in his column 'Swaminomics' of 19 October 2015, 'Modi's ploy seemed to evade the beef thuggery question via insincere homilies. He wants to appear non-communal without categorically condemning his colleagues or the Dadri murder.[21] Another well-known columnist, Chaitanya Kalbag explained, 'Modi has chosen to not speak at all about last week's lynching of a Muslim man in the outskirts of Delhi. This is because he finds himself on the horns of the dilemma. He has attacked cow slaughter, cattle smuggling, and the "pink revolution" of meat exports, both as Gujarat Chief Minister Modi and as PM candidate, Modi.'[22]

HATE CRIMES IN THE NAME OF GAU RAKSHA

Cow slaughter has been a core ideological issue for the RSS. In fact, the mouthpiece of the RSS, the weekly magazine *Panchjanya*, in its cover story provided justification for Akhlaq's lynching by stating that his killing over the beef consumption rumours could not have been without reason. It further stated, 'The Vedas order killing of anyone who slaughters the cow. Cow slaughter is a big issue for the Hindu community. For many of us it is a question of life and death.'[23] Sensing serious charges might be brought against the organisation, the RSS immediately distanced itself from the Panchjanya article and refused to admit that the magazine was their mouth piece: 'The report that the RSS supports the Dadri incident is false and baseless.'[24]

The Dadri incident was not a standalone case, however. In the name of cow protection, Muslims and Dalits were being routinely terrorised and brutally beaten. According to a report published in the *Times of India*, dated 30 June 2017, 'A review of media reports shows 32 cases of attacks by mobs or vigilante groups on Muslims since May 2014. In these attacks 23 people were killed including women and children. This is a conservative estimate as many attacks may not have been reported in the national media … The target of cow vigilantes has extended to Dalits and tribals too. And in some cases police personnel and government officials also.' Seasoned journalist Aakar Patel wrote in his column, 'Akarvani', in the *Times of India* that 'the data journalism website IndiaSpend has reported that 97 per cent of lynching murders by Gau Rakshaks have come after 2014.'[25] Of these, according to a recent IndiaSpend analysis (the initiative being the country's first journalistic watchdog for data and facts), twenty-six attacks were also carried out on non-Muslims.

Among these attacks, a few in particular caught the attention of the national media. In the month of March 2017, two Muslim persons, Muhammad Majloom and Azad Khan (a minor), were mercilessly beaten and most horrifically hanged to death from a tree in the Balumath forests in Latehar district, Jharkhand. Their bodies were strung up, with their hands tied behind their backs and mouths stuffed with cloth. According to Latehar SP Anoop Birthary, 'The manner of their hanging showed that assailants were led by extreme hatred.'[26]

In another incident, the whole country was traumatised by the chilling video of seven Dalit persons being beaten up by a cow vigilante group in the Una town of the Gir Somnath district of Gujarat. The video of the victims being attacked with iron rods and sticks was circulated on social media. Their crime was that they were skinning a dead cow.

Similarly, a Dalit boy of sixteen was tied to a tree by a group of upper-caste boys in Agra district, UP, and whipped till he fell unconscious. Petrol was poured over his private parts and the perpetrators tried to inject toxic drugs into his body. He was blamed for stealing a buffalo, an accusation which proved to be untrue.

Another troubling incident was the killing of Pehlu Khan near Alwar, Rajasthan. Fifty-five-year-old Pehlu Khan was returning to his village, along with four others, including his two sons, from a cattle fair organised by the Jaipur Municipal Corporation. The group was returning with three cows they had purchased. He had all the necessary documents to prove that the cows were not being taken to slaughter but had been bought as milch cattle. 'We had municipal corporation permits. We paid tax and an amount to the police for checking the cows,' said his son Irshad, who was thrown to the ground during the 1 April attack and beaten till he lost consciousness.[27] This incident rocked the parliament, and the government was forced to put out an assurance that the culprits would not go unpunished.

Junaid Khan was another of the unfortunates who met a similar fate. He belonged to Ballabhgarh district in Haryana. Junaid Khan and three of his brothers had boarded a Delhi–Mathura train from the national capital. According to reports, for three-and-a-half hours, they were abused, humiliated and assaulted by a mob of around twenty people who passed communal remarks and accused them of carrying beef in a bag. Finally, nineteen-year-old Junaid was stabbed to death and another of the boys also received stab injuries before they were thrown out of the train. After Junaid's murder, civil society organised a protest at Jantar Mantar in Delhi, under the banner 'Not in My Name'.

What has been surprising is that despite assurances by the BJP governments in the states and at the Centre, punitive action did not follow in most cases, except for the Latehar lynching, where the eleven accused were held guilty and a life sentence was pronounced. In the Dadri incident and other cases, attempts were made to either derail the investigation or openly help the accused. In the Dadri case, at the behest of the local Member of the Legislative Assembly (MLA), Tejpal Singh Nagar, the accused youngsters were promised employment under the Maharatna scheme in the National Thermal Power Corporation (NTPC) site situated near Bisada village, once they got bail from the Allahabad high court. In Dadri, the Hindutva forces, by way of the Hindu Raksha Dal and Akhil Bharatiya Kshatriya Mahasabha, shamelessly demanded that one of the accused, Ravin Sisodia, who died in police custody of organ failure, be declared a martyr. VHP leader Sadhvi Prachi made provocative speeches and accused the UP government of protecting the Akhlaq family. At that time, the Samajwadi Party was in power in the state. Mahesh Sharma, still a minister in the Central government then, visited Bisada, paid his respects and posted his picture with Sisodia's body wrapped in the tricolour on Twitter for the world to see. Did he forget that Ravin was a murder accused?

Mahesh Sharma is not the only minister to have displayed such controversial affiliations. On 6 July 2018, his colleague, the Harvard educated Union Minister of State for Civil Aviation, Jayant Sinha garlanded the eight men convicted by the fast track court in the killing (by lynching) of Alimuddin Ansari in Ramgarh, Jharkhand, in June 2017. The men had been granted bail by the high court. He proudly shared photographs of this and defended himself against criticism by saying that he was honouring the due process of law. He later expressed regret after being severely criticised.

In the Pehlu Khan case, a fact-finding team suggested monumental inefficiency on the part of the police or a deliberate attempt to weaken the case against the accused gau rakshaks. The FIR did not invoke Section 307 of the Indian Penal Code (IPC) for the offence of murder, which provides for imprisonment of ten years to life. Instead, the FIR invoked only Section 308, which takes cognisance of culpable homicide not amounting to murder, prescribing an imprisonment of three to seven years.[28] The independent investigation also revealed that the accused named in Khan's dying declaration were not arrested. The police also failed to defend the arrests they made in court, as five out of the seven accused were able to get out on bail.[29]

The fate of Junaid's case was no different. In less than three months, four of the six accused were out on bail, as the Haryana Railway Police withdrew the charges of rioting, unlawful assembly and common intention noted against them in the charge sheet. Just as he had after the Dadri killing, this time too Prime Minister Modi remained ambivalent. When the popular outrage reached deafening proportions, he decided to say a few words, but refused to make a categorical statement or send a strong message. After the Una incident, Modi's statement was very feeble. He said, 'Some people are running a business in the name of Gau Raksha. I feel so angry … I have seen that some people who indulge in antisocial activities through the night don the robes of Gau Rakshaks by day …'[30] When he spoke next year at the Sabarmati Ashram in Ahmadabad, Gujarat, once again there was no open condemnation of 'cow vigilantism'. All he said was, 'This is the country where Mahatma Gandhi taught us the lesson of non-violence. What has happened to us? … Whether anyone is guilty or not, the law will take its course. No person is allowed to take the law in his hands.'[31]

The Modi government did send an advisory to the state governments in 2016 stating, 'No person can, under any circumstances, take the law in their hands. Any person or persons, doing so, have to be dealt with strictly under the relevant laws and brought to justice in the quickest possible fashion, for the strictest punishment.'[32] But later, most surprisingly, the government washed its hands of the matter and lobbed the ball over to the state governments. When the matter was referred to the supreme court, Solicitor General Ranjit Kumar told the court, 'It is the state government which has to take action in such cases, law and order comes within the state domain, and the centre has no role to play.'[33]

Modi is no ordinary leader. First of all, he is the only prime minister in the last thirty years who had a majority in the Lok Sabha on his own, unlike, say, Atal Bihari Vajpayee. Rajiv Gandhi was the last prime minister to have had the same privilege. That means his government is not dependent on others for support. Secondly, unlike Vajpayee, Modi has total control over the government and the party. Vajpayee's power was constrained by his allies—by L.K. Advani within the party, and by the RSS, led then by K.S. Sudarshan, within the Hindutva fold. He was engaged in a running battle with the VHP, Bharatiya Mazdoor Sangh (BMS), Bharatiya Kisan Sangh (BKS), Swadeshi Jagran Manch (SJM) and other affiliates of the RSS. Modi, on the other hand, has an excellent relationship with the RSS. Mohan Bhagwat, the current chief, does not interfere in the day-to-day functioning of the government. He does not make damaging statements about the government, the way Sudarshan used to. Thirdly, today the BJP commands more states than Vajpayee could even imagine controlling in his time. In the month of March 2018, the BJP led the government, or was part of the government, in twenty-two states. In these states, Modi's words are mantra. Fourthly, Modi is feared, whereas Vajpayee was not. No leader of the BJP or the RSS can afford to take him lightly or defy him.

So to say that the Centre is helpless in enforcing law and order in a state such as UP can only be termed as hiding behind the word and not the spirit of the constitution. In reality, if Modi wanted to put an end to cow vigilantism, all he had to do was to pick up the phone and say 'Stop this nonsense,' for it to end without a murmur.

But this is not happening. Why?

Vigilante groups of any shade can have no place in a civilised society. The presence of an extra-constitutional authority such as the Bharatiya Gau Raksha Dal is a symptom of the weakening of the state.

Can a different leadership be held responsible for the vigilantism? Within the RSS folds, the sarsanghchalak is the supreme leader. His authority is above question. The RSS works on the premise that once the chief has spoken, his diktat has to be followed, come what may. Like Modi, though, Mohan Bhagwat remains ambiguous. In his annual Vijayadashami address to the RSS swayamsevaks in 2016, Bhagwat had said, 'Gaurakshaks are good people but they should work under the law and constitution.'[34] Bhagwat thus ended up praising the vigilantes in a covert fashion, almost granting them a certificate of good conduct.

By the following year, Bhagwat did realise that cow vigilantism was adversely affecting the image of the RSS and the other Hindutva organisations. He therefore tried to dissuade the cow vigilantes. He said, 'Nothing should be done while protecting cows that hurts the belief of some people. Nothing should be done that is violent. It only defames the efforts of the cow protectors.'[35] This statement stems from the understanding that the vigilante violence did annoy a few of the group's own supporters.

Seshadri Chari, a former editor of the RSS mouthpiece, the *Organiser*, and a member of the BJP's national executive body, was one such person within the Hindutva fold who voiced his annoyance after Pehlu Khan's murder. He said, '[the] cow is [a] very respectable animal, and I don't want a single abattoir in the country but that does not mean you bash up people. This is completely unacceptable.'[36]

Yet the ambivalence exhibited by Bhagwat and Modi is understandable. For a long time, the protection of the cow has been an instrument of mobilisation for the RSS. Gau rakshak bands (or 'dals') have been formed and nurtured by the champions of Hindutva. There is no denying that the idea has a certain amount of traction among Hindus, especially in rural and semi-urban areas. As a child, whenever I visited my village in Gonda district, UP, I overheard two abusive terms which had religious overtones. If one had to abuse a Hindu person, the slur of choice was '*gaikhani*', meaning they ate cow meat; if the person belonged to the Muslim community, they were addressed as '*suwarkhani*', someone who ate pork. My village had a mixed population. Hindus and Muslims have lived together for generations and there has never been any history of communal clashes.

At school in Lucknow, I remember that we were asked to write an essay on the cow many a time. The first sentence was almost always, 'गाय हमारी माता है (The cow is our mother).' Sometimes we would joke in rhyme, saying, 'गाय हमारी माता है, हमको कुछ नही आता है। (The cow is our mother and we know nothing other than that).'

It is not only the RSS that has projected the cow as a divine animal; since the Vedic age, Hindus have treated it as sacred and maternal. This is a part of their religious belief system. In the Puranas, it is depicted as Kamdhenu, the cow which fulfils people's every wish, including that for nourishment. However, the RSS goes a step further when it insists that eating beef was never a practice among Hindus, contrary to historical claims. So to kill a cow and eat it is not an ordinary crime, but an irreligious act, a sin for Hindus now. When performed by others, it becomes an act that involves hurting the religious sentiments of Hindus. In contrast, Muslims have no such inhibitions as they are not constrained by the diktats of their religion when it comes to the cow. Eating beef is normal for them—or so it used to be.

Historians, as mentioned, don't agree with the RSS's insistence that Hindus have never consumed beef. Experts on the Hindu culture are of the opinion that there is ample evidence to support the argument that the cow and its progeny were not only sacrificed but also eaten by Hindus, especially Brahmins. 'Babasaheb' Bhimrao Ramji Ambedkar, in his treatise *The Untouchables: Who Were They and Why They Became Untouchable*, wrote, 'When learned Brahmins argue that the Hindus not only never ate beef but they always held the cow to be sacred and were always opposed to the killing of the cow, it is impossible to accept their view. There is clear and ample evidence in the *Rig Veda* as well as *Brahmanas* and *Dharma Sutras* that the Hindus at one time did kill cows and eat beef.'[37] Babasaheb further wrote, 'For generations Brahmins had been eating beef. In a period overridden by ritualism, there was hardly a day on which there was no cow sacrifice to which a Brahmin was not invited by non-Brahmins. The Brahmins were therefore the greatest beef-eaters.'[38]

Swami Vivekananda is considered to be an icon by Hindutva warriors. Yet when he addressed his American audience at the Shakespeare Club, Pasadena, California, on 2 February 1900, he said, 'You will be astonished if I tell you that according to the old ceremonials, he is not a good Hindu who does not eat beef. On certain occasions he must sacrifice a bull and eat it.'[39]

Professor D. N. Jha, who has done a systematic study on the subject, also says, 'The Rig Veda frequently refers to the cooking of the flesh of the animals, including that of the ox, as an offering to the Gods, especially Indra. In most Vedic yajnas, cattle were killed and their flesh eaten. Although some post-Vedic texts recommend the offering of animal effigies in lieu of livestock, ancient Indians continued to kill cattle and eat beef, which was the favourite food of Yajnavalkya, the respected sage from Mithila. He made the obdurate statement that he would continue to eat the flesh of cows and bullocks so long as it was tender.'[40]

Jha suggests that in the post-Mauryan age, there emerged some kind of disapproval of cattle killing, though the *Manusmriti* (200BC to 200AD) allowed the consumption of flesh, the only exception being camel, not cow. Jha further elucidates, '*Yajnavalkyasmriti* (100BC to 300AD) also discusses lawful and forbidden food and endorses the Vedic practice of killing animals and eating the consecrated meat, but unlike the *Manusmriti*, it clearly states that a learned Brahmin should be welcomed with a big ox or goat, delicious food and sweet words.'[41] But references get rarer and rarer in the post-Gupta era, he notes, and later it becomes totally forbidden. The *Vyasasmriti* categorically states that a cow killer is untouchable and that one incurs a sin by even talking to them.[42]

Hence, to say that eating beef has never been a practice among Hindus is not true. It had been a practice in ancient India but as history progressed, examples of beef being consumed by Brahmins became rare. Babasaheb Ambedkar disclosed his opinion on the reason for the decline of cow-killing and beef-eating by Brahmins—the rise and phenomenal growth of Buddhism. He said, 'Buddhism had rejected the Brahmanic religion which consisted of Yajnas and animal sacrifice, particularly of cow. The objection to the sacrifice of the cow had taken a strong hold of the minds of the masses especially as they were an agricultural population and the cow was a very useful animal. The Brahmins in all probability had come to be hated as the killers of cows.... That being the case, Brahmins could do nothing to improve their position against the Buddhists except by giving up the Yajnas as a form of worship and the sacrifice of cows.'[43] So it would seem rejecting beef and resorting to cow protection instead was a strategic move by the Brahmins to fight back, retrieve their religious ground and win back the confidence and trust of the people who had gone over to the Buddhists in the post-Mauryan era. It was the survival instinct of the Brahmins, and to call it a religious or divine intervention would be falsifying history. Indeed, Brahmanism succeeded in its endeavour. Buddhism evaporated from the land of its origin and Brahmanism again became the dominant religion of South Asia, but the Brahmins had to sacrifice eating beef for good and, since then, the cow has become a sacred animal for them. Paradoxically, though, large sections of the Hindu community, especially people from the depressed castes, Shudras, tribals and others, did continue eating beef. It was this section of people who were declared outcaste by Brahmins and were treated as Untouchables.

With the arrival of the Muslim invaders who were traditionally beef eaters, the conflict was inevitably renewed, this time between Brahmins and Muslims. Occasional tensions have been mentioned in history. Akbar was sensitive to the feelings of non-Muslims and he issued orders against the slaughter of animals, including the cow, on specific occasions, a policy which was continued by his son Jahangir.[44]

It is also a fact that the cow became a symbol of identity for the upper-caste Hindus only after 1857, which saw the First War of Independence. Mangal Pandey, a Brahmin, revolted against the British as the cartridge which was supplied to the army by the British was rumoured to be laced with tallow from cattle and had to be torn using teeth. It was this incident which apparently triggered the mass rebellion. Pursuant to this, in 1882, Swami Dayanand Saraswati formed a Gaurakhshini Sabha. It was during this time that communal clashes between Hindus and Muslims were reported for the first time. India had not had a history of communal riots before this. It was at this time that in the Punjab, the Sikh Kuka or Namdhari movement used the cow as a symbol for mobilisation among both Hindus and Sikhs against the British.

For all this history, surprisingly the cow held no attraction for the original mentor of the Hindutva brigade, V.D. Savarkar. For him, the cow was merely a useful animal, which should be protected for economic reasons, but he was against attributing religious qualities to it. For him that was 'anti-intellect' (sic) and a sign of 'weakness'.[45] He preferred the lion to the cow as a symbol of Hindutva. Savarkar said, 'Whilst considering the cow to be divine and worshipping her, the entire Hindu nation became docile like the cow. It started eating grass. If we are to now found our nation on the basis of an animal, let that animal be the lion.'[46]

Mahatma Gandhi was also confronted with the question of cow slaughter. Once the announcement was made that India would be a free country, there were many Indians who believed that a ban on cow slaughter would be true freedom. Yasmin Khan records an interesting anecdote in her book *The Great Partition: The Making of India and Pakistan.* She writes, that responding to fellow Congressman, Rajendra Prasad, who told Gandhi that he had received around 50,000 postcards, 30,000 letters and many thousand telegrams from all over the country, demanding a ban on cow slaughter, Gandhi said, 'In India, no law can be made to ban cow slaughter.... It will mean coercion against those Indians who are not Hindus ... How can I force anyone not to slaughter cows unless he is himself so disposed? It is not as if there are only Hindus in the Indian Union. There are Muslims, Parsees, Christians and other religious groups. The assumption of the Hindus that India has now become the land of the Hindus is erroneous. India belongs to all who live here.'[47]

If Gandhi envisioned a plural India, an India of diversity, where every faith had freedom, then Golwalkar was on a different page. His interpretation of history and his vision for India were vastly different. For him, India's history was a clash of two religions, Hinduism and Islam, and the followers of these religions could never live together in peace. In 1966, when he was asked how cow slaughter began in our country, his reply was, 'It began with the coming of the foreign invaders to our country. In order to reduce the population to slavery, they thought that the best way would be to stamp out every vestige of self-respect in Hindus. They took to various types of barbarism such as conversions, dashing our temples and mutts. In that line cow slaughter also began.'[48]

Following Golwalkar's lead, the RSS continued to give the issue of cow slaughter a religious slant, attributing divinity to the animal and insisting its protection was a sacred act. The first chief of the RSS, K.B. Hedgewar, wanted the Congress Party to pass a resolution against cow slaughter in its annual convention in 1920, held at Nagpur. Hedgewar was with the Congress at the time. Moreover, for the RSS, cow slaughter is not just about respecting the religious sentiments of the Hindus over the non-Hindus or specifically Muslims, but about fighting a stigma. Golwalkar said, 'Cow slaughter began in this country with a foreign domination. Mohammedans started it and the British continued it. Therefore, it is a stigma on us. We have now achieved independence and with it all such stigmas ought to be removed. Otherwise, we will be still labouring under mental slavery.'[49] Like Savarkar, he too contested the consumption of beef in the Vedic era, insisting that the supposed references were in fact misinterpretations of the word *gou*, which should be understood to indicate the *indriya*s, the senses. Golwalkar claimed, that when Yajnavalkya said that he would 'eat gou' he had, in fact, meant that he would conquer the senses and make himself invincible.[50]

On 7 November 1966, a massive rally was organised in Delhi with RSS support, demanding a ban on cow slaughter. Around 10,000 people, led by Hindu gurus and sadhus, blockaded the parliament. To control the mob, the police had to open fire; many protesters were injured and a few succumbed to their injuries. This was the first serious mobilisation on the issue of cow slaughter. Gulzarilal Nanda, then home minister, had to resign as it was presumed that he was sympathetic to the protesters' cause. To further quell the rising anger against cow slaughter, Prime Minister Indira Gandhi formed a high-powered committee headed by the former Chief Justice of India, Amal Kumar Sarkar, to study the issue of cow slaughter and make recommendations. Golwalkar was a member of the committee, along with the *shankaracharya* of Puri and Verghese Kurien (the 'milkman' of India). Pushpa Mittra Bhargava, the eminent scientist and Padma Bhushan awardee, was asked to appear before the committee to scientifically explain the relevance of the ban on cow slaughter. However, the committee, which was supposed to submit its report within six months, could not complete its deliberations over twelve years and finally had to be disbanded by Morarji Desai during his tenure as PM.

Three decades later, Bhargava went to see Kurien in Anand, Gujarat, along with a friend. When Bhargava reminded Kurien about the committee, Kurien told him that over the years, he and Golwalkar had become close friends and the latter had admitted to him that the cow protection agitation was only a political manoeuvre, which he had started only to embarrass the government.[51] Kurien narrated this conversation with Golwalkar in his biography *I Too Had a Dream*:

> One day after one of our meetings when he had argued passionately for banning cow slaughter, he came to me and asked, 'Kurien, shall I tell you why I am making an issue of this cow slaughter business?'
>
> I said to him, 'Yes, please explain to me because otherwise you are a very intelligent man. Why are you doing this?'
>
> 'I started a petition to ban cow slaughter actually to embarrass the government.... If this nation does not take pride in what it is and merely imitates other nations, how can it amount to anything? Then I saw that the cow had the potential to unify the country—she symbolises the future of Bharat. So I tell you what, Kurien, you agree with me to ban cow slaughter on this committee and I promise you, five years from that date I will have united the country. What I am trying to tell you is that I am not a fool, I am not a fanatic. I am just cold-blooded about this. I want to use the cow to bring out our Indianness. So please cooperate with me.'[52]

Golwalkar's statement offers a different perspective on the seeming ambivalence of Bhagwat and Modi—that it is a deliberate, well-calculated and cold-blooded political move, not a matter of faith. There is nothing religious about it, it is just a political tool, a part of a bigger plan.

Ambivalence is a strategic feature of the ideology whose grand project is to make Hindus appear macho and aggressive as a community. India is a democracy and constitutionalism is the basic principle of the polity, which abhors the use of violence as a political tool. Any justification for preaching of violence is not legally permissible, and is indeed a punishable offence. Hence the delayed responses, vague articulations and strategic silences are effective ways to covertly promote or support the actions of the foot soldiers. Prime Minister Modi's delayed and mild response to the Akhlaq lynching is a good example. Modi linked the Dadri episode with the scrapping of Pakistani ghazal singer Ghulam Ali's concert in Mumbai and Pune. Speaking to the Bengali newspaper *Anandabazar Patrika*, he said, 'The Dadri incident and cancellation of Ghulam Ali's concert are sad and unfortunate. The opposition is accusing the BJP of being communal but by doing so, is not the opposition responsible for this politics of polarisation?'[53] He not only avoided issuing an outright condemnation, but tried to turn the tables on the opposition.

Bhagwat's response to the killing of Pehlu Khan is equally indicative. By calling cow slaughter a vice that needs to be removed, Bhagwat enabled a stepping up of cow protection efforts across the country. To avoid adverse publicity, however, Bhagwat advised supporters that, many states where the RSS functionaries were in power had enacted a law on the ban of cow slaughter ... and that other state governments should follow suit. BJP governments in the states were more than willing to follow the diktats of the top boss. That year, a series of orders and instructions were passed by BJP-led governments in the states, on banning consumption of meat, cow slaughter and sale of beef, closing down abattoirs and undertaking raids on places where beef was supposedly served or eaten. These events had a direct bearing on the Muslim and Dalit citizens. The BJP-led Brihanmumbai Municipal Corporation (BMC) imposed a four-day ban on the sale of meat during the Jain fasting period of Paryushan, which was cut down to two days by the Bombay high court. At the same time, in Chhattisgarh, the BJP government ordered an eight-day ban on the sale of meat, which was, also, later revised to two days.

The ambivalence of the top leadership cannot be viewed in isolation from the direct and indirect support extended by members of the Hindutva fold to the killers of Akhlaq, Pehlu Khan, Junaid and others. The omissions and oversights can be interpreted or inferred by those opposed to Hindutva as a part of a bigger whole, designed to shield and incite the foot soldiers of the ideology.

As the demand for a beef ban was getting shriller, the Delhi police raided Kerala House, the official state mission for Kerala in the national capital, in the last week of October 2015, on the pretext of having heard beef was served there for lunch and dinner. Kerala House is a property of the Kerala government. The Delhi Police in fact have no jurisdiction there and may not enter without written permission. As a result, the raid was construed as an attack on the federal structure of the constitution. It's interesting to note that in Kerala, the BJP did not officially support a beef ban. In stark opposition to the central leadership's approach, the Kerala state unit president Vellamvelly Muraleedharan spoke his mind: 'The party won't interfere with what people eat and what they wear.'[54] The Goa chief minister and senior BJP leader Laxmikant Parsekar also did not support the ban on beef. These two gentlemen echoed the popular sentiments of their respective states instead. This attests to the resilience of the ideology, even as it affirms that the demands for a ban on cow slaughter and beef consumption are only a strategic tool, not a core value of the ideology—exactly what Golwalkar had told Kurien.

IDEOLOGY VERSUS DEMOCRACY

These episodes triggered a flurry of debates on faith versus reason, freedom versus religion, the limits of the state machinery versus the rights of citizens, citizenship versus identity, majoritarianism versus minoritarianism, liberalism versus obscurantism. The challenge to the Indian State was grave. The conversations were not merely about banning beef or not eating meat; they revolved around limiting the freedom of an individual, restricting the choices of citizens, imposing the wishes of one over another, dictating what the ideological others may or may not do, setting a single moral barometer for all, and intruding into the hitherto private spaces of persons. In the course of its evolution, democracy has tended to sharpen the process of individuation, constructing an idea of the individual as one who is complete in themselves, who is the master of their own universe and who does not want to be told what they should or should not do at every turn. In a democracy while, the rights of every individual are to be respected, it is equally important to be mindful of not infringing on the rights of others. The ban on beef came to be seen as an attempt to reverse that process of individuation and coerce the individual to be a part of a collective, where much of their freedom, aspirations, ambitions, privacy, desires and rights are subordinated to the collective will.

It was in this context that the Bombay high court rightly intervened and reversed the Maharashtra government's year-old law placing a total ban on beef across the state. The ban on beef consumption was struck down as unconstitutional as the court allowed the possession and/or consumption of beef that had been brought in from outside the state. The court said that the state could not dictate a citizen's choice of food.[55] However, this was a small victory. A bigger assault on the march of democracy was yet to come. In UP, the BJP had just won an unprecedented majority. Immediately after assuming power, the BJP government led by Yogi Adityanath, a five-time MP and head of the Gorakhnath Math in Gorakhpur district, ordered the closure of 'illegal abattoirs', a move that created mayhem. The state government justified its actions by citing an order from the National Green Tribunal. Adityanath said, 'Those(abattoirs) which are violating the orders of NGT and playing with the health of the public would not be spared.'[56] The slaughterhouses were mainly run by Muslim citizens. Meat shops are also mostly managed by Muslim citizens. Selling meat has often been their traditional business for generations. After the UP government's orders, they had no idea what to do.

Swaminathan S. Anklesaria Aiyar's letter of 2 April 2017 to Prime Minster Modi makes a moving account of the whole affair. He writes, 'In one sense, closing illegal units is good governance. Yet millions of hawkers make a living by illegally occupying pavements and paying no taxes. Millions of enterprises flout dozens of rules. Millions of squatters illegally invade cities. The answer can't be to shut down everything and expel everybody. We need a gradual formalisation of millions of informal enterprises plus tough administration for big rule breakers. By targeting abattoirs and meat processors, you effectively target two groups associated with this trade, Muslims and Dalits—the very opposite of Sabka Sath, Sabka Vikas.'[57]

The UP government's crackdown had a cascading effect with the Jharkhand government following its example. A sudden closure of abattoirs, without any notice, was accompanied by a crackdown on roadside mutton and chicken shops. This suddenly rendered lakhs of people jobless and left them facing a bleak future. The Gujarat government passed the harshest law to ban cow slaughter, raising the maximum jail sentence from seven years to fourteen years. The Chhattisgarh chief minister Raman Singh, in an apparent bid to outdo everyone said that those who would kill cows would be hanged in his state.[58]

What was further shocking was the Centre's notification to ban the sale of animals for slaughter in livestock markets, though this was ostensibly formulated to follow the supreme court's instructions to check the smuggling of animals to Nepal and Bangladesh. Many believed that the Centre's notification was ill-advised, as cross-border smuggling of animals is a law-and-order problem that needed to be dealt with as such, and a notification could not be the solution. Interestingly, again, the notification elicited the sharpest reaction from 'God's own country', Kerala. In what can be perceived to be a strong political statement, the ruling Left parties as well as the opposition held beef festivals on the first day of Ramadan. Malayalis took to social media to post pictures of beef dishes in an open contempt of the ban.[59]

Finally, the supreme court stayed the Centre's notification on 16 July 2017. The *Times of India* reported that the SC order was a big relief for the Muslim community, which had a large presence in the abattoir business, and could allay fears that the rules amounted to dietary restrictions and were intended to appease the Hindutva constituency. Yet, this did not deter the Maharashtra government to move the supreme court to seek the revival of a draconian law whose provision allowed any police officer to stop and search a person suspected of possessing the meat of cow or its progeny slaughtered outside Maharashtra.

The entire fracas took place at a time when India was the leading beef exporter in the world, its export value having quadrupled from $1.15 billion in 2009–10 to $4.78 billion in 2014–15. This was also a time when rural distress had acquired mammoth proportions and economists had been warning that a beef ban campaign would adversely affect India's economy, lead to unemployment and make farmers more desperate. Yet such is the power of the Hindutva ideology that such warnings fell on deaf ears. Maybe the annihilation of the enemy is more urgent in the visionary world than a bid to make India great again!

THREE

Victimhood No More
Dalits versus Hindutva

THE BRIDEGROOM'S PRIDE

'Am I not a Hindu?' asks Sanjay Kumar.

Over the past few months of 2018, the 27-year-old Dalit youth from Basai Babas village in Hathras district of western UP, has shot off letters to every government office-bearer, from the local police inspector to the state director general of police (DGP), the chief minister to the SC/ST Commission, approached local dailies to media outlets, and released videos on social media, seeking help to take out his baraat through his bride's Thakur-dominated village. On 15 March 2018, he moved the Allahabad high court.

'When the constitution says we are all equal and chief minister Yogi Adityanath says we are all Hindus and he heads a Hinduvadi party, why am I facing such a situation?' asks Kumar, a Block Development Council member. 'Am I not a Hindu then? There cannot be separate rules for people governed by one constitution.'[1]

The couple in question belong to the Jatav community. District Magistrate of the area, R.P. Singh, and Superintendent of Police, Piyush Srivastava, visited Kumar's bride Sheetal's village and advised them not to insist on having the wedding procession pass through the main streets of the village, both sides of which were flanked by Thakur households. No Jatav wedding procession had taken that route in the last twenty years and it was best avoided, they warned.

However, the bride's family was as determined as the groom's, and insisted this was about samman (family honour) and were loathe to back down.

Launching an offensive, the Thakurs cut off the water supply to the Jatav fields and procured the bride's school certificate that showed she was two months short of turning eighteen, and hence still a minor. Meanwhile, none of the officials came to the groom's aid. Instead, they all kept trying to convince the couple to accept the usual route adopted by the local Dalit families.

> District Magistrate. Singh, an upper caste himself, is unapologetic about where he stands. 'The two groups should not be fighting with each other. They are not Hindus and Muslims, they both are Hindus,' he says. 'Unlike a Muslim wedding, which is essentially a contract, a Hindu wedding is a bhawna (emotion). There is no concept of a juloos (procession). The Jatavs simply want to pick up a fight where there isn't one. We cannot change parampara (tradition).'
>
> Noting the stand taken by the authorities, BSP leader Ajay Kumar says Dalits like Kumar have few options, with the traditional channels of compromise mediated by village elders tilted against them. 'Dalit families have for long wanted to celebrate weddings in a grand manner but they would suppress their desires. But this time the groom is adamant,' Ajay says.

The responses may be unsurprising. Sheetal's family had expected opposition to begin with, which was why they sought permission from the village elders for the grand ceremony—and were denied. However, the family decided to persevere since they were upwardly mobile and keen to shed their past association of servitude to the Thakurs. Everyone in the family had completed their schooling, benefitted from reservation policies and now were mostly employed in government jobs. According to the bride's father they wanted it established that they didn't work for the Thakurs anymore.

The story caught my attention when it appeared on the front page of *Indian Express* on 1 April 2018. Finally, after much national outrage, the family was granted permission to take out a barat (groom's procession) through the main village streets. The story is simple and underlines a few points.

1. Educationally and economically, the Dalits are moving up the ladder.
2. They are aware of their rights, as ordained by the constitution.
3. Their rising consciousness has made them bolder and more assertive.
4. Traditional society is still in resistance mode vis-à-vis the Dalits.

5. Savarna resistance is leading to social conflict.²
6. There is a perception that the BJP is an upper-caste party.

It is a potentially explosive situation, likely to create a huge upset in Indian politics, enough to make the BJP nervous and Prime Minister Modi sweat.

The 2014 parliamentary election in Uttar Pradesh (UP) was a turning point in India's political history. The Dalits, who had earlier been voting en masse for the BSP led by Mayawati, deserted her and went with the BJP. Amit Shah, who was then in charge of the BJP in UP, successfully executed the necessary social engineering to sway the Dalit vote bank. Knowing that the BSP leadership was mostly dominated by the Jatavs, he wooed the other Dalit castes—Pasis, Dhobis, Valmikis, Khatiks and Dusadhs. Sixty non-Jatav candidates amongst the Dalits were given tickets across the country. Badri Narayan, one of the leading experts on Dalit politics, wrote, 'The Dalits were told that Mayawati, who heads the BSP, was indifferent towards them. At the same time, the BJP and RSS campaign also appropriated (Babasaheb Bhim Rao) Ambedkar and other Dalit heroes, promised a Bharat Ratna to Kanshiram, launched a social harmony project and organized meetings in Dalit hamlets with the help of social organizations such as Sewabharati and Vishwa Hindu Parishad, linked with the RSS.'³ The local cadre of the RSS mobilised the Dalits by playing up their Hindu identity. It was propagated that whatever the differences, Dalits were Hindus and at a time when Muslims were organised along religious lines, it was important to vote for a party that could protect Hindu interest. Dalits were told that Modi was a 'true' Hindu and at a time when a 'true' Hindu leader could become the prime minister, Dalits should not waste their votes. The strategy worked. The BJP-led NDA won seventy-three seats, whereas Mayawati scored a zero.

In the 2017 assembly elections in UP, history was repeated and the BJP romped home with an unprecedented majority. But a lot has changed since then. In 2018, the BJP contested four assembly elections—Karnataka, Rajasthan, Madhya Pradesh and Chhatisgarh—and it failed to win in any of the states. In Karnataka, Congress and the Janata Dal (Secular) formed the government, while Congress snatched Rajasthan, Madhya Pradesh and Chhatisgarh from the BJP. There is now a definite unease among the Dalits, leading to serious social conflicts. The story above is just the tip of the iceberg.

THE SCHOLAR'S DESPAIR

Long before Sanjay and Sheetal's struggle for a grand marriage, thousands of kilometres away from western UP, in Hyderabad, a brilliant research scholar who was also from the Dalit community, Rohith Vemula, revolted in the most tragic fashion against upper-caste domination. He committed suicide. Dalits are neither honoured in life nor in death, however. Their life is mocked, their death is ridiculed. Typically, a Dalit person committing suicide occasions no furore. But Vemula's suicide made the headlines. It forced people to think. In his suicide note, Vemula wrote:

> I would not be around when you read this letter. Don't get angry on me. I know some of you truly cared for me, loved me and treated me very well. I have no complaints on anyone. It was always with myself I had problems. I feel a growing gap between my soul and my body. And I have become a monster. I always wanted to be a writer. A writer of science, like Carl Sagan. At last, this is the only letter I am getting to write.
>
> I always wanted to be a writer. A writer of science, like Carl Sagan.
>
> I loved science, stars, nature, but then I loved people without knowing that people have long since divorced from nature. Our feelings are second handed. Our love is constructed. Our beliefs coloured. Our originality valid through artificial art. It has become truly difficult to live without getting hurt.
>
> The value of a man was reduced to his immediate identity and nearest possibility. To a vote. To a number. To a thing. Never was a man treated as a mind. As a glorious thing made up of star dust. In every field, in studies, in streets, in politics and in dying and living.
>
> I am writing this kind of letter for the first time. My first time of a final letter. Forgive me if I fail to make sense.
>
> My birth is my fatal accident. I can never recover from my childhood loneliness. The unappreciated child from my past.
>
> Maybe I was wrong, all the while, in understanding world. In understanding love, pain, life, death. There was no urgency. But I always was rushing. Desperate to start a life. All the while, some people, for them, life itself is curse. My birth is my fatal accident. I can never recover from my childhood loneliness. The unappreciated child from my past.
>
> I am not hurt at this moment. I am not sad. I am just empty. Unconcerned about myself. That is pathetic. And that is why I am doing this.
>
> People may dub me a coward. And selfish, or stupid once I am gone. I am not bothered about what I am called. I don't believe in after-death stories,

ghosts, or spirits. If there is anything at all I believe, I believe that I can travel to the stars. And know about the other worlds.

If you, who is reading this letter can do anything for me, I have to get 7 months of my fellowship, one lakh and seventy five thousand rupees. Please see to it that my family is paid that. I have to give 40 thousand to Ramji. He never asked them back. But please pay that to him from that.

Let my funeral be silent and smooth. Behave like I just appeared and gone. Do not shed tears for me. Know that I am happy dead than being alive.

'From shadows to the stars.'

Uma anna, sorry for using your room for this thing.

To ASA family, sorry for disappointing all of you, you loved me very much. I wish all the very best for the future.

For one last time.

Jai Bheem.

I forgot to write the formalities. No one is responsible for my this act of killing myself.

This is my decision and I am the only one responsible for this.

Don't trouble my friends and enemies on this after I am gone.[4]

Vemula is gone. But his spirit remains alive—alive with his questions. These questions need answers. Why has the value of a person been reduced to an 'immediate identity and nearest possibility'? Why did he say his birth was a 'fatal accident'? Why was he 'just empty'?

In his last days, Vemula would have had reasons to be a bitter man. He was thrown out of his hostel room along with four other students. He desperately wanted to get his life back on track but his pleas were rejected by the officials at the University of Hyderabad. Yet he did not blame anyone—neither for his expulsion nor for his death. Instead he wrote, 'No one is responsible for my this act of killing myself.' He could have easily blamed the University Vice Chancellor, Appa Rao Podile, or the Akhil Bharatiya Vidhyarthi Parishad (ABVP) student member Nandanam Susheel Kumar, on whose complaint he was expelled. He could have mentioned in his letter, the name of Smriti Irani, then minister for Human Resource and Development (HRD) at the Centre, given that her ministry wrote four letters to the university authorities asking what action was taken against the students who had organised a protest rally against the hanging of Yakub Memon. He could have blamed Bandaru Dattatreya, a central minister and local MP, for putting pressure on Smriti Irani. Yet, he did no such thing. Was he assigning his birth as the cause of his emptiness? Or perhaps, as Santhosh S. so eloquently put it, 'By stating that *no one* is responsible for this act of killing himself, he redistributes that responsibility to *everyone*. This (re)distribution, or the refusal to name, is a reclamation of the sacredness of his act ...'[5]

To try and trace the genesis of Vemula's questions, one might note he was originally a Marxist, a member of the Students' Federation of India (SFI), but later became an Ambedkarite. He wrote in his personal journal: 'The shift of my political identity from Marxism to Ambedkarism is a conscious move to build a new future on the foundation of a more humane and inclusive society. I intend on compelling this stratified society, perforce, to take off its elitist mask of generosity and solidarity, which is a product of seamless majoritarian cultural unity or nationalism.'[6]

We know Vemula was born into a Dalit family and brought up by his mother single-handedly. He had a fire in his belly. Despite his young age, he was already a highly educated man. He joined the university not on the reservation quota but through the mainstream admission process. He had a dream—he wanted to break his shackles and change the oppressive social structures: 'My core intention is to challenge and expose the upper class hypocritical advocacy of progressiveness which shamelessly maintains its ties with the oppressive structures of class, caste and gender.'[7]

So why was Vemula expelled from his hostel? He was allegedly involved in a brawl with Nandanam Susheel Kumar, an activist of the ABVP, the student wing of the RSS. Kumar had allegedly referred to members of the Ambedkar Students' Association (ASA) as goons on Facebook. Vemula was an active member of the ASA. An argument ensued when members of the ASA confronted Kumar who later complained that its members had assaulted him. The proctorial board initially gave Vemula and the four other scholars implicated a clean chit. Apparently the board could not find any evidence of misdemeanour. However, ABVP students approached Dattatreya, who obliged them by writing a letter to Irani, calling these students 'casteist, extremist and anti-national'.[8] Irani must have felt obliged to write to the university authorities to take action, and action did follow. The students found no relief on appealing to the high court of Hyderabad either. Their fellowships were stopped.

The students were up against a formidable establishment—two central ministers, the vice chancellor, the proctorial board and an army of the RSS's student wing, the ABVP. Also, Vice Chancellor Appa Rao Podile who had been chosen and appointed over thirty-five other candidates, had reportedly rusticated ten Dalit students when he was the hostel's chief warden in 2002.[9] Vemula had no money, he had no place to live and he was called 'anti-national'. How was he supposed to continue fighting? He took his life. His death finally provoked the required discourse and highlighted the questions he had raised.

Is justice even possible for Dalits in the Brahmanical order perpetuated by the RSS–BJP ideology? Will there ever be a social order in which everyone is equal? Is social democracy, and not just a political democracy, possible? And finally, what Babasaheb Ambedkar had said about constitutional equality and liberty was all very well and good, but what about fraternity? Could it be a mere coincidence that Dalit agitation is picking up momentum alongside the rise of an aggressive and masculine Hindutva?

Vemula's suicide caused the first major Dalit revolt against the Modi government. It united the entire political landscape minus the BJP and the RSS. Congress, the Aam Aadmi Party (AAP), the Leftists, All India Trinamool Congress (TMC) and the liberals, all demanded the removal of Irani and Dattatreya. Noted writer Ashok Vajpeyi returned the DLitt degree he had been awarded by the University of Hyderabad. He said, 'A dalit student, Rohith Vemula, who wanted to be a writer was driven to commit suicide ... I have decided to return the award in protest against university authorities, (who were) presumably acting under political pressure.'[10]

In a most unfortunate reaction, a one-man judicial enquiry commission, set up by the HRD ministry reported that Vemula was not from the Dalit community at all. Dalits across India were enraged and social media provided them a platform to articulate their anger. This single incident united Dalits of all shades. In one voice they said that Dalits had no future under the present regime. The echo was heard in other educational institutions too. A literal caste war broke out in the prestigious Indian Institute of Mass Communication (IIMC), Delhi, when a group of eighteen students and three professors held a meet on 18 January 2016, expressing their solidarity with the plight of Rohith Vemula. Offensive posts were written by a few upper-caste students in response. The BJP blamed the opposition for politicising the incident, while the RSS viewed it as a turf war between the liberal Left and Hindutva to dominate educational institutions.

If Rohith Vemula's suicide was the trigger point for a radical rise of consciousness among the Dalits, then the brutal beating of Dalits in Una, Gujarat, on the pretext of cow protection, became the spark for the first organised mass upsurge by Dalits against the Modi government. On 11 July 2016, a video surfaced on various TV channels with horrific visuals of four men being mercilessly beaten. These Dalits of Mota Samadhiyala village, near Una in Gir Somnath district, were accused of killing a cow. When confronted by the cow vigilantes, they explained that they were only skinning a cow that had died, per their customary livelihood. The vigilantes responded by tying them to their car and beating them up with sticks and iron rods. One of the accused filmed the whole incident himself. Unsurprisingly, the video went viral. The Dalit family were then dragged to Una town and beaten again, until the police took charge of them while the assailants sped away in their car. As the entire nation witnessed the brutality, the infuriated Dalit community organised a protest in Una. The matter was raised in parliament. Protests spread to other parts of Gujarat. Twelve Dalit youth tried to commit suicide to protest against the incident; one of them died. Finally, sixteen perpetrators were arrested and four policemen were suspended. I had visited Una at the time with Arvind Kejriwal to meet the victims. We were told that such incidents had been happening for a long time, but the difference was that this time people outside Una had learnt of it due to the media attention.

By now, the Dalits were too angry to be subdued by punitive action alone. In a powerful message to the BJP government, they initiated the Dalit Asmita Yatra from Ahmedabad to Una and organised a huge rally in Ahmedabad, attended by thousands. Jignesh Mevani, an articulate firebrand of a man in his thirties, with Left leanings, emerged as the new face of the movement. His words—'We have had enough. We will break their hands and legs if the upper-caste exploiters torture us any more,'[11]—echoed the sentiments of Dalits brutalised over generations.

This organised response to the institutional torture of Dalits was remarkable for several reasons:

1. The entire protest was spontaneous. It was organised without the support of any political party. Darshan Desai, a senior journalist who has been a keen observer of Gujarat politics, wrote, 'This was the

first time that as many as 30 Dalit groups from across Gujarat came together to raise a plethora of issues that the community has faced for decades.'[12]
2. This kind of collective assertion had never been seen before. Gujarat is the original laboratory of Hindutva. No other state has been polarised along communal lines the way Gujarat has. The RSS controls every aspect of life in the state. Under Modi's thirteen-year rule, the BJP government has almost finished off every other popular movement, blunted the edge of every other organisation, and nipped every other leader in the bud. It was evident this was not a government habituated to countenancing any voice of dissent. In a state like this, where Dalits are only 7 per cent of the population, the mobilisation on such a large scale was a stupendous achievement. Mevani said, 'That they came, no-holds barred with an unprecedented and unseen confidence. We spoke and spoke with freedom, with our heart. This has never happened, and this is the precursor of what is in store.'[13]
3. The rally also hinted at a polarisation of a different nature, which could take the shape of an all-India phenomenon in the future. This rally was attended by Muslims too. The Jamiat-Ulema-e-Hind participated in the rally. Slogans like 'Dalit–Muslim ekta zindabad, fansiwad murdabad (Long live Dalit–Muslim unity; down with fascism)' reverberated throughout the grounds.

THE THIRD WAVE

The name is Chandrashekhar Azad. He is popularly known as Ravan and has a thick moustache he loves to twirl. He was released from jail in September 2018 after more than a year. Two years ago, he was a non-entity. He shot into prominence when he put up a board in his village that said, 'Here lives the Great Chamar.'[14] The local Rajputs objected. How dare an untouchable use the word 'great' with his name? Now Chandrashekhar is another face for the Dalit community to rally behind.

Chandrashekhar Azad belongs to Saharanpur and heads the Bhim Army. On 14 April 2017, BJP MP Raghav Lakhanpal of Saharanpur insisted on taking out a procession in the name of Babasaheb Ambedkar on his 126th birth anniversary, travelling through the local Muslim neighbourhood, along with activists from the Hindu Yuva Vahini, an organisation founded by Yogi Adityanath before he became the chief minister. As the procession was passing through the neighbourhood, provocative slogans were shouted. Radheshyam, the district president of Rashtriya Dalit Mahasabha, said, 'What I found odd was that instead of Jai Bhim, they were raising slogans of 'Jai Shri Ram (Hail Lord Ram)' and 'Mandir wahin banayenge (We shall build the temple only there)'. This angered the Muslims.'[15] A violent confrontation ensued.

Not too long after, on 5 May 2017, in a seemingly unrelated incident, a local Rajput youth took out a procession in Shabbirpur village nearby, commemorating the Rajput king Rana Pratap, during the course of which the village head objected to the blaring music. The Rajputs did not like this. Verbal altercations escalated into a physical fight. Dalit households were torched, the local Ravidas temple was attacked and idols desecrated. One Rajput lost his life. The Bhim Army, co-founded by Chandrashekhar Azad of Saharanpur, called for a mahapanchayat meeting on 9 May. The police declined permission for the gathering. Nonetheless, defiant Bhim Army supporters tried to congregate at the venue. The police initiated a lathi charge to disperse the crowd. A manhunt for various Bhim Army activists, including Azad, followed.

A few days later, Azad appeared at Jantar Mantar in Delhi, at a rally organised by the Dalits to protest against the police atrocities in Saharanpur. He coined a new aspirational slogan: 'Mere saath kaho—hum desh ke shashak hain. (Say with me—we are the rulers of the country.)' The rally sent out a strong message that Dalits would not cower down any more. Unfortunately, the Modi government did not seem to grasp the seriousness of the issue. By the time Azad was arrested in Himachal Pradesh, his stature had grown. Mayawati rushed to Saharanpur. Her visit was followed by another round of violence due to caste tensions between Dalits and upper-caste Rajput men, which led to two deaths and more than a dozen people being injured. Azad was granted bail by the Allahabad high court, which considered the charges against him frivolous and politically motivated, but before he could be released, the BJP government of UP under Yogi Adityanath invoked the draconian National Security Act (NSA) to keep him in jail.

As in Gujarat, the Dalits of western UP have also been trying to form a grand alliance with Muslims and other backward classes (OBCs) in the area.

Azad spoke of it at Jantar Mantar. Ravi Kumar Gautam, the twenty-six-year-old president of the Bhim Army's youth wing, said, 'We are not the only ones who suffer. Brahmin tyranny has made victims out of Muslims and OBCs as well. Our appeal to them is to join hands with their Dalit brothers and sisters.'[16] Amrish Chotala, who holds an MA degree, says, 'Right-wing forces try to tell us that Muslims are our enemies. But we don't think so. Muslims never deny us entry into mosques but Brahmins stop us from entering temples. So who is our real enemy?'[17]

The Saharanpur riots serve as a reminder that this third wave of Dalit radicalisation is igniting the minds of a supressed class towards a new battle. If the first one was led by Babasaheb Ambedkar during the Indian freedom struggle, Kanshiram was the architect of the second wave in the 1980s and the 1990s. The third wave is radicalising a whole new generation of articulate, educated and more confident Dalits who are not dependent on any one leader or individual. This is a self-generated social movement with people like Chandrashekhar Azad at the forefront.

After Saharanpur, Bhima Koregaon in Maharashtra was the next flashpoint. Bhima Koregaon is known for the Third Anglo–Maratha War in 1818, which took place between the Maratha peshwa's troops and the British army. The peshwa lost the battle and, with this defeat, the Maratha rule touched its nadir. Babasaheb visited the place in 1927 to pay his respects at the Bhima Koregaon war monument, and since then it has been a place of annual pilgrimage for many people from Dalit communities across the country. The year 2018 was the 200th anniversary of that historic battle, a special occasion. The Dalits therefore assembled in great numbers that year. However, before detailing the violent clash between Dalits and pro-Hindutva forces that followed, a slight digression into history and the Hindutva view on historicity is warranted for context.

HINDUTVA, DALITS AND DIVERGENT HISTORIES

One may ask why the defeat of the peshwa by the British, should be celebrated by the Dalits. The answer lies in the composition of the victorious army. The British army was much smaller than the 30,000-strong force of the last peshwa, Baji Rao II. However, the British side included Mahars in large numbers in its regiments.[18] The credit for the defeat of the peshwa went to the valour of these Mahar soldiers. As Thomas Crowley put it in his article '200 Years of Anti-Caste Struggle', for the Dalits, the peshwa's defeat signalled the end of the oppressive Brahmanical regime. 'For Ambedkar, the battle of Koregaon did not represent a British victory, but the end of the tyrannical peshwas and the assertion of Mahar strength and dignity. Recognising Mahar valour was part of the transition from Untouchable to Dalit.'[19]

In contrast, the peshwa's loss was interpreted by the Hindutva forces as the end of Hindu rule. M.S. Golwalkar contested Ambedkar's interpretation of the Bhima Koregaon battle and portrayed 'the Peshwas as Proto-nationalists'[20] Obviously, Hindutva elements do not like the annual congregation of Dalits in Koregaon. But there is also a subtext that runs alongside the main text of the Bhima Koregaon conflict.

Chhatrapati Shivaji Maharaj's son Chhatrapati Sambhaji Maharaj was killed by the Mughal emperor Aurangzeb in 1689. At his execution, it was also announced that if anybody was found performing any last rites for Sambhaji, they too would be put to death. Govind Gopal Gaikwad, of the Mahar caste, defied Aurangzeb's diktat and performed the last rites—and was accordingly executed. Thus Gaikwad became a symbol of Mahar valour and courage. A tomb was erected in his memory in the village of Vadhu Budruk, Pune, opposite the tomb of Sambhaji. However, this version of the Mahars' history is contested by the Marathas. Sambhaji was a Maratha himself, of course. Another memorial stands in Vadhu Budruk, this one dedicated to the Shivale Deshmukhs, who the Maratha residents of the village believe performed Sambhaji's last rites.[21]

On 30 December 2017, a board that declared Gaikwad had performed the last rites of Sambhaji Maharaj was set up near the tomb. However, some people, who believed that it was actually their ancestors who had performed the last rites, tried to forcibly remove the board and it led to a confrontation.[22] It was alleged that two organisations, the Sambhaji Brigade led by Sambhaji Bhide and the Hindu Ekta Aghadi led by Milind Ekbote, had been active in the area for a week prior to the annual congregation for the Bhima Koregaon anniversary and had been instigating villagers against Dalits' assembly. Stones were pelted at the congregation by pro-Hindutva elements, which triggered violence and caused the death of one. The Dalits retaliated with vengeance: 'The Dalit outfits took to the streets over the incident and vandalised buses in Pune, Thane, Kalyan, Dombivli and Ulhasnagar. Many private vehicles and more than 134 state transport buses in Chembur were damaged.'[23] A call for a Maharashtra bandh was issued by Dalit groups the very next day. Violent protests again erupted on 3 January. The bandh paralysed life in Mumbai, Pune, Pimpri–Chinchwad, Nagpur and Aurangabad.

The Maharashtra government was run by the BJP at the time. Instead of recognising the sensitivity of the issue, the BJP government tried to twist the facts and blamed the 'breaking India brigade'—a term it uses to refer to ultra-Leftists and Naxals—for the agitation. An order was issued to register cases against Dalit leaders Jignesh Mevani and Umar Khalid under sections 153 A, 505 and 117 for disturbing the peace—they had been present in Shaniwar Wada, where they had delivered speeches at Elgar Parishad—an event to commemorate the 200th anniversary of the battle of Koregaon—on 31 December 2017. The RSS also placed the blame on 'anti-India elements'. Manmohan Vaidya, the joint general secretary of the RSS, said, 'The breaking India brigade had raised anti-India slogans at JNU in 2016, and is now trying to divide the Hindu society …'[24] Dalit leaders, on the other hand, demanded the arrest of Sambhaji Bhide and Milind Ekbote for inciting violence.

The battle of Koregaon is a sore point for the Hindutva warriors. The loss not only brought on the demise of the Maratha empire but also heralded the death of the first Hindu kingdom. To Hindutva ideologues Indian history is a continuous religious war between the Hindu and others, from the Vedic era to the present. In their analysis, the Maratha empire led by the peshwas deserves pride of place because for the first time the Hindus had established such a vast empire, comparable in its geographical reach to any foreign empire on Indian soil. Savarkar, who had done a brilliant systematic study of Indian history from the Hindutva point of view, contextualised the Maratha empire accordingly. From his perspective, it is a farce to claim that Hindus as a nation are a recent phenomenon. He argues that the inhabitants living between the Sindhu (Indus) river and the Sindhu ocean, with their rich culture and great value system, have always been a nation—theirs is a glorious tradition that existed even before Christianity and Islam were born. In the Vedic era, when other civilisations were still in their dark ages, the Hindus already had a well-developed system of knowledge, he argued—their philosophy was rich and their language and traditions were highly evolved. It was the Hindu golden period. Foreign invasions disrupted that great tradition and as Hindus digressed from the Vedic ways, the decline of their civilisation began.

Alexander was the first invader to break down the boundaries of the great Hindu nation but it has to be noted that the Greeks were also the inheritors of an equally great civilisation. They had a developed system of knowledge and learning, which continues to be enlightening. Hindu ideologues use good words for them, but in a somewhat miserly fashion. In the eyes of Savarkar, Indians were far superior to Greeks. 'They proved to be powerless before the Indians and hence was this ignoble retreat,' Savarkar says, discussing Alexander's retreat.[25]

In the period following the Greeks' departure, Savarkar praised Chandragupta Maurya and his guru Chanakya, who established the Maurya dynasty, but loathed the very name of King Ashoka, who is typically hailed as one of the greatest rulers in history. Ashoka's conversion to Buddhism and thereafter his state protection of Buddhism was understood by Savarkar as the main reason for the decline of Hinduism. Savarkar believed that the Buddhist onslaught was so severe that Hinduism almost reached its deathbed, but King Pushyamitra Shunga helped revive its vitality between 184 BC and 149 BC. Savarkar wrote with glee that Pushyamitra was not content with the peaceful revival of Hindu rites, but indulged in a savage persecution of Buddhism.

Pushyamitra Shunga was originally commander-in-chief in the Mauryan army, when he assassinated King Brihadratha Maurya, and ascended the throne. This event has been seen by a section of historians as a revolution in Indian history. Pushyamitra was a Brahmin and his coronation planted the seeds of revival of Brahmanism. Buddhism retreated. Babasaheb Ambedkar, while tracing the origin of untouchability, wrote, 'Its significance can't be measured by treating it simply as a change of dynasty. It was a political revolution as great as the French Revolution, if not greater. It was a bloody revolution engineered by the Brahmins to overthrow the rule of Buddhist kings.'[26] Ambedkar further wrote that in order to justify the killing, 'This triumphant Brahmanism was in need of many things. It is of course needed to make Chaturvarna the law of the land the validity of which was denied by the Buddhists. It needed to make animal sacrifice which was abolished by the Buddhists, legal … Triumphant Brahmanism wanted on a sacred text, infallible in its authority to justify their transgressions.'[27] And thus the controversial Manusmriti came into existence.

Hinduism could only regain a portion of its former glory during the Gupta period from AD 240 to AD 605. The Gupta kings were patrons of Brahmanism, but this was hugely different from the Hinduism of the Vedic period. Ambedkar stated that there was no untouchability in the Vedic era. Untouchability could not be found in recorded history until AD 400. Untouchability, as per Ambedkar, was the result of the struggle for supremacy between Buddhism and Brahmanism. In order to defeat Buddhism and capture the minds of the people, Brahmanism adopted a few practices from Buddhism. Since Buddhists did not eat animal flesh, Brahmins also decided not to eat meat. The Gupta kings made cow slaughter a sin and a capital offence. This hit people at the lowest strata of society badly, as meat, especially the flesh of cattle, was a key nutritional resource for them. Ambedkar explained, 'Since the cow became sacred and the Broken Men (Dalits) continued to eat beef, there was no other fate left for the Broken Men except to be treated unfit for Association i.e. as Untouchable.'[28]

It must be noted that the caste system was already an integral part of Hinduism. It existed even in the Vedic era, but was based on occupation then. Within the caste hierarchy, upward and downward mobility was possible, depending on the profession one was engaged in. But following the advent of Buddhism and with the emergence of the Manusmriti, the caste system degenerated and turned rigid. It became inherent—one inherited a caste; movement within the structure stopped and the system became oppressive and dehumanising. Shudras or the 'foot-born' were treated as less than human.[29] Since the tradition had the sanction of religion, it was impossible for them to receive justice or salvation within the caste system. Ambedkar said, 'Hindu looks upon the observance of untouchability as an act of religious merit, and non-observance of it as sin.'[30] He asked, 'Why will not a Hindu touch an Untouchable? Why will not a Hindu allow an Untouchable to enter [a] temple or use the village well? Why will not a Hindu admit an Untouchable in the inn? The answer to each one of these questions is [the] same. It is that Untouchable is an unclean person, not for the social intercourse.'[31]

Hindu ideologues apparently do realise that untouchability is a bad practice and do dub it a curse. Savarkar said that it would be ungrateful on our part if we desisted from criticising with sufficient severity the unlimited harm done by this caste system and the irrational and obstinate pride that Hindus took in it.³² Golwalkar called untouchability a 'religious perversion'.³³ RSS thinker Rakesh Sinha cites a letter written by Golwalkar to senior RSS leader, K Suryanarayana Rao, in which he wrote, 'We have to completely eliminate untouchability and distinctions of higher and lower caste.'³⁴ His successor 'Balasaheb' Madhukar Dattatraya Deoras's speech in 1974 in Pune is always cited by the RSS as proof of their commitment to the amelioration of Dalits. He said, 'Untouchability is a most painful and unfortunate aspect of social inequality in our society ... If Untouchability is not a sin, nothing is.'³⁵ Interestingly, the RSS takes great pride in telling its critics that it organised a regional convention of the VHP in 1969 in Udupi, where a resolution was passed, which, frankly, conveys nothing except the organisation's concerns about the unity of the Hindus.

It wouldn't be too harsh to say that the RSS's concern for the untouchables is only lip service. Had it not been so, given the kind of human resources it controls as an organisation, it could have successfully launched a movement for the upliftment of Dalits and for the elimination of untouchability; but it did not do that and never will. From their past actions, it appears that Dalits are not a part of their agenda. The RSS and Hindutva forces firmly believe in the caste system. It is so entrenched in their thought process that they have refused to move beyond it. The RSS believes that it is due to the robustness of the caste system that Hindus could survive as a religion for thousands of years, that Hindus could withstand the onslaughts of several civilisations and could regain freedom and independence despite so many foreign invasions. For the RSS adherents, caste grants social cohesion and unity. Any attack on the caste system makes them paranoid and they smell a conspiracy to weaken Hinduism. In fact, they blame the British for developing awareness of caste inequity in pursuit of their policy to divide and rule.

Golwalkar, while he did not condone untouchability, opined, 'Society was conceived of as the fourfold manifestation of the Almighty to be worshiped by all, each in his own way and according to his capacity. If a Brahaman became great by imparting knowledge, a Kshatriya was hailed as equally great for destroying the enemy. No less important was the Vaishya who fed and sustained society through agriculture and trade or the Shudra who served society through his art and craft. Together and by their mutual interdependence in a spirit of identity, they constituted the social order.'³⁶ He challenged critics and claimed that if the caste system had really been the root cause of weakness, then people would have succumbed to foreign invasions and converted to other religions, abandoning Hinduism; yet this had not happened. He added, 'Separatist consciousness breeding jealousy and conflict is being fostered in sections of our people by naming them Harijans, Scheduled Caste, Scheduled Tribes and so on and by parading the gifts of special concessions to them in a bid to make them all their slaves with the lure of money.'[37] One is tempted to ask how Golwalkar could be so blind to the plight of Dalits. Why could he not see the dehumanising dimension of the caste system and the torture visited on Dalits, historically and in the present? Why couldn't he see the pain of a community whose mere shadow was believed to pollute an 'upper-caste' person, the futility of expecting a sense of community and belonging for a person who was barred entry to the temple and treated as less than human?

Savarkar went a step yet further than Golwalkar. He brazenly supported the Manusmriti, which said that a Shudra who insults a high-caste man with gross invectives should have his tongue cut out, for the former was of low origin; that if he arrogantly taught Brahmins their duty, the king should cause hot oil to be poured into his mouth and into his ears; that a low-caste man who tried to place himself on the same seat with a man of high caste should be branded on his hips and be banished or the king should cause his buttocks to be gashed.[38] Of this same text, Savarkar said, 'Manusmriti is that scripture which is most worshipable after Vedas for our Hindu nation.'[39] Did Savarkar mean that in his ideal Hindu nation, Dalits or Shudras or untouchables would have no place? His only concern seemed to have been that Dalits should not abandon Hinduism and embrace Islam. During his time, there were 7 crore Dalit citizens, a rather large number. But, under his leadership, the Hindu Mahasabha openly said that it would not insist on framing laws to explicitly allow the entry of untouchables into temples.

The demand for a separate identity for Dalits and the fight for their rights continues to unnerve the RSS. But why blame only Savarkar and Golwalkar? The caste system always had an exalted position in mainstream Hinduism. The social reform movements of the nineteenth century did not believe in the abolition of the caste system, though in many respects these movements were progressive enough to severely criticise many evils of the Hindu tradition. Vivekananda was so radical in his definition of God and religion that he went to the extent of saying, 'I don't believe in a God or a religion which can't wipe the widow's tears or bring a piece of bread to the orphan,' but even he defended the caste system.[40] He said, 'Caste system was one of the greatest social institutions the Lord gave to mankind … India fell because you prevented and abolished caste.'[41] Swami Dayanand Saraswati, who believed that India's salvation lay in going back to the Vedas, was also a great supporter of the caste system. However, neither Saraswati nor Vivekananda approved of the caste system in its current form. They both rejected the idea of caste privileges and hereditary caste identity. Yet, the Hindutva brigade did not have the courage to openly denounce the caste system based on birth, adhering instead to Brahmanism, which can never accept Dalits into its fold. So it is no wonder that the Hindutva brigade would rather lament the peshwas, than celebrate the valour of the Dalit opponents who trounced them in Bhima Koregaon.

The Maratha empire founded by Shivaji did initially recruit the untouchable Mahars into its army, allowing them to attain a position of respectability; but with the arrival of the peshwas, who later emerged as the de facto rulers of the Maratha empire, the Mahars were again marginalised and oppressed. The peshwas were Brahmins—the first two were Deshastha and the rest Chitpawan.[42] The peshwas were great warriors and were the reason for the decline of the Mughal empire. Savarkar thus termed Maratha's resurgence as the victory of the Hindu nation. He wrote, 'Their (the Marathas') sole objective was to liberate Hindu religion and Hindu nation … and to establish all over India a sovereign Hindu power.'[43] Savarkar's praise of the peshwas did not find support from Ambedkar, of course, who himself was a Mahar. For him, the *peshwashahi* symbolised a Brahmin raj, an oppressive regime in which Dalits were treated as untouchables.

Ambedkar wrote, 'Under the rule of the Peshwas in the Maratha country, the untouchable was not allowed to use public streets if a Hindu was coming along lest he should pollute the Hindus by his shadow. The untouchable was required to have a black thread either on his wrist or in his neck, as sign or a mark to prevent the Hindus from getting themselves polluted by his touch through mistake. In Poona, the capital of the Peshwa, the untouchable was required to carry, strung from his waist, a broom to sweep away from behind the dust he treaded on, lest a Hindu walking on the same should be polluted. In Poona the untouchable was required to carry an earthen pot hung around his neck wherever he went, for holding his spit, lest his spit falling on the earth should pollute a Hindu who might unknowingly happen to tread on it.'[44]

So for Ambedkar, unlike for the Hindutva ideologues, the defeat of the peshwas at Bhima Koregaon was a liberation. His visit to Bhima Koregaon in 1927 was a symbolic gesture. For the Hindutva forces, this perspective is treasonous and unpatriotic, as the peshwas were defeated by foreigners, the British.

HINDUTVA WANTS THE DALITS, BUT NOT AS ITS OWN

It is then not surprising that the RSS refused to take a stand on the issue of violence that occured in January 2018 in Bhima Koregaon, Pune and other places. It only condemned the violence and demanded strict action against the perpetrators, whereas other Hindutva organisations called the Dalit congregation anti-national. Instead of being sympathetic to the cause of Dalits, attempts were made to give the whole incident a different colour. It was declared a Naxal act. On 28 August 2018, five prominent civil and human rights' activists—Sudha Bhardwaj, Varavara Rao, Arun Ferreira, Vernon Gonsalves and Gautam Navlakha were arrested. The Maharashtra police said, 'We have been able to recover several CDs, hard drives and letters. There are credible links with the Elgar Parishad organised in Pune and the violence thereafter and these people have been on the watch list for quite some time.'[45] BJP president Amit Shah unhesitatingly said, 'In the context of the Naxals, those who have been held face serious charges like conspiring to purchase arms, helping Naxals and plotting to kill the prime minister.'[46]

What was most surprising was that despite clear evidence, Manohar Bhide and Milind Ekbote, whose names figured prominently in the first FIR registered on 1 January 2018, had not been arrested. The police had in fact, in a counter affidavit, told the supreme court that they posed a threat to the witnesses. Times Now on 1 September 2018 reported, 'The report compiled by a ten-member committee formed by the Pune police has blamed Hindutva activists Sambhaji Bhide and Milind Ekbote for orchestrating violence that took place on 1 January in which one person was also killed.'[47]

This clearly underlines the fact that the BJP government at the centre, and in Maharashtra, were shielding the main culprits because of ideological affinities whereas those who were sympathetic to the Dalit cause were targeted.[48] The Bhima Koregaon conflict was termed an act of Naxalism instead of viewing it as a Dalit assertion. This leads us to the question—is the rise of Hindutva antagonistic to the assertion of the rights of Dalits?

To be fair to the RSS, Deoras, when he took charge, did try to break away from the past. In his famous speech in Pune in 1974, Deoras talked about eradicating social inequality in each and every form and called for adoption of roti–beti vyavahaar—breaking bread and inter-marrying between castes; but even he was unable to urge his followers beyond mere symbolism. Yes, it is true that in 1989 the VHP, an affiliate of the RSS spearheading the Ram mandir agitation, organised the shilanyas (laying of the foundation stone) by a Dalit person. It was an effort to send a serious message. But it ended up being mere tokenism.

Still, the RSS had been seriously jolted by the Meenakshipuram episode in 1981 when thousands of Dalits converted to Islam. In 2014, the RSS did mobilise Dalits to vote for the BJP and after coming to power, Modi tried to reach out to the Dalit community through Dalit entrepreneurs while party president Amit Shah was seen visiting Dalit hamlets and breaking bread with them. But even these attempts failed to leave any lasting impact. I have directly asked RSS leaders, on multiple occasions, why the organisation is unable to attract the Dalit population in large numbers when it stands for the unity of the Hindus. Every time I was told that the 'upper-caste mindset' was a big stumbling block. I was also told that the entire leadership of the organisation is dominated by Brahmins and they control every operation. As Nilanjan Mukhopadhyay writes in *Economic Times*, 'Insiders in the Parivar accept that since January when the government challenged Vemula's Dalit identity, the latent "savarn-mansikta" or Upper Caste mentality has repeatedly surfaced in BJP with support from a section within RSS.'[49]

The filthy language used to refer to BSP leader Mayawati, in 2016, by BJP vice president in UP, Dayashankar Singh, is one reflection of this mentality. Singh was thrown out of the party on the eve of the UP elections; but it was merely an exercise in damage control. Singh's wife, who had not been active in politics until then, was given a ticket for the assembly elections, and later made a minister. After the assembly elections, Singh was admitted back into the party, and he is now back in the vice president's chair as well. It is this absence of an honest and cohesive approach that makes Modi's claim of being an 'Ambedkar bhakt' unconvincing.

NEW DALIT IDENTITIES AND NEWER DISCRIMINATIONS

Three generations have passed since Ambedkar launched the Mahad agitation in 1927.[50] India has also progressed. Indian society is more literate, more open, more confident, more competitive, more aspirational and more deeply engaged with new ideas and technologies. Dalits have also moved with the times. Now more and more Dalits aspire to go to colleges and universities. 'Our parents never went to school and faced unbearable atrocities at their villages,' says Dontha Prasanth, one of the four students to have been suspended along with Rohith Vemula. 'We have left those villages and reached the university campus. But here we find new and modern forms of discrimination. But we are not going to be slaves to oppression here as well. We will assert our identity and fight for it.'[51] The new, educated generation of Dalits have compulsorily read Ambedkar's writings or are at least aware of his struggles—they are very well acquainted with his ideas and his revolt against the Hindu establishment. For them, he is a great inspiration. Ambedkar revolutionised the Dalit self-identity but the community itself did the rest. Today, they are no longer diffident and submissive. Dalit thinker Chandra Bhan Prasad says, 'This generation feels free, feels that no one owns them and they are masters of their own destiny. My generation saw humiliation and lost their "manobal" (self confidence) ...'[52]

The economic reforms since 1991 have also helped revolutionise their psyche. They have opened up new avenues and instilled new confidence in the idea that if one is meritorious and competitive, caste is no barrier. According to Prasad, who is an advisor to the Dalit Indian Chamber of Commerce & Industry (DICCI), economic liberalisation has opened up new possibilities and held for economic parity with the mainstream for young Dalits, but the mainstream society is yet to catch up with the changing social order.[53]

This dichotomy is deepening the new social order, a violent reflection of which was seen in different parts of Maharashtra after the Bhima Koregaon conflict. Indeed, within three months, Dalits again went on the warpath when the supreme court decided to dilute the provisions of the Scheduled Castes and Scheduled Tribes (Prevention of Atrocities) Act (SC/ST Act), 1989. It declared that the arrest of an accused under the SC/ST Act would no longer be mandatory. It also said that there could be recourse to coercive action only after a preliminary inquiry and sanction by the competent authority. Further, the court said that there is no absolute bar against anticipatory bail in cases filed under this act, if no prime facie case could be made out, nor where on judicial scrutiny the complaint is found to be prima facie mala fide. The court order made it clear that under the act, no arrest could be made without the permission of an appointing authority, in case of a public servant, and that of a senior superintendent of police in case of a member of the general public.[54] Originally, the act—legislated for affirmative action and to be a safety net for the Dalit and tribal citizenry against any form of discrimination by the powerful—mandated the immediate arrest of the accused and denial of anticipatory bail. No doubt, this act was misused on occasion, but in the larger historical and civilisational context, it had served as a great saviour to the oppressed communities against the tyrannical social order. The act's dilution by the court was seen as an effort to bring back the old social order.

This revived the Dalit community's memories of past injustices. The Modi government failed to comprehend the fallout. In fact, the government was seen as complicit in diluting the act for concurring with the court order. During the hearing, Additional Solicitor General Maninder Singh, who is a law officer for the government, argued in favour of granting anticipatory bail if no prima facie case could be found; he argued that more than 90 per cent of cases were not genuine and that the government was worried about people taking advantage of the act. In fact, the government had instructed on 19 March 2015 that in such circumstances, wherein false cases are lodged, the IPC should be invoked for punitive action against such persons who exploit the law and the justice system for ulterior motives.

Dalits' rage over the dilution of the SC/ST Act again spilled over onto the streets on 2 April. Their anger was especially directed against the Modi government and the BJP. The BJP-ruled states bore the brunt of it. Madhya Pradesh and Rajasthan suffered the most. Twelve people were killed in episodes of arson. The Modi government was at its wits end. It changed its stance and pleaded the court for a review. But it was too late. The damage had been done.

It leads me to wonder: Are the RSS and the BJP so naive that they don't understand the feelings of the Dalits or is there a serious disconnect between the two sides? An organisation which claims to have taken up the civilisational project of Hindu unity cannot afford to be naive. It is mature enough to know what it is doing. In every incident related to the Dalits—be it Vemula's suicide, the Una beatings, the Saharanpur riots, the Bhima Koregaon violence or the SC/ST Act—latent indifference to Dalit issues is palpable. The reactions have not been empirical or situational; they are ideological.

Ideological organisations typically have a heightened sense of righteousness and high-sounding principles. The RSS and BJP derive their aggression from Hindutva, which is greatly influenced by the Brahmanism of the past, which never accepted Dalits into its folds. Savarkar and Golwalkar's ideological articulations and cherry-picked historical facts exemplify this. Ambedkar, on the other hand, advocated the destruction of the Hindu religion because he believed that unless the caste system was gone, Dalits would not find justice in Hinduism, and one could not simply wish it away because the caste system was at the core of the Hindu religion. 'You must not forget,' he said, 'that if you wish to bring a breach in the system, then you have got to apply the dynamite to the Vedas and the Shastras, which deny any part to reason; to the Vedas and Shastras which deny part to morality. You must destroy the religion of the Shrutis and the Smritis.'[55]

Will the RSS ever agree with Ambedkar's thesis? Never. Given that there is no meeting ground between the two, a fight between the Ambedkar army and the followers of Savarkar and Golwalkar is inevitable. Bhagwat being the fountainhead of that ideology and Modi the chief executive officer, both have pressed the buttons that create this resentment in the minds of Dalits and are responsible for the fights that have ensued. So the story will go on despite all the tokenism and symbolism.

FOUR

Hindutva at War with History

The eight-year-old was gang raped thrice inside the 'Devasthan' or prayer hall after the mastermind had 'performed rituals'. One of the rapists was called from Meerut to 'satisfy his lust'. The girl was confined using sedatives, then strangled and hit on the head twice with a stone—'in order to make sure' she was dead. But not before another accused, a police personnel, asked the others to 'wait because he wanted to rape' her one last time.

And all this, to 'dislodge' a group of Bakherwal Muslim nomads from Rasana village in Kathua near Jammu.[1]

This was not the end of the story. Worse was to come. This incident happened in the month of January. In April, when the crime branch of the police was about to file an eighteen-page charge sheet against the eight accused in court, local lawyers obstructed them. When they failed to prevent the filing of the charge sheet, the next day the High Court Bar Association of Jammu and Kashmir (J&K) called for a Jammu bandh, supported by the newly formed Hindu Ekta Manch. Lawyers marched on the roads of Jammu with the tricolour in their hands, shouting, 'Bharat mata ki jai! (Victory to Mother India!)'. The bandh and the Hindu Ekta Manch were both supported by two BJP ministers in the J&K government. The BJP even supported the Jammu Bar Association's demand that the Union-government-controlled CBI investigate the case afresh, despite the fact that the state crime branch had already completed its investigation and filed a charge sheet.

The mastermind mentioned in the report, Sanji Ram, was against the settlement of the members of the Bakarwal tribe in the tehsil and had been urging members of the Hindu community to deny them the use of land for grazing. According to a report published in the *Times of India* on 12 April

2018, the Hindu community was under the impression that the Bakarwals indulged in cow slaughter and drug trafficking. This belief had led to tension between the two communities. The abduction of the girl was a retaliatory act by Sanji Ram, abetted by his juvenile sons and local police personnel to teach the Bakarwals a lesson.[2]

'Those who commit love jihad will meet the same fate,' said Shambhu Lal Raigar, father of three daughters.[3] Towards the end of 2017, the thirty-eight-year-old Raigar from Rajsamand, Rajasthan, assaulted a man called Mohammad Afrazul with a pickaxe and then burnt him alive, over a neighbour's daughter's eloping, while his fifteen-year-old nephew, coached by him, filmed the whole incident. The horrifying footage was released on social media. Raigar was later arrested, but when he was to be produced before the court in Udaipur, hundreds of people with saffron flags clashed with the police, leading to a pitched battle on the road. More than thirty police officers were injured, including an additional superintendent of police. Saffron-clad men unfurled a saffron flag at the entrance to the district court.

Raigar was eventually sent to jail but remained unrepentant. From his jail cell, he released two videos that went viral on social media. He said, 'I have no regrets for whatever I did; I don't care for my life, love jihad is dangerous for the country.'[4] Later, in the last week of March 2018, in a Ram Navmi procession in Jodhpur, a tableau was dedicated to Raigar. The tableau depicted a person dressed as Raigar holding a pickaxe and another man posing as Afrazul lying on the ground.

PURITY AND AGGRESSION

Horrific as these incidents are, the most ghastly aspect is that they can happen anywhere in India. Sanji Ram and Shambhu Lal Raigar can be found in any community by other names. To say that such creatures are born only in the Hindu community would be erroneous and false. However, what is most surprising in these two cases is the communal support they elicited after the incidents. The bandh called in Jammu and the unfurling of the saffron flag in Udaipur, in support of these criminals, needs deeper introspection by the community. Why were these horrific acts projected as acts of nationalism, performed to make 'Bharat Mata' safe? Why were these seen as steps to eliminate the enemy within, carried out by devout Hindus to teach Muslims a lesson? How was it that those who condemned these acts or supported the victims, even the eight-year-old gang-rape victim Asifa, were termed anti-nationals?

Since the Modi government came into existence, the discourse around 'love jihad' and cow slaughter has been used as a major tool to forcefully purify the Hindu civilisation, which has supposedly been afflicted with foreign influence for centuries. The ideological justification by the bigots should be a matter of great concern. The hate and the venom against Muslims that has been spreading like wildfire since 2014 has been the main reason for such perversions finding popular support. An illusion has been created that Hindus are in danger and that violence is the only way to confront and subdue the enemy, or the Other, if India as a nation is to become a world power.

The ideological hate mentioned by Sardar Patel in his letter to Golwalkar as the main reason for the murder of Gandhi in 1948 has resurfaced with a new virulence.[5] Not that this hate was non-existent before 2014, but now it is emboldened due to the belief that a friendly government is at the centre and that there is a strong leader who endorses these attempts to make the land of Hindus a great nation. Earlier, the state was not perceived to be an accomplice in such crimes against humanity. Pitirim Sorokin, the Russian-American sociologist, based on his own experience in Vladimir Lenin's Russia, described such acts in words that are ironically poetic and apt for contemporary India: 'People are bewitched by ... great illusions. They are hypnotized and do not see what actually takes place around them. All around, ferocity and slaughter reign supreme. They don't perceive it and believe that on the morrow the revolution will bring not only plenty, but the beatitude of paradise to all. All around, morality crumbles away, license, sadism and cruelty are everywhere—the masses call it moral regeneration.'[6]

Richard Overy, a prominent British historian of national socialism, too undertook an elaborate study on communist Russia and Hitler's Germany. Both the regimes thrived on the twin weapons of hate and violence. Anyone who opposed the state was persecuted. In Soviet Russia, millions were sent to concentration camps and annihilated. Germany established a monster state in the name of purity of race. Both countries were convinced that they were in the pursuit of national redemption. Overy writes, 'The death of the race was presented by the National Socialists as the end of everything for Germany; successful counter-revolution in the Soviet Union was regarded as a disaster that would confirm the malign and unrelenting power of the bourgeoisie even in the face of their historical collapse ... Fear of the hidden enemy helps to explain one of the central characteristics of the two dictatorships. Both were animated by profound hatreds and resentments.'[7]

The Indian state is certainly not comparable in every respect with either Germany or the Soviet Union. Those were totalitarian states that had total control over the life and death of all their citizens. Lenin's untimely death brought in Joseph Stalin. But the state which was created by the October Revolution in 1917 was not a democratic state. It was the dictatorship of the proletariat. The party was the state and there was no place for the voice of dissent. Every institution of the state had to serve the ideology and was to be subordinated to the Communist Party, which was headed by the general secretary. When Stalin became the general secretary, he systematically wiped out all his rivals in the party.

Germany, before Adolf Hitler, was undoubtedly a democratic state. Elections were held to elect its leaders. Hitler was the product of a democratic process too, but once he acquired power, he killed all the institutions and within two years of assuming power, he became the state. He was addicted to power and was convinced that he was destined to make Germany great. In fact, the most trusted man in his cabinet, the famous propaganda minister Joseph Goebbels said in no uncertain terms: '[O]nce we have power, we will never give it up. They will have to carry our dead bodies out of the ministries.'[8] And in the end, that was exactly what happened.

Thankfully, India does not show even the remotest possibility of that situation as yet. Indian democracy is vibrant. Regular elections are the hallmark of the democratic tradition; debate and discussion are the soul of the state; and freedom of the press and independence of the judiciary are the surest bets to keep democracy alive—and these are still maintained in India. However, certain alarmingly authoritarian traits have become visible over time, and several democratic institutions are feeling the heat and are under severe pressure. This pressure is the product of Hindutva, the guiding ideology of the government at the centre, that also controls more than twenty states out of a total of twenty-nine.

This ideology has been in existence since before Independence and has been banned twice—once in 1948 and then again in 1975—but it has grown phenomenally over the years. The fundamental problem of this ideology is that its idea of national redemption is based on hate and that it does not hesitate to use violence as an instrument of civilisational justice. It is also a fact that it shares the belief with national socialism that history is a continuous war between civilisations. English historian Sir Ian Kershaw writes, 'Hitler was not a just a propagandist, a manipulator, a mobilizer. He was all those. But he was also an ideologue of unshakable convictions ... integrated by the notion of human history as the history of racial struggle. His "worldview" gave him a rounded explanation of the ills of Germany and of the world and how to remedy them.'[9] It is an accident of history that the ideologues of Hindutva share the same idea of nation, nationhood and of national awakening. It is not a coincidence that Golwalkar's analysis of Indian history has a remarkable resemblance to Hitler's worldview. He writes in his book *We or Our Nationhood Defined*, '[The] Hindu nation is not conquered. It is fighting on. Ever since that evil day, when Moslems first landed in Hindusthan, right up to the present moment the Hindu nation has been gallantly fighting on to shake off the despoilers. It is the fortune of war, the tide turns now to this side, now to that side but the war goes on and has not been decided yet.'[10]

For Golwalkar, the attainment of India's freedom in 1947 was not the end of the civilisational fight; the war had to continue till the enemy was defeated and in his understanding that enemy comprised the Muslims or, to look at the bigger picture, the real enemy was Islam. Hindutva's mandate was to keep fighting this war against the enemy religion, till it emerged victorious. Golwalkar was confident that the Hindus would ultimately win: 'Nor is there any fear of its being decided to our detriment. The race spirit is awakening. The lion was not dead, only sleeping. He is rousing himself up again and the world has to see the might of the regenerated Hindu nation strike down the enemy's hosts with its mighty army.'[11] Golwalkar's identification of Muslims as the enemy is stark and unhesitating.

Hitler also had a similar theory about the 'internal enemy' and how it was important to identify them if the nation or the race was to win the war against them.[12] He admitted that Germany had no dearth of good leaders but felt that the destiny of the nation was endangered as the leaders only saw the symptoms of the disease and not the disease itself: 'Even in those days when the destinies of the nation were in the balance, the internal enemy was not recognised; therefore all efforts to resist the external enemy were bound to be in vain.'[13] In Germany, the Jews were recognised as the internal enemy and once Hitler captured power, the liquidation of the Jews en masse began, in what came to be known as the Holocaust. Golwalkar's grouse with history was that in the past, Hindus had been too soft and had conceded ground to the internal enemy. In his opinion, this was the reason that the great civilisation had declined and been conquered by foreigners. He was adamant that this process be stopped: 'In our self-deception, we go on seceding [sic] more and more, in hopes of "Nationalising" the foreigners and succeed merely in increasing their all-devouring appetite.'[14] On this point, Golwalkar had a serious issue with the spirit of the freedom movement and with the father of the nation, Mahatma Gandhi. The Hindutva ideologue believed that Gandhi was too accommodative of the Muslims. To Golwalkar and others, Gandhi's inclusive approach was self-defeating. Gandhi was of the opinion that India's political freedom should follow social freedom. In his scheme of things, Hindus, Muslims, Sikhs and Dalits would present a united front and would fight as one. In 1918, Gandhi told Mahadev Desai, 'Though we do say that Hindus and Muslims are brothers, I can't conceive of their being brothers today ... Something within tells me that Hindus and Muslims are going to unite as brothers one day, that there is no other course open to them and they have but to be brothers.'[15] As far as Golwalkar was concerned, this was a recipe for disaster. He believed that Hindus and Muslims were two nations and could never be one. But Gandhi was determined to prove otherwise.

In 1919, Gandhi's support for the Khilafat movement was an attempt to forge a bond between the two communities and foil the British game of divide and rule. This has been severely criticised by the Hindutva warriors, who see it as the first attempt by the Congress Party to appease Muslims. This was also the time when Bal Gangadhar Tilak and Gopal Krishna Gokhale, two stalwarts of the freedom movement, had died and the leadership of the Congress Party had passed from the Brahmins to a Bania, Mohandas Karamchand Gandhi. It was not accidental that in 1923, Savarkar's book *Hindutva* was published and in 1925, the RSS was formed. It should also be noted that the founder of the RSS, K.B. Hedgewar, was in Congress until he left in 1920 and joined the Hindutva bandwagon.

ONE NATION, TWO NATIONALISMS

The fight between Golwalkar and Gandhi was a clash of ideas on how India as a nation should be conceived. On one side was Golwalkar, who believed, 'There are only two courses open to the foreign elements, either to merge themselves in the national race and adopt its culture, or to live at its mercy so long as the national race may allow them to do so and to quit the country at the sweet will of the national race.'[16] On the other hand was Gandhi, who believed that Hindus and Muslims were his two eyes. After the Partition, when riots broke out, Gandhi had a feeling that a few Congressmen wanted Muslims to leave India, so while addressing the All India Congress Committee (AICC), he said, 'We would be betraying the Hindu religion if we did evil because others had done it ... violent rowdyism will not save either Hinduism or Sikhism ... Hinduism can't be saved by orgies of murder.'[17] It was at this time that he was informed of the role of the RSS in the Delhi riots. He confronted Golwalkar, who said that the 'RSS did not stand for the killings of Muslims.'[18] Gandhi told Nehru that he did not find Golwalkar convincing. The carnage continued. Hindus and Muslims were both butchered. Nehru, too, persisted with Gandhi's line. He professed that it was the responsibility of the majority community to make the minority feel safe. Gandhi and Nehru were colossi and the RSS was too weak at the time to confront the Congress Party. However, times have changed. Since the late 1990s, the Hindutva ideology has gained immense support and there has been a severe attack on the Gandhi–Nehru vision of the nation. The Hindutva brand of new nationalism that has currency today, supports Golwalkar's idea of Muslims as the internal enemy and believe that those who support them are anti-nationals.

A debate about nationalism can always encompass many positions and nationalism can be defined in many ways, depending upon the ideas one cherishes. Bhagat Singh's idea of nationalism, for instance, was different from Gandhi's. Subhash Chandra Bose had a different understanding from that of Nehru's of Indian nationalism and the way nationhood should be achieved. In turn, Nehru's idea of Indian nationalism differed from Sardar

Patel's, though both of them were dear to Gandhi and were partners in the government. If Bhagat Singh and Subhash Bose were in favour of violence as a tool to attain freedom, then Gandhi, Nehru and Patel always persisted in the path of non-violence. If Bal Gangadhar Tilak used religion and the Ganesh festival to mobilise Indian masses, then Swami Vivekananda and Sri Aurobindo believed that the country needed a religious renaissance for the regeneration of India in general and the Hindus in particular. Vivekananda continues to be a great source of inspiration for the Hindutva brigade, but his idea of nationalism was vastly different to theirs. It was inclusive, all-encompassing and accommodative. It was not confrontational. He used to say, 'In India, religious life forms the centre, the keynote of the whole music of national life.'[19] He did say that Hinduism was the mother of all religions. However, in his idea of Hinduism and nationalism, there was no place for hate. Though he did say that temple after temple had been destroyed, he also added that they had all been resurrected again and again and that was the strength of Hinduism.[20] Unlike Golwalkar and Savarkar, he embraced Islam, Christianity and Buddhism. He went to the extent of saying, 'Hinduism can't live without Buddhism nor Buddhism without Hinduism … this separation between the Buddhists and the Brahmins is the cause of the downfall of India.'[21]

Another great inspiration for the Hindutva brigade was Sri Aurobindo, but even his nationalism was not exclusive, though he did advocate the 're-Aryanisation' of Indians.[22] He was a romantic but believed that Indians needed to revive the concept of manhood, the 'Chhatriyavad'; yet he did not preach hate for Islam and other religions. Aurobindo, unlike Golwalkar, said, 'Our idea therefore is an Indian nationalism, largely Hindu in its spirit and traditions, because the Hindu made the land and the people and persists, by the greatness of his past, his civilisation and his culture and his invincible virility, in holding it, but wide enough to include the Moslem and his culture and traditions and absorb them into itself.'[23] It is true that another great thinker of Hinduism, the social reformer Dayanand Saraswati, was harsh on Islam and Christianity; but he was harsher on Hinduism. He went to the extent of calling the writer of the Bhagwat a 'shameless creature' and went on to say, 'Oh why did not the writers of Bhagwat and other Puranas die in their mother's womb or as soon as they were born? Had the people been saved from the hands of these popes, they would have been scared of the pain and suffering that they are afflicted with.'[24]

So, it was not only Gandhi and Nehru who differed with Golwalkar and Savarkar in their idea of nationalism; the majority of the members of the Indian leadership did not buy their convoluted arguments and demands for exclusion either. In fact, Savarkar was so diabolical in his fanaticism for the construction of nationalism that he went to the extent of justifying rape to defeat the enemy—the Christians and the Muslims. Purushottam Agrawal says, 'Even a rapist dare not attribute morality to rape, but through his concept of perverted virtue, Savarkar destroys that dilemma of the rapist.'[25] Savarkar spoke of Ravana to convey his point: 'After Ravana abducted Seeta and Shree Ramachandra marched on him, some of his well-wishers advised the demon king ... that he should send Seeta back because it was highly irreligious to kidnap her. "What?" cried the wrathful Ravana. "To abduct and rape the women folk of the enemy, do you call it irreligious? (राक्षसानमपरोधर्म: परदाराविघषर्णम्) To carry away the women of others and to ravish them is itself the supreme religious duty of the Rakshasas."'[26] Savarkar's biographer Dhananjay Keer writes, 'He said that abduction and rape of Indian women by the inhuman acts of Pakistan can only be stopped if the similar act was done with them too.'[27] So would it be correct to assume that Savarkar believed in *rakshasdharma* (law of the demons)?

I am not saying that the RSS openly propagates this but Savarkar, who is the greatest icon of Hindutva, and is to the followers of Hindutva what Karl Marx is to communists the world over, did provide an ideological justification for such hateful acts. What happened in Kathua is dreadful, a blot on the face of humanity. The entire country is ashamed, but a few Hindutva warriors see virtue in this act and find reasons to support the rapists. The only reason is that all the accused are Hindus and the girl is a Muslim. Their ideological training teaches them to read a conspiracy even where there is none. Two BJP leaders who supported the criminals were ministers—Lal Singh Chaudhary was a minister for forests, environment and ecology and Chander Prakash Ganga was a minister for industries and commerce in Mehbooba Mufti's cabinet. They attended the rally organised by the Hindu Ekta Manch in March and spewed venom from the stage. Two more MLAs from the BJP, Rajiv Jasrotia and Kuldeep Raj Gupta, are active supporters of the Manch. The local unit of the RSS and the VHP support the Hindu Ekta Manch. Surprisingly, the BJP is in the state government and its own police is in charge of the investigation, and yet they did not trust the police investigations. The state president of the BJP in Madhya Pradesh, Nandkumar Singh Chauhan, even invented a Pakistani conspiracy in the incident.

How can anybody support rapists? These individuals are the creatures of an ideology that believes in continuing the civilisational war with Islam, and believe that the Hindus have to teach the enemy of the nation a lesson by any means possible.

CONSTRUCTING THE ENEMY, LAYING A TRAP

The 'enemy of the nation' syndrome has been carefully constructed since 2014 by the Hindutva regime, with the active support of its cadre. It has been refashioned as a very potent weapon to flog and brutalise opponents, create stereotypes and vilify the 'other'. Muslims are easy victims of this strategy, as they have been projected to be the monsters of society to be kept away from the mainstream till they decide to leave the country or surrender their political power and live like second-class citizens. It is a constant refrain that Muslims don't chant 'Bharat mata ki jai', and that they have problems with saying 'vande mataram', all of it to suggest that though they live in India, their minds and hearts lie somewhere else; that even if they are valid citizens of the country, they are not loyal sons and daughters of the nation. According to these divisive forces, India is not the first love of the Muslims and their loyalties will always lie primarily with the rest of the Muslim world.

In such a crisis, leaders such as Asaduddin Owaisi, the chief of All India Majlis-e-Ittehad ul Muslimeen, provide easy opportunities to further beat Muslims with the ideological stick and provide a readymade justification for the dangerous designs that the Hindutva brigade harbours. Owaisi has a personality that tends to invite controversies. In the month of March 2016, he said that he would not say 'Bharat mata ki jai' even if someone were to put a knife to his throat. He was responding to RSS chief Mohan Bhagwat's assertion that every Indian should say 'Bharat mata ki jai'. This became a huge controversy. It was an easy trap that Owaisi walked into. Owaisi defended himself saying the constitution did not require anyone to chant 'Bharat mata ki jai' and that Bhagwat could not force anyone to utter those words either.[28] His party member and MLA in Maharashtra, Waris Pathan, joined Owaisi and was suspended by the assembly for refusing to articulate

'Bharat mata ki jai.' Owaisi was supported by the Islamic seminary Darul Uloom Deoband and Jamaat-e-Islami Hind. Darul Uloom issued a fatwa. Signed by eight muftis, the fatwa said, '"Bharat Mata" deifies India as a goddess with a trident in one hand and Islam does not allow idol worship ... Hindus treat Bharat as a goddess and worship it. We Muslims see India as our motherland and have all our love for it, but Islam sees only Allah as God ... Chanting slogans for the goddess goes against the tenets of Islam.'[29] Seminary spokesperson Arshad Usmani clarified, 'We had been receiving thousands of letters from all over the country seeking clarification on the chanting of the slogan. To clear the air on the issue, the muftis sat together and studied the matter under the light of the Hadees teachings and the holy Quran. We then arrived at a consensus that the slogan which is in the reverence of a goddess is un-Islamic.'[30] He said that the Prophet Muhammad was the most revered figure in their faith, yet their religion did not allow them to worship the Prophet. The Jamaat-e-Islami Hind's chief, Syed Jalaluddin Umri called the fatwa correct and supported it saying, 'There are also chants of "Bharat ki jai" which is accepted by all ... but saying "Bharat mata ki jai" is not permissible ...'[31]

This raised another controversy: Did chanting 'Bharat mata ki jai' fall under the domain of religion? Despite the fatwa issued by Deoband, the biggest seminary of Muslims in India, other Muslims scholars and leaders disagreed, being more strategic in their thinking. Parvez Lakdawala, Mumbai chief of the Indian Union Muslim League, said, 'India is our motherland and there is nothing wrong in praising the motherland or saluting it even if our constitution doesn't make it binding on the citizens.'[32] Other Muslims clearly see the trap and want to sidestep it. Imtiaz Ahmed, noted political thinker, says that the deification of Bharat as mata (mother goddess) is an essential element of Right-wing nationalism. He elaborates, 'At the moment, the BJP is trying to set up certain symbols as hallmark of nationalism which is in contradiction to religious and social ethos of certain communities. The real question is: does everybody have a right to hold on to their theological positions without being called anti-national?'[33] All India Milli Council's M.A. Khalid quotes the great Urdu poet Allama Iqbal, who migrated to Pakistan, to convey his perspective on the motherland: पत्थर की मूर्तों में समझा है तू खुदा, खाके वतन का मुझको हर ज़र्रा देवता है। (You look for God in stone idols/For me, every corner of the homeland is God).[34]

It is interesting to note that Owaisi's party, the All India Majlis-e-Ittehad ul Muslimeen, has a slightly problematic past. After Independence, the Nizam of Hyderabad did not want to join the Indian state. The anti-India Razakars fought a bitter battle with the Indian forces that had gone to liberate Hyderabad from the oppressive Nizam at the prompting of Sardar Patel (then home minister).[35] The Razakars killed several of the nationalists before they lost the battle and their leader Qasim Rizvi fled to Pakistan. After his departure, the organisation was run by Owaisi's grandfather. The only change he brought in was to add 'All India' to the name—formerly MIM, it became the AIMIM. Journalist Rajesh Ramachandran writes, 'In Dr B R Ambedkar's original draft of the constitution, the first article said, "India that is Bharat, shall be a union of states." While discussing this article the slogan Bharat mata ki jai came up in the Constituent Assembly as a Congress member Seth Govind Das pointed out that, "We fought the battle of freedom under the leadership of Mahatma Gandhi by raising the slogan of Bharat mata ki jai." The traditionalists within the Congress wanted to drop India altogether while the ultra Hindus weren't happy with the name "Bharat" either; V D Savarkar found Sindhusthana and Hindusthana more authentic than Bharat. It is interesting to note that Savarkar's disciples now have completely appropriated the Nehruvian or Gandhian nationalist slogan of Bharat mata ki jai, probably realising that Savarkar's coinage has been discarded by the vast majority of the new nation.'[36]

DEFINING MUSLIMS AND OTHER ANTI-NATIONALS

We can harbour no illusions that in the eyes of Hindutva, the patriotism of the Muslims will ever be above suspicion. Ignoring the religious sensibilities of the Muslims and their sense of insecurity over losing their faith in a majoritarian regime, Hindutva forces constantly pressurise Muslims to prove their patriotism. One such incident was seen in UP in the month of August 2017 after Yogi Adityanath became the chief minister. His government came out with an order that all state-aided madrasas must celebrate Independence Day and if they didn't, punitive action would follow. The madrasas were also asked to provide video footage of such celebrations. Not surprisingly, other government schools were not required to furnish video evidence of celebrations. If the idea was to instil a sense of patriotism in all children, then surely a similar order should have been sent to all schools, including the Saraswati Shishu Mandir schools run by the RSS. Obviously a clear distinction was being made. It couldn't be more obvious that the assumption was that Muslims don't celebrate Independence Day. This circular by the UP government was not only discriminatory but also humiliating. This was an attempt to stigmatise Muslims, while delivering a larger message that Muslims were not patriots but they would be forced into becoming patriotic, against their will, if need be. The BJP's national spokesperson Guntupalli Venkata Lakshmi Narasimha Rao said that minority appeasement that had continued for decades had led to such a decline that even celebrating Independence Day was now viewed through a communal prism by certain elements in the Muslim community and the political class.[37]

The addition of the phrase 'political class' to 'Muslim community' by the BJP spokesperson is part of the ideological design of the Hindutva brigade to paint the entire political establishment except the BJP and RSS as supporters of anti-nationals and by that logic, call them anti-nationals as well. This logic is part of the bigger picture where Hindutva proponents insist on rewriting history to declare Rana Pratap the victor of the Battle of Haldighati (as was done by Rajasthan's BJP government) and to label the great Mughal emperor Akbar, hailed in history as a secular king, a loser. This same ideology led to the violent disruption of a literary seminar in Ramjas College in Delhi and the arrest of young leader Kanhaiya Kumar in Jawaharlal Nehru University (JNU) on the pretext of a disputed video clip. Yet, to assume that only Muslims or the minority are their targets will be reading history the wrong way. The ideological state does not stop with persecuting just one community or a few specific communities; in their paranoia, it gradually ends up calling everyone an enemy who does not subscribe to its world-view. It would be erroneous to believe that Hindus are immune to being targeted or will be safe under a majoritarian Hindutva regime. The concept of the 'internal enemy' can take on diabolical dimensions.

As great pundits who have studied the ideology understand, the enemy that is few in number cannot survive in the nation unless actively supported by traitors within the majority community. Golwalkar gave a vivid description of such people. He wrote, 'Wishful thinking born out of lack of courage to face realities, mouthing of high-sounding slogans by the persons at the helm of affairs to cover up the tragedies overtaking us one after another, and opportunistic alliances of parties and groups with the hostile elements to further their narrow self-interest, have all combined to make the threat of internal subversion of our national freedom and security very acute and real.'[38] Nehru, who was responsible to a large extent for the creation of a vibrant democracy, was consistently blamed by Golwalkar for collaborating with anti-national elements: 'And in order to justify their blatantly anti-national move, Pandit Nehru gave the Muslim League a clean chit of patriotism ...' He continued: 'Everywhere the Muslims are being abetted in their separatist and subversive activities by our own government, our leaders and political parties ... How is it that they dare to carry on these offensive and anti-national practices openly? It is because our government too overtly and covertly supports them.'[39]

Therefore the attack on a prestigious institution like JNU, a place where Hindutva has always been severely criticised, is almost to be expected. The intellectual space in JNU has always been dominated by the communists, who are the other enemy of the state according to Golwalkar. Therefore, to first discredit, then dislodge and finally dominate that space is rather high on the Hindutva agenda. The attack on JNU in the garb of nationalism was vicious and nearly fatal. Though a Hindu, Kanhaiya Kumar's crime was that he belonged to the All India Students Federation (AISF), an organisation allied with the Communist Party of India (CPI), was a non-believer in Hindutva and was a friend of Umar Khalid, a Muslim. The lawyers who beat him up inside the court premises of Patiala House were doing so in the service of the greater cause of 'nationalism'. One of them, Surinder Tyagi, later bragged to the press, 'In the heart of India, sitting here in the national capital, how can we allow someone to plunge a knife into Mother India? Anti-nationals like Kanhaiya Kumar must be taught a lesson immediately so that others dare not commit treason.'[40] Another attacker, lawyer Vikram Singh Chauhan, was felicitated by a group of lawyers in Shakarpur, and at the event he said that the felicitation was for 'the good work' he had done for the community. He also declared his irritation with journalists and their 'stance on nationalism' and said he had attacked them because of it.[41]

WHAT'S WRONG WITH KANHAIYA KUMAR

In February 2016, a video clip from JNU surfaced rather mysteriously on the Zee News channel, in which a few students were heard shouting, 'भारत, तेरे टुकड़े होंगे, इंशाअल्लाह, इंशाअल्लाह (God willing, India, you will be divided into a thousand pieces)' and 'अफ़ज़ल, हम शर्मिंदा हैं, तेरे क़ातिल ज़िंदा है (Afzal, we are ashamed that your killers are still alive)'. The clip was soon all over other channels and a loud debate ensued on every news show. The BJP and RSS said that JNU had become a den of anti-national elements and that the protesting students should immediately be arrested and taught a lesson. It was alleged that on 9 February 2016, a demonstration was organised on the JNU campus against the hanging of Afzal Guru, the accused in the terrorist attack on the parliament in 2001. The local unit of the ABVP took out a protest march opposing the event. Another group of students also marched to the Ganga Dhaba, a popular eatery on the campus, where a slanging match escalated into a clash between the two groups. The video was apparently shot there. It was later revealed that the joint secretary of the JNU Students' Union (JNUSU), Saurabh Sharma, who belonged to the student wing of the RSS, the ABVP, had got the ZEE News camera crew on campus to shoot the footage. Later, a BJP MP from the national capital, Mahesh Giri, complained to the police. An FIR was registered under Sections 124A (sedition) and 120B (criminal conspiracy) of the Indian Penal Code at the Vasant Kunj police station near the campus. The home minister, senior BJP leader Rajnath Singh, instructed the Delhi police to take strong action. As a follow-up, the Delhi Police arrested JNUSU president Kanhaiya Kumar, a bright PhD student from Bihar, on charges of sedition. The police told the court that slogans were raised against the Indian army, in favour of Pakistan, Afzal Guru, and Maqbool Bhat, the Kashmiri terrorist hanged in the 1970s. Kumar claimed he was innocent, saying that he had only gone to the gathering to calm tempers down in his capacity as the JNUSU president and reiterated that he had not shouted any anti-India slogans. Along with Kanhaiya, five others—Umar Khalid, Anant Prakash Narayan, Rama Naga, Ashutosh Kumar and Anirban Bhattacharya—were also named in the FIR. A furious civic debate ensued. Society was sharply divided. One group, led by the Left and the liberals, called the police action a witch-hunt, a conspiracy to discredit JNU and liberal voices, and an attempt to crush the voices of dissent and alternative thinking. The other group, led by the Hindutva brigade, called the incident in the video an attack on the Indian nation. The atmosphere became so vitiated that rational debate seemed impossible. Things were so bad that one felt that one could be lynched even inside the TV studio simply for having divergent opinions. Congress vice-president Rahul Gandhi, CPI(M) general secretary Sitaram Yechury and other opposition leaders addressed JNU students on the campus and extended support to them.

On 15 February, when Kumar was produced before the Patiala House court, all hell broke loose. A group of very hostile and violent lawyers spared no one, thrashing students and teachers from JNU and journalists who were covering the event. A Delhi BJP MLA, Om Prakash Sharma, was caught on camera beating up a JNU student. For the benefit of the readers, I am reproducing a report by the *Economic Times* journalist Akshay Deshmane, who was present on the spot:

> Walking in from Gate No 2 I saw some lawyers pacing around hurriedly, shouting slogans. One of the slogans was, 'Hindustan Zindabad, JNU Murdabad'. Inside the courtroom, lawyers could be seen arguing and shouting at the JNU professors. The lawyers, also shouting slogans, wanted the professors and anyone associated with JNU thrown outside the courtroom. The police appeared to be in a mood to concede to the lawyers' demand, even though the professors (mostly women) were in no mood to relent.
>
> On our part, reporters stood in one corner and witnessed the increasingly tense verbal exchanges. Soon, all JNU professors were forced out by the police and then the lawyers turned towards us. A senior TV reporter repeatedly told the lawyers and the police present that the hearing had not been declared in-camera, so unless the judge asked us, we will not leave. All of us were forced to show our ID cards by the lawyers and police. One of them shouted loudly, without any provocation, 'You show pro-terrorist news!' In some time, one of the staff of the judge's staff came forward and asked us to leave.
>
> Outside, Professor Rohit Azad of JNU told me that some lawyers had slapped him. Within minutes I found AISF General Secretary, Vishwajit Kumar writhing in pain, his shirt was torn apart. Kumar tried to get police help but the officers seemed content as bystanders.

Within minutes, I witnessed my friend and Bureau Chief of a Marathi channel, Amey Tirodkar, being beaten up severely by the lawyers ... I tried to intervene and asked the lawyers beating him, why they were beating up a journalist? ... One of them asked if I am a journalist too and on hearing an affirmative answer joined his colleagues in landing a hailstorm of blows on my legs and back. It's hard to recall exactly how many of them were around, but they were enough to constitute a ferocious mob ...

For a minute, somehow, I walked out of that trap and towards the gate. At the same time, I saw Tirodkar still being beaten and forced towards the gate. I turned back in anger, for the briefest of moments, and that was enough to provoke the mob of black coats following me ...

The provocation had already been made. Behind my back, I heard one voice say, 'Aankhen dikha raha hai?' Soon, fresh blows landed on me and I was pushed down on a patch of grass. One black coat came up to me and seemed to be in the mood to hit me some more. Next, I heard from him what is possibly the most ridiculous rhetorical question ever asked to me by anyone. 'Pakistan Zindabad, ha?' I can't tell what got me scared more, his bigotry or ignorance. But somehow the scared feeling made me utter helplessly, 'Do you know what you are talking about? Who you are attacking?'

I wanted to tell him that I was not one of those who shouted stupid slogans; am a journalist here to cover the proceedings. I was also worried that, as it happened before, he would only be more provoked. Mercifully, another lawyer intervened and told him to let me go. Yes, I was luckier than Manu Shankar of Kairali TV who was allegedly beaten up inside court premises and had to be admitted. In the absence of anything redeemable, I guess I should thank my luck for this small mercy.[42]

There are a few remarkable things to be noted about this incident:

- The temple of justice, the court's own premises, were turned into a battlefield.
- Those meant to fight for human rights, the lawyers, had turned into goons.
- The protectors of law and of civilians, the police, had turned collaborators in the crime.
- A lawmaker, an MLA, had morphed into a law-breaker.
- The fourth pillar of democracy, the press, had become the victim of their attack.

- The creators of the future, professors of one of the nation's leading universities, were helpless.

The party in power at the centre, the BJP, called its MLA's hooliganism a 'natural reaction' and the police chief called the incident 'minor' in nature. Yes, violence on the court premises was a minor thing for Police Commissioner Bhim Sain Bassi, who was to retire in a few days and was possibly aspiring to be obliged by the government after retirement for 'services' rendered, by way of a post-retirement posting.

The BJP's indifference was understandable, as it planned to take the debate on nationalism to the masses rather than to the court. On 17 February 2016, the *Economic Times* reported, 'The nationalism issue has not just enthused the BJP but also Sangh fountainhead RSS, and a roadmap for wooing the people towards it in the name of patriotism is being prepared.'[43]

On 18 February again, the *Times of India*'s headline screamed 'Emboldened by inaction, lawyers beat up JNUSU president & journalists at court in 2nd Assault in 3 days'. Also highlighted in bold type was the insult added to injury: 'Cops give goons a free hand. Again.' This was the day when Kanhaiya Kumar was produced in court again. He was mercilessly beaten up in the courtroom itself, despite the express order of the supreme court to provide security after the violence of a few days before.[44] The senior lawyers of the country informed the supreme court about the second round of violence and the court sent a team of six eminent lawyers to report back on the incident. These lawyers were not spared either and they too were abused and jostled. The audacity of the lawyers who took the law into their own hands was such that the police took three hours to finally get Kanhaiya out, through a rarely used gate that was presumably forgotten by the mob. Don't forget that all this happened while the supreme court was monitoring the event. Lawyers openly mocked the journalists while thrashing them: 'Where is the supreme court?' Despite all the uproar by civil society, political parties from the opposition and media in possession of visual evidence, none of the rogue lawyers were arrested immediately. MLA Sharma continued to roam free. The police took its own sweet time to register cases, applying the most harmless sections of the IPC to arrest the rowdy elements so that they were granted bail in only a few hours. The police chief was patted on the back for managing the situation well. Alas, even the supreme court of the nation was left helpless when the judicial and judiciary systems decided to collude with the ideology in power.

There was yet more to come. Two contradictory reports were produced before the supreme court on whether Kanhaiya Kumar was beaten inside the courtroom. The supreme court constituted a committee of eminent lawyers—Kapil Sibal, Rajeev Dhavan, Dushyant Dave, Harin Raval, A.D.N. Rao and Ajit Kumar Sinha—who informed the court that Kumar had been beaten. In the words of Rajiv Dhavan: 'A gentleman, if he could be so referred, had entered the court and sat near Kanhaiya, who was sitting near the registrar general. He suddenly got up and boxed the accused before walking away. The registrar general repeatedly asked the police to arrest the person but they did not.'[45] The committee apparently handed over a video interview of Kumar, who spoke about being beaten inside the courtroom. However, in his own report, the registrar general denied that any such incident had taken place.[46] Later, the Delhi Police also denied that Kumar was thrashed inside the courtroom. It's a different matter that all the media houses reported the incident the next day and TV channels did so the same day, corroborating that he was beaten up inside the courtroom. In fact, Kumar informed the judge hearing his case, right after the assault, that he had been attacked by a person wearing dark glasses. The JNU students' counsel also protested that the attackers had left the premises easily.[47]

No one knows—or perhaps the supreme court does—what happened to the report and why no action was ever taken. Neither did the court issue a statement on whether Kumar was beaten inside the courtroom or not. The mystery continued, but the whispers among the legal fraternity were loud: to keep the dignity of the institution intact, it was better that this matter was buried, the truth left covered. Yet the truth was naked and stark; it was dangerous and horrifying; it was the whisper of a different kind of monster—people understood that the system had caved from within.

And yes, I did hear the prime minster say a few days after this incident, 'सुबह शाम मेरे खिलाफ तूफान चलता है। ये लोग षड्यंत्र करते हैं कि मोदी को कैसे खत्म किया जाये। कुछ एनजीओ से हिसाब माँगा, सारे इकठ्ठा होगये मेरी सरकार को गिराने केलिये। (There is a storm against me day and night. These people plan and plot about how to finish Modi. I held some NGOs accountable and they all ganged up to topple my government.)'

The RSS did react, of course—against JNU. It passed a resolution in its highest decision-making body, the Akhil Bharatiya Pratinidhi Sabha (ABPS). The RSS's second-in-command, Suresh 'Bhaiyyaji' Joshi, said, 'The acceptance of the nationalist discourse has been gaining steadily and the resultant unease among the anti-national and anti-social forces has come to light through certain incidents. The anti-national activities at the Bhagyanagar (Hyderabad) and the JNU have thoroughly exposed their conspiracies.'[48]

HISTORY REPEATED AT RAMJAS

The furore seemed to die down to a simmer. Then, exactly a year later, history repeated itself. This time the battleground shifted to the University of Delhi. Ramjas College was the place where the confrontation took place. The provocation, if one can call it that, for the 'nationalist' forces was a seminar whose topic was 'The Culture of Protest', in which Umar Khalid was to participate. The date was 23 February. Permission for the seminar had been initially granted, but was later withdrawn, only to be granted again, with a caveat. The condition was that Umar Khalid, the JNU student accused of shouting the slogan, 'India, you shall be divided into a thousand pieces,' in the disputed video clip, would not be the guest speaker. The seminar began—and that was when the Delhi University Students' Union (DUSU), dominated by the ABVP, the nationalist student wing of the RSS, began to play loud music and allegedly threw stones and bricks through the windows of the conference hall, breaking many a pane. The seminar had to be called off. The police had to intervene to calm things down. The next day, students of Ramjas College, led by the All India Students' Association (AISA)—the student wing of the CPI(ML)—and other student organisations called a protest march against the attack on their freedom of expression and the alleged hooliganism of the ABVP.

This was the signal for more drama to unfold. The protest march was to begin at 1.30 p.m. Instead, those assembled at the gates in preparation for the march were brutally attacked by alleged ABVP activists. Several students and faculty members of Ramjas College were injured. A teacher of English at the university, Prasanta Chakravarty, was taken to the hospital. The march could not take place at all and intermittent clashes continued between the AISA and ABVP supporters. The police maintained a facade of standing vigil. Around 6.30 p.m., the police suddenly began to attack journalists covering the event right in front of the Maurice Nagar police station. The attacking police officers, not in uniform, slapped, punched and kicked journalists. 'Journalists assaulted by cops on campus,' screamed the eight-column headline of the *Times of India* the next day.[49] More than thirty persons (including ten police officers) were injured and eighty protesters were taken into custody.

Civil society, led by the the liberal Left, once again rose up in anger. Once again, heated arguments about nationalism dominated the discourse while society stood divided. Lynch mobs roamed the roads and apparently went on a rampage in TV studios and on social media, trying to throttle each other by the throat, literally and figuratively. If men were abused in the filthiest language possible by the 'nationalist' forces, then women were threatened with rape and intimidated with sexual slurs on social media. The whole atmosphere was one of extreme hostility, bitterness, abuse, intimidation—indeed, near insanity. It was impossible to hold a genuine debate on 'nationalism'.

THE 'MISGUIDED' DAUGHTER OF A MARTYR

The situation turned uglier still when a twenty-year-old woman from Delhi University, Gurmehar Kaur, dared to challenge the nationalist edifice with a placard on social media, stating, 'I am a student from Delhi University. I am not scared of ABVP. I am not alone. Every student of India is with me.'[50] Her father had been an army officer, martyred during the Kargil war. The post, which really riled the 'nationalist' elements, was an old video of hers from a year ago. She had participated in a peace campaign back then, holding a placard that read, 'Pakistan did not kill my dad, war killed him', amongst others. The young woman was taunted, abused, threatened not only by ordinary folks but also by top celebrities, senior politicians and ministers. Legendary cricketer Virender Sehwag tweeted a photo of himself with a similar placard: 'I didn't score two triple centuries, my bat did'. Kaur responded, 'I am heartbroken, these are the people you yell for in matches and they troll you at the expense of your father's death.'[51] For the Hindutva nationalists, clearly the word 'Pakistan' triggers an obsessive compulsive reaction; it is their raison d'être and cause for their 'nationalism'. BJP MP Pratap Simha from Mysuru tweeted, 'At least Dawood did not use the crutches of his father's name to justify his anti-national stand.' The central minister of state for home affairs, Kiren Rijiju, asked, 'Who is polluting this young girl's mind?'—as if the 'young girl' could not have a mind of her own. It was as if the young woman's daring was so dangerous that she had to be infantilised, if she could not be intimidated into silence. A few voices rose in her defence. Famous poet and celebrated scriptwriter Javed Akhtar tweeted, 'If a hardly literate player or a wrestler troll a pacifist daughter of a martyr its [sic] understandable but what's wrong with some educated folks'. A traumatised Kaur, however, withdrew herself from social media after a barrage of rape threats: 'I am withdrawing myself from the campaign. Congratulations everyone ... I said what I had to say ... this is all my 20 year self could take ...' Later that year, *Time* magazine called her a 'free speech warrior' and placed her on a list of the next generation's leaders.

Meanwhile, readers might be intrigued to learn that Gurmehar Kaur once used to hate Pakistan and Pakistanis because her dad had been killed by a Pakistani soldier. She was a child then. She was horrified when she found out that her maternal grandmother had been a Pakistani. She cried, asking her mother how a Pakistani could have lived in their house? Her mother told her the story of the tenth Sikh guru, Gobind Singh. The First Battle of Anandpur Sahib was on in 1704 and the Sikhs were fighting the Mughal army. One Bhai Kanhaiya's duty was to attend to all the injured with water to quench their thirst, after the fight had ended for the day. Though Sikh himself, he attended not only to the Sikh soldiers but also to the wounded Mughals. The other Sikhs called him a traitor and complained to the guru. Guru Gobind Singh summoned Kanhaiya and asked if the complaint was true. Kanhaiya replied, 'Yes, my Guru, what they say is true. But Mehraj, I saw no Mughal and Sikh on the battlefield, I only saw human beings. And Guru ji, don't they all have the same God's spirit? Guru ji, have you not taught us to treat all God's people as the same? Our Sikh heroes destroy the enemy by killing them, but I destroy the enmity by saving them.' Gobind Singh smiled when he heard this. 'You have understood the true message of the Gurbani,' he told Kanhaiya, 'From tomorrow, carry balm and mend the wounds of the soldiers too.'[52] Her mother then told Kaur that her father did what he had to do as a soldier, killing the enemy, but that she had to do what Bhai Kanhaiya did—kill the enmity.

In comparison, I dread what Savarkar would have told Gurmehar Kaur. For him, her mother's teaching would likely have been a 'perverted virtue', a sign of weakness and the reason for the downfall of Hindu nationalism over the centuries, something to be discarded if India wants to rule over the world.[53]

THE SHADES OF PAST NATIONALISMS

Contemporary India is clearly caught between these two kinds of nationalism—the one taught by Guru Gobind Singh, Vivekananda and Gandhi, and the other that has swayed the Hindutva 'nationalist' warriors, inspired by Savarkar and Golwalkar. Golwalkar disagreed with the nationalism of the freedom fighters led by Gandhi during the freedom movement too. He used to call that nationalism 'reactionary' and 'shallow patriotism'.[54] He rubbished the Indian National Congress, which spearheaded the freedom movement, as a 'safety valve to seething nationalism' that was created by the British for that purpose only. 'The congress that they founded as a safety valve to seething nationalism, as a toy which would lull the awakening giant into slumber, as an instrument to destroy national consciousness, has been as far as they are concerned, a success,' he said.[55] He was of the opinion that this type of nationalism was merely predicated on a negative, being based on anti-British sentiments: 'Anti-British sentiments were equated with patriotism and nationalism. This reactionary view has had disastrous effects upon the entire course of the freedom struggle, its leaders and the common people.'[56]

Interestingly, the RSS largely did not participate in the freedom struggle. None of its top- or middle-ranked leaders went to jail, except Hedgewar, even as lakhs of people sacrificed their lives, abandoned lucrative careers, faced the lathis and bullets of the British, and endured insufferable torture in jails, sometimes not seeing their loved ones for years. It is ironic that the RSS are fighting for Mother India, or Bharat Mata, with so much vigour now, given that it is a matter of historical record that the RSS discouraged its volunteers and supporters from participating in the freedom movement. Golwalkar himself confessed, 'In 1942 also there was a strong sentiment in the hearts of many. At that time too the routine work of Sangh continued. Sangh vowed not to do anything directly.'[57] It is difficult to fathom why the RSS had such a low opinion of the Gandhian agitation that revolutionised the minds of a sleeping population and ultimately led to Independence. Yet there it was: 'Definitely, there are bound to be bad results of struggle. The boys became unruly after 1920-21 movement ... after 1942, people often started thinking that there was no need to think of law.'[58] Yes, it is indeed ironic.

Another stalwart of the Hindutva brigade, Syama Prasad Mookerjee, who founded the Bharatiya Jan Sangh, an earlier avatar of the BJP, had in fact written to the British governor of Bengal, telling him that as the deputy chief minister of the province, he would crush the Quit India movement in 1942. At that time, Savarkar's Hindu Mahasabha was in the government with Muhammad Ali Jinnah's Muslim League. Yes, the present generation will find it difficult to digest this fact that Savarkar and Jinnah, who created Pakistan and purportedly caused the death and displacement of millions of people, joined hands for the sake of power—indeed, Savarkar seemed happy in Jinnah's company. Savarkar was then the leader of the Hindu Mahasabha; Mookerjee was part of it and wrote, to the astonishment of the freedom fighters, 'The question is how to combat this movement (Quit India) in Bengal? The administration of the province should be carried on in such a manner that in spite of the best efforts of the Congress, this movement will fail to take root in the province.'[59] Mookerjee's biographer Tathagata Roy, the controversial former governor of Tripura and now of Meghalaya, tried to justify his attitude: 'So what account [sic]for Dr Mukherjee's disapproval of these fearless acts of freedom fighters? Was it Dr Mookerjee the constitutional politician thinking? Or was it Dr Mookerjee the humanist who knew that the iron hand of British imperial power will in no time descend with all its terrible might on these foolhardy young men, and so was he trying to soften the blow by prevailing upon Herbert, the governor, reasonably, and sensibly, with a little mercy? Probably it was mixer of both and an exhibition of his political sagacity.'[60] But this argument does not hold water. Mookerjee's letter simply cannot be justified. However, I leave it to the wisdom of history to call it opportunism, survival instinct or fear of the colonial power.

It is a tragic irony. The nationalist Bhagat Singh sacrificed his life at a young age for 'Bharat Mata', berating his father for petitioning the British government for clemency. Meanwhile, the 'nationalist' Savarkar wrote four letters to the British Empire seeking forgiveness, promising to never indulge in anti-British activity if his life imprisonment was commuted and to remain loyal to the British government. Indeed, once he was out, Savarkar did not participate in the freedom struggle. Today, it is paradoxical that the RSS with the Hindutva brigade are trying to appropriate the great tradition of the freedom movement and its heroes, except the Nehru–Gandhi family; it is also interesting that the people popularly recognised as great martyrs were 'failures' to the RSS: 'There is no doubt that such men who embrace martyrdom are great heroes ... All the same, such persons are not held up as ideals in our society. We have not looked upon their martyrdom as the highest point of greatness to which men should aspire. For, after all, they failed in achieving their ideal, and failure implies some fatal flaw in them.'[61] In the eyes of the RSS, there must have been something wrong with the martyrdom of Bhagat Singh, Rajguru, Sukhdev Thapar, Ashfaqulla Khan, Chandra Shekhar Azad and Ram Prasad Bismil because they all failed to achieve independence in their lifetimes.

Not only did the RSS rubbish the martyrs of the freedom struggle but also did not accept the tricolour as the national flag. The Hindutva brigade wanted a saffron flag instead, because for them that alone symbolises India's past and its Hindu culture. They had a problem with the colour green in the tricolour because it is associated with Islam, and viewed its inclusion as an attempt to appease Muslims. The Hindutva brigade went to the extent of saying that the tricolour was inauspicious as it had three colours and in Hindu culture, three is seen as a bad omen and therefore India would never accept it.[62] It is not a mere coincidence that the RSS did not hoist the national flag at its headquarters in Nagpur for fifty-two years. Yet today, they are apparently the biggest champions of the tricolour and anybody found wanting in 'respect' for it is immediately branded an anti-national. How ironic!

Meanwhile, I ask, should the RSS and the BJP, Golwalkar and Savarkar be called anti-nationals because of their minimal role in the freedom struggle? Can they be named as collaborators of the British, people who weakened India's struggle for freedom? Can it be said that they were not patriots because none of them went to jail, nor faced bullets or suffered the wrath of British batons? Above all, can one call them anti-national because, not only did they not participate but also derided and obstructed the movement?

Yes, it is tempting to do just that. But that would be wrong. It would be an overgeneralisation and resorting to the same fallacy and narrow-mindedness that afflict the Hindutva brigade.

In a democratic mass movement, several streams are bound to run parallel to each other. They may even work at cross-purposes to each other, with different and sometimes antagonistic interpretations of history and social forces, with different strategies to deal with the main adversary. During the freedom struggle, the Gandhian movement was the mainstream, which believed that freedom could only be achieved by the spiritual awakening of the national consciousness, by shedding fear. It was aptly described by Nehru in *The Discovery of India*: 'The essence of his teaching was fearlessness, not merely bodily courage but the absence of fear from the mind.'[63] Bipan Chandra writes, 'National leaders from Dadabhai Naoroji, Surendranath Banerji and Tilak to Gandhijee and Nehru accepted that India was not yet fully a structured nation but a nation in the making and that one of the major objectives and functions of the movement was to promote the growing unity of Indian people through a common struggle against colonialism.'[64] The RSS and the Hindu Mahasabha did not share that perspective. They believed that India had always been a great nation, despite many upheavals. Similarly, Babasaheb Ambedkar had a different understanding of the Indian nation and of nationalism.

Ambedkar's thesis was that India was not prepared for independence per se. He believed that at this time, independence would only be a change of regime from the British to the upper castes for rulers; that the oppression of the depressed classes would continue. He said, 'The demand for independence, we may dismiss from our consideration. It is impracticable and in my opinion it will be disastrous in the present state of the country. It is only people, cemented by the feeling of one country, one constitution and one destiny who may take the risk of being independent. No one can deny that this country is miles distant from that position.'[65] Ambedkar also castigated the mainstream patriots: 'India is a peculiar country and her nationalists and patriots are peculiar people. A patriot and a nationalist in India is one who sees with the open eyes his fellowmen treated as being less than man. But his humanity does not rise in protest … The patriot's one cry is power and more power for him and his class.'[66]

Ambedkar's thoughts were also shared by E.V. Ramasamy 'Periyar', the founder of the Justice Party and originator of the self-respect movement in south India. He too believed that freedom from the British would only be a change of regime from British to Baniya–Brahmins. In 1925, he resigned from the Congress Party as he believed that Congress was only serving the interests of Brahmins and north Indians. He evolved the theory of the Aryan–Dravidian dichotomy. In his understanding, India's freedom would lead to the rule of Aryans over Dravidians. In 1940, he demanded a separate nation called Dravida Nadu, as he feared north Indian domination after Independence. Much to the discomfort of the Hindutva forces, Periyar praised Islam and termed it an emancipator: 'Muslims are following the ancient philosophies of the Dravidians. The Arabic word for Dravidian religion is Islam. When Brahmanism was imposed in this country, it was Mohammad Nabi who opposed it by instilling the Dravidian religion's policies as Islam in the minds of the people.'[67]

The leftist movement was also strong during the freedom struggle. It too viewed the mainstream freedom movement as a bourgeois movement and its leaders as sharing the same class character as the British, implying that no qualitative change would occur after Independence and the ruling class would keep serving the interests of the capitalist class.

Should we then club Ambedkar, Periyar and the leftist leaders with the Hindutva brigade and call them all anti-national? No. We cannot and we should not. That would be a travesty of justice; it would go against the basic spirit of our democratic tradition and constitutionalism; it would be an attempt to monopolise entire thought processes. It would be dictatorial.

Swami Vivekananda beautifully summarised the outer boundaries of modern nationalism when he defined the elements of the practical Vedanta. He spoke of a nationalism that had space for every thought and religion, which had no place for hate and hate mongers, which recognised no caste hierarchy and which was truly egalitarian, which remained in continuity with the national past but was not a prisoner to the past, which spoke about valour but endeared itself with compassion, which revered diversity of India and respected the voice of dissent. He said, 'We conceived that this ideal had to be spread. And not only spread but made practical. That is to say, we must show the spirituality of the Hindus, the mercifulness of the Buddhists, the activity of the Christians, the brotherhood of Mohammedans by our practical lives.'[68]

Unfortunately, Hindutva remains caught in the web of the past. Brahmanic undertones define its nationalism, in which Dalits and other 'backward' classes, minorities and women feel suffocated, threatened or ostracised. Today, it is the dominant ideology, hegemonic in nature, so one can hardly say with any confidence that Kathua won't be repeated or another Kanhaiya Kumar won't be thrashed inside a courtroom again. Such is the time we live in.

FIVE

The Kashmir Question

The mere existence of the state of Jammu and Kashmir is a test for the RSS ideology. Its existence mocks the RSS's pompous articulation of a masculine Hindu nationalism. That it further has the audacity to challenge the Indian state and defy it, ridicules the basic premise of the nation as understood by the adherents of Hindutva.

But for those who stand outside the Hindutva fold, the dynamics around J&K underline the hollowness of Hindutva, its ideological opportunism and its brittleness of character vis-à-vis the lust for power. It exposes the inner confusion of Hindutva, its cluttered mind and the superficiality of its convoluted thinking. Worse, it hints at the dangers of a diabolical ideology, which, if not understood in its historical context, will lead to a humanitarian crisis of unforeseen proportions. For if Kashmir is a test of human patience and resilience and a testimony of defiance against the might of the Indian state, then it is also a test of a thought process that threatens the very existence of India's past, present and future—the Hindutva ideology. If Kashmir's history is indicative of its people's past resilience, their tenacity at present and uncertainty around their future, then it is also a curb on the idea that homogenises the diversified Indian mind. The battle is interesting, and also frightening.

THE KASHMIR OF THE PAST

Since 1947, the Indian state has been carrying the legacy of the freedom movement in the diversity and dignity of its citizens, its civilisational democracy and the historically assimilative spirit of its social forces.

This nation was established around the idea of inclusivity. That idea is now being strongly challenged and there is an attempt to write and establish an alternate narrative. In the history of a nation, such challenges are not new; what is new is the method being used to usurp the nation's legacy. The Modi government stands for a Hindu Rashtra, be it by peaceful methods or through war. And Kashmir, of course, is already at war.

The war is not new. Kashmir had once been a peaceful state, but since 1931, its mood has been belligerent. Kashmir used to be ruled by a Hindu king whose ancestor, Raja Gulab Singh, bought Kashmir for a hundred years from the British by a sale deed for seventy-five lakh Nanak shahi rupees. This was in 1846, and even then, it was a Muslim-majority state. With Independence, the monarchy ended in Kashmir and it demanded recognition of its identity. Sheikh Abdullah, once the blue-eyed boy of the Indian nationalist leaders and a friend of Nehru (himself a Kashmiri) turned rebel—and there the problem began.

Abdullah's contemporary, the Hindu raja Hari Singh was also ambitious and wanted the state for himself, knowing well that the Hindus were in minority here. Yet with Hindus as rulers, they were deeply entrenched in the state apparatus. With the onset of modern thinking and advocacy of constitutionalism, the majority community, the Muslims, began to feel alienated from the Hindu monarchy that was Kashmir, and demanded a dominant share in the power, according to the region's demographics. The logic was simple—if Hindus could have the majority say in the power structure of the rest of India, why should the Muslim majority be denied its democratic rights in their own state?

While Abdullah was close to Nehru, Hari Singh was close to Sardar Patel. If Nehru, the idealist, wanted the people of Kashmir to decide for themselves whether they wanted to accede to Pakistan or India, Patel was a realist in his view that the ruler and not the people should take the decision on the merger. However, Raja Hari Singh was confused—or one might say, he preferred not to choose, since his true ambition was to remain the monarch of an independent state. Rajmohan Gandhi sums up his state of mind beautifully: 'If the Sardar was indifferent, the Maharaja was unable to decide. Unwilling, as a Hindu, to accede to Pakistan, Hari Singh seemed equally reluctant to join India. He feared that the state's Muslim majority might not like it, and he knew that he would not like the elevation of Abdullah, which Nehru was bound to ask for. Joining neither India nor Pakistan, he hoped for the acquiescence of both in Kashmir's independence.'[1]

Abdullah was a modern man. He was not communal and was liked by the Indian leaders, but when the United Kingdom Cabinet Mission toured India in 1946 to decide the nation's fate, he asked that the future of Kashmir be decided by the people of Kashmir. He presented his case before Gandhi and the others and sent a memorandum called Naya Kashmir to Raja Hari Singh. Naya Kashmir or New Kashmir was a charter of demands presented in the form of a political manifesto to Raja Hari Singh by Abdullah's political party, the National Conference, in 1944. This document was approved by Jawaharlal Nehru. The document talked about the new vision for Kashmir as a state, and promised to fight for the oppressed. It assured the safeguarding of the rights of women, workers and the weaker sections of society. Abdullah said that this document was to build a new personality of every man and woman in New Kashmir. It opposed monarchy and demanded power be given to the people. When he did not get a favourable response, he sent a telegram to the Cabinet Mission: 'This is a historic moment. The future of the Indian people is being determined, while the Cabinet Mission is working out a constitutional framework of the country. The right of accession is a contentious issue between three parties, the people, the rulers and the federation. We Kashmiris have to put it in its historical perspective. A sale deed does not have the status of a treaty. Therefore, after the termination of British rule, Kashmir has the right to become independent. We Kashmiris want to inscribe our own destiny and we want the cabinet mission to reaffirm the correctness of our stand.'[2]

Abdullah's defiance was not appreciated by Raja Hari Singh. He was arrested and that angered the people of Kashmir. The Indian nationalist leaders were also disturbed, especially Nehru. It has to be underlined that the leadership of what Abdullah had proposed as Naya Kashmir, was aware that accession of the state to Pakistan was not a good option. According to Abdullah's account in his autobiography, colleagues in the National Conference were not convinced that the people's vision of a New Kashmir would be accepted by the newly created Pakistan: 'Chains of slavery will keep us in their continuous stranglehold. But India was different. There were parties and individuals in India whose views were identical to ours. By acceding to India, then would not we move closer to our goal? The other choice was an independent Kashmir but to keep a small state independent while it was surrounded by big powers was impossible.'[3] Yet Abdullah said in a public meeting, 'Our first priority is to get rid of the Dogra domination. Then if the people decide to accede to Pakistan, I will be the first one to sign my name.'[4] This despite the fact that there was no love lost between Abdullah and Jinnah; neither had Abdullah ever endorsed Jinnah's two-nation theory. In his opinion, the demand for Pakistan was an escapist device.

A myth about Kashmir is that it eventually remained with India because of Patel. The truth was that it was Nehru's doing. Rajmohan Gandhi hints that Patel was willing to let go of Kashmir: 'Visiting Kashmir between June 18 and June 23, Mountbatten had told Maharaja Hari Singh "that if Kashmir joined Pakistan this would not be regarded as unfriendly by the government of India. According to V.P. Menon, Mountbatten said to Hari Singh "that he had a firm assurance on this from Sardar Patel himself." We should note that Mountbatten was quoting Vallabhbhai and not Nehru.'[5] This was also corroborated by Abdullah: 'He (Mountbatten) had given him (Hari Singh) Sardar Patel's message that were he to accede to Pakistan, it would not be considered an unfriendly act.'[6]

The struggle over Kashmir continued until October 1947. The situation during this time was extremely uncertain. Before any decision could be taken, providence intervened by way of Pakistan's attack on Kashmir, in the guise of raiders. The raiders' attack forced the decision. To save Kashmir from falling to Pakistan, Hari Singh finally agreed to sign an instrument of accession to the government of India. The Indian army marched into the valley when the raiders were only forty kilometres away from Srinagar.

Kashmir was saved, but a large portion now remained with Pakistan, what is now called Pakistan-occupied Kashmir (PoK). There was a twist in the instrument of accession. A point was conceded by both Nehru and Patel on an 'offer of plebiscite to be held once law and order had been restored' and it would be included in the 'acceptance of accession.'[7] Lord Louis Mountbatten, then governor general of India, added another proviso, which was to become a sore point in the future. Mountbatten wrote to Hari Singh, 'Under the special circumstances mentioned by you, my government accepts the accession of Kashmir to the Indian Dominion, in the case of states where the question of accession is a controversial one, it should be accomplished by the will of the people. My government feels that as soon as the raiders are beaten back and peace is restored in Kashmir, the question of accession should be settled by a reference to the people.'[8]

However, a mere five days before the raiders' attack, a rather unfortunate incident had taken place, which raises a big question mark over the roles of Raja Hari Singh, the RSS and also Sardar Patel. In October 1947, approximately two lakh Muslim citizens were killed in the Jammu area. It is alleged that Raja Hari Singh and his militia, along with Hindutva elements, were responsible for the inhumanity. The massacre was so ruthless that the Muslims in the Jammu region, who were formerly 61 per cent of the population, were reduced to only 34 per cent and became the regional minority. It is alleged that the whole exercise was a conspiracy to 'save Jammu' from going to Pakistan if a zonal plebiscite took place. The incident has been largely underplayed in history books. Eminent journalist Saeed Naqvi writes in his book *Being the Other: The Muslim in India*,

> The lid on these massacre was lifted by Ved Bhasin and a few journalists of that time ... Here I am again quoting from his paper presented at the Jammu University in 2003. 'Communal tension was building up in Jammu soon after the announcement of the Mountbatten plan with the Hindu Sabha, RSS and the Muslim Conference trying to incite communal passion. Tension increased with a large number of Hindus and Sikhs migrating to the state from Punjab and NWFP [the North-West Frontier Province] and even from areas now under Pakistan's control ... The Maharaja's administration had not only asked all Muslims to surrender their arms but also demobilised a large number of Muslim soldiers in the Dogra army and the Muslim police officers whose loyalty it suspected ...'
>
> Bhasin reports the large-scale killing of the Muslims in Udhampur district, particularly in Udhampur proper, Chenani, Ramnagar and Reasi areas. Even in Bhaderwah a number of Muslims were victims of communal marauders. According to Bhasin, the RSS played a key role in these killings, aided by armed Sikh refugees ... Some of those ... later joined the National Conference and some even served as ministers. There were reports of Muslims massacred in Chhamb, Deva Batala, Manawsar and other parts of Akhnoor ... In Kathua district too there was the large-scale killing of Muslims and reports of women being raped and abducted.
>
> ...Bhasin alleges that instead of preventing these communal killings and fostering an atmosphere of peace, 'the Maharaj's administration helped and even armed the communal marauders' ... Terrible carnage took place later

when the Muslims in Talab Khatikan area were asked to surrender. They were shifted to the police lines at Jogi Gate ... Instead of providing them security, the administration encouraged them to go to Pakistan for safety. The first batch of several thousands of these Muslims were loaded in about sixty lorries to take them to Sialkot .... The vehicles were escorted by troops. But when they reached near Chattha on Jammu Sialkot road, in the outskirts of the city, a large number of armed RSS men and Sikh refugees were positioned there.

They were pulled out of the vehicles and killed mercilessly with soldiers either joining [in] or looking on as idle spectators. The news was kept a closely guarded secret. [The] next day another batch of these Muslim families were similarly boarded in the vehicles and met the same fate. (T)hose who somehow managed to escape the wrath of killers reached Sialkot to narrate the tale of woe. The state administration denied it had any role in the massacres. It even feigned ignorance of any plan to change the demography of the Jammu region.[9]

Ved Bhasin did not agree with the government's stance. He was of the firm opinion that the entire exercise was done to change the demographic character of Jammu:

As the general secretary of the student union, I had issued an appeal entitled 'Insaniyat Ke Naam Par' asking people to maintain communal peace and harmony in the best interest of the state and join in the efforts for providing relief to the Hindus, Sikh and Muslim sufferers of the communal orgy. We had also formed students' peace committees. I was summoned by the then governor of Jammu, Lala Chet Ram Chopra, at his official residence at Kachi Chowni. Though polite, he warned me of dire consequences ... he first warned me by saying that 'I could have put you behind bars for your nefarious activities. But since you also happen to be a Khatri like me and are also related to me, I am simply giving you advice. It is not the time to form peace committees and work for peace but to defend Hindus and Sikhs from the Muslim communalists who are planning to kill them and destabilise the situation. We have already formed a Hindu and Sikh Defence Committee. You and your colleagues better support it.' Then he added, 'We are imparting armed training to Hindus and Sikh boys in Rahari area. You and your colleagues should better join such training.' When I sent a colleague to the training camp the next day he found that some RSS youths and others were being given training in the use of .303 rifles by soldiers.[10]

One can readily surmise from this that the massacre was part of a larger design and that Raja Hari Singh's administration was likely involved. Christopher Snedden's controversial book *Kashmir: The Unwritten History* suggests that not only were at least two lakh Muslim men, women and children killed, an estimated twenty-seven thousand women were abducted.[11] It is ironic that BJP leader and minister Lal Singh, who had to resign for supporting the accused of the heinous gang rape of an eight-year-old in Kathua, had in May 2016 threatened a delegation from the Gujjar community with a reminder of the 1947 carnage: '*O Gujron, 1947 pulligaya hai tuse qe?* (Oh Gujjars! Have you forgotten 1947? Why have you come here?)' He later denied having said this and claimed he was referring to the high temperature in 1947.[12]

Abdullah also referred to this massacre in his book. He wrote, 'Upon reaching Jammu, Maharani Tara Devi and he [Singh] distributed arms among communal Hindus and RSS volunteers. The Muslims of Jammu were assured of a safe conduct to Pakistan but were massacred at a place called Saubha. No doubt these killings were organised by the Maharaja, his bigoted wife and Mehr Chand Mahajan.'[13] He also mentioned a confrontation with Sardar Patel on this issue. In a meeting in Delhi, also attended by Maulana Abul Kalam Azad, N. Gopalaswami Ayyangar and Nehru, Patel told Abdullah, 'A few days ago, the Maharani of Kashmir came to see me. She fainted while relating her suffering because Maharaja Hari Singh had been asked to leave the state.' Abdullah retorted, 'You are so concerned about your Maharaja and Maharani ... have you any sympathy for the thousands of innocents who were butchered by them in Jammu?' Sardar answered, 'It would probably be best if we part company with them.' Abdullah replied that the people of Kashmir had opted for India because of a similarity of ideals, but 'let me make clear to you that we did not elect to be with you but with the people of India.'[14] Nehru had to intervene to cool tempers.

Abdullah was convinced that Sardar Patel never liked him. He also believed that Sardar Patel was a 'staunch reactionary' and helped Hindu revivalists.[15] It is true that Patel did seek the help of M.S. Golwalkar. Walter Andersen and Shridhar Damle note in their book *The Brotherhood in Saffron*, 'Home minister Patel solicited Golwalkar's help in an effort to convince the Hindu Maharaja of Kashmir to merge his princely state with India. Golwalkar met the Maharaja in October 1947 and urged him to recruit Punjabi Hindus and Sikhs into his militia.'[16] It is important to ask the reason for this martial advice. Raja Hari Singh was the king of a princely state at that time and commanded an army in which one third of the soldiers were Muslims; so why did he need to have a private militia apart from that? It is true that a certain number of the Muslim soldiers and police officials revolted and changed sides, fighting alongside the Pakistani raiders due to religious reasons; however, that does not justify a private militia.

THE HINDUTVA VIEW

To this day, the RSS believes that it played a historic role during that crisis and that it was due to Golwalkar's influence that Raja Hari Singh decided to cede Kashmir to India. For the RSS, Raja Hari Singh was a devout Hindu and J&K was a Hindu state. On 2 November, 2014, the mouthpiece of the RSS, the *Organiser*, reproduced an editorial, first published in its pages on 6 November 1947, titled 'The Importance of Kashmir'. That article offers an insight into the RSS's thinking, as cited by eminent writer and jurist A.G. Noorani:

> The inclusion of Kashmir State into the Indian Union will bring us the unflinching loyalty of the Dogra clan which is most warlike, intelligent and efficient in military tactics and to which the present ruler of Kashmir belongs ... Kashmir has vast space for the expansion of population. If industrialized, it can absorb crores of people ... Above all, Kashmir has a historic importance too. Not a thousand years back, it was a seat of Hindu culture and learning. At every step in Kashmir there lie our worship and a sacred place.[17]

This excerpt establishes three things:

1. The RSS extended support to Raja Hari Singh purely on religious grounds.
2. Similarly, the RSS wanted to protect Kashmir because, according to its understanding, the state was a seat of Hindu culture.
3. The RSS had a plan for Kashmir and that was to tilt the demographic balance in favour of Hindus.

The editorial totally ignored the fact that 77 per cent of the population at that time was Muslim. The RSS had no love for them and, in fact, would not acknowledge that these Muslims were now Indian citizens. They also seemed to forget that along with Raja Hari Singh, Abdullah, a mass leader of Kashmir, who was a Muslim, had supported the Instrument of Accession and that without his support the accession would not have been possible. The RSS ignored the historic role played by the Kashmiri Muslims, plotting instead to turn them into a minority in their own home state. The RSS's demographic policy was akin to Stalin's nationality policy, wherein he deliberately manoeuvred the migration of Russians to small republics to balance the local nationalities, and, if possible, turn the latter into a minority. Yet the Soviet Union was an obviously totalitarian state while India purported to be a functioning democracy.

It was because of Abdullah's support that Kashmiri Muslims rejected the lure of Pakistan; that religion could not bind them to Jinnah. In fact, it was Kashmir that proved Jinnah's two-nation theory wrong. The whole world took note of the news that a Muslim-majority state did not find the idea of Pakistan an attractive proposition. India was proved right: Jinnah's demand was proved a politically motivated one and his differences with the Indian leadership more of an ego battle than representing warring nationalities.

It is rather strange that the RSS and the Hindutva forces had no opinion on how the Dogra kings treated their subjects in their rule of hundred years. The RSS found the Dogra rulers intelligent and efficient, yet history judges them differently. In their rule, Muslims were treated like second-class citizens and discriminated against. Pandit Prem Nath Bazaz said, 'The Dogras have always considered Jammu as their home and Kashmir as the conquered country ... they established a sort of Dogra imperialism in the state in which the Dogras were elevated to the position of masters and all non-Dogra communities and classes were given the humble places of inferiors.'[18]

Sir Albion Rajkumar Banerji, who was a member of the Dogra raja's council of state, and also the prime minister of Kashmir between 1927 and 1929 said, 'Jammu and Kashmir State is labouring under many disadvantages, with a large Muhammadan population absolutely illiterate, labouring under poverty and very low economic conditions of living in the villages and practically governed like dumb driven cattle.'[19] Alastair Lamb's account is even more of an eye opener. He wrote, 'In every aspect of the State's life there was discrimination against the Muslim majority and the application of legislation expressly designed to favour Hindus ...

The administration of the state was dominated at all levels by the Pandits, Kashmiri Brahmins, who were notoriously corrupt and avaricious ... Hindus, alone, were allowed licenses to possess firearms in the Vale of Kashmir; and Muslims from the Vale were carefully excluded from service in the state's Armed Forces where the higher ranks were reserved for Dogra Rajputs.'[20] Other than the religious affinity, the ban on cow slaughter and capital punishment for that offence under Dogra rule would certainly have won the hearts of the RSS and Hindutva brigade.

There is no denying that the Dogra rule was unpopular and did not have the support of the majority Muslim population. Abdullah's first mass movement was against the recruitment policy of Raja Hari Singh—his relentless opposition to it made him the most popular leader in the state. It seems logical enough that the hundred years of repression under a Hindu raja had helped construct a negative image about Hindus in general in the minds of the Kashmiri Muslims. For the Muslim psyche, it was deeply ingrained that Hindus are generally discriminatory and not only do they treat Muslims as the other but also consider them inferior and deny them justice.

That said, despite the affinity between Raja Hari Singh and Sardar Patel and various Hindutva leaders, the raja preferred the idea of an independent state. Similarly, Abdullah, who openly praised the secular ideology of the freedom struggle, enjoyed a close friendship with Nehru and had deep respect for Mahatma Gandhi, was also not comfortable with the idea of a merger with India. Abdullah was aware of the apprehensions of Kashmiri Muslims about aligning with the Indian state, which was dominated by Hindus.

On 15 August 1947 India became independent. Pt Nehru became its first prime minister and J&K acceded to India. Pakistan was created as a new state. But the question of Kashmir hung in the balance. Under Article 370, Kashmir was accorded a special status with a constitution of its own, something that the RSS did not approve of. After Gandhi's death, the RSS was banned in February 1948, and its chief, M.S. Golwalkar, was arrested. The ban was lifted a year later. The RSS realised that it needed political power to spread its message of Hindutva. It was with this understanding that it helped form the Bharatiya Jan Sangh, a right-wing political party, which came into being in October 1951, with Syama Prasad Mookerjee, one time leader of the Hindu Mahasabha, as its first president. Over the years, the Bharatiya Jan Sangh has morphed into the Bharatiya Janata Party (BJP), but its political affiliations to the RSS remain.

For the RSS–BJP, the creation of a Hindu Rashtra—a nation where Muslims are aliens—has always been the final goal. Talking of the Bharatiya Jan Sangh in 1952, Mookerjee said in no uncertain terms that 'The new party will be for a Hindu India, to be a Hindu Rashtra ...'[21] In this context, Abdullah was a suspicious person for the Hindutva forces. His loyalty to the Indian republic was questioned time and again. The RSS and the Jan Sangh also vehemently opposed the proposed plebiscite in Kashmir, and wanted the United Nations to withdraw any involvement in the Kashmir situation. It believed that the integration of J&K was unequivocal and no questions on this issue should be entertained. It also clamoured for the abolition of Article 370, which was the sole condition for the integration of J&K into the Indian state.

To the Hindutva elements, it was anathema that Kashmir had been bestowed with a special status, with the option to draw up a separate constitution, and choose a separate flag other than the tricolour; that it had the right to have its own prime minister rather than a chief minister, and a sadr-i-riyasat as its head of state rather than a governor; that the Indian government could not make laws for Kashmir other than on the subjects of defence, foreign affairs, finance and communication without the concurrence of the state assembly. In defiance of Article 370, the Working Committee of the Bharatiya Jan Sangh, under the leadership of Mookerjee, passed a resolution on 14 June 1952 that, emphasised that Jammu and Kashmir was an integral part of India and declared that the decision of the State Constituent Assembly concerning an elected president and separate flag were in violation of India's sovereignty and the spirit of India's constitution.[22]

By 1951, Abdullah was growing increasingly frustrated with the situation. He was bitter that India was not ready to hold the plebiscite and was moving in the direction of a complete merger with J&K. Abdullah's antipathy towards Raja Hari Singh was also playing on his mind. A local Hindu party, the Jammu Praja Parishad—formed in 1947 by former RSS adherent, Balraj Madhok—had launched a campaign for the merger of J&K, which Abdullah believed to be financed by Raja Hari Singh. Even Nehru supported the Praja Parishad's cause, though he disagreed with their brand of agitational politics. Abdullah had fought a monarch before Independence. Now, his rebelliousness was arraigned against the modern government of India. Abdullah was talking about the sovereignty of J&K and there were also whispers that he was lobbying in foreign countries, especially the United States of America, to facilitate J&K's independence. Abdullah termed these rumours a conspiracy to unseat him.[23] He said, 'We are a hundred percent sovereign body. No country can put spokes in the wheels of our progress—neither Indian parliament nor any other parliament outside the state has any jurisdiction over us.'[24] Mookerjee was livid on hearing this and said in parliament, 'You can't have divided loyalty. Abdullah has said: "We shall treat both flags equally." You cannot do it. It is not a question of fifty–fifty, it is not a question of parity. It is a question of using one flag for the whole of India—an India that includes Kashmir. There is no question of having a separate Republic of Kashmir having a separate flag.'[25] He also raised the slogan, 'एक देश में दो विधान, दो प्रधान, दो निशान नहीं चलेंगे. (In one country, two constitutions, two prime ministers and two flags shall not be tolerated)'. Mookerjee decided to go to Kashmir in person, setting out for Jammu on 8 May 1953 by train. As he crossed the J&K border two days later, he was arrested on the pretext that he did not have a permit to enter the state. He was taken to a cottage near the Dal Lake. There he stayed for forty days and died in police custody. His supporters smelt foul play.

The Hindutva forces take a lot of pride in the 'Kashmir movement' and the 'martyrdom' of Syama Prasad Mookerjee.

A couple of months after Mookerjee's death, Abdullah was also dismissed from the office of prime minister by the sadr-i-riyasat, Karan Singh, who happened to be the son of Hari Singh. The claim was that he had lost the confidence of the cabinet. This was followed by his arrest for anti-national activities, also in 1953, and then in 1955, in what has come to be called the 'Kashmir conspiracy case'. Under this, Abdullah was accused of conspiring with Pakistan against the government of India, to declare Kashmir independent. Abdullah along with twenty-three others was jailed and a case filed in the court of law by the government of Kashmir and the government of India. The case was framed in 1958 and the trial began formally in 1959.

Abdullah remained in jail for the next decade on that charge, apparently estranged even from Nehru, who did not dismiss the charges against him and order his release until the case was almost ready for judgement. Mookerjee's biographer Tathagata Roy writes, 'Thus Nehru used Abdullah to get rid of Dr Mookerjee, refused an inquiry into his death and then got rid of the expendable Abdullah.'[26] This, it seems, set in motion an unending war. Even though Abdullah's own clan has compromised with the Indian state now, others have donned Abdullah's mantle, adding embroidery of their own.

THE PRESENT PERSPECTIVE

Mookerjee's death in doubtful circumstances certainly drove a bigger wedge between Hindutva nationalism and Kashmiri nationalism. Though nothing is impossible in politics, the current differences are so sharp as to seem irreconcilable. The RSS–BJP's communal agenda and anti-Muslim tirades have always been viewed with suspicion by Muslims across India. From the Kashmiri Muslims' perspective, the events subsequent to Independence validated their beliefs about Hindu high-handedness and proved their apprehensions right. Not staging a plebiscite despite the written agreement, the sacking of Abdullah's government in 1953, putting him in prison for eleven years, the installation of a puppet government in Srinagar like that of Bakshi Ghulam Mohammad, Khwaja Shams-ud-Din and Ghulam Mohammad Sadiq, and finally the deliberate dilution of Article 370 added fuel to the fire.

The situation improved slightly only after the Sheikh Abdullah–Indira Gandhi agreement in 1974, which resulted in Abdullah becoming the chief minister of Kashmir. However, the dismissal of Farooq Abdullah's government in the mid-1980s reignited their age-old fear of persecution and resulted in allegations of electoral sabotage and rigging in 1987, becoming an ultimate trigger for revolt. I will not dissect the merits of the Kashmiris' perspective or debate whether these were received perceptions or observed facts. However, the truth is that this perception proved decisive in defining their relationship with the Indian state.

In this context, Modi's decision to form a government with the People's Democratic Party (PDP) led by Mufti Mohammad Sayeed could be viewed with great suspicion. Though the PDP–BJP government was hailed as a historic and innovative alliance, it was in reality a blunder of Himalayan proportions on the Modi government's part.

It is true that in the late 1980s, the J&K National Conference, the principal Kashmiri party at the time, had cooperated with the BJP when opposition leaders banded together to dislodge Rajiv Gandhi from the post of prime minister. Later, in the 1990s, they even participated in the Vajpayee government. However, Vajpayee's image was somewhat different from that of the Hindutva brigade in general. He was considered large-hearted and liberal and is remembered for his attempts to improve diplomatic relations between India and Pakistan. He had the experience of interacting and intermingling in a plural democracy, having been in national politics since the days of Syama Prasad Mookerjee. The RSS leadership was not very comfortable with Vajpayee, and time and again, the leaders and affiliates critiqued him in his capacity as prime minister.

In almost direct contrast, Modi had never been active in national politics until his debut in Gujarat, and his experience of a plural democracy is very limited. He had never even entered the parliament before 2014. However, he personifies Hindutva nationalism in this milieu and enjoys an excellent relationship with the RSS leadership. One of the reasons is that the worldview of the RSS leadership and of Modi match perfectly, especially on the issue of Muslims. Thus, the BJP and PDP alliance of 2014 was even more unnatural, given that Modi hardly had the trust of the Kashmiris in the way that Vajpayee might have had. The alliance undermined the credibility of the PDP in its own state, where it had been seen to be sympathetic to the alienation of Muslims, and peddling soft separatism since its very formation. This alliance also enhanced the people's suspicion about the BJP's motives.

Kashmiri nationalism already had plenty of reasons to view Modi with suspicion. Modi epitomises Hindutva nationalism, which is founded on an adversarial attitude towards Muslims and believes that India's history is one of Hindus being tortured in their own homeland for thousands of years because of the ruthlessness of Muslim rulers. Unsurprisingly, the abolition of Article 370 has been on the top of the RSS–BJP agenda. For Kashmiri nationalists, Article 370 is an emotional issue. It is the constitutional guarantee that their identity would not be subjugated to the larger Indian identity. The fact that senior BJP leaders and ministers in the central government have called for discussions on not retaining Article 370 has not helped gain trust of the people of Kashmir. It has also been a cause for concern for the people of Kashmir that since Modi has a majority in the lower house of parliament, unlike Vajpayee, he can move in the direction of abolition of Article 370.

Indian Muslims in general also evaluate Modi in the context of the 2002 Gujarat riots—despite being exonerated by the courts, he is still perceived as having orchestrated it all from behind the curtains. Since Modi came to power, the attack on Muslim sensibilities and security have increased many times over, as seen in earlier chapters. There is a sense of helplessness growing in the Muslim community and the Modi government has not made any attempt to allay their fears.

Indeed, as an extension of the constant questioning of Muslim allegiances by the upholders of Hindutva, an illusion has been created through hostile media discourse, that Kashmiris are anti-nationals; that their demands are unjustified; that they collude with India's arch enemy, Pakistan; that they have linkages with international jihadis; and that debate and discussion with them is futile, so that a military solution is the only option to deal with their situation. These ideas have been a part of the Hindutva narrative of nationalism for a long time, but they have visibly and monstrously materialised since 2014.

Kashmiri nationalism thus found it difficult to understand the PDP's alliance with Modi, in what was called the 'bringing together of the North pole and South pole' by Mufti Mohammad Sayeed.[27] Until then, these two had been antagonistic forces: The BJP had accused the PDP in general and Mehbooba Mufti (Sayeed's daughter) in particular of pursuing a separatist agenda and being hand in glove with the Kashmiri militants. Yet the BJP changed its colours overnight and joined hands with the those who they refer to as the enemy of the state.

Certainly, the PDP had more to lose, including popular support. This was apparent at the funeral of Mufti Mohammad Sayeed—PDP leader and the chief minister in office as well as the architect of the healing touch policy—that was attended by a surprisingly low number of people.[28] With only 5,000 people in attendance, including officials and party leaders, the PDP was forced to acknowledge the drop in its popularity after its alliance with the BJP.[29]

In fact, Sayeed had been a bitter man in his last days. He felt betrayed by the Modi government. Sayeed had been an astute politician who dealt with national leaders for forty years. After his death, Mehbooba Mufti took over the leadership of the party. Mufti was new yet considered more of a hardliner. She was aware of the problem and the depth of the danger her party faced, and thus took her time before taking on the mantle of chief minister of Jammu and Kashmir. Indeed, there was a constant battle between the two parties: '[The] BJP has managed to pinprick PDP on every politically volatile issue—hoisting of Pakistani flags, a beef ban, the Armed Forces (Special Powers) Act, 1958, or AFSPA, which has been in force since 1990, Article 370, return of Kashmiri Pandits, and the release of separatist leader Masarat Alam Bhat. "They (BJP) are sitting on our throats," a senior PDP leader told ET Magazine.'[30]

Mufti was worried and did not want to take a decision in haste. She did think about breaking the alliance with the BJP but it was too late by then. She waited for three months but eventually decided to form a government with the BJP. Commentators at the time noted that the alliance was an uneasy one for PDP since it brought into question its ideological existence. In fact, they were also accused of 'facilitating the institutional entry of RSS in Kashmir'.[31]

Forming a government is easy. To run it stably and successfully in Kashmir is a huge undertaking. Kashmir is a complex space. Pakistan's involvement has made it even more complicated. Since 1987, terrorism has given it a new dimension. Over a period of time, the demand for Kashmir's independence turned into a cry for a merger with Pakistan. In turn, Pakistan tried its best to keep Kashmir simmering, with terrorist outfits supported and funded by Inter-Services Intelligence (ISI) making every effort to thwart all meaningful peace initiatives. Modi, with good intentions but without any long-term strategic thinking, first invited Pakistan's prime minister, Nawaz Sharif, to his swearing-in ceremony and later dashed off to Lahore to wish him a happy birthday. However, attacks on strategic Indian locations—the Dinanagar police station and the Pathankot air base in Punjab, the Nagrota and Uri army camps in J&K—aggravated international relations.

No meaningful talk could happen between India and Pakistan in this atmosphere. The Modi government was trapped by its own macho image. During Manmohan Singh's regime, Modi had said that terrorism and talks could not go together. He had given the impression that Pakistan would desist from its frequent attacks and subterfuge, only if India presented a firm stand. Now it became apparent that Modi's own government lacked planning and was caught in a web of confusion. If it hazarded a surgical strike across the border to demolish seven terrorist launch pads with a lot of fanfare and machismo, then it was also guilty of inviting the ISI to the Pathankot air base to investigate its own crime; something that had never been done before. If the same invitation had been extended by any other government, the RSS–BJP leaders would have hit the roof.

If Hindutva's own history was a heavy baggage for Modi, then the inherent machismo of the ideology and his self-image as a strong leader became an entrapment. The fundamental mistake was to give in to ideological pressure and term the Kashmir movement for independence anti-nationalist. This stance now left no space for a soft power approach or indeed for any political manoeuvring. Hindutva had shunned strategic politics in favour of a military solution when other governments were in power. In fact, in 2014, the Modi government had called off talks initiated by Pakistan at the level of the countries' respective foreign secretaries after the Pakistan High Commissioner's meeting with Hurriyat leader Shabir Shah.

Probably it was this ideological pressure that had the Modi government going after the All Parties Hurriyat Conference (APHC). The Hurriyat has been viewed as an alternative to the traditional political outfits by earlier governments. As a political outfit, it also worked to prevent secessionist forces from monopolising the separatist space, and functioned as a buffer between the centre and the militants. Now, it was totally sidelined by the Modi government and mainstream right-wing TV channels declared it anti-national. Hurriyat leaders were hounded like never before. They were arrested. Cases of money laundering were thrust upon them to try and obstruct their funding. Government officials did not talk to them directly and frowned on those who did. Earlier governments, including the Vajpayee-run NDA, had had no problems if Pakistan wanted to talk to the Hurriyat leaders. Now this was offered up as proof of anti-national activities.

Kashmir was now witnessing a bizarre situation. Its political leadership had considerably shrunk due to the marginalisation of the Hurriyat, the PDP being discredited because of its alliance with the BJP and the irrelevance of the National Conference in Kashmir politics. Policy initiatives had become a zero-sum game under the Modi government. This created an unprecedented void on the ground, which fed the anxiety of the average Kashmiri. A total breakdown of trust between the centre and the inhabitants of the state gave rise to an explosive situation. The killing of twenty-two-year-old Hizbul Mujahideen militant Burhan Wani on 8 July 2016 triggered a massive uprising.[32] Wani became a new symbol of martyrdom in Kashmir.

The *Indian Express* report on Burhan Wani's funeral is eye-opening: 'Braving heavy rain, defying curfew, clashing with the police and Army, screaming slogans of azadi and shouting Burhan Muzaffar Wani's name, people from across Kashmir streamed into Tral through Friday night and all of Saturday, walking dozens of miles to attend his funeral. The ceremony was to start at 11.30 am Saturday. But by 10 am, every inch of the Eidgah in Tral, a ground measuring 18,500 sq m, twice the size of a soccer field, was filled. Outside, the roads were packed with more people struggling to get in.'[33] Another report said, 'In widespread protests and violence of the kind rarely seen in the last two decades over a militant's killing, 11 people were left dead by Saturday evening, and over 200 injured. All of the deaths happened in south Kashmir. More than 50 of those injured have bullet wounds. By the end of the day, the protests had intensified.'[34] Prime Minister Modi's appeals fell on deaf ears. Chief Minister Mufti tried to blame vested interests for the violence. Nawaz Sharif said, 'Massacre and genocide in Indian occupied Kashmir is extension and re-enactment of ethnic cleansing started by Modi in Gujarat.'[35] Secessionist leaders Syed Ali Shah Geelani, Mirwaiz Umar Farooq and Yasin Malik said the 'nation was facing a do-or-die situation'.[36] The violence, arson and anarchy continued for more than two months. More than eighty people died. Wani, whom some had called a paper tiger, turned out to be more deadly in his death than in his life.[37] Pakistan meddled in the affair as well.

Meanwhile, certain mainstream TV channels with a right-leaning agenda, played up the incident to further incite people's sentiments. Wani's photo was circulated along with that of Shah Faesal, the 2009 topper of the Indian Civil Services, who has recently resigned from the servies. The IAS officer's angry reaction is a telling comment on the insensitivity of certain TV channels. According to news reports: 'He accused a section of the national media of being a "sadistic propaganda machine" indulging in "conventional savagery that cashes on falsehoods, divides people and creates more hatred" at a time when Kashmir was "mourning its dead".'[38]

Even after one-and-a-half months, the situation was so grim that in four districts of south Kashmir—Pulwama, Shopian, Kulgam and Anantnag—it was virtually a free-for-all. The police had left the area and of the thirty-six police stations in these districts only three still functioned. Most police personnel had abandoned their stations since the mob attacks began and some stations were even set ablaze.[39] Use of pellet guns did not help matters either, instead aggravating the situation.

Wani's death thoroughly exposed the Modi government's Kashmir policy. This incident reminded people of the period between 1989 and 1992, the early years of militancy in Kashmir. It should be noted that normalcy had slowly returned to the Valley during Manmohan Singh's time. Tourists had started flocking to the Dal Lake again. Sonamarg and Gulmarg were again vibrant. Business and trade had improved. Yet, it all changed after 2014. The situation on the ground deteriorated. Even more worryingly, militancy in the area has also changed its character over the past years. Now more and more educated youth are joining the ranks. Tellingly, these are people born and brought up in the insurgency era. Local militants are starting to outnumber outsiders. The Hizbul Mujahideen and Lashkar-e-Taiba are still active, but the latest uprising seems more home grown. Support from the local population is also on the rise.

Dileep Padgaonkar, who was a member of the Kashmir interlocutors' committee appointed by the Manmohan Singh government, says, 'There was a time when New Delhi could justifiably argue that the population of the Valley was by and large indifferent, if not hostile, to the militants on account of their depredations—intimidation, wanton killings, maltreatment of women etc. Today the huge crowds that turn up for the funerals of slain militants, the attacks on the security forces by ordinary civilians (including, most tellingly, by women), the strict observance of hartals and shut-downs decreed by separatist leaders and so forth tell another, altogether alarming story.'[40]

There was another serious development. Kashmir's independence movement was never communal; radical Islam never had traction among the Muslims of Jammu and Kashmir. Kashmir's separatist movement had its own peculiarities. Despite Pakistan's best efforts, it had little to do with radical Islam. In fact, the Jammu Kashmir Liberation Front (JKLF), which started the insurgency in Kashmir, was secular in its ideology. It did talk about independence but it was not guided by radical Islam. It was to mitigate its influence amongst the Kashmiri people that Islamist organisations like

Hizbul Mujahideen were propped up. However, even these organisations did not propagate the establishment of an Islamic state and could be said to be more or less secular in nature.

Even when Raja Hari Singh tried to play the Hindu–Muslim game, Sheikh Abdullah and the National Conference stuck to the secular ethos. In the early 1990s, when foreign mercenaries migrated from Afganistan into the Kashmir Valley in the name of jihad, Kashmir did not opt for radical Islam, though the exodus of the Kashmiri Pandits remains a severe blot on its face.[41] Now, however, the radicalisation of Islam in Kashmir is a serious issue.

Salafi madrasas have mushroomed over a period of time with Saudi funding; Pakistan is also indulging in this game. Muzaffar Hussain Baig, former deputy chief minister of J&K and a Harvard law graduate, warns about the latest danger: 'It [the Kashmir movement] was not part of a world vision for the revival of Khilafat (the movement for an 'Islamic state') and hegemony of religious extremism. Now, there's danger of it becoming a part of the international struggles. Until now, the older and rural population voted in Kashmir. Now, that may be in danger because this new uprising has gone into rural Kashmir. It appears religious extremism is infecting the hearts and minds of youths.'[42]

After Burhan Wani's death, the Modi government was facing flak from all quarters. To quell criticism, Home Minister Rajnath Singh was sent to the Valley. His two-day trip was a damp squib. He did talk about Kashmiriyat (Kashmiri culture and consciousness of belonging), insaniyat (humaneness) and jamhooriat (democracy), but it was of no use.[43] It was also said that pellet guns would henceforth be rarely used, but it was too little and too late. Efforts to win over the Kashmiris continued and yet another delegation comprising members of various parties, led by Rajnath Singh, again visited Kashmir in the first week of September 2016. This too proved to be a futile exercise.

Finally, the government had to clarify that it was willing to talk to all the stakeholders of Kashmir, including the All Parties Hurriyat Conference. By then more than 500 people had been injured by pellet guns, creating more alienation in the Valley. The army was called in to control the situation and it took up positions in the four worst-affected districts of south Kashmir. Since 2014, this was the first time that the army had to be requisitioned for this job.

With tensions still running high, the country next witnessed the big terrorist attack on the Uri army camp, along the Line of Control (LoC) between India and Pakistan. Nineteen soldiers were killed, thirteen were burnt alive. This was on 18 September 2016. Pressure for the military option was growing again. As an icon of masculine and martial nationalism, Modi was in a fix. Manoj Joshi wrote in the *Economic Times,* 'This is largely the outcome of heightened political-psychological expectations that the Narendra Modi government will give Pakistan a "muh-torh jawab" (a jaw-breaking response).' Joshi further explains the problem of the ideological blindness of the Modi regime: 'This government's goal in Kashmir and with Pakistan are maximalist: nothing short of a complete "integration" of J&K into the Indian Union, with no room for dissent of the kind being witnessed. Likewise with Pakistan, success is complete surrender by Islamabad and its assimilation into the larger civilisational entity called India, or Bharat.'[44] By now, TV channels that thrived on a daily dose of masculine nationalism had already killed Pakistan many times over. Instead of being sober and calm in this hour of national crisis, they were hysterical in search of that prize called TRP (target rating point). Revenge was the flavour of the season. Demanding suspension of the Indus Waters Treaty or withdrawal of 'most favoured nation' (MFN) status for Pakistan seemed too mild for Modi's persona. Emotionalism and not national interest became the prime mover behind India's foreign and domestic policies. Blood was boiling on the other side of the border too: Pakistan's defence minister Khawaja Muhammad Asif even threatened India with nuclear war.

Modi's India was left with no option but to cross the line. 'Surgical strike' had become the new buzzword in the war against terrorism. Indian commandos crossed the Line of Control around 12.30 a.m. on 29 September and the strike began around 2.30 a.m., destroying seven terrorist launch pads. The operation was over by 4.30 a.m. Forty to fifty terrorists were reportedly killed. The whole operation was hailed a great success. India's diplomats also did a good job. World powers such as Russia, the USA, the UK, France and Germany supported India's action. To Pakistan's disappointment, support even flowed from Muslims countries such as Saudi Arabia, the United Arab Emirates (UAE), Qatar and Bahrain. Pakistan felt isolated. Modi and the RSS–BJP now had legitimate reason to tom-tom their military success in the assembly elections that were held in February and March 2017 in UP, Uttarakhand, Punjab, Goa and Mizoram. Still, the big question was how often would this action need to be repeated, knowing Pakistan and the nature of terrorist groups in general. The attack on Uri would not be the last one; would India resort to the same action after every audacious act of terrorism?

No, the terrorists did not stop, and neither, seemingly, did Pakistan learn a lesson. They continued to hog the headlines: 'Pak-based Terrorists kill Indian Army Jawan on LOC, Mutilate body','8 Civilians Die in Heavy Pak Shelling along Border, LOC', 'Indo-Pak Tensions Escalate as Terrorist Behead Soldier', '7 Army Men Killed as Terrorists Strike Military Base Yet Again', '3 Soldiers Killed in J&K Ambush, 2 Officers Injured', 'Pak Soldiers Cross LOC, Kill and Behead 2 Indian Jawans', 'Kashmiri Army Officer on Leave Abducted, Killed by Terrorists', 'LeT Terrorists Kill 6 Cops then Mutilate Face with Bullets', '7 Amarnath Yatris from Guj Killed in J&K Terror Strike', '5 Jawans Killed After Jaish Terrorists Storm CRPF Camp', 'Capt among 4 Soldiers Killed as Pak Pounds Rajouri Sector', 'Jaish Targets Sleeping Families at Army Camp, 2 Soldiers Killed', '3 More Soldiers Die in Attack on Jammu Army Camp'. The 2 per cent voter turnout during the repolling in thirty-eight polling booths in Budgam district on 26 May 2017 for the parliamentary by-election was a pointer to the militancy's continued stranglehold.

Sadly, the government and the army compounded the Kashmiris' alientation by justifying a shocking choice by army personnel to use a local youth as a human shield. The young man, Farooq Ahmed Dar, was tied to an army jeep to ensure safe passage for a five-vehicle convoy running the gauntlet of a stone-pelting mob. Naturally, the incident did not help the Kashmiri people's confidence in the government, given that they had long felt violated and victimized. However, the army and the Hindutva nationalists justified the unjustifiable, saying that this strategy had facilitated the movement of the army convoy through hostile terrain without a single bullet being fired. The army chief was so jubilant about this 'innovative idea' that he decided to award Major Leetul Gogoi of the 53 Rashtriya Rifles a COAS (chief of the army staff) commendation card even before the army court of inquiry could complete its investigation. This was nationalism of a new kind. BJP MP and famous film actor Paresh Rawal had a 'brilliant' suggestion to tie writer and activist Arundhati Roy, who is known for her radical opinion on

Kashmir—she favours self determination for Kashmiri people—to the jeep instead of a 'stone pelter'. Fortunately, the national security agencies did not feel compelled to act out his morbid idea. However, what seems clear is that Kashmir is certainly not reassured by the army's presence there.

Army chiefs in India have always maintained a low profile, unlike their counterparts in Pakistan. In India, their job is to ensure the safety and security of the nation and let the political leadership do the talking. Even during wartime and in insurgency areas, the army has rarely breached this tradition. The country has always been proud of its dignified conduct. However, with the appointment of General Bipin Singh Rawat as chief of staff in 2016, superseding two senior generals (something that has happened only for the second time in Indian history), the line between strategic articulation and political statements has been increasingly blurred. Indian army generals were known for their operational successes and their leadership on the ground; but General Rawat is in the news quite often because of his political utterances, which betray the constitutional requirement. It is not known whether his statements come at the prompting of his 'ultimate' boss or are self-motivated. In either case, he is setting a bad precedence and treading a dangerous path that helps no one—neither the government whom he represents, nor the foot soldiers whom he leads.

Kashmir is the site of an old wound and whether we like it or not, the fact remains that the army and the security forces are not welcome there. They are perceived as an occupying force. To change this mindset of Kashmir the army has to change its attitude towards Kashmiris as well. It has to reassure the civilians that it is there for their benefit. Mufti Mohammad Sayeed was right in articulating the healing touch policy. Vajpayee and Manmohan Singh maintained the policy of 'strategic restraints' despite grave provocations.[45] They never allowed their generals to make political statements and the army operated on the understanding that Kashmir might be a hostile terrain but it is not an enemy land, that its citizens are members of the Indian state.

General Rawat, it appears, treats the Kashmiri youth as enemies instead. He said of the human shield incident, 'In fact, I wish these people, instead of throwing stones at us, were firing weapons at us. Then I would have been happy. Then I could do what I (want to do). Adversaries must be afraid of you and at the same time your people must be afraid of you. We are a friendly army, but when we are called to restore law and order, people have to be afraid of us.'[46] This can't be the language of the army operating within its own national boundaries. What's more, General Rawat seems to be advocating an eye-for-an-eye policy, which is not only a departure from the past but also an aggressive stand to take against the citizens of your country.

Nor is his definition of maintaining law and order the usual one. Commenting on the basic education structure of Kashmir, General Rawat said: 'The other issue is the madrassas and masjids—what is being informed to them (the students) or incorrectly informed to them is through the madrassas and masjids. I think some controls have to be exercised there and that is what we are looking at.'[47] He commented, too, on the fact that two maps—one of India and another of the state of Jammu and Kashmir—were used in classrooms. Managing education is not usually in the army's purview. Yet, Rawat continued: 'What does it mean to children that I am part of the country but I also have a separate identity. So, the basic grassroots problem lies here is the way the education in Jammu and Kashmir in government school has been corrupted [sic].'[48] This was an offensive statement. It was not only highly political, which is beyond his constitutional brief, but also hurts the federal spirit of the constitution. The J&K government immediately took offence and reacted strongly. It asked him to do his own job and not meddle in the affairs of the state.

A NEW HOPE

It appears that by the latter half of the year 2017, the Modi government had realised that masculine nationalism and warmongering had their limitations and that instead of showing positive results, the situation had gone from bad to worse. It decided to appoint an interlocutor, a low-profile officer who had been the chief of the Central Intelligence Bureau, Dineshwar Sharma. The government said he would have complete freedom to talk to all groups and individuals. Till now, interlocutors have not had much success in Kashmir, except the architects of 1974 who were responsible for the Indira Gandhi–Sheikh Abdullah accord, which led to him becoming the CM of Jammu and Kashmir after eleven years. Despite that, this was a welcome move since dialogue is always a step in the right direction.

It is yet to be seen whether Sharma can overcome the serious handicaps of the historical legacy of the RSS, the ideological blindness of the Modi government and the masculine nationalism of the rabid Hindutva elements. Above all, he has to convince Kashmir that the government no longer treats the citizens of the state as anti-national elements and that Kashmiris are citizens of this great country called India and not enemies of the state. It is probably the toughest assignment any officer in independent India has ever undertaken.

Dineshwar Sharma's appointment was followed up by two good moves by the Modi government. One, after consultations with the Home Ministry in Delhi, the chief minister of J&K, Mehbooba Mufti, announced the amnesty scheme for first-time stone pelters on 22 November 2017. Under this scheme, cases against first-time stone pelters were withdrawn. It was also announced that those injured by the pellets would be rehabilitated and ₹5 lakh would be given to the families of those who were killed during the unrest in 2016. Till then the stone pelters had been treated as a category of militants and accordingly penalised. The arrests of stone pelters had become one of the major reasons for the growing unrest in the Valley, as locals believed that security forces were victimising innocent youth in the garb of stone pelting. In a move that would bring some relief to the Valley and its people, Mehbooba Mufti, informed the assembly on 3 February 2018, that 9,730 people will be granted amnesty.[49]

Secondly, on 16 May, 2018 the Modi government announced the unilateral suspension of anti-terror operations in the month of Ramzan. The government said, 'Ramzan is in the true sense, the month of worship, purity and peace. It should be our collective endeavour to isolate those, who bring a bad name to Islam by their senseless acts of terror and violence.'[50] The government stressed that it was not declaring a ceasefire, and made it very clear that security forces would not initiate an attack but neither would they hesitate to retaliate if challenged by terrorists.

During his visit to Kashmir, Home Minister Rajnath Singh, expressed the government's readiness to talk to any group or person including members of the Hurriyat Conference. He said, 'I appeal to people of J&K, for peace of the state please come forward. It should not happen that one more generation of J&K gets lost in darkness. Dialogue can happen with everybody.'[51] But Rajnath Singh had no idea what was to happen in a fortnight. On 14 June 2018, Shujaat Bukhari—respected journalist and the editor-in-chief of the newspaper, *Rising Kashmir*—was gunned down along with his two security guards by three assailants. This was a serious setback to the peace initiative by the Modi government. Events unfolded rather fast after this. Bukhari's murder proved to be the last trigger for the collapse of PDP–BJP government. On 19 June 2018, BJP decided to withdraw support from the Mehbooba Mufti government. She had no option but to resign. Ram Madhav, the general secretary of the BJP blamed Mehbooba for the 'increased violence' in the region and cited it as the reason for the BJP's withdrawal of support.[52]

But the real reason was more ideological. It is true that the Modi government made seemingly sincere efforts for peace in Kashmir in the latter part of 2017 but these initiatives—amnesty for stone pelters, rehabilitation plans for the injured, unilateral halt of anti-terror operations—created tremendous unease amongst the core supporters of the RSS and BJP. The Modi government, which was expected to teach the militants a lesson, was seen to be surrendering. It was seen to be compromising on the hard-line nationalism pursued by the Hindutva brigade.

The murmur was getting stronger within the RSS that the Modi government was no different than the Manmohan Singh government, and was handling the militants with kid gloves. BJP's state unit had been expressing its annoyance vis-à-vis the centre's changed Kashmir policy even before the withdrawal of support from the PDP. While speaking to the *New Indian Express*, on 12 May 2018, BJP spokesperson Arun Gupta had voiced his disapproval of the amnesty granted by the J&K government and also said that he was not in favour of talks with those who did not respect the constitution.

At a time when assembly elections in three major states—Rajasthan, MP and Chhattisgarh—were due, to be followed by the parliamentary elections in 2019, the Modi government could not afford to be seen as weak. The softer approach in Kashmir had been a well-calculated gamble by the Modi government to refurbish his image but the government and party imprisoned by the Hindutva ideology could only walk this far. Beyond a point, it can't be seen fraternising with the purported enemy of the country. Let's not forget that the Hindutva brigade views Kashmir from the point of view of a civilisational warfare. Golwalkar, quoting Prof Arnold Toynbee, wrote, '… he had unequivocally stated that the creation of Pakistan is the first successful step of the Muslims in this 20th century to realise their twelve-hundred-year-old dream of complete subjugation of this country. Their direct aggression, whetted by their first success, then turned against Kashmir. There too they met with success, though partial.'[53]

I do not need to reiterate that ideology can make a tactical retreat for strategic gains, but it can't be seen to surrender before the forces it is committed to annihilate, because it knows that such an action can be suicidal.

On 21 August 2018, the governor of Bihar, Satya Pal Malik, was transferred to Jammu and Kashmir to take charge of the state as the governor. A seasoned politician, Malik, unlike his predecessor N.N. Vohra, is not constrained by the bureaucratic approach. His appointment is proof that the Modi government does not want to experiment anymore. Malik is expected to ensure that the political equilibrium is intact and law and order is in check. Because, in an election year, the Modi government would not like its image of aggressive masculine nationalism to be dented.

SIX

The Line between Nationalism and Terrorism

The history of terrorism in India and the rise of politics based on religion run almost parallel to India's transformation from a socialistic economy with extensive government participation, to a more market-based model where government participation was reduced. As its economy grew and India got linked to the global market, secular politics weakened. Terrorism in J&K and the BJP's rise in Indian politics should be viewed in this context. Today, 'secularism' has become a dirty word and polarisation around religious identities is the stark reality. Indianness as a macro identity is being dominated by religious identities.

The problem is when the state, which by definition has to be secular, is governed by a party with a particular religious affiliation and the system of administration is blinded by that religious ideology.

The Modi government is the first of its kind to experiment with this as a new normal. If J&K has suffered because of this experiment, then other parts of India are not untouched either. Ideally, the Modi government should have one yardstick while dealing with the menace of terrorism, but the illusion of cosmic warfare has blurred its vision. So two approaches, both detrimental to the larger question of national security, are being exercised, one for Kashmir and the other for Hindu terrorism.

In the first decade of the twenty-first century, India witnessed the spread of jihadi terrorism beyond the boundaries of J&K. Hardly any major city was spared. Delhi, Mumbai, Ahmedabad, Hyderabad, Varanasi, Lucknow, Surat, Baroda, Pune, Bengaluru all bore the brunt of jihadi terrorism. These attacks were supposedly engineered and sponsored by cross-border terrorist groups supported by Pakistan. A series of attacks in Mumbai in 2008, now imprinted in public memory as 26/11, was the arguably the most audacious of these incidents and shook the foundation of India's secular democracy. Shivraj Patil, the home minister at the time, was considered too soft, and after intense criticism, resigned from his post. The country needed a strong and efficient minister and P. Chidambaram was chosen for the job. It was at this time that a new revelation surprised everyone.

AN ENEMY WITHIN?

It turned out that a few of the blasts—the Samjhauta Express bombing, the Mecca Masjid blasts in Hyderabad, the Ajmer Sharif Dargah blast and the Malegaon blasts—carried a different signature. Investigations concluded that these were not engineered by jihadi groups as suspected earlier, but were triggered by groups with Hindutva leanings. This led to the arrests of Swami Aseemanand, Lt. Col. Shrikant Purohit, Sadhvi Pragya Singh Thakur and others. It was found that an organisation called Abhinav Bharat, an extreme right-wing group, was involved. The BJP, the RSS and other organisations with Hindutva leanings blamed Chidambaram and the Congress (then the ruling party) for deliberately twisting facts and targeting Hindu organisations. They lamented that it was a part of a bigger conspiracy to defame and discredit the RSS and others.

The Samjhauta Express blast took place on 18 February 2007. Sixty-eight passengers were killed. In Mecca Masjid, the blast was triggered on 18 May 2007 and sixteen citizens lost their lives. At the Ajmer Sharif Dargah, a powerful blast went off on 11 October 2007, killing three people. In Malegaon, the first series of blasts occurred on 8 September 2006; the death toll was thirty-seven. Another blast took place two years later, on 29 September 2008, killing six people. After initial investigations by agencies such as the CBI and the state police, all the Hindutva-related matters were handed over in April 2011 to the National Investigation Agency (NIA), which was Chidambaram's brainchild to specifically deal with terrorism. But the investigation took a questionable turn after the Modi government took over from Manmohan Singh.

Judgement has been pronounced in two cases—the Mecca Masjid case and the Ajmer Sharif Dargah blast. In the Mecca Masjid case, all the five accused were exonerated, including Swami Aseemanand, who had initially been considered the kingpin of the entire operation. In the Ajmer blast case, three of the accused—Devendra Gupta, Bhavesh Patel and Sunil Joshi—were found guilty but Aseemanand was once again acquitted.

TURNAROUND ON AJMER SHARIF AND MECCA MASJID

Aseemanand's acquittal is surprising because he had confessed to his role in the terror blasts not only before the police but also before the media. On 18 December 2010, he told the magistrate, 'I know I can be sentenced to death but I still want to make the confession.'[1] His interview with the *Caravan* and his forty-two-page confession published in *Tehelka* are testimonies to his alleged involvement and the larger conspiracy hatched by a few top Hindutva leaders.[2] Aseemanand told the court that the Mecca Masjid in Hyderabad had been targeted because during the Partition, the Nizam of the erstwhile princely state had opted for Pakistan. And the reason the Samjhauta Express was chosen for bombing was because it was mostly used by Pakistanis. Aseemanand later retracted his statement.[3]

In cases such as these, the trial hinges mostly upon circumstantial evidence, the confessions of the accused and the statements of witnesses. It is difficult to find direct material evidence. If witnesses turn hostile or the accused retracts their confession, the case falls flat. The court summoned ninety-three witnesses in the Ajmer blast case. Out of them, nineteen key witnesses retracted their statements. The public prosecutor in the Ajmer case, Ashwini Sharma, showed his annoyance at the way the NIA conducted itself during the trial. Sharma spoke at length to Scroll.in:

> 'Since several witnesses were acquaintances of the accused, they were liable to be influenced by the defence lawyers,' said Sharma ... 'But it was the task of the investigating agency to ensure that did not happen', he added. At the very least it could gather evidence to show that witnesses were being influenced by the defence. For instance, during their cross-examination, Sharma had asked the witnesses for their mobile numbers. 'The NIA could have procured their call records which would show that they were in touch with the lawyers of the accused,' he said. He passed on the name of the hotel where he heard a group of witnesses had been lodged by the defence. In their cross-examination, the witnesses had claimed to have spent the night in Jaipur at the railway station. 'If the NIA got a copy of the hotel register, it would show that the witnesses were lying,' he said.

He even suggested that the NIA obtain copies of the CCTV footage of the court building to 'show the witnesses were meeting the defence lawyers and discussing the case with them'.

But his suggestions were ignored.

When a senior NIA official was contacted he unofficially maintained that the agency's job was limited to investigation and gathering evidences, what happens in the court is outside its preview.[4]

The officer quoted conveniently forgot that to take the investigation to its logical conclusion, and ensure that the guilty are punished, is also the responsibility of the investigating authority so that the course of justice is not hijacked. In this case, it is evident that justice was subverted while the safe keepers of democracy looked the other way.

In the Mecca Masjid blast case, all five accused—including Swami Aseemanand, head of the Vanavasi Kalyan Ashram, affiliated to the RSS; Devendra Gupta, head of the RSS in Jamtara district of Jharkhand; Lokesh Sharma, an RSS worker; Bharat Mohanlal Rateshwar of the Hindu Vichar Manch; and Rajendra Chaudhary, a farmer with the aliases Samundar and Dasharath—walked free.[5] Amongst these men, Devendra Gupta and Lokesh Sharma had been convicted in the Ajmer blast case. As the investigation played out in court, however, it looked like a big farce. A total of 226 witnesses were named, of which 66 were critical. Most of them were from Jharkhand and Indore, the very places where the accused belonged. These were small traders and teachers who had earlier said that they knew about the blast plans. Now fifty-four of them retracted their statements. Aseemanand had already written to the NIA claiming he had been pressured by the earlier investigating agency, the CBI, to confess to the crime.

Before the NIA and the CBI had stepped in, the Hyderabad police had arrested 200 people, mostly Muslims, and it was assumed that the terrorist organisation Harkat-ul-Jihad-al-Islami (HuJI) of Bangladesh was behind the blast. Once the investigation shifted focus to Hindutva groups, they were all discharged. Now nobody really knows who took those sixteen precious lives.

It is rather coincidental that just two weeks before the Mecca Masjid verdict, the case-in-charge Pratibha Ambedkar was abruptly transferred elsewhere. Why? It is also strange that when Aseemanand was granted bail on 23 March 2017, NIA officials in Hyderabad believed that his bail should be challenged in a higher court, but could not get clearance from top officials in Delhi. The *Indian Express* quoted an official in Hyderabad saying on the condition of anonymity, 'There were sufficient grounds to challenge the bail order of Aseemanand and the high court was at liberty to reject the agency's move if there were no merits in the appeal. Among investigators, the opinion to appeal was very strong.'[6] The news website Wire interpreted this to indicate 'that the top officials gave clear orders asking them not to pursue the matter further.'[7] Why this reluctance? It is to be noted that when Aseemanand was granted bail by the Chandigarh high court in the Samjhauta Express blast case in August 2014, the NIA did not challenge his bail. Aseemanand was represented by Satya Pal Jain at the time, then chief of the legal cell of the ruling BJP government; he is now the additional solicitor general of India.

On the day of the Mecca Masjid judgement, NIA officials hinted at the agency's unwillingness to challenge the acquittal of all five. It was said that it would be a futile exercise as there was no material evidence in the matter and circumstantial evidenced based on confessions had already been retracted. Similarly, the NIA did not make any effort to challenge the acquittal of Aseemanand in the Ajmer blast case either.

THE MALEGAON MYSTERIES

Along with Swami Aseemanand, Sadhvi Pragya Singh Thakur and Lt. Col. Shrikant Purohit were considered to be the main players in the blasts carried out by Hindutva extremists. The role of the NIA in the 2008 Malegaon blast case turned out to be the most curious. On 13 April 2016, the NIA filed a supplementary charge sheet in the special court and gave a clean chit to Thakur and five others due to want of enough prosecutable evidence. It also told the court that Purohit and the eight other accused should not be tried under the Maharashtra Control of Organised Crime Act (MCOCA) but under the Unlawful Activity Prevention Act (UAPA). This was not all. In a rather dramatic fashion, the NIA also informed the court that the Anti-Terrorism Squad (ATS) of Maharashtra had planted RDX explosives to frame Lt. Col. Purohit. It must be remembered that the ATS, at the time, had been led by the joint commissioner of police (JCP) of Mumbai, Hemant Karkare, who laid down his life fighting terrorists in one of the most shocking terror attacks on India—26/11. This was a serious charge against the martyred officer.

Sadhvi Pragya Singh Thakur was a member of the ABVP, the student wing of the RSS. Thakur holds a postgraduate degree in history and belongs to the Bhind district in Madhya Pradesh. She grew up in a family of RSS followers. In her student days, she had been an active member of the ABVP and afterwards she joined the Durga Vahini, the women's wing of the VHP. The major charge against her was that she allowed Ramji Kalsangra to use her LML Freedom motorbike in the 2008 Malegaon blast. Kalsangra, also one of the accused, has been absconding ever since. The NIA concluded that the motorbike was given to Kalsangra two years before the blast based on the statement of a witness, a motor mechanic. Thakur was accused of attending a meeting in Bhopal to plan the blast in Malegaon but this was denied by the two witnesses, Yashpal Bhadana and R.P. Singh.

Along with the motorbike, the ATS had gathered more evidence against Thakur, such as the intercepts of phone calls and a transcript of the meeting in which the conspiracy for the blast was supposed to have been hatched. Reportedly, all this evidence disappeared. According to the *Caravan*, 'On 3 November 2008, the ATS, which claimed that it had tapped Thakur's phone for three months, produced transcripts from those conversations before a Nashik court. In one exchange, Thakur asked another suspect, Ramchandra Kalsangra, "Meri gaadi se blast kiya to itne kam log kaise mare? Gaadi bheed mein kyun nahi lagayi? (If my vehicle was used for the blast, how come only few people died? Why didn't you park it in the crowd?)" To this, Kalsangra replied, "Bheed mein khadi karne nahi diya (They didn't let me park it in the crowd)".'[8] These were crucial bits of evidence. Later, it was reported that copies of the transcripts were produced before the court.

Prior to this, Thakur was also one of the accused in the murder of RSS pracharak Sunil Joshi, who purportedly had a violent streak. He was gunned down a few metres from his one-room house in Dewas district of Madhya Pradesh, on 29 December 2007. At the time, he was in hiding, wanted for the murder of a local Congress leader. Joshi was also supposed to have been one of the main conspirators in the Hindutva terror blasts. Aseemanand, in his confession, had admitted that Joshi was a key figure in the entire operation and alleged that he and Thakur often used to visit his ashram to discuss ways to retaliate against terror attacks on Hindu temples.

Sunil Joshi's name figured prominently in the Ajmer blast case, in which he was convicted posthumously. Joshi's death remains a big mystery. A diary recovered from his home had contact numbers of many top leaders of the RSS. It is believed that he was killed because he knew too much and was ready to reveal all: 'The RSS leader was also tired of being a mere foot soldier. Joshi wanted to play a more pro-active role in society and leave terror activities behind. He had even contemplated surrendering to police, but his intentions scared those working with him. They tried to talk Joshi out of it, but ended up making him more adamant about his decision to change his life, says the NIA.'[9]

Initially, Joshi's murder was assumed to have links with the blasts, so the case was handed over to the NIA along with other terror cases. Manmohan Singh was the prime minister at the time. The NIA had almost completed its investigation and was about to file a charge sheet when the government changed. By the time the NIA filed the charge sheet in August 2014, Narendra Modi had become the new prime minister. The charge sheet named eight people, including two of Joshi's own associates—Lokesh Sharma and Rajendra Chaudhary, who were also accused in the terror blasts. However, the charge sheet underlined that the alleged motive for the murder was 'Joshi's sexual advances towards Pragya'[10] The NIA had concluded that Sunil Joshi's murder had no connection with the blasts.

The case therefore passed from the NIA's special court to the Dewas court in September 2014, which acquitted Thakur on 1 February 2017. However, the additional district and sessions judge Rajiv Madhusudan Apte severely criticised both the investigating agencies while pronouncing the verdict: '… it is evident that the two organisations, the MP police and the NIA, did not conduct the investigation with the required seriousness due to reasons not known to this court … conflicting evidence provided by the two government organisations instead has the effect of placing doubt on the case presented by the prosecution and is inadequate to prove the guilt of the accused.'[11] It should be noted that in Madhya Pradesh, the police reported to a BJP government that had no inclination whatsoever to pursue the Hindutva angle of enquiry in the blasts. I will elaborate on this later.

Despite getting a clean chit from the Dewas court on Sunil Joshi's murder and being discharged by the NIA in the Malegaon investigations, Thakur's problems were far from over. The special court did not agree with the NIA's suggestion that there was not enough evidence against her in the 2008 Malegaon blast case. The court ruled that Thakur and Purohit would face charges of terrorism. This order came in on 27 December 2017. To the utter dismay of the NIA, presiding judge S.D. Tekale observed, 'There is evidence to suggest that the accused number one (Thakur) had knowledge about involvement of her motorcycle.' The ruling also noted that Thakur 'had also expressed dissatisfaction about causing less casualties in the blast'.[12] The court ordered that charges be framed against her as well as Purohit, Sudhakar Dwivedi, Ramesh Upadhyay, Ajay Rahilkar, Sudhakar Chaturvedi and Sameer Kulkarni under sections 16 and 18 of the UAPA and IPC, for crimes punishable by life imprisonment and death. The court also rejected a contention by Purohit that he was present in the meetings in Faridabad and Bhopal for counter-intelligence purposes.

Purohit's role in the Malegaon blast is almost out of a Hollywood movie. From a middle-class family in Pune, Lt. Col. Shrikant Prasad Purohit joined the army in 1994 and served in counter-terrorism operations in J&K from 2002 to 2005. Purohit was the first serving army officer to be arrested on the grave charge of terrorism; at the time of his arrest he was working in military intelligence. He was accused of floating the militant organisation Abhinav Bharat with another retired army officer, Major Ramesh Upadhyay, to plan and execute terror blasts seeking revenge on the Muslim community for the jihadi attacks on India. When he was caught by the ATS in Maharashtra, his defence was that he had infiltrated Abhinav Bharat, that his seniors knew about it and that he had kept them informed about his activities. The court refused to believe that he was on duty and wondered whether his superiors had any clue about the discussions in the meetings held at Abhinav Bharat.

Purohit was known among colleagues for his ultra-nationalistic views. In fact, in 2008, sometime before his arrest, he had made a slide presentation to his senior officers in military intelligence in which he was 'highly critical of the political masters of the time, alleging they were dreamy, lacked vision, were heavily corrupt, and had failed to understand and identify the "enemies" threatening India's national security in various manifestations …. Purohit also spelt out a clear solution to carve out Abhinav Bharat, based on "hard-core nationalism", by indoctrinating the young generation with nationalistic feelings, inducting them into the civil services, and by making training in self-defence techniques mandatory for all citizens.'[13] The slideshow was incorporated in the NIA's charge sheet. The NIA charge sheet further stated, 'Purohit had proposed theory for a separate constitution for Hindu Rashtra with separate flag (Bhagwa flag), the constitution of Abhinav Bharat, and discussed about the formation of Central Hindu Government (Aryawart) against the Indian government and put forth concept of forming this government in exile in Israel and Thailand(sic).'[14] His concept of a government in exile was innovative but seditious and falls within the realm of waging war against the state and planning to overthrow the government of the day.

One of the other serious charges against him was that he accessed sixty kilograms of RDX from the army, which was used in the blasts. The NIA, in its report, had submitted to the court that the RDX was, in fact, planted by the ATS. It claimed to have recorded the 'testimony of an Army major and a subedar on how they "caught" Maharashtra ATS officer Shekhar Bagade emerging from accused Sudhakar Chaturvedi's "locked" house at Devlali before the ATS raided it and recovered RDX traces.'[15]

Once Purohit's name cropped up in connection with the Malegaon blasts, the military ordered an enquiry by the director general of military intelligence (DGMI). Retired Brigadier Raj Kumar, a former deputy DGMI who was the nodal officer for the case on behalf of the army, said in an interview to *India Today*, 'Purohit had very clearly told us that he had not supplied it, nor there are any proof and our investigation suggest this(sic), certainly Purohit had boasted in one of the meetings that he can get it.'[16] This does not mean that he was exonerated by the DGMI, as Brigadier Kumar added, 'This is what we heard but there is nothing to corroborate that his involvement is not there in supplying RDX.'[17]

In 2011, the DGMI report indicted him on two counts. He was caught in possession of illegal weapons at his residence and his meetings with various leaders of Abhinav Bharat and others at different times were found to be illegal, implying his participation in these meetings took place without the knowledge of his superior officers and was thus not authorised by them. According to a detailed report in the *Indian Express*, 'Between March 3 and March 15, 2008, the report said, Purohit met "RSS chief Sri Sudershanji (former RSS chief K.S. Sudarshan) at Jabalpur and apprised him on (RSS leader) Indreshji's linkages with ISI". In the same period, the report said, during his stay in Pune, Purohit received one 9 mm pistol, along with 12 rounds of ammunition from Rakesh Dhavde, an accused in the Malegaon case. He also directed Ajay Rahirkar, Abhinav Bharat's treasurer, to give 3.2 lakh to Dhavde for weapon procurement, the report said. "This was an illegal activity undertaken by the offr [sic]," the report said.'[18]

As for his seniors knowing about his activities concerning Abhinav Bharat, it came to light that he did inform his seniors, but only when he feared that the Malegaon case might be cracked. The *Catch News* website cited from the DGMI report: 'That Purohit informed his superiors about Sadhvi Pragya and her alleged involvement in the Malegaon blast only after he got wind of the ATS cracking the case.' According to the *Indian Express*, 'In addition, on 13 Oct 08, on receiving confirmation from his informers about apprehension of Sadhvi by ATS, he telephonically informed CO SCLU, IO SCLU (Devlali) and initiated a written report to CCLU Team at Jabalpur intimating involvement of Sadhvi Pragya Singh in the Malegaon Bomb Blast.' The paper, while quoting the report also stated that 'Between 07 and 24 Oct 08, he used these mobile nos to warn his associates through direct calls and SMS. His close associates were told to switch off mobile no. and take new sim ...'[19]

This story of being a mole also does not hold ground for the simple reason that military intelligence is tasked with operating only in areas where the army is authorised to fight insurgency. Bahukutumbi Raman, one of the country's most celebrated intelligence officers, writes, 'The military intelligence is authorised to collect tactical intelligence through human and technical means in areas where the Army has a counter-insurgency role, as in Jammu & Kashmir and the North-East. In areas where it has no counter-insurgency role, it is not permissible for the military intelligence to collect intelligence through any means—particularly through the penetration of Indian organisations run by Indian citizens. Only the Intelligence Bureau of the government of India and the intelligence wings of the State Police are authorised to run such operations. Even the Research and Analysis Wing (R&AW) is not empowered to do so.'[20] So if this operation was beyond the jurisdiction of the army, then it could not have authorised one of its senior officers to infiltrate Abhinav Bharat for information gathering. No wonder the DGMI report terms Purohit's meetings illegal.

Even if one were to believe his version to be true, then another question arises: If he was a mole and knew about the conspiracy, then why did he not facilitate the arrest of the conspirators before they could execute the conspiracy and trigger the blast? That would have saved so many lives. Indeed, why—even after the blasts—did he not help apprehend the conspirators? In the absence of answers to these questions, Lt. Col. Purohit's mole story does not stand up to scrutiny.

The NIA's role in the Malegaon blast investigation raises some serious questions. Special public prosecutor Rohini Salian, in an explosive interview to the *Indian Express*, revealed that she was asked by an officer to go soft on the accused: 'Soon after the NDA government came to power last year, she said, she got a call from one of the officers of the NIA ... asking to come over to speak with her. "He didn't want to talk over the phone. He came and said to me that there is a message that I should go soft" ... Matters came to a head this month, on June 12, she said, when just before one of the regular hearings in the case in the Sessions Court, she was told by the same NIA officer that "higher-ups" did not want her to appear in the court for the State of Maharashtra and that another advocate would attend the proceedings.'[21] Cut to three months later Salian made a further revelation: '"I am told that a criminal contempt petition is filed before this Honb'le court and in administration of justice and as an officer of the court, I am disclosing the name of the NIA officer, who had tried to interfere with the delivery of the administration of justice, as a messenger. His name is Suhas Warke, SP, NIA, Mumbai branch," Salian said in her affidavit.'[22] As it usually happens in such cases, the NIA denied that any pressure was put on her; however, she had indeed been removed from the prosecution panel. Salian had no reason to lie. She later said that it was very clear that the government did not want 'favourable orders', which meant that the accused should go free.[23] The question remains, who were these 'higher-ups' who tried to pressure her?

Not only Salian, even the special public prosecutor appointed to replace her, Avinash Rasal, was unhappy. When the charge sheet was filed in the special court, he was not informed or shown the content. Instead, another public prosecutor, Geeta Godambe, submitted the charge sheet. It is believed that Rasal was not in favour of dropping charges framed under the MCOCA against all the Malegaon blast accused. Again, it is imperative to ask why this happened. The NIA sought the legal opinion of Attorney General Mukul Rohatgi on dropping the MCOCA charges. This is baffling, since the case was already sub judice and it could have been left to the wisdom of the court.

The special treatment given to NIA chief Sharad Kumar by the Modi government also raises questions. He was granted two extensions of one year each on a contractual basis after he had reached retirement age as deputy director general of the NIA, which goes against convention. This is the first such commutation since the application of the Sixth Central Pay Commission. There is no doubt that he is an efficient officer. However, it is also said that he had a tiff with the Congress government when he was posted in Haryana and was superseded for the post of state DGP because he was close to BJP leaders. After retirement from the NIA, he was on track to be appointed to the National Human Rights Commission, a move vociferously opposed by several NGOs, who submitted a memorandum to President Ram Nath Kovind. He is now the vigilance commissioner in the Central Vigilance Commission (CVC), as of June 2018. His appointment was challenged in the supreme court by former Navy Chief Admiral (Retd.) L. Ramdas and others but the bench led by Justice Ranjan Gogoi dismissed the petition saying the petitioners were not the aggrieved persons.[24] After his appointment, Sharad Kumar thanked the government by saying 'I am grateful to the government for reposing faith in me. I will try and do the job to the best of my abilities."

THE STRANGE MATTER OF SAMJHAUTA

Among all the blasts discussed in this chapter, the 2007 Samjhauta Express bombings were the most lethal. The blast ripped apart two railway coaches, killing sixty-eight people near Diwana station, close to Panipat in Haryana. This twice-weekly train service between Delhi and Attari in India and Wagah and Lahore in Pakistan was started in 1976 as a goodwill mission between the two countries.

The blast occurred a day before Pakistan's foreign minister Khurshid Mahmud Kasuri was to reach India for peace talks. The attack was seen as an attempt to disrupt the dialogue. For a very long time, investigating agencies and the government were convinced that the blast was the handiwork of Pakistan-based terrorist organisations. The Lashkar-e-Taiba was the major suspect. Local organisation, the Students' Islamic Movement of India (SIMI) was also on the agencies' radar. In fact, a narco-analysis was carried out on SIMI operative Safdar Nagori. However, the recovery of an unexploded suitcase from the blast site turned the investigation on its head. Trying to trace it to its source, the special investigation team (SIT) of the Haryana police reached Indore, a business hub in Madhya Pradesh. The suitcase had been bought from a shop in Indore. The shopkeeper told investigators that the buyers were Hindus. This was a turning point in the case.

Vikas Narain Rai, the head of the SIT, said in a video interview to the Wire, that the investigating team was told by the shopkeeper that the dialect of the two 'boys' who came to purchase the suitcase indicated that they were locals to Indore. The team was able to locate all the items used to assemble the explosive device within a radius of one kilometre. Indore, Rai noted, was gaining notoriety at the time for both Hindutva and SIMI's activities. There was a BJP government in Madhya Pradesh at the time, and Rai claimed that they got little cooperation from the local police though unofficially a few officers hinted that they were on the right track.

In the course of the investigation, which extended to Bhopal, the team became aware of a Hindutva group headed by Sunil Joshi; but by the time they began investigating him, Joshi was murdered.[25] Rai added that it was while comparing notes with officials investigating blasts at the Mecca Masjid and Malegaon that they realised the signatures were the same. Vikas Rai's submission again proves the importance of Joshi, who was also pronounced guilty in the Ajmer blast case. In fact, Home Secretary R.K. Singh, who later joined the BJP and became a minister in the Modi cabinet, had claimed that ten names that had surfaced in the investigation were connected to the RSS. He too mentioned Joshi, Kalsangra and Dange.

The question that died with the death of Sunil Joshi was whether Joshi acted on his own or was simply a foot soldier controlled, monitored, trained and tutored by someone else. It leaves another question to be answered: Was he eliminated to protect the bigger names?

As the investigation proceeded, with the arrest and interrogation of a few RSS leaders and workers, a prominent name appeared on the horizon. This was Indresh Kumar, a very senior leader of the RSS: 'Vasudev Parmar, who was arrested by the Madhya Pradesh police in December (2010) for allegedly killing Joshi ... told his interrogators that though the group had contacted a number of RSS leaders for help, it was Indresh who supported them by providing ₹70,000 for the entire operation to bomb the Pakistan-bound train.'[26] Swami Aseemanand had also spoken of Indresh Kumar's role in the blasts in his confessional statement before a Delhi court, which he later retracted: 'Indreshji told me that this responsibility (bomb-for-bomb) has been given to Sunil and whatever help Sunil needs would be provided by him,' claimed Aseemanand in his confession before the court.[27]

Indresh Kumar was quizzed by the CBI on 23 December 2010 in the Mecca Masjid case. At that time, it was speculated that he could be arrested at anytime but that did not ever happen. Later, the NIA mentioned in its charge sheet that Indresh Kumar did meet Sunil Joshi just before the Malegaon blasts in 2008 but when Joshi sought his help to carry out the blasts, Kumar told him that he did not support such acts. The NIA also gave him a clean chit in the Ajmer blast case in April 2017, along with Sadhvi Pragya Singh Thakur. Kumar has always denied these charges and called them a bunch of lies. The RSS has consistently said that this was a conspiracy by the United Progressive Alliance (UPA) government to malign the name of the RSS and discredit the organisation.

The most curious twist to the case, however, was given by Aseemanand and Purohit, who apparently believed that Indresh Kumar was an ISI mole in the RSS, who had amassed fake currency to the tune of ₹21 crore from a Pakistani agency and had to be eliminated. Purohit, during his joint interrogation by the ATS Maharashtra, the Intelligence Bureau and the Directorate of Military Intelligence between 29 and 30 October 2008, confessed, 'a Pune-based rich, staunch RSS supporter, Shyam Apte, was roped in to finance the plot to kill ISI agent Indresh with a fraud Sharda Peeth Shankaracharya alias Dayanand Pandey jumping onto the bandwagon to make money.'[28]

THE COURSE OF JUSTICE

Now the narrative that emerges is very interesting. It is crystal clear that people related to the RSS and other Hindutva groups were involved in each of the four blasts. In the Mecca Masjid case, all the accused were given a clean chit by the NIA special court. But in the Ajmer blast case, three have been convicted and out of the three, two have direct links with the RSS—

Sunil Joshi, who is mysteriously dead, and Devendra Gupta, who is serving a life sentence. Judgements in the other two cases are pending.

There are strong doubts that attempts have been made to save the accused. The NIA's role is not above suspicion. Its investigations, after the BJP formed the government under the leadership of Narendra Modi, leave much to be desired, with little claim to being clean and objective. The NIA has to answer why so many of its witnesses have turned hostile and why it did it not make any effort to protect its witnesses. Why did Salian say that she was asked to go soft in the Malegaon case? Why was the other special public prosecutor not shown the charge sheet before it was submitted in court? It is beyond understanding why the NIA is so rigid in its refusal to challenge the acquittal of Aseemanand in the Ajmer blast case or the acquittal of all the accused in the Mecca Masjid cases. Two courts—the Dewas court in the case of Sunil Joshi's murder and the NIA special court for Malegaon— have hinted that the NIA's investigation has not been carried out in the true spirit of justice. The Dewas court's observation indicts both the Madhya Pradesh police, which works under a BJP government, and the NIA; the NIA special court did not subscribe to the NIA's insistence that Sadhvi Pragya Singh Thakur should be discharged, showing that the court believed Thakur's role in the blast was not above suspicion. It appears ultimately as though Sunil Joshi was the prime mover in the entire operation and he was eliminated with a definite purpose. His death needs to be reinvestigated, and it remains to be seen if the new Congress government in the state supports this investigation.

Former home secretary R.K. Singh went on record in a television interview, saying, 'We have names of at least 10 persons ... who were associated with the RSS.'[29] Now, a minister in the Modi cabinet, he has a reputation of being a no-nonsense officer. He has also altered his stance: 'Any official at any ministry, when he gives an official statement, that statement is based on information provided by the agencies under it. In these cases, the investigation agency was NIA.'[30]

A home secretary is not merely a politician. He is the topmost officer responsible for law and order in the country. It was Singh's responsibility in that role to lead, coordinate and monitor the actions of the NIA. If the NIA was wrong in the investigation of such a sensitive matter, which had a direct bearing on the issue of national security, then the responsibility lay with him.

Can he get away with saying that he simply relayed whatever information was given to him by the NIA? Or should he, rather, come out and admit that he was pressurised to take the investigation in a particular direction to avoid maligning the image of Hindutva forces and the RSS?

Terrorism is terrorism; it should not be seen through the prism of religion. Whether it is Jihadi terrorism or Hindutva terrorism, both are dangerous for the country, and perpetrators should not be shown any mercy. But such is the colour of ideology that administrative blindness is just a minor side-effect of the malaise which has seeped into Indian politics.

SEVEN

Matters of Statecraft

Machiavelli was not a great thinker. He was not in the same league as Plato, Aristotle, Karl Marx, Immanuel Kant or Shankaracharya. He was not a man for epistemology. He was a politician who was practical and wrote treatises for kings and princes on how to conduct statecraft. In that, he was similar to Chanakya. Machiavelli blurred the line between moral and immoral; he was a worshipper of power and believed that if a king or leader had to resort to any vices to preserve the kingdom, then so be it. Virtue had no meaning for him if it led to disaster. Unlike Machiavelli, ideologies and ideologues are mostly not realistic; they chase dreams and are guided by high morals for the betterment of the universe. Narendra Modi is a rare breed of politician. He is a purveyor of an ideology that dreams of making India a Hindu Rashtra; on the other hand, he is also a technician of power, if I may borrow the phrase from Isaac Deutscher.[1] In his tenure as chief minister and later as prime minister, Modi has ruthlessly married the idealism of ideology to the pragmatism of politics. For him, his politics provides the ecosystem in which his ideology of Hindutva can attain its goal.

CLOSE FRENEMIES?

Atal Bihari Vajpayee was also a product of the same ideology as Modi; but he failed to create an organic mix of ideology and politics. His conviction tilted more towards virtue than power. For Modi, power defines virtue and paves the way for an ideological empire. Vajpayee was conflicted whereas Modi is clear-headed. It was this conflict, which filled Vajpayee with guilt when the Gujarat riots took place. He was anguished and wanted to punish Modi to cleanse the taint which became his lifelong companion. He was also not convinced about the demolition of the Babri Masjid, therefore taking a back seat and letting L.K. Advani take the lead.

Modi's journey is that of a loner, his dream his only partner; the rest of his peers are only facilitators. Emotionalism and vagueness are anathema to him. A person can either stand with him or must be against him. He trusts no one and owes nothing to anyone. Power is his only friend and his only deity. It is not surprising that after becoming prime minister, his first move was to seat his one-time mentors L.K. Advani and M.M. Joshi in the august gallery of the marginalised. The Margdarshak Mandal was a beautiful creation to show them their place, as well as show the world, his party, and its leaders who the real boss was—they were the past and he the present.

It was not surprising that when he was to choose a presidential candidate, the CBI filed an appeal in the court that the conspiracy case of the Babri demolition be reopened after seventeen years. It was, many believed, a deliberate move by Modi.[2] Let us not forget that it was Advani who saved him from certain removal from the seat of chief minister, after the Gujarat riots. Had he been sacked then, Modi would not be where he is today. For that, Modi should have been eternally obliged to Advani; but Advani made the mistake of opposing him when Modi had already positioned himself as the prime ministerial candidate of the party.[3] Advani had crossed him and needed to be taught a lesson. While Vajpayee could probably never have done this, Modi did it without any hesitation. Modi knew that Advani was the only one with the stature and the personality to be able to put a damper on his ambitions and he ruthlessly tackled the problem by plucking Advani out of the presidential race.

At the time of the presidential election, there was a strong expectation that Advani would throw his hat into the ring and be the candidate of the opposition. A section in the BJP and the RSS was also of the opinion that Modi had become too powerful and it was imperative to put some chains around him. This section of the BJP thought that Advani had the requisite stature to stand up to Modi, due to his political standing and also because of the paramount role he played during the Ayodhya movement. Had he decided to contest the presidential election, it could have led to a moral dilemma for many in the Hindutva fold and it would also have been difficult for Modi to ignore his candidature.

I know for a fact that the anti-Modi team in the BJP, which is quite substantial though discreet, was upbeat about the prospect. Members of the Advani family were contacted and a secret meeting did take place to discuss whether he would be amenable. Several opposition leaders of various parties were in touch with him on a regular basis. Several trips outside Delhi were also made. A consensus was emerging. Although some parties were reluctant to accept him due to his involvement in the Ayodhya movement and the rath yatra (chariot procession), they were also concerned that every party would face a tough time ahead if Modi continued to have a free run. Many leaders were concerned about their own futures and clearly said that if Modi continued in this manner, most of the leaders would end up in jail and their parties would be liquidated. One of them, a very senior leader in the opposition, said to me, 'We all criticise Mrs Indira Gandhi for imposing emergency and putting leaders in jail, but she did take good care of us in jail; only our freedom was restricted, otherwise there was no problem as such. We had total freedom inside.' He added, 'Modi is fascist. He can go to any extent to finish us. Indira Gandhi had not forgotten that she was Nehru's daughter. She had democratic bones in her body but Modi carries none. Though there is no declaration of emergency now but it is worse and leaders are treated like worms.' He cited the example of the AAP, the way its leaders were arrested and the CBI raided the chief minister's office. He said that the opposition should forget all differences among themselves and unite to fight Modi.

There were indications that Advani was willing. Some of his well-wishers indicated that several BJP leaders would support him and a demand for his candidature could arise from within the party. I am not aware if any of the opposition leaders had an opportunity to speak to him personally, but I am certain that the channel of communication was open from both the sides. It is in this context that on 2 March 2017, the supreme court opined in the Babri Masjid case against Advani, that the conspiracy charges had been dropped merely on a technicality.

After the mosque's demolition, two sets of cases had been filed—one in the Rae Bareli court and the other in the Lucknow court. In the Rae Bareli court, the trial was against the big leaders of the RSS–BJP: L.K. Advani, M.M. Joshi, Uma Bharti and eleven others, whereas in the Lucknow court, the proceedings were against the unknown kar sevaks. The CBI had charge-sheeted Advani and others under sections 153A (promoting enmity between classes), 153B (making or publishing any assertion prejudicial to national integration) and 505 (making or publishing false statements, rumour circulation to disturb the peace). The CBI later added a charge of criminal conspiracy against Advani and others. The special court quashed this charge, a decision that was upheld by the Allahabad high court.

On 2 March 2017, during the hearing in the supreme court, the CBI surprisingly demanded the revival of the conspiracy charges. The additional solicitor general appearing for the CBI, Neeraj Kishan Kaul, 'stuck to the stand taken during the tenure of the UPA government, seeking revival of conspiracy charges and said the agency was agreeable to clubbing both the trial proceedings.'[4] If the CBI was called a caged parrot by the supreme court during the Manmohan Singh regime, under Modi it had surrendered completely and did not even breathe without permission.[5] Therefore, the CBI demanding conspiracy charges to be revived came as a bolt from the blue. The Ayodhya matter is a serious one for the RSS–BJP and one which had the direct involvement of senior leaders like Advani and Joshi. Surely, the CBI dare not touch them without a nod from the top? The additional solicitor general can hardly have uttered a word without clearance from the Prime Minister's Office (PMO).

The CBI further pleaded before the supreme court, on 6 April 2017, that 'BJP leaders L.K. Advani, Murli Manohar Joshi and Uma Bharti had conspired with other accused for the demolition of Babri mosque in 1992 ... should also face prosecution for criminal conspiracy'.[6] The CBI said, 'All the accuse [sic] worked in tandem and they should be prosecuted together.'[7] The supreme court not only revoked the lower courts' decision, but also ordered the clubbing of both the Rae Bareli case and the Lucknow case. What complicated the matter further for Advani was the order of the supreme court that the sessions court in Lucknow should finish the hearing in two years' time and pronounce the verdict. Lalu Prasad Yadav, the president of Rashtriya Janata Dal, said, 'The CBI is under the influence of Prime Minister Narendra Modi. It ... sought permission to run trial against Advani and others ... Since Advani's name was in circulation as a probable for the post of president, Modi through well thought out politics struck out his (Advani's) name.'[8] On 3 May 2017, Advani, Joshi and others appeared before the court in Lucknow; charges of criminal conspiracy were framed against them and the court granted them bail. The case is still pending before the supreme court with a deadline of April 2019. But the damage had been done. Ram Nath Kovind became the president of India.

Lalu Prasad Yadav's sarcasm was short-lived too. Soon he was to face the biggest and most traumatic challenge of his political life.

THE SCATTERING OF THE YADAV CLAN

Lalu Yadav was a man who had stood like a rock against communal politics and, despite various corruption charges, he was one leader who did not succumb to the might of the RSS–BJP. As chief minister of Bihar, on 23 September 1990, he stopped a rath yatra led by L.K. Advani in the Samastipur district and arrested him. The Ayodhya movement was then on the rise and Advani was the new symbol of Hindutva assertion. Advani's arrest led to the fall of the Vishwanath Pratap Singh government. V.P. Singh had implemented the recommendations of the Mandal Commission that granted a 27 per cent reservation to OBCs.[9] Yadav championed the cause of the OBCs and emerged as the new leader of the backward classes in his own right. He was mocked, ridiculed, lampooned, humiliated and insulted by the upper-caste politicians and intelligentsia, but he continued to rule Bihar for fifteen years.

Yadav's time as chief minister will undoubtedly be remembered for the lawlessness and jungle raj that pervaded, but it is also a fact that the consolidation of OBCs, Dalits and Muslims because of Yadav was so strong that Bihar did not witness communal riots during his time. He did not let the RSS–BJP grow enough to stand on their own feet. His defeat in 2005 was the beginning of communal politics in Bihar. Yadav's rival in Bihar politics from the OBC fold, Nitish Kumar, partnered with the BJP to form the government. However, he broke his alliance with the BJP on the eve of parliamentary elections in 2014, and later aligned himself with his arch-rival Lalu Prasad Yadav for the assembly elections, defeated the BJP and continued as the chief minister. He is now back with the BJP.

The NDA, led by the BJP, won thirty-two seats in the 2014 parliamentary elections, but as time passed, Modi realised that it would be difficult to repeat the performance and that if Yadav and Kumar remained together, the BJP's seats could quite possibly be reduced to a single digit. The

Machiavelli in him inferred that the alliance had to be decoupled. There were murmurs that Nitish Kumar was not too happy in the company of Yadav, after all. His alliance with the BJP had been smoother. Kumar has a weakness. He is image conscious and projects himself as someone who has zero tolerance for corruption. Suddenly, Yadav was being bombarded with all kinds of corruption charges—the income tax department, the CBI and the enforcement directorate targeted Yadav and his entire family in a coordinated manner.

Despite his impeccable secular credentials, Yadav carries the image of a corrupt politician. He had earlier been jailed over a fodder scam and had had to resign the chief ministership in 1997.[10] He was convicted in the fodder scam case in 2013 and sentenced to five years' imprisonment each under the Prevention of Corruption Act (PCA). He had also been charged in a disproportionate assets case but was acquitted later in 2006 by the court.

Yadav and his family are now facing new charges of corruption. He has been accused of acquiring benami properties.[11] A *Times of India* report on 7 June 2017 carried a list of Yadav's benami properties as alleged by BJP leader Sushil Kumar Modi:[12]

1. A mall being developed near Saguna Mor in Patna.
2. A petrol pump fraudulently allotted to Lalu Prasad Yadav's son, Tej Pratap Yadav.
3. Around 45 decimal lands in Aurangabad, allegedly bought by Tej Pratap Yadav.
4. Three plots in Patna, bought by AK Infosystems, allegedly a shell company floated by the Yadav family.
5. Land given to Rabri Devi Yadav (Lalu Prasad Yadav's wife) by the former union minister, Kanti Singh.
6. Land in Gopalganj transferred to Lalu Prasad Yadav's sons Tej Pratap and Tejashwi Yadav as gifts by former union minister Raghunath Jha.
7. Land in Danapur gifted to Rabri Devi by one Lalan Choudhary.

Sushil Modi also alleged that Rabri Devi acquired eighteen flats in Patna, worth ₹18 crore, through dubious means, and that her son Tejashwi owns twenty-six properties. The income tax department booked Rabri Devi and several of the couple's children—Misa Bharti, Chanda, Rohini, Tej Pratap and Tejashwi Yadav—as well as their son-in-law Shailesh Kumar Yadav over benami properties.[13] Three of Misa Bharti and her husband's alleged properties were searched, they were summoned for questioning by the Enforcement Directorate and they were finally charge-sheeted under the Prevention of Money Laundering Act.

Lalu Prasad Yadav is also accused of having rigged the tender process for running railway hotels when he was the railway minister, to benefit private companies. Apparently in connection with this, three acres of land were sold to a company owned by Yadav's associates at a throwaway price and later this company, Delight Marketing (now known as Lara Projects), was transferred to Lalu Prasad and Tejashwi Yadav. The CBI registered an FIR against Lalu Prasad, Rabri Devi and Tejashwi Yadav in September 2018.

Meanwhile, a two-judge bench of the supreme court, comprising Justice Arun Kumar Mishra and Justice Amitava Roy, revived the conspiracy charges against Lalu Prasad Yadav in the fodder scam, which had been quashed by the Jharkhand high court. The high court had also ordered that all the fodder scam cases should be tried as one; however, the supreme court ordered that all the cases of fodder scam would be tried separately. The Court further ordered that all the cases should be wrapped up in nine months.

After the supreme court verdict, the CBI court pronounced Lalu Prasad Yadav guilty in three more cases of fodder scam. On 6 January 2018, he was sentenced to three-and-a-half years each, under the IPC and PC acts. On 24 January, he was sentenced to five years each under the IPC and PC acts. On 24 March, he was again sentenced for seven years each under the IPC and PC acts by Judge Shiv Pal Singh. The three earlier sentences were concurrent but surprisingly the last one was consecutive, which meant Yadav has to serve two sentences of seven years, one after another. So in this case alone, he will be jailed for fourteen years, which seems a disproportionately long term in comparison to convictions in earlier cases of a similar nature.

Yadav and his family are obviously demoralised. I have had occasion to meet Tejashwi Yadav and Misa Bharti during the case, in fact after the first conviction. They were of the opinion that a part of the reason for the allegations was to wean Nitish Kumar away from Lalu Prasad Yadav, and also to tarnish the image of the Yadav family and turn them into hate figures. They were also apprehensive that before the elections in 2019, half the family might be in jail and nobody would be left to lead and campaign for the party. However, paradoxically, if this was indeed a conspiracy, the strategy seems to have backfired. I have had occasion to be in Patna quite a few times and can say that now Yadav and his family are seen as victims. The alleged involvement of his family members, especially his sons and daughters, is believed to be part of a bigger conspiracy by the upper castes to finish off a less-privileged leader. OBCs, Muslims and a section of Dalits are galvanised and a new consolidation of the three different sections of society is taking shape, which could destabilise Modi's applecart. Lalu Prasad and Tejashwi Yadav in particular have played up their victimhood, and sympathy for a 'victimised' Lalu has catapulted Tejashwi to the post of a mass leader.

SAYING BOO TO BANERJEE

Like Lalu Prasad Yadav, Mamata Banerjee also has reason to believe that she has been regularly targeted since the Modi regime came into power. Banerjee is a feisty woman and deserves credit for dislodging the Left Front government in West Bengal, which had ruled the state for thirty-five years. The TMC has thirty-four MPs in the lower house of the parliament. Banerjee is in the forefront of those opposing the Modi government and never minces words. She did try to cobble together all the opposition parties into a united front. In one such meeting where I was present, she expressed two main concerns—first, that Modi has dictatorial tendencies; his ideology is dangerous for the country and the minorities are scared in his rule. Second, Modi does not want any kind of opposition. He will work to destabilise every government formed by an opposition party and will ultimately send all the opposition leaders to jail.

Under Modi's leadership, the BJP has certainly been expanding its base in regions where it has traditionally been weak or even non-existent. West Bengal is one such region. The Left's social base has been shrinking. Its cadre has shifted to either the TMC or the BJP. The Congress is almost redundant in West Bengal now. There is an opportunity for the BJP to occupy the opposition space and it has made serious inroads in the state. BJP's national president Amit Shah has made many visits. Bengal, after a very long time, is witnessing the mobilisation of the masses on religious lines. Communal tension is on the rise and some clashes have occurred already. The RSS–BJP are leaving no stone unturned to project Banerjee as a leader who cares only for Muslims and to portray the TMC as an anti-Hindu party.

The acrimony between Banerjee and Modi had grown so bitter that Banerjee accused the Modi government of planning a coup in West Bengal to unseat her with the help of the army. She alleged that the Modi government was trying to 'intimidate the state by stationing army trucks on national highways and at toll posts and raising the spectre of a "civil war".'[14] The Modi government vehemently denied these charges.

Banerjee believes that corruption cases have been levelled against TMC leaders deliberately, so as to weaken her resolve to fight Modi and to sully her image as an honest politician. Three major scams—the Narada bribery scandal, the Rose Valley scam of ₹17,000 crore and the Saradha scam for ₹2,500 crore—have hurt her image of being an upright politician.

In the Narada bribery case, twelve senior members of the TMC were booked by the CBI on 17 April 2017. The website, Narada News, had published the results of a sting operation in which cash worth about ₹5 lakh was given to the TMC leaders by a representative of a fake Chennai-based company called Impex Consultancy, ostensibly with the intent to call in some favours in the future.[15] Senior leaders such as Mukul Roy, the former railway minister who later joined the BJP; Madan Mitra, a former West Bengal minister; and Lok Sabha members Saugata Roy, Aparupa Poddar, Sultan Ahmed, Prasun Banerjee and Kakoli Ghosh Dastidar were named. It was alleged that they had been caught on camera either accepting money or asking for money to be handed over to someone else: 'Others named in the CBI FIR as accused include West Bengal state urban development minister Firhad Hakim, transport minister Suvendu Adhikari, environment minister Sovan Chatterjee, panchayati raj and rural development minister Subrata Mukherjee, MLA Iqbal Ahmed and IPS officer Saiyaad Mustafa Hussain Mirza.'[16] Banerjee was furious. She termed the CBI FIR a political vendetta. Mukul Roy, who was once the second most powerful leader in the TMC, was apparently pressurised by the BJP leaders to cross over and help the BJP build the party in the state; otherwise, he would end up in jail. He moved to the BJP. The BJP was happy to admit a tainted leader in its fold.

The Rose Valley and Saradha scams both centred around Ponzi schemes. In the Rose Valley case, TMC's Rajya Sabha MP Tapas Paul and the party's parliamentary leader in the Lok Sabha Sudip Bandyopadhyay were arrested, whereas in the Saradha scheme verdict, TMC's Rajya Sabha MPs Kunal

Ghosh and former MP Srinjoy Bose, former West Bengal police chief and party vice president Rajat Majumdar and former transport minister Madan Mitra went to jail. It should be noted that the CBI investigation of the Saradha scheme was directed by the supreme court in May 2014.

Mamata Banerjee was particularly shaken after Sudip Bandyopadhyay's arrest. She said, 'I couldn't think that they would arrest Sudip da. From what I gather from my sources in the Enforcement Directorate and CBI, instructions are coming from the top to go for our ministers and MPs .... They are also after my family members .... I know why they are doing this. They had put pressure on me to keep silent. But you know me, I don't buckle under pressure.'[17] She also tweeted, 'We strongly condemn the political vindictive attitude of Narendra Modi and Amit Shah. For no reason arrests have been made. Only reason is #NoteBandi.'[18] The BJP also reacted strongly. Siddharth Nath Singh, the BJP in-charge of West Bengal, said, 'CBI is investigating the Ponzi scams under the directives of the supreme court' and went on to hit back: 'Under Mamata there is no democracy in Bengal, only violence and riots.'[19]

AAP: AN ANTIPATHY

Like Mamata Banerjee, the Arvind Kejriwal government in Delhi and the AAP were also subjected to the ruthlessness of state power. Some fifteen MLAs were arrested on frivolous charges; many of them were arrested multiple times. Most of them were later exonerated by the court. Chief Minister Arvind Kejriwal's office was raided. His principal secretary was arrested and put in jail for two months. His house was also raided by the Delhi Police. Deputy chief minister Manish Sisodia was questioned by the CBI. Health minister Satyendra Jain was accused by the income tax department and the enforcement directorate of engaging in money laundering and hawala transactions. His residence was searched many times and his wife was also questioned, leaving his image maligned.

Since Delhi is not a full state and power is shared by the lieutenant governor, elected governments of Delhi do not have the police under their jurisdiction. The Centre has vast powers to interfere in the union territory's affairs. Control over the Anti-Corruption Bureau (ACB), which had proved phenomenally effective in curbing corruption during the first stint of the

AAP government was snatched away with the help of paramilitary forces during the AAP government's second stint on 8 June 2015. The power to appoint and transfer officers in the Delhi government was also taken away. The Delhi government's powers were so curtailed that it was not even allowed to appoint a peon. Senior secretaries in the chief minister's office were arbitrarily transferred without consulting the chief minister. Senior bureaucrats were threatened by the lieutenant governor to not cooperate with Delhi's elected government. The Delhi government's orders were routinely declared null and void or were delayed to make them ineffective. The bills passed by the Delhi assembly were routinely kept in abeyance by the lieutenant governor or by the Central home ministry, whose signature is a must for the bill to become law. The Delhi government was rendered powerless by an absurd order of the high court of Delhi that the lieutenant governor was not bound by the aid and advice of the elected government. This order was challenged in the supreme court, which (after reserving judgement for six months) has upheld that the lieutenant governor indeed is bound by the aid and advice of the council of ministers. It is more than evident that the Modi government has made governance in Delhi by the elected government a farce.

The AAP and Kejriwal have been paying the price for inflicting the most humiliating defeat on Modi in his entire political career. The BJP could win only three seats out of seventy in the Delhi assembly elections in 2015. The AAP has also paid the price for being the most outspoken critic of Modi. To begin with, representatives of the AAP delved into national politics by severely criticising the inhuman killing of Mohammad Akhlaq in Dadri for allegedly consuming beef, visited Hyderabad after the suicide of Dalit student Rohith Vemula and visited Una, where Dalits were brutally beaten up by upper-caste men for alleged cow slaughter (see chapter 2). The AAP also did not spare Modi on the issue of demonetisation. It was also the first party to raise the issue of the rigging of electronic voting machines (EVMs) and called the BJP victories a result of EVM manipulation.[20]

It is not that the AAP did not try to seek cooperation from the Central government. After forming the Delhi government, Arvind Kejriwal and Manish Sisodia had visited Modi and sought his cooperation. At one of the ceremonial dinners at Rashtrapati Bhavan where the Delhi chief minister was invited as per protocol, Kejriwal was told in as many words that he should not spread his wings beyond the boundaries of Delhi. Kejriwal was seated next to the national security adviser, Ajit Doval, who is thought to be very close to the prime minister. Doval asked him, 'Arvind, why are you going outside Delhi?' He assured the chief minister that there would be no problems for his government or his party if Kejriwal confined himself to Delhi. 'Otherwise,' he said, 'you know Modi ji …' It was clear that Modi wanted to make a deal with the AAP. This was at a time when the AAP was rated very highly and was seen as an all-India alternative. Analysts were betting that the AAP would replace the Congress nationally. In early surveys by the *India Today* magazine, Kejriwal had been seen as a serious challenger to Modi and found to be the second most popular leader after him. In the popularity stakes, Kejriwal was clearly ahead of Sonia Gandhi and Rahul Gandhi. And among the chief ministers he was rated as the most charismatic CM.[21]

Subsequently, the relationship between the two soured so much that Modi refused to acknowledge Kejriwal and Sisodia at public functions and stopped reciprocating their pleasantries. Many BJP leaders told me that Modi would see to it that the AAP as a party was ruined and that Arvind Kejriwal was finished as its leader. Delhi police chiefs and lieutenant governors were more than willing to play Modi's game. Police Chief B.S. Bassi was ready to do anything to please his master. I was told by a very senior police officer close to the BJP that once Modi happened to witness a press conference by AAP's senior leader Sanjay Singh, who later became a Rajya Sabha MP, where he said something about the 'Gujarat model'. Apparently Modi called up one of his senior cabinet colleagues right away and told him that it was getting too much and that Singh should be booked for casting aspersions upon a particular community. The very next day, a meeting was called that brought the cabinet minister together with Bassi and additional solicitor general Pinky Anand. There, Anand was entrusted with the responsibility of preparing a legal case and Bassi was asked to make arrangements for Singh's arrest. Bassi was ready to pick him up at any time. He discussed the matter with his senior colleagues as well. When Modi was apprised of the entire plan, he asked Bassi to wait for a day. His enthusiasm had waned a bit by the next day, and then the day after that, it had lessened some more. The plan was never executed. I was told that Modi was not very sure how the situation would unfold after arresting such a senior person. He was apprehensive of it boomeranging back at him.

JARRING: THE JAYALALITHAA STORY

The story in Tamil Nadu was equally jarring. As long as Jayaram Jayalalithaa was alive, Tamil Nadu seemed to be safe from the wrath of the Central government. After her unfortunate death, the state went into a turmoil apparently choreographed by the Centre. Within two weeks of the chief minister's demise, the residence and offices of the chief secretary of state, P. Rama Mohana Rao, were raided by the income tax department. The IAS officer was supposed to be one of Jayalalithaa's most trusted officers and it was alleged that the Centre wanted to remove him and let one of its trusted people control the administration. Rao's son and other relatives were not spared either. The raid was linked to the arrest of the sand-mining baron J. Sekhar Reddy. The All India Anna Dravida Munnetra Kazhagam (AIADMK) reacted sharply: 'It's hardly 17 days since Amma (Jayalalithaa) passed away. It's betrayal by BJP. It looks like the NDA government has a larger game-plan.'[22] The BJP just said that no one had immunity from IT raids.

After Jayalalithaa's death, her closest confidant V.K. Sasikala and her entire family took charge of the party. She tried to not only become Jayalalithaa's successor but also the chief minister of the state. Senior AIADMK leader O. Panneerselvam was made the chief minister after Jayalalithaa was admitted to hospital, however.

Sasikala did not have a clean reputation and had gone to jail along with Jayalalithaa on corruption charges. Yet, though Jayalalithaa had her thrown out of her residence twice, she was the one who commanded the maximum control over the party and in the government. Modi and the BJP did not want Sasikala to emerge as Jayalalithaa's successor, as it was assumed that she would be quite independent and would not be easy to handle. It was obvious from day one that a weak leader would suit Modi and the BJP better. Panneerselvam, who had served as chief minister thrice already, was the ideal candidate for Modi to bet on.

Meanwhile, Sasikala was moving fast. She not only got herself appointed the general secretary of the party, the post held by Jayalalithaa, but was also chosen unanimously as the leader of the legislative party. One the same day, that she was elected leader of the AIADMK, Panneerselvam resigned from his post as chief minister. It appeared that Sasikala was only a step away from the chief minister's seat.

If Jayalalithaa had been convicted in four corruption cases, Sasikala had been convicted in three. Like Jayalalithaa, she had also escaped conviction in two cases. However, there was one pending case of disproportionate assets to the tune of ₹66.65 crore. The supreme court had reserved its judgement on it on 7 June 2016; judgement was to be pronounced before May 2017, as one of the judges was to retire by then. A week before her installation as the party leader, news broke: 'Madras high court set aside Sasikala's discharge in at least four Enforcement Directorate-investigated cases, thereby exposing her to trial in all these cases.'[23]

But that would come later. Two things happened within three days of Sasikala becoming a candidate for the chief ministership in the AIADMK legislative party. First, O. Panneerselvam revolted and announced that he would withdraw his resignation letter. That meant he would challenge Sasikala for the top post. Now Sasikala had to save her MLAs from the Panneerselvam camp. Around hundred MLAs were bundled into buses and taken to an undisclosed location. Secondly, Governor Chennamaneni Vidyasagar Rao, senior BJP leader from Andhra Pradesh, absented himself from Tamil Nadu, thus delaying an invitation to Sasikala to form the government in Tamil Nadu. He was said to be busy in Maharashtra. Nobody knew when he would come back to Chennai. BJP national secretary H. Raja clarified, 'These are just rumours, the BJP has nothing to do with the governor's absence. Although there is nothing unusual about the governor taking some time to consult with legal and constitutional experts in Delhi before arriving in Chennai.'[24] Newspapers reported the next day, 'According to government insiders … it is unlikely that [the governor] would rush to take a final call before supreme court gives its verdict in the corruption case involving Sasikala.'[25]

Now the moot point is how the governor could possibly know when a judgement would be pronounced, given that it had been reserved for more than eight months. Nor is the governor supposed to know the content of the judgement in advance. So surely it was impossible for him to be sure that Sasikala would be jailed? The Indian judiciary is supposed to be independent of the legislature, as constituted by the principle of separation of powers, and the supreme court is supreme—the Central government cannot dictate terms to it. The supreme court pronounced its verdict within a week of Sasikala being elected as leader of the AIADMK legislative party.

On 14 February 2017, it set aside the Karnataka high court's judgement and upheld the conviction of Sasikala by the trial court. Now Sasikala had to spend three years, ten months and twenty-seven days in jail. The biggest thorn in the BJP government's side was out.

Sasikala's exit paved the way for Edappadi K. Palaniswami to be sworn in as the next chief minister of Tamil Nadu. He was Sasikala's choice.

Meanwhile, in her absence, Sasikala's nephew T.T.V. Dinakaran, who had appointed himself the deputy general secretary of the party, was also arrested by the Delhi Police on the charge of trying to bribe officials of the Election Commission to allot his faction of the AIADMK, the 'two-leaf' symbol, the party symbol of the AIADMK. In March 2017, the Election Commission had decided to 'freeze' the symbol, prohibiting its use by either of the two factions of the AIADMK, led by Sasikala and Panneerselvam respectively, for the by-elections in Chennai.

After being released from jail, Dinakaran decided to contest elections from the Dr. Radhakrishnan Nagar (popularly known as R.K. Nagar) constituency for the assembly seat which was vacant since Jayalalithaa's demise. Five days before the polling, the income tax department most dramatically raided the home of health minister C. Vijayabaskar. Officials claimed that he was distributing cash to buy votes for Dinakaran. A few other AIADMK MLAs were also questioned. The by-poll in R.K. Nagar was countermanded. Dinakaran cried foul. But when polling did take place, he was declared a winner. It is common knowledge that the income tax department does not report to the state government; it is monitored and controlled by the Centre. However, it is not a secret that since 2014, the department has been led by the diktats of the Modi government.

There are many questions that arise at this juncture. Was it just by chance that after Jayalalithaa's death, the residence and office of the chief secretary of Tamil Nadu were raided? Was it not a beautiful coincidence that just as Sasikala was poised to become the chief minister, she was sentenced to imprisonment for four years? Was it also not serendipitous that Sasikala's successor Dinakaran was arrested for bribery, and the income tax department raided a minister close to Dinakaran just days before polling so that the by-election was countermanded? Was Mamata Banerjee right to lambast the Central government on the raids on the residence of the chief secretary, saying, 'Earlier the Principal Secretary of Arvind Kejriwal was raided and harassed. Now I read Chief Secretary of Tamil Nadu has also been raided. Why this vindictive, unethical, technically improper action? Is it only to disturb the federal structure? Why don't they raid Amit Shah and others who are collecting money?'[26]

CHIDAMBARAM: ATTACK AD HOMINEM?

If Jayalalithaa's succession involved too many revolving doors, the lot of her once arch-rival, P. Chidambaram, has been practically a one-man courtroom drama.

For a good ten years, P. Chidambaram was one of the most powerful persons in India. The senior Congress leader, who had held the posts of finance minister and home minister of the country under Manmohan Singh and been a minister under prime ministers Rajiv Gandhi, P.V. Narasimha Rao, H.D. Deve Gowda and Inder Kumar Gujral, now feels hounded by the central agencies that once used to report to him.

On 23 February 2018, Chidambaram moved the supreme court to seek protection from the agencies. In his writ petition, he wrote, 'The CBI and ED [Enforcement Directorate], as part of political vendetta, have made vexatious searches, issued repeated summons, unreasonably questioned persons for unconscionably long hours, unlawfully attached fixed deposits, maliciously leaked false information to the media and otherwise caused extreme harassment, anguish and humiliation to me and my son, and to other persons who are normal business and social friends of my son.' His 100-page petition declared, 'The writ petition is being filed to defend and protect the petitioner's fundamental rights under Article 114, 19 and 21 of the constitution and to defend his right to privacy and the right to live, along with members of his family, in dignity.'[27]

Within five days of filing this petition, Chidambaram's son Karti Chidambaram was arrested at the Chennai airport by the CBI, on his arrival from London. He was accused of 'demanding and accepting' a bribe of $1 million or approximately ₹6.5 crore from the INX Media company. The week before, on 17 February 2018, the CBI had recorded the statement of the former director of INX Media, Indrani Mukerjea, under Section 164 of the Code of Criminal Procedure, in which she said that Karti Chidambaram had demanded and accepted the bribe money. Any statement recorded under Section 164 is admissible as evidence in a court of law. It should be noted that at the time of recording her statement, Mukerjea was under arrest in Mumbai jail for allegedly killing her daughter along with her husband Peter Mukerjea.

An FIR was lodged against Karti, his company Chess Management Services and also Advantage Strategic Consulting on 15 May 2017. The very next day, his residence and fourteen locations in Chennai, Delhi, Mumbai and Gurugram were raided by CBI officials, and several hard disks, e-mails and documents were seized. According to the FIR, Karti was accused of having 'hatched a criminal conspiracy with INX Media Private Limited (now called 9X Media) to "scuttle" an investigation into the company's irregularities. In return, Karti was "paid" by the company for "resolving" the issue "amicably" with the finance ministry officials …'[28]

Less than a year later, Karti Chidambaram was arrested: 'It is alleged that Karti exercised his influence over the Foreign Investment Promotion Board (FIPB) unit officials to help INX Media wriggle out of a probe proposed by the Department of Revenue into an alleged unapproved 26% down-streaming of foreign investment in INX News, received from three Mauritius-based companies in 2007. INX Media had got FIPB approval for ₹4.62 crore influx, but received ₹305 crore by selling its shares at a premium of ₹800 per unit. For down-streaming of funds, the company re-applied as advised by the FIPB and got a separate approval later, allegedly by concealing the fact that it had already been made. The agency alleges that in lieu of the "services" rendered to INX Media by Chess Management Services, payments were received through Advantage Strategic Consulting and other entities located abroad.'[29]

Though P. Chidambaram was not named in the FIR, the CBI mentioned that the '"deceitful and fallacious" foreign investment proposal was "favourably considered" and "approved" by Chidambaram and the officials of the finance ministry at the time.'[30] In his weekly column that appears in the *Indian Express*, Chidambaram openly criticised the government and said, 'The government, using the CBI and other agencies, is targeting my son and his friends. The government's aim is to silence my voice and stop me from writing.' Finance Minister Arun Jaitley rebutted the charges, saying,

'Now people in high positions acquiring assets through shell companies is not a small matter and I think the day of reckoning has come for many, they will all be held accountable.'[31]

Karti also faces another case in the Aircel Maxis matter related to the 2G spectrum scams, in which the CBI and Enforcement Directorate had registered a case. The supreme court has granted an interim stay order on his arrest.

HOME STATE SECURITY

If in Tamil Nadu the invisible footprints of the Modi government could be felt, then in Gujarat the footprints were quite visible. In Modi and Shah's home state, Congress president Sonia Gandhi's political secretary Ahmed Patel, once considered the third most powerful person in the country after Sonia Gandhi and Manmohan Singh, was to be the candidate for the Rajya Sabha. Initially, it was considered a cakewalk for him—the Congress had fifty-seven MLAs, more than the required number for election to the upper house. But it got tricky when during the presidential elections, eleven Congress MLAs did not tow the party line and voted instead for the BJP candidate, Ram Nath Kovind. Shankarsinh Vaghela, the leader of the opposition in the Gujarat assembly, was leading the rebellion. He was allegedly in touch with Amit Shah.

Before I proceed, it is interesting to note that on 17 June 2015, Vaghela's house in Gandhinagar was raided by CBI officials for nearly twelve hours in connection with a corruption case. Vaghela was minister for textiles in Manmohan Singh's cabinet. He was accused 'of selling prime land belonging to the National Textile Corporation in Mumbai's Parel area to a firm, allegedly causing a loss of ₹709 crore to the state exchequer in 2007-8'.[32] Vaghela accused the BJP government of pursuing vendetta politics. However, an FIR was lodged against him and an enquiry set up.

There were loud whispers in the corridors of power that after the CBI raid, Vaghela knew that it would be difficult to continue his tirades against Modi and Amit Shah. He was reconciled to his political career being over. I had occasion to meet him a few times while he was thinking of quitting the Congress. He was unhappy with the Congress leadership. But it was not the Vaghela I knew who engineered a vertical split in the BJP's legislative party in 1995, exported 47 MLAs from Gujarat to Madhya Pradesh and came back only when the BJP removed Keshubhai Patel as chief minister.

Vaghela used to be a powerful leader credited with establishing the BJP in Gujarat from scratch. But in our meetings, he appeared a pale shadow of his former self. He was not sure about his future course—should he form a party of his own or should he join another party? He toyed with the idea of joining the AAP too but later backtracked. I could feel something was amiss; it seemed there was something weighing on him. I could also sense that he was worried about his son Mahendrasinh's political career—he wanted him to settle down in the BJP fold, if possible, which his son finally did.

There were speculations on the eve of the Gujarat elections that Vaghela was pressurised into leaving the Congress and helping BJP win. After his resignation, six other Congress MLAs resigned from the party on the eve of the Rajya Sabha election. The Congress Party was worried. It decided to herd its MLAs out of Gujarat. Karnataka was the place. The MLAs were kept at a resort owned by Karnataka urban development minister D.K. Shivakumar. On 2 August 2017, like a ghost, the income tax department suddenly appeared and raided thirty-nine places in Karnataka, including the resort where the Congress MLAs were staying. The raiding party did not seek help from the state police, nor did it inform the state government in advance about the raid; instead, it sought the services of the Central Reserve Police Force, which is directly controlled by the Central government. In protest, the Congress disrupted parliament and 'alleged the raids were meant to intimidate the MLAs and objected to the use of Central Reserve Police Force to accompany I-T sleuths'.[33] The BJP unleashed finance minister Arun Jaitley in its defense. He said, 'Searches were not conducted in the resort where Congress MLAs were staying. Tax sleuths visited the resort only to take Shivakumar [the Karnataka minister who was in charge of 'guarding the Gujarat MLAs] to his residence.'[34]

On the day of the polling, a bigger drama was to be enacted. By now it was crystal clear that Ahmed Patel's election had become a prestige issue for Modi and Amit Shah, and they would go to any extent to stop him from being elected. For the Congress also, it was a do or die situation. It was said that Amit Shah believed that he had been sent to jail in the Sohrabuddin encounter case because of Ahmed Patel.[35] He was not only out to settle a score with Patel but also wanted to prove that Gujarat was his citadel and that the speculation that the BJP was on a sticky wicket in the assembly elections was only a rumour. Two of the rebel Congress MLAs, who had voted for the BJP showed their votes to BJP functionaries while coming out of the booth. This was technically wrong. As per the rules, party members are supposed to show their votes to the authorised functionaries of their party. The rebel Congress MLAs committed a blunder. Ideally, their votes should have been declared invalid. However, because the matter was so high-profile, local authorities passed the buck to the Central Election Commission, which again could not decide till midnight.

High-power delegations of the BJP and the Congress both presented their cases before the Commission. The BJP's was led by Jaitley, law minister Ravi Shankar Prasad, Piyush Goyal, who later became the railway minister, and Nirmala Sitharaman, who was to be appointed defence minister in the future. The Congress was represented by former finance minister P. Chidambaram, Kapil Sibal, leader of the opposition in the upper house, Ghulam Nabi Azad and Anand Sharma. Finally, the Election Commission declared those two votes invalid. Patel won; but it was not the end of his troubles. The enforcement directorate was waiting in the wings to slap a money-laundering case against him, his son Faisal Patel and son-in-law Irfan Siddiqui. One Sunil Yadav employed by the Sandesara Group, had alleged that he used to deliver a huge amount of cash on behalf of the group to Faisal's driver, which was meant for Ahmed Patel.[36]

UPSETS IN UTTARAKHAND

The situation in Uttarakhand over the last two years also does not reflect well on the Modi government.

Nine Congress MLAs, led by the former chief minister Vijay Bahuguna and Harak Singh Rawat, rebelled against their own government, led by Harish Rawat. The Congress alleged that the BJP used the lure of money and muscle power to engineer the defections. Rahul Gandhi, then vice president of the Congress, accused Modi on Twitter: 'Toppling elected Govts by indulging in horse trading & blatant misuse of money & muscle, seems to be BJP's new model, after failure in Bihar.'[37] Rahul's statement also highlighted the plight of Arunachal Pradesh, where the government had been sacked, which I will discuss later. As per the constitutional requirements, the governor of Uttarakhand, Krishan Kant Paul asked Chief Minister Rawat to prove his majority on the floor of the house before 28 March 2016. However, just a day before, on 27 March, president's rule was suddenly imposed in Uttarakhand and Rawat was denied the opportunity to prove his majority. The pretext was a sting operation that had surfaced on a TV channel, allegedly showing Rawat offering money to rebel MLAs for extending support to his government during the floor test. It was a stunning development. The sting operation recording was handed over to CBI for further investigation.

The Congress challenged the dismissal of the government and imposition of president's rule in the Uttarakhand high court. Justice U.C. Dhyani ordered a floor test. It was a severe jolt to the Modi government. The high court's decision was challenged before a division bench. Meanwhile, two Congress MLAs accused the BJP of offering them ₹50 crore to defect. On 7 April 2016, the division bench of Justice K.M. Joseph and Justice V.K. Bisht warned the Modi government against any 'hanky panky' while they heard the matter.[38] It was brought to the notice of the high court that the Modi government might lift president's rule and the BJP might try to form the government through defection. On 21 April, the high court overturned the Modi government's order regarding president's rule, revived the assembly, restored the Rawat government and ordered it to prove its majority on the floor of the house on 29 April 2016.

The HC was very critical in its pronouncement. It said that 'even the president can be terribly wrong' and noted that the 'draconian 356 should not have been imposed'. The bench added, 'The said party (BJP) was a direct beneficiary of Article 356, which was not justified as there was no riot or violence in the state. The central government has to work in a completely non-partisan manner and without bias.'[39] It was probably the biggest setback inflicted by the judiciary on the Modi government. The high court's verdict was immediately challenged in the supreme court.

As the country waited for the supreme court's verdict, the CBI became very active. It summoned Harish Rawat to appear before it on 9 May. Rawat cried foul and alleged that the Central government was misusing the government agencies to harass him. Rawat said, 'The timing of the CBI probe and my being summoned (just before the floor test) raises serious questions over the functioning of the probe agency. I am being watched as if I am an anti-national. The telephones of all Congress leaders ... are being tapped. Our MLAs are being approached by their relatives and acquaintances who are giving them lucrative offers and threatening them.'[40] The BJP state president Ajay Bhatt mocked him: 'He is the first former CM who has been served summons by the CBI. There is no smoke without a fire. It is another indication that he has done something wrong.'[41]

On 10 May, Rawat proved his majority on the floor of the house.

So what can one deduce about the CBI summoning Harish Rawat a day before the floor test? The only inference that can be drawn is that it was trying to unsettle him and interfere in the democratic process. It is also interesting to underline that the CBI dared to summon him even when no FIR was registered in this case. Rawat was summoned by the CBI in the same case once again after six months, on 24 December 2016. What is baffling was that the CBI had still had not registered an FIR and he was summoned only on the basis of a preliminary enquiry (PE). The *Times of India* reported, 'This may be a unique case where a sitting CM has been summoned by the CBI during its probe of a PE. The PE is the first step during which the agency verifies the facts in the complaint received by it. During a PE, the agency usually only "requests" a person to "join the probe" and does not summon him, carries out searches or makes any arrests.'[42] Why was this done, then? Well, this was the time when preparations for the assembly elections were in full swing and the dates for it were about to be announced. Though Rawat and his party lost badly in the assembly elections, that is a different story. The issue is why a chief minister was treated this way.

And yes, one more story unfolded in 2018. The Uttarakhand high court's chief justice K.M. Joseph, who was a part of the bench that had overturned the president's rule imposed by the Modi government, had to face the consequences for his audacity when the president did not approve the supreme court collegiums' recommendation to promote him to the office of a supreme court judge. The file was returned on 30 April though the Collegium had recommended his name on 10 January. Finally after a long tiff between the supreme court and the Central government, he was appointed as a supreme court Judge on 3 August 2018.

ARUNACHAL: A DIFFERENT STORY

If the supreme court's rollback of president's rule left them red-faced, the Modi government suffered another humiliation when the Court restored the Congress government in Arunachal Pradesh. The crisis originated when twenty-one of forty-seven Congress MLAs rebelled against their own government led by Nabam Tuki. Governor Jyoti Prasad Rajkhowa did not act in the spirit of the constitution. He pulled forward the assembly meeting from 14 January 2016 to 16 December 2015 without consulting the chief minister. Tuki's government was sacked, with the union cabinet recommending president's rule, and after some time, the rebel leader Kalikho Pul was sworn in as chief minister even though the matter was pending before the supreme court. Eleven BJP MLAs supported Pul's government. The supreme court pronounced its verdict on 13 July 2016, The five-judge bench observed, 'The Governor must keep clear of any political horse-trading, and even unsavoury political manipulations, irrespective of the degree of their ethical repulsiveness. Who should or should not be a leader of a political party is a political question, to be dealt with and resolved privately by the political party itself.'[43]

UNFREEDOM OF THE FOURTH ESTATE

The government seems to be so intent on overcoming all opposition and criticism that even the media has not been left untouched.

News channel NDTV, which had not succumbed to the charms of the government, was also subjected to the tyranny of the Centre's agencies. The information and broadcasting ministry directed the channel be shut down, along with Newstime Assam, for airing news content during the Pathankot terror attack. The ministry viewed the channels' content as not being in accordance with the government's guidelines. NDTV asked why these two were the only channels targeted when the same content was aired by all channels. One of the doyens of Indian journalism, T.N. Ninan said, 'It's inherently wrong and dangerous for a government committee to have the power to take a TV channel off air.'[44] After a lot of hue and cry, the ban on NDTV was put on hold.

NDTV had to face another assault the following year when the CBI raided the residence of co-founder and executive co-chairperson Prannoy Roy. It was alleged that ICICI bank had suffered a loss of over ₹48 crore, arising out of 'unlawful/undue favour and profit transferred' to the Roys and RRPR Holding.[45] This turned out to be a loan between two private parties and the government should have had nothing to do with it. The loan had been mutually adjusted between the Roys (Prannoy and his wife and co-founder of NDTV, Radhika Roy) and ICICI Bank seven years ago, but an FIR was nonetheless entertained by the CBI. Information and Broadcasting Minister Muppavarupu Venkaiah Naidu said, 'If somebody does something wrong simply because they belong to media, you cannot expect the government to keep quiet.'[46]

Teesta Setalvad, who fought for the victims of the Gujarat riots, was also hounded by the Central agencies. The registration of her NGO Sabrang Trust was suspended and all foreign funding blocked. The trust was alleged to have spent more than 50 per cent of the funds on administrative expenses, in violation of the Foreign Contribution Regulation Act (FCRA). With CBI cases pending against her, she had to run to the supreme court to avoid being arrested.

Noted lawyer Indira Jaising's NGO, Lawyers' Collective, also had its licence cancelled by the government and it was claimed that there were 'discrepancies in the foreign contributions cited by the association in its returns filed with the MHA [ministry of home affairs]'.[47] It might be worth noting that Jaising has been a vocal critic of the government.

It should also be considered that there are right-wing news channels that openly air communal content but have never been hauled up by the government. Noted historian Ramachandra Guha tweeted, 'The UPA regime was defined by the cronyism and corruption; this BJP government by vengefulness and vindictiveness. The UPA was desperately keen to favour its friends and relatives; this government is consumed by the desire to punish its critics and rivals.'

SOMETHING IS ROTTEN

It is the responsibility of the government to act against those who indulge in wrongdoing and punish those who violate the law of the land. The government is expected to strictly follow the principle of fair play and objectivity in the discharge of its duties. It is not expected to be partisan.

Discrimination in the execution of law is not the mandate of the constitution. The law does not prescribe selective implementation of a government order. In the eyes of the law, every citizen is equal and should be treated equally. If there is a perception that the critics of the government are being targeted, then something is wrong.

Unfortunately, there is a growing perception that the Modi government is discriminatory and selective in the execution of the law. The role of the government agencies in the cases mentioned above does not inspire confidence or suggest that they are impartial. Why should it not be inferred that instead of serving the people of India, they were serving their political master? I am not getting into the merit of each of the cases. I only ask why these various agencies shied away from taking similar action when similar charges were made against the friends of the government.

Anar Jayesh Patel is the daughter of the former chief minister of Gujarat, Anandiben Patel. Her business associate's little-known company Wildwoods Resorts and Realties, was given 250 acres of public land adjacent to the Gir lion sanctuary at a throwaway price of ₹15 per square metre. 'Soon after the land was allotted and permission granted for developing a resort in Dhari, shares of WWR [Wildwoods] were transferred to Anar's current business partner, Daxesh Rameshchandra Shah, and two others. Two companies owned by Anar's partner, Anil Infraplus Ltd and Parshwa Texchem (India) Pvt Ltd, acquired 49.5% shares each in Wildwoods. Later, Anar's company Anar Projects, and Relish Pharma (in which she is a business partner) joined [Wildwoods] by acquiring equity through various business transactions recorded with the Registrar of Companies.'[48]

What is most intriguing is that this land falls within a radius of two kilometres of the Gir sanctuary, in the eco-sensitive zone where according to the rules, no commercial activities can be undertaken. Yet this rule was changed and instead of two kilometres, the radius was reduced to one-and-a-half kilometres. When the land was allotted to Wildwoods, Anandiben Patel was the revenue minister and Modi was the chief minister. Later, another 172 acres of agricultural land were given to Wildwoods, with their land use changed to non-agricultural. Despite vociferous demands for a probe, no action was ever initiated. Anar and Anandiben Patel did not respond to the allegations. The BJP called all the charges baseless.

JAY SHAH AND OTHER TALES

The son of BJP president Amit Shah, Jay Shah runs a company named Temple Enterprise. As reported by the Wire, the turnover of the company rose 16,000 times, from ₹50,000 in 2014–15 to ₹80.5 crore in 2015–16, the year after Narendra Modi became prime minister and Amit Shah the BJP president.[49] The company wound up next year, citing losses. Jay Shah called the charges false and defamatory, saying that his business was fully legitimate and conducted in a lawful manner. The opposition demanded a probe, which was never ordered. However, a ₹100-crore defamation suit was filed in the court against the Wire.

Piyush Goyal was the railway minister in 2018. He has been accused of 'impropriety and conflict of interest'.[50] The main opposition party, the Congress, has demanded that he should be sacked and that allegations should be investigated by an enquiry committee headed by a sitting supreme court judge. The Congress alleged, 'Goyal was chairman and whole-time director of Shirdi Industries from April 25 2008 to July 1 2010 during which the company took a loan of ₹258.62 crore from a consortium of banks headed by Union Bank of India. Goyal later resigned from the company's board and the company was subsequently declared sick due to its inability to repay loans. However, after the Modi dispensation assumed power at the Centre, 65 per cent of the outstanding loan amount of ₹651.87 crore was "shockingly" waived by the consortium of banks without any objections …. [Veerappa] Moily claimed that Asis Industries, a sister concern of Shirdi Industries, granted an unsecured loan of ₹1.59 crore in 2015–16 to Intercon Advisors, a company owned by Piyush Goyal's wife Seema Goyal.'[51]

Piyush Goyal was also flagged in another case of impropriety. According to the Wire, it was alleged that he sold a company, jointly owned by him and his wife, at nearly '1,000 times the face value' to the privately-owned Piramal Group, after becoming part of PM Narendra Modi's cabinet in 2014.[52] The report also alleged that 'the Piramal Group has interests in new and renewable energy, as well as the power sector. At the time of the alleged sale, Goyal was a minister of state with independent charge for power, coal and renewable energy.' While the Congress was gunning for his resignation, the BJP defended Goyal and responded by saying that the Congress was running a malicious campaign against him and that there was no truth in the allegations and 'no wrong doing or irregularity' on Goyal's part.[53]

Pankaja Munde is the daughter of BJP's senior leader and former deputy chief minister of Maharashtra, Gopinath Munde. She is the minister of rural development and women and child development in Maharashtra. She has been accused of giving out twenty-four contracts in a day without any tendering process to procure items such as chikki, water filters and medicines to the amount of ₹206 crore. The opposition demanded an enquiry. Instead, the ACB gave her a clean chit and declared that she did no wrong. The ACB—no surprises here—reports to the BJP government and therefore its independence as an institution is doubtful. The matter is pending in the Maharashtra high court.

Raman Singh is the third-time chief minister of Chhattisgarh. He is popularly known as 'Chawalwale Baba' (rice god). His public distribution scheme (PDS) has been praised even by his critics and some have tried to imitate the scheme in their own states. But the Raman Singh government has also been accused of a scam of thousands of crores of rupees. It is alleged that poor-quality rice has been procured by the government and diaries have been recovered in which the names of Raman Singh, his wife, sister-in-law and cook figured, with allegations of them receiving benefits.[54] The opposition has demanded a supreme court-monitored enquiry. The state government's ACB arrested fourteen people but no action has ever been initiated against Raman Singh and his associates. Raman Singh refused to resign, calling the allegations a figment of the opposition's imagination.[55] The Modi government was quiet. Raman Singh's son Abhishek Singh's name also figured in the Panama Papers.[56] Abhishek Singh allegedly has undisclosed foreign bank accounts and owns assets in the British Virgin Islands. Once again, this has been vehemently denied by Abhishek Singh.

Eknath Khadse is one of the seniormost leaders of the BJP in Maharashtra. He was also a pretender to the chief minister's seat when the BJP won the assembly elections. Later, he became the revenue minister. The charge against him was that he bought three acres of land in Bhosari from the Maharashtra Industrial Development Corporation at a throw away price of ₹3.78 crore.[57] The market value of the land was around ₹40 crore. Khadse was asked to resign, but the ACB later pronounced him not guilty, absolving him of any wrongdoing.[58]

Since the Modi government came into power, there have been serious allegations against foreign minister Sushma Swaraj and Rajasthan chief minister Vasundhara Raje Scindia for helping the fugitive Lalit Kumar Modi. Despite a lot of media hype, no action ever followed.

The Vyapam scam has claimed more than forty lives in Madhya Pradesh, with accusations reaching the doors of Shivraj Singh Chouhan, the chief minister of Madhya Pradesh. However, he has never been put through the rigours of an investigation by any agency.

STIFLING THE OPPOSITION

In contrast, in cases related to its opposition leaders and dissenting voices, the government and its agencies have been very free in summoning persons of interest—as with Harish Rawat, the chief minister of Uttarakhand, who was summoned twice without any FIR being lodged; in questioning and interrogating them innumerable times—like in the case of the family members of Lalu Prasad Yadav, P. Chidambaram and Satyendra Jain; in raiding the premises of the accused on such a scale as to give the impression that a major crackdown is happening—as evident by the IT raids on D.K. Shivakumar in Bengaluru or on the residence of the chief secretary of Tamil Nadu. The residence of the chief minister of Himachal Pradesh, Virbhadra Singh, was raided on the day his daughter was getting married. The cancellation of registration for Indira Jaising's NGO was done on a Sunday.

Arrests on frivolous charges have become so common that they have lost their relevance. In Delhi, AAP MLA Dinesh Mohania was arrested from a live press conference. AAP minister Jitender Singh Tomar was arrested as if he was a terrorist. Karti Chidambaram was picked up from the airport. Cases are so mercilessly pursued and so many charges are made that it will take years to be rid of them.

A twenty-four year old Patidar leader Hardik Patel who was spearheading the Patidar Community's agitation, demanding reservation, was kept in jail for almost a year. The Gujarat Police pressed sedition charges against him. Dalit leader Chandrashekhar Azad (Ravan) from western UP was arrested and when he was about to get bail, charges under the National Security Act were slapped on him and he languished in jail for more than a year. Lalu

Prasad Yadav is in jail and now his entire family—wife Rabri Devi Yadav, sons Tejashwi and Tej Pratap Yadav, daughters Misa Bharti, Chanda and Rohini Yadav and son-in-law Shailesh Kumar Yadav are—are all facing cases. Similarly, Chidambaram's wife, his son and daughter-in-law have been booked by the income tax department. Agencies have been ever so generous in leaking information on these cases. Confidential papers easily reach the favourite TV channels, who run it like the most exciting breaking news while the accused's reputation goes for a six. But when it comes to BJP leaders and their friends, nothing seems to move. There is no urgency in summoning, no questioning and no interrogation takes place, no arrest happens and if it does happen, then bail is granted in a few hours, as in the case of Delhi BJP MLA, O.P. Sharma, and the Patiala House court lawyers who beat up Kanhaiya Kumar.

In totalitarian states, such things are normal. Hitler and Stalin were ruthless rulers who never hesitated to liquidate their enemies. Hitler had flown to Munich to arrest his old friend Ernst Röhm, whom he perceived to be a threat to his regime in the long run. He stormed into his bedroom with a revolver in his hand and shouted at him, 'You are under arrest, you pig.'[59] He was taken to prison and asked to shoot himself with a gun placed in his cell. When he did not shoot himself, the guard shot him in the chest at point-blank range. Stalin also chased his enemies into foreign lands.

It would be naive on my part to think about contemporary India on these lines. India is a functioning democracy. It has a rich democratic tradition. Yet in the last few years, its institutions have shown signs of dangerous fragility. Today investigating agencies have literally become tools in the hands of the ruling regime at the Centre. Modi as prime minister has shown the tendency to attach all powers to himself. Officers in the CBI, Enforcement Directorate, income tax department and the police in Centre-administered areas are handpicked and they are loyal only to the king.

Earlier, Indira Gandhi had advocated the concept of a committed bureaucracy. She demanded that the bureaucrats serve the ideology of the ruling party, which then meant the Congress, because people had elected that party to form the government. During the Emergency, she did brutalise the system. Fundamental rights were curtailed, top leaders of the country were jailed and political activists were tortured in police custody. There was no space for criticism. The voice of dissent was crushed.

Today, there is no emergency. So such measures are not warranted. Yet opposition leaders and workers are terrorised by the blatant use of state power and attempts to break the spirits of the dissenting voices. These are not good symptoms. If this is part of the exercise to make India an 'opposition-mukt Bharat' on the pretext of making India 'Congress-mukt', then democracy is in peril.[60] The 'Congress mukt' statement by BJP president Amit Shah is quite dangerous. It provides an opportunity to peep into the minds of those who control the levers of power in India right now. Let us not forget that the opposition is equally important for a vibrant and dynamic democracy. It is a diabolical ideology that requires democracy for its survival but once at the helm of affairs, kills the very system that propelled it to the top. India is moving in that direction. Hitler did exactly the same thing. He too was a product of democracy.

EIGHT

Wheels of Justice Squeaking and Squealing

The date was 12 January 2018. It was 10.45 in the morning. Delhi was cold and sunny. I received a message saying that the four most senior judges of the supreme court were going to hold a press conference. I was surprised and did not take the message seriously. I was sure that in this age of social media–propagated hoaxes, this was just another rumour, the product of some fertile but warped imagination. I had never heard of judges holding a press conference, after all. They rarely speak to the public. Silence is their biggest armour.

I did, however, know that there was simmering discontent in the higher levels of the judiciary. I had also heard that the supreme court was a house divided and there were serious differences within the collegiums. Senior journalists on the legal beat had told me that the chief justice of India had failed to win the confidence of the senior justices. There were murmurs in the corridors of justice that the chief justice was under tremendous pressure from the government and his closeness to the ruling establishment was discussed in hushed tones. Nonetheless, I was not willing to believe that an open rebellion was possible in the judiciary. An hour and a half passed in which I tried to talk to a few of my friends and was told that a presser was a real possibility and that TV channels were waiting, ready to go live. This was a shocker. Yet even then, the media had no clue why the presser had been scheduled, what the provocation was.

I switched on the TV and waited anxiously. By 12.20 p.m., the anchors announced that they were going live at Justice Jasti Chelameswar's residence. I could see cameras lined up and some very senior editors roaming about the lawn, talking to each other. Everybody seemed anxious and impatient.

Tension was writ large on all faces. The four justices walked in slowly. I could see Justice Chelameswar, followed by three more justices I did not immediately recognise. I later learnt they were Justice Ranjan Gogoi, Justice Kurian Joseph and Justice Madan Bhimrao Lokur. All four justices together formed the collegium that is entrusted with the task of choosing the judges for the supreme court and the high courts. Justice Chelameswar was the most senior and was to retire on 22 June 2018. Justice Ranjan Gogoi was in line to succeed Justice Dipak Misra as the next CJI.

Justice Chelameswar was leading the group. He opened the session: 'We tried to persuade the CJI that certain things are not in order. Unfortunately, the efforts failed. We are convinced that unless corrective steps are taken immediately, the judiciary will lose its strong and independent tag, an essential hallmark of a vibrant democracy … We wanted a particular thing in a particular manner. That thing was done but that raised further questions about the integrity of the institution. Today also we went to meet the CJI and pointed out that a particular thing was not in order and requested him to rectify it. Despite senior most colleagues requesting him to correct the anomaly, he was not amenable to correct it.'[1]

The press was told that the collegium had written a letter to the chief justice two months back and had requested him to correct a few things, but they had failed to get any response. Therefore, they had met the chief justice again that morning and had tried to convince him. They were disappointed yet again. The justices told the media that they were left with no other option than to talk to the public: 'Things less than desirable have happened in the supreme court. We tried to collectively persuade the CJI so that he takes remedial measures but our efforts have failed. Four of us are convinced that for the survival of democracy, an impartial judge and judiciary are needed.'[2] This was explosive stuff.

Everybody was dying to know what the immediate provocation had been. At the press conference, however, the justices tried to be discreet and did not go into the specifics. They basically hinted that the judiciary seemed to be in turmoil over the selection and allotment of politically sensitive cases to the respective benches. What they did not say but only hinted at was that the allotment of benches was being done to seek favourable verdicts and it was done at the behest of the ruling party. It was an enormous accusation. After a lot of pestering, Justice Gogoi finally said that the matter could be related to the death of Justice Brijgopal Harkishan Loya: 'It is about assignment of a case. Whatever Justice Chelameswar said is enough. It is a discharge of debt to the nation and we have done it.'[3]

That morning at 10.15, all the justices had met the chief justice, requesting him to transfer a politically sensitive case from a particular bench to a bench led by one of the most senior justices. The chief justice had not obliged. He apprised them that in November 2017, a five-judge bench had decided that the CJI was the master of the roster and it was only he who should decide which case should go to which bench and what the composition of the bench should be. After this altercation, all four justices met separately and decided to go public on the issue.

The rebellion by the justices immediately evoked serious debate. Justices addressing the media directly, outside the courtroom context, was historic and unprecedented. The legal fraternity had sharp reactions. One section was of the opinion that the justices had no business going to the public and behaving like politicians. If there were any issues, they should have been sorted out within the four walls of the judiciary, they felt. Justice R.S. Sodhi went to the extent of demanding that all four should be impeached. Former attorney general, Soli Jehangir Sorabjee, was very disappointed and said that conducting a press conference was 'inappropriate', and that there were other ways of doing this.[4] The more radical group, on the other hand, welcomed the move. Senior advocate Prashant Bhushan said, 'Somebody had to confront the situation, where the CJ (chief justice of India) is blatantly misusing his powers, hence the unprecedented step.'[5] Justice Mukul Mudgal said that there must have been very compelling reasons if they had had to resort to a press conference.[6]

THE HEART OF THE MATTER

Tensions had been brewing within the collegium for some time. What aggravated the matter was a medical scam case in which there were veiled accusations against the higher judiciary, including the chief justice. The matter was related to a Lucknow-based medical college, Prasad Institute of Medical Sciences, which (along with forty-five other colleges) had been barred by the central government from admitting students due to its substandard facilities. A retired judge of the Orissa high court, Justice Ishrat Masroor Quddusi, along with five others, was arrested by the CBI in connection to the case. According to the CBI, the supreme court bench headed by CJI Dipak Misra had instructed the government to review its decision about barring the Prasad Institute of Medical Sciences and decide afresh. The government, after a review, once again debarred these colleges. The Prasad Institute then got in touch with Justice Quddusi, who promised a favourable judgement from the supreme court. *India Today* reported, 'The CBI FIR further says that the Prasad Institute challenged the government order in the [supreme court] afresh. However, a few days later, on the advice of Justice Quddusi, the petitioner withdrew the plea from the supreme court and moved to the Allahabad high court. The Allahabad high court provided temporary relief to the petitioner staying the debarment order.'[7] The Medical Council of India challenged the high court's verdict in the supreme court. The Prasad Institute also filed a writ petition in the court. At this stage, Justice Quddusi contacted Biswanath Agarwal from Bhubaneswar, who presumably had contacts in the supreme court. Justice Dipak Misra was chief justice in the Orissa high court before being promoted to the supreme court.

The matter took a curious turn on 8 November 2017, when an NGO called Campaign for Judicial Accountability and Judicial Reforms (CJAR) filed a public interest litigation (PIL) suit before Justice Chelameswar, seeking an urgent and independent investigation of the medical scam as the matter was related to corruption in the higher judiciary. Chelameswar scheduled the matter for a hearing on the day after, that is, on 10 November. Meanwhile, through the supreme court registry, as was routine, the matter reached the CJI, who assigned the case to Justice Arjan Kumar Sikri. However, the petitioner's counsels Dushyant Dave and Prashant Bhushan again mentioned the matter before Chelameswar the very next day. Chelameswar constituted a five-member bench of the most senior judges, including the chief justice. The petitioners requested that the chief justice not be on the bench as he had already heard the matter in the past. Chelameswar left this matter to the wisdom of the chief justice.

As Chelameswar was about to pass the order, the chief justice intervened and transferred the matter to another court. However, 'Justice Chelameswar interpreted the draft order differently. Citing Article 143(3), he observed that the matter relating to the SIT probe can be heard by a constitution bench without the CJI passing a specific order.'[8] This was not taken kindly by the chief justice. He asserted his authority as the master of the roster and decided to set up a seven-judge bench to hear the order passed by Chelameswar. Two justices recused themselves from the bench. The remaining five judges went on to cancel Chelameswar's order. The bench also decided that no one else could decide which bench was to hear which case—it was the prerogative of the chief justice of India as the master of the roster. The bench then assigned the case to another bench.

This episode clearly established that there was a serious lack of trust between the chief justice and the four most senior judges. The other judges believed that since there were veiled accusations against the chief justice, he should therefore not get involved in the matter and let the others settle it to clear all doubts. This was important to preserve the credibility of the institution. In their opinion, the chief justice insisting on technicality relating to the roster had not done justice to the larger cause of the judiciary's credibility.

However, an even bigger issue was the relationship between two of the three wings of governance defined by the constitution—the executive and the judiciary. Since 2014, there had been growing apprehensions that the independence of the judiciary was not appreciated by the executive beyond a point. Certainly, the chief justice of India seemed to be under some kind of pressure. It is in this context that the allotment of the benches to decide politically sensitive cases became a serious cause of conflict: 'Privately, the senior judges shared their anguish over the CJI not reposing trust in any of them with important cases. Later, the non-assigning of important cases to them, culminating with the petition on Loya's death, triggered the public outburst.'[9]

Judge Brijgopal Harkishan Loya would have died a silent death and nobody would have noticed except his friends and relatives if on 20 November 2017, the *Caravan* magazine had not published a shocking report, implying that his death might not be a simple heart attack and that he might have been a victim of some conspiracy. At the time of his death as a CBI judge, Loya was hearing the controversial Sohrabuddin fake encounter case in which, along with senior Gujarat police officials, BJP president Amit Shah was also one of the accused.

On 25 July 2010, Amit Shah was arrested and jailed for more than three months. Later, he was barred by the supreme court from entering Gujarat for two years. Amit Shah had been charged with murder, extortion and kidnapping in the case of the killing of Sohrabuddin and his wife Kausar Bi in 2005. Amit Shah had always been thought to be very close to the Gujarat chief minister, Narendra Modi. When Narendra Modi became prime minister, Amit Shah also moved with him to Delhi. He was appointed the BJP president. An absolute workaholic, Amit Shah became the most powerful person in India after the prime minister in no time. In my memory, there have not been many politicians envied and feared by their peers quite as much. He was undoubtedly admired for turning the BJP into an unbeatable electoral machine. He was favourably compared with former Congress president Kumaraswami Kamaraj, who is credited with selecting two prime ministers—Lal Bahadur Shastri and Indira Gandhi—when the Congress was at the zenith of its political power. If Amit Shah is known for his strategic genius, he is also known for his ruthlessness in pursuit of his goals.

On 30 November 2014, Loya had gone to Nagpur to attend the wedding of a fellow judge's daughter. On 1 December 2014, however, his family was informed that he had died of a cardiac arrest. According to his family, he had been a healthy man and had had no history of heart trouble.[10] Since he complained of chest pain, he had been taken to Dande Hospital where he was given some medication. In a few hours, though, Loya was shifted to the Meditrina hospital, where he was declared brought dead. When his body was taken to his native village, Gategaon in Latur, Loya's niece Nupur Biyani and his sister Sarita Mandhane noticed something unusual: 'A diary entry by Biyani from the time reads, "There was blood on his collar. His belt was twisted in the opposite direction, and the pant clip is broken. Even my uncle feels that this is suspicious." Harkishan (Loya's father) told (Caravan), "There were bloodstains on the clothes." Mandhane said that she, too, saw "blood on the neck". She said that "there was blood and an injury on his head ... on the back side," and that "his shirt had blood spots." Harkishan said, "His shirt had blood on it from his left shoulder to his waist."'[11]

This story created a huge uproar. The family demanded an inquiry, which was supported by many. It was alleged that Loya's was not a natural death, that he might have been murdered.

The supreme court had shifted the Sohrabuddin encounter case from Gujarat to Mumbai, where Loya sat. However, the court had originally ordered that one judge should hear the case from start to finish. Judge J.T. Utpat had been assigned to this case in Gujarat. Despite Amit Shah's larger-than-life image, Utpat had been rather strict with him. 'On 6 June 2014, Utpat had reprimanded Amit Shah for seeking exemption from appearing in court. After Shah failed to appear on the next date, 20 June, Utpat fixed a hearing for 26 June. The judge was transferred on 25 June. On 31 October 2014, Loya who had allowed Shah the exemption, asked why Shah had failed to appear in court despite being in Mumbai on that date. He set the next date of hearing for 15 December.'[12] He was dead on 1 December.

The next judge gave Shah a clean chit and the verdict was never challenged in the higher courts by the CBI.

The *Caravan* magazine did a series of articles on its in-depth investigation of Loya's death, which later became the basis for a PIL in the Mumbai high court and in the supreme court. This investigation raised some serious questions, for which no satisfactory answers have been found:[13]

1. When Judge Loya complained of chest pain, it was claimed that he was taken to the hospital in an auto rickshaw. Two judges accompanied him. The guesthouse where they were staying, Ravi Bhavan, was in a location where it was difficult to find an auto rickshaw even during the day; then how was one found at midnight? Three judges were staying there and surely some other vehicle should have been there to help ferry them?
2. Ravi Bhavan did not have any entry in its register in the name of Loya, though the guesthouse was supposed to be very strict with identity verifications.
3. Loya's body was not taken to Mumbai where he lived with his family. Instead, it was sent to his ancestral home in Latur. Ideally, it should have been transferred to his current address. No reason was given.
4. It was also mysterious that the family was not informed immediately when his condition deteriorated. Why was the family informed only in the morning?
5. It was surprising that nobody except the ambulance driver accompanied Loya's body. The two judges who had insisted on Loya attending the wedding did not bother to accompany the body of

their fellow judge. Judge Vijaykumar Barde, who informed the family about his death, also did not bother to accompany the body. Why?

6. An RSS worker (the RSS later denied that he belonged to them), Ishwar Baheti, organised the arrival of the body in Latur. He is not related to the family in any way. What did he have to do with Loya?

7. Loya's phone was not returned immediately to the family. It was returned after two days and all call details and messages were deleted, except one. Was this phone with Baheti? Why did he keep the phone with him?

8. Loya's body was recognised by one Dr Prashant Bajrang Rati, according to the inquest panchnama. Rati later admitted to the *Caravan* that he did not know Loya, had never met him and never had any contact with him. Why did the Nagpur police rely on a stranger to recognise his body?

9. The post-mortem was conducted without the concurrence of Loya's family members. His family members should have been called and the post-mortem should have been conducted in their presence. What was the hurry? Why was the post-mortem conducted without waiting for the arrival of his immediate family members?

10. The post-mortem report is vague about the bloodstains. It simply writes 'dry' in the concerned column. What could be the reason for that?

11. According to one of the judges who took him to Dande Hospital, the ECG machine there was not functioning. His sister, Dr Anuradha Biyani, had also said that the family was told that no ECG was done on him as the ECG machine was not working. Even the state intelligence department, which made a discrete inquiry about the death, did not mention any ECG test in its report. However, a chart from the medical team was published by the *Indian Express* and *NDTV*, which claimed to be authentic. The time and date on the chart mentioned were 6.15 a.m. of 30 November 2014, whereas he actually died a day later. Dande Hospital later called this discrepancy a 'technical glitch'. Were the records fudged?

12. The bill served by Meditrina mentions ₹1,500 for neurosurgery. Now, if Loya died of a cardiac arrest, why was the neurosurgery

done? His family did notice bloodstains and a cut on his head. Was something hidden from the family?
13. According to Loya's friend, Uday Gaware, a senior lawyer, Loya was tense when Gaware met him the last time. He told Gaware that he wanted to resign and return to the village and that he would rather take up farming than give a wrong judgement. Now the question was, who was putting pressure on him to give a wrong judgement?
14. According to Loya's sister, Anuradha Biyani, her brother confided in her that the former chief justice of Mumbai high court, Mohit Shah, offered Loya a bribe of ₹100 crore to give a favourable judgement. Loya's father also said that bribe offers were made to Loya. There is no reason for a dead man's sister and father to make such false statements. Indeed, on whose behalf was such a large sum offered and what was the favourable judgement sought?

On 25 November, the Latur Bar Association passed a unanimous resolution and demanded an independent enquiry into the matter, to be led by a judge of the supreme court or a high court. This demand was never met. The Lawyers Association of Maharashtra also filed a petition in the Maharashtra high court. Ultimately, a PIL was moved in the supreme court. The supreme court bench, led by Justice Arun Mishra, asked that the matter be heard by another appropriate bench. After the four senior justices' presser, newspapers reported that Arun Mishra was extremely hurt and aggrieved by the charge that his was a 'bench of preference'.[14] Mishra apparently confronted the four justices in a regular meeting later and said that they had ruined his reputation. After Mishra's recusal, Chief Justice Dipak Misra brought the Loya case to his own bench.

Misra's bench 'emphatically ruled that there was no "reasonable suspicion" in the death of district judge B.H. Loya and slammed the petitioners seeking an independent probe for attempting to mislead the court while seeking to raise doubts over the judge's demise … the SC bench not only rejected their claims but described the petition as a frontal attack on the judiciary through a spate of scurrilous allegations. Referring to the petitioners' approach of levelling baseless charges against judicial officers and HC judges, the SC said this was nothing but "a veiled attempt to launch a frontal attack on the independence of judiciary and to dilute the credibility of judicial institutions".'[15]

A fresh petition was filed. However, with such a forceful outburst from the supreme court, the matter seemed to have ended though the mystery continues. In the medical college scam, Allahabad high court judge, Justice S.N. Shukla, was found guilty by the in-house enquiry committee of the supreme court and was asked to either resign or take voluntary retirement. However, before the supreme court verdict on the Loya case could sink in, seven opposition parties—the Nationalist Congress Party (NCP), the CPI, the CPI(M), the Samajwadi Party, the BSP, the Indian Union Muslim League (IUML) and the Congress Party—moved an impeachment motion against the chief justice of India, Dipak Misra, signed by sixty-four members of the upper house of parliament.

THE BATTLE OF THE BENCHES

Impeachment motions have been brought against the supreme court and high court judges in the past, but the day of the press conference was the first time the chief justice of India was in the dock. Since it was the very next day after the Loya judgement, it was easy to infer that they were linked.

Four serious charges had been pressed in the motion. First, the opposition questioned Justice Dipak Misra's role in the medical college scam, citing several audio conversations between the retired justice Quddusi and a middleman. The conversation had veiled references to Justice Misra. Second, he was charged with antedating a note: It is a practice in the supreme court that when the chief justice of India is sitting in a constitution bench, then a petition can be moved in the court of the next most senior judge. Accordingly, a petition was moved in Justice Chelameswar's court. Chelameswar listed it for a hearing on the same day, i.e., 9 November. When he went to pronounce an order, he was restrained by a note from the supreme court registry dated 6 November.[16] The note was antedated, which is a serious offence and amounts to forgery or fabrication. Third, it was alleged that the chief justice had bought a piece of land by tendering a false affidavit when he was practising as a lawyer in Allahabad. Fourth, he was also accused of abusing his position as master of the roster, allocating matters not on the basis of merit but by preference. This was the same charge that was made by the rebel justices in the press conference. The impeachment motion was an extremely serious development and vastly damaged the dignity of the institution that is the chief justice of India.

The government went out of its way to protect Justice Misra. Finance minister Arun Jaitley was pressed in to defend the chief justice. He called the entire exercise a 'revenge petition'.[17] He did not shy away from linking the impeachment motion with the rejection of the probe in the Loya case: 'If intimidatory tactics of institution disruptors and impeachment motion are threats to judicial independence, the single greatest threat is the divided court itself ... The four judges who held the controversial presser are all experienced judges and, in my view, men of high integrity. Did they check up the facts of judge Loya case before commenting on it, even though only as a listing issue? ... Is the impeachment motion filed today a direct result of the press conference? Does this impeachment set a precedent that political parties in India will use impeachment as an instrument to intimidate judges hearing controversial matters?'[18]

Jaitley did not realise that if the opposition was wrong, as he understood it to be, in moving for impeachment, then his veiled attack on the four senior justices could also be bracketed in the same category. His attack on the opposition was part of the usual political ping-pong, but he failed to understand why four justices were forced to go public to express their anguish. Did Jaitley realise that if there was a perception that important, politically sensitive cases were not distributed according to merit but on preference, then this was a serious matter and it raised serious questions as to the independence of the judiciary? It was the duty of the government to find out the reasons behind the presser, yet it decided to brush these under the carpet. Why? This is itself a big question.

The office of the chairman of the upper house, Venkaiah Naidu at the time, was swifter in its dismissal of the opposition's impeachment motion. Within seventy-two hours, it had rejected the motion. Naidu, a senior BJP leader, wrote in his order, 'I am of the view that the allegations are neither tenable nor admissible ... allegations emerging from the present case have a serious tendency of undermining the independence of the judiciary.'[19]

In another seventy-two hours, the Modi government had returned the collegium file to promote K.M. Joseph to the supreme court, though it did accept the appointment of senior lawyer Indu Malhotra. Let us not forget that as chief justice of the Uttarakhand high court, Joseph had declared the president's rule imposed by the central government (due to the defection of a few Congress MLAs) invalid, to the great discomfiture of the Modi government. The government raised the issues of seniority and over-representation. It was said that Joseph was not senior enough among the high-court justices since he ranked forty-second in the seniority list. Kerala was already represented in the supreme court by another judge and promoting Joseph would not sit well with other states at a time when ten states had no representation in the supreme court.[20] Lastly, it was argued that there were no judges from a scheduled caste or tribe (SC/ST) in the court.

These arguments made no sense. The sole principle for appointment in the higher judiciary is merit, based on understanding of the law and the constitution. The judge must be a person of impeccable integrity, who would not be cowed by extraneous pressures. Seniority and representation certainly should be looked into while appointing a judge, but they can't be a disqualification for a competent candidate. Indeed, if the government was so concerned about over-representation, how could it explain the promotion of Malhotra to join the supreme court, making him the fourth judge from Delhi. Kerala is in no way smaller than Delhi, either in terms of geography or demography. Kerala's population is 3.48 crore whereas Delhi's is approximately 1.9 crore. By this yardstick, Delhi should not have more than one judge in the supreme court either.

It should also be noted that the other judge from Kerala, Kurian Joseph, was to retire in November 2018, so the two judges from Kerala would only have overlapped for a few months. Secondly, Joseph might have been forty-second in seniority among high-court justices in general, but among the chief justices of the high courts, he was the most senior, being at least two years senior to the next senior high court chief justice. Indeed, as the most senior among the chief justices he was the most eligible candidate. His judgement on the president's rule in Uttarakhand also proved that he was a man of conviction who decided constitutional matters solely by the spirit of the constitution. All of this makes him an ideal candidate. Yet, in the present political scenario, one is forced to wonder whether it might not have been his biggest disqualification. Was he denied the nod for daring to go against the wishes of the central government? Law minister Ravi Shankar Prasad 'denied "insinuations" that the government was acting under influence and reiterated that its decision to send back Justice Joseph's proposal for appointment to SC had nothing to do with the latter's judgement overturning president's rule in the state.'[21]

What was more of a concern is the fact that despite reiteration that Joseph's name would be sent up again, it could not be done immediately. It was leaked to the press that the collegium was divided on the issue and apparently the chief justice was adamant that Joseph's name alone should not be sent.[22] Many meetings of the collegium took place and more than a month passed, but the matter was kept hanging. It is in this context that Justice Chelameswar's statement that Justice Gogoi might be superseded as chief justice becomes very relevant. Chelameswar said 'he would be surprised if Justice Ranjan Gogoi, who is in line to succeed Justice Misra, does not get to helm the top court as punishment for being part of the tumultuous press conference on January 12. "I think it will not happen. But if it happens, it would prove the issues raised by us and what was said in our letter."'[23] To kill all rumours and safeguard the integrity of the judiciary as independent of the executive body, Chief Justice Misra should have sent back the name of Justice Joseph immediately. It is unfortunate that it did not happen and thus the whispers grew louder, acquiring more political overtones that the judiciary had failed to live up to its reputation under his leadership.

However, Justice Chelameswar and Justice Joseph both set a new precedent and announced that they would not accept any post-retirement assignments. If others follow their example, it will go a long way towards establishing the independence of the judiciary. I wish the former chief justice Palanisamy Sathasivam had not accepted the governorship of Kerala from the Modi government immediately after retirement.

JUSTICE BLINDED AND GAGGED?

Of course, this is not the first time that two arms of the government have fought each other or that the executive has tried to overpower the authority of the judiciary. This battle has a long history. Similar allegations had been levelled even during the tenure of the first prime minister, Jawaharlal Nehru, and later in the time of Indira Gandhi.

Nehru was a democrat. When he assumed leadership of the country, idealism was the nectar of the masses. India became a republic on 26 January 1950. As quoted in *Working on a Democratic Constitution*, a newspaper wrote, 'Today India recovers her soul after centuries of serfdom and resumes her ancient name.'[24] Nehru was so phenomenally popular that once he himself acknowledged that all it needed was 'a little twist and he would turn into a dictator'. But nobody could question his loyalty to democracy.

In 1950, India was experimenting with new concepts and new structures were being laid down. Nobody had any idea how the institutions would shape up and how people at the helm would ensure the sanctity of the constitution. Everything was fluid, and yet to evolve. This was also a time when experts were predicting doom for the country. It was prophesied that India would not survive as a nation. It was a country of the poor and the illiterate; most of India was living in villages. The father of the nation, Gandhi, was also gone. India did not have a strong army, its police forces were outdated and the country was trying to recover from the pain of Partition. A new nation had been born but it had yet to learn to walk.

It was a time when even the president of India was confused about his powers and the dynamics of the relationship between him and his cabinet. Rajendra Prasad was the first president, a Gandhian and also a Hindu at heart. He sought opinions from legal luminaries: To what extent was he bound by the advice of the cabinet? Could he refuse to accept its advice? Could he exercise his discretion? He and Nehru had had major differences on the issues of the Hindu code bills, property rights and the Somnath temple. Many a time, Nehru had threatened to resign over these differences, but had not done so. Major differences cropped up with the judiciary as well: Who would be the guardian of the constitution—the parliament or the judiciary? Who would have the final say in a matter of law or of the constitution? Would the judiciary have the power to review the functioning of the legislature in all matters? Could fundamental rights be circumvented for the directive principles? Could the parliament have the power to change the constitution or amend it at will?

The independence of the judiciary and the interference of the executive in the selection of judges was extensively discussed in those days as well. After the death of the first chief justice of India, Harilal Jekisondas Kania, the next most senior judge was Justice Mandakolathur Patanjali Sastri. However, he was not Nehru's choice, who was instead keen on Justice Sudhi Ranjan Das, who was fourth in seniority after Justice Sastri, Justice Mehr Chand Mahajan and Justice Bijan Kumar Mukherjea. According to sources, all six judges of the supreme court threatened to resign if Sastri was superseded. Good sense prevailed and Justice Sastri was appointed chief justice. Similarly, after Justice Sastri, Nehru did not want Justice Mahajan, who he had taken a dislike to since the days he had been the prime minister of J&K, and pushed for Justice Mukherjea instead. Again, Nehru was prevailed upon. It was the strength of the democracy that did not let Nehru tinker with the judiciary. It also has to be said that Nehru had the character and the humility to accept the counter arguments and submit. His daughter, though, was of a different mettle.

Unlike her father, Indira Gandhi was a practical politician. Idealism was not her forte. Her father had had a towering personality and was respected by his peers, but Gandhi had to fight her way to power and consolidate her gains. She was chosen to be the prime minister because the powerful leaders of the party thought they could control her. She began her innings with a weakness as she did not have a social and political base of her own; she was considered a lightweight who could be easily manipulated; insecurity was her primary trait. To assert her control over the party, she had to fight the very forces that had anointed her in the prime minister's chair. She painted her opponents as right-wingers and switched to the Left. She surrounded herself with advisers who were either socialists or communists. She was enthused by the theory that social revolution needed total control over the state apparatus, that individual rights should surrender to social needs and that the judiciary should act as a facilitator for the realisation of socialist goals. The nationalisation of banks and the abolition of privy purses were political moves to marginalise party bosses, yet she was also ideologically convinced that these had to be done to bring about the necessary changes in society.

Therefore, when the supreme court put fetters on her, Gandhi was furious. In fact, the curtailment of property rights was the beginning of a serious confrontation between her government and the judiciary. In the Golak Nath case on 27 February 1967, the supreme court held that the parliament did not have the power to abridge fundamental rights.[25] It was a serious setback to the supremacy of the parliament; the judiciary had asserted its independence. Granville Austin writes, 'Thus the Golak Nath case began the great war, as distinct from the earlier skirmishes, over parliamentary versus judicial supremacy.'[26]

Mrs Gandhi's vengeance was swift. She came out with the twenty-fourth, twenty-fifth and twenty-ninth amendments to the constitution to establish parliamentary supremacy and limit the powers of the judiciary to review laws passed by the parliament. This battle finally culminated in the Kesavananda Bharati case.[27] A thirteen-judge bench of the supreme court, maintaining the balance between the legislature and judiciary, decided that the parliament had the power to amend but could not change the basic structure of the constitution. By now, Gandhi was convinced that something more needed to be done to tame the beast called 'the judiciary'. The very next day, after the Kesavananda Bharati judgement, she appointed Justice Ajit Nath Ray the next chief justice of India to take over after the retirement of Justice Sikri, bypassing three senior judges.

Under the influence of her communist friends, Gandhi had been propagating the theory of a committed bureaucracy and judiciary, which found its first resonance in the speech of Jagjivan Ram, the first president of the Indira faction of the Congress after the split, what was called Congress (I) at the time. Speaking in Mumbai in 1969, Ram said, 'We need an apparatus with purpose in mind. We need a service committed to the ideals of democracy, socialism and secularism.'[28] Gandhi's closest adviser, steel minister Mohan Kumaramangalam, took it to another level: 'Scholars have coined the term "Kumarmangalam [sic] doctrine" to explain this ideology of the government to populate the court with judges who were believed to be supportive of the government policies.'[29] Kumaramangalam made this famous statement in the Lok Sabha: 'We will take the forward-looking judge and not the backward-looking judge.'[30]

Justice Ray's appointment was the most serious assault on the judiciary. The three superseded judges—Justice Jaishanker Manilal Shelat, Justice Kawdoor Sadananda Hegde and Justice A.N. Grover resigned with immediate effect.

There is another story also. Mrs Gandhi's election was challenged in the Allahabad high court and she was expecting an adverse judgement. She wanted a friendly chief justice who could bail her out. Justice Hegde had earlier rejected Mrs Gandhi's appeal to the Allahabad high court to not admit certain evidences in her case. She knew that with Hegde at the helm, she would be in great danger of losing her prime-ministership. Justice Ray was toeing the government line in major cases such as the nationalisation of banks, the abolition of privy purses and the matter of Kesavananda Bharati. With Ray at the top, Gandhi had the judiciary in her pocket. L.K. Advani records in his biography, 'According to [Bishan] Tandon, [H.R.] Gokhale [Law Minister] had met Indira Gandhi on 3 June 1974—nine days before Allahabad HC judgement—and afterwards, discussed her case with A.N. Ray. The Chief Justice of India told him that "if the Allahabad HC gave an adverse ruling, there would be no difficulty in getting an absolute stay". Tandon observes: 'I kept thinking; had Hegre or one of these three been the Chief Justice, would Gokhale have had the temerity to speak to him?'[31] When Mrs Gandhi imposed the Emergency, it was the supreme court which went out of its way to justify it.[32] Justice Hans Raj Khanna was the only one who dissented; the rest of the big names simply surrendered to Empress Gandhi.

SUPERSEDING AUTHORITY

No other chief justice incumbent has been superseded since Indira Gandhi's government. However appointments of favourable and pliable judges remains a contentious issue. Governments blocking recommendations from the collegium by delaying notification, continuing with acting chief justices for months, expecting that such judges would oblige the government because they were hoping to be made the chief justice, returning files without any valid reasons—all these have happened under all the regimes. Be it Justice Yeshwant Vishnu Chandrachud or Justice Prafullachandra Natwarlal Bhagwati or Justice Raghunandan Swarup Pathak, various chief justices have expressed their frustration with the central government. For example, Justice Bhagwati has said that his experience with the government regarding appointments was 'absurd and humiliating'. Bhagwati is reported to have said, 'I cannot help saying that the non-appointment of judges to the supreme court for several months has operated as an act of cruelty to the existing judges who are carrying an intolerable burden.' Bhagwati's concern was valid since at the time he retired on 21 December 1986, only fourteen judges were working, against a sanctioned strength of twenty-six.[33]

The Modi regime is no different. One was not surprised when eminent lawyer Gopal Subramanium's appointment to the supreme court was blocked by the centre. Subramanium is one of the country's most respected lawyers. His understanding of the constitution and of law is second to none. The supreme court would have been richer for his joining the bench, but the recommendation of his name by the collegium, led by Chief Justice Rajendra Mal Lodha, was not acceptable to the government. The reason was never spelt out but it was obvious that his role in the Sohrabuddin encounter case was not appreciated by Modi and Amit Shah. While his name was sent back for reconsideration, his integrity and honesty were questioned through selective leaks in the media. He withdrew his name and wrote a letter to Chief Justice Lodha alleging that 'he was being targeted for displaying "independence and integrity" when he assisted the court twice in a case involving the 2005 encounter killing of Sohrabuddin Sheikh in Gujarat, then ruled by Narendra Modi. Amit Shah, Gujarat's former minister of state for home affairs, was facing legal scrutiny in the case—and on Subramanium's suggestion, the supreme court had barred Shah from entering Gujarat in 2010; he was allowed to return to Gujarat two years later. In his letter, Subramanium said he was "sorry that the supreme court did not stand by me".[34]

Justice Jayant Patel's case is also similar. He was the second most senior judge in the Karnataka high court to be elevated to either acting chief justice or chief justice within two weeks, but he was abruptly transferred to the Allahabad high court where he was the third in seniority. Obviously his transfer was seen as an attempt to block his promotion in the Karnataka high court. He resigned in protest. Justice Patel originally belonged to Gujarat. The Bar Council of Gujarat wrote a scathing letter to the supreme court collegium, saying the 'transfer had shaken its belief in the independence of the judiciary', and it had decided to abstain from work for a day on 27 September 2017.[35] Senior lawyer Yatin Oza wrote, 'During the (Ishrat Jahan) encounter cases, (former) Chief Justice Mukhopadhaya had assigned all the matters to Justice Patel. There are people who are critics of Justice Patel, but none of his critics can say that he is a judge who will compromise his honesty and integrity. They wanted Justice Patel to act according to their wishes. But he is one judge who will never, ever ditch the constitution.'[36]

In the early days of Modi's government, the supreme court valiantly asserted its authority. It struck down the National Judicial Appointments Commission (NJAC) Act passed unanimously by the parliament and sixteen other state legislatures and revived the collegium system. The NJAC for the appointment of judges comprised the chief justice and the next two most senior judges of the supreme court, the law minister and two eminent persons picked by the selection committee comprising the prime minister, the chief justice and the leader of the opposition in the Lok Sabha. The supreme court took exception to the presence of the law minister and feared that it would be the beginning of direct interference in the selection of judges in the higher judiciary. The government took offence and called the judgement a challenge to parliamentary sovereignty, forgetting the simple fact that sovereignty lies only with the people, the parliament only reflects the will of the people and the Indian constitution is based on the separation of powers. That means that the power of the parliament is not supreme and it should not expect the other two wings of governance—the executive and the judiciary—to play a subservient role. For the constitution to function properly, the equilibrium among the three wings should not be disturbed and none of the three should try to dominate the other two, nor any two rise above the third.

It was so ironic that the government that had been keen from day one to erase the memory of the first prime minister, Nehru, inadvertently quoted him in its defence. Finance Minister Arun Jaitley said, 'While quashing the same, it relegislated the repealed provisions of Article 124 and 217 which only the legislature can do ... The court can only interpret—it can't be the third chamber of the legislature to rewrite a law.'[37] Nehru had eloquently spoken on this topic in the constituent assembly on 10 September 1949: 'Within limits, no judge and no supreme court can make itself a third chamber. No supreme court and no judiciary can stand in judgment over the sovereign will of parliament.'[38]

Nehru too had hinted about a 'committed' judiciary. He had said, 'If courts proved obstructive, one method of overcoming the hurdle is ... the executive which is the appointing authority of judges begin to appoint judges of its own liking for getting decisions in its own favour.'[39] However, Nehru was a true democrat. He never tried to trample over the judiciary. He listened to the voices of sanity and surrendered to the larger will of the people. Indira Gandhi was the real danger. She had an authoritarian streak. Her communist advisers, such as Kumaramangalam, had no sympathy for constitutional democracy.

Kumaramangalam was a member of the CPI before he joined the Congress. To Kumaramangalam, the judiciary was a great impediment in the path of the socialist revolution. Austin writes, 'Kumaramangalam and ex-Communists in the Congress Forum held an extreme position in their willingness to sacrifice constitutional democracy and civil liberty to the social revolution ... And the Congress party allowed Kumaramangalam's extreme position to stand on its own. Explaining Article 31C, he said, "The clear object of this amendment is to subordinate the rights of individuals to the urgent needs of the society."'[40]

Now read Kumaramangalam's statement with that of Andrey Vyshinsky, the architect of the judicial system of the communist Soviet Union. He was Stalin's most loyal lieutenant in the field of law. He said, 'The Soviet Court participates directly in the historic venture of the construction of the communist society.'[41] Vyshinsky's words were neatly enshrined in the constitution of the Soviet Union. They read: 'The Article 3 of the 1958 USSR Fundamental Principles of Court Organisation provides: By all its activity, the court shall educate citizens in the spirit of loyalty to the motherland and to the cause of communism.'[42] The Soviet concept of law and constitution discards the basic function of the courts as understood by the rest of the world, that of 'a mediator among the conflicting societal interests'.[43] Within the communist system, courts were not free entities. They were not accorded equal status vis-à-vis the executive or the Communist Party. It was the party which was to articulate and interpret the doctrine of the state and the doctrine of the state was communism—that is, to create a classless society; it was the responsibility of the courts to work in that direction. Maddock and Grzybowski say, 'The Communist Party establishes and maintains the philosophy and inspires all actions and control, directly or indirectly, all departments of governance, including the administration of justice. An independent judiciary and professional Bar simply have no place in such a society.'[44] Therefore, in a communist system, the courts have a subordinate status. During Indira Gandhi's time, a serious attempt was made to roll the wheels of history in that direction. Austin was compelled to write, 'Mrs Gandhi's attack on judicial independence struck at democracy's heart as parliament acquired a rash presumption of omnipotence.'[45]

The problem was that Indira Gandhi was dictatorial. What made this worse was the borrowed ideology of her advisers. During her time, there was a real danger of India converting into an ideological state. People like Kumaramangalam were spearheading this evolution. However, Gandhi did not succeed for two reasons, despite imposing the Emergency. First, she was not trained in totalitarianism. Being the daughter of Nehru, someone who grew up in the company of Mahatma Gandhi and other freedom fighters for whom democratic values were supreme, she did not have enough conviction to carry her half-baked ideas forward. Secondly, by mid-1975, Indian democracy had deepened its roots in the psyche of the people. People revolted against her regime.

However, Modi and the RSS are made of a different clay. Hindutva as an ideology is the antithesis of everything that is Gandhian and Nehruvian. Democracy is not its basic tenet. The nature of the RSS's organisational structure is dictatorial. The word of the RSS chief is final and it has to be followed. Moreover, Modi is not Vajpayee. He has dictatorial traits of his own and has spent all his life in the RSS ecosystem. Hindutva is a strong conviction in him. Since he took charge of the party and the government, as with Indira Gandhi, he alone is the cabinet, he is the government and he is the parliament. Modi's personality and Hindutva make a deadly cocktail. It is in this context that his government's attack on the judiciary is far more lethal than Indira Gandhi's was. It is more systematic. It is part of a larger goal.

JUSTICE SWINGING IN THE BALANCE

The forty-third chief justice of India, Tirath Singh Thakur, was the last chief justice who resisted the pressure imposed by the government. Even he was left in tears, while addressing a gathering that included Prime Minister Modi in the audience.[46] Chief Justice Thakur did cry in the presence of Prime Minster Modi. 'Chief Justice of India, T S Thakur on Sunday came down heavily on the government, saying the latter was sitting over at least 170 recommendations sent by the apex court collegium two months ago for appointment of high court judges, when many of the HCs were working at 50% of their strength.'[47] The government was not moved by the tears.

Less than two months later, in the first week of June, the government rejected, for the second time, the recommendations of the collegium for the appointment of chief justices to the high courts. This was unprecedented. It was done in contravention of the relevant constitutional provisions. The government can reject the collegium's recommendation once, but if it is reiterated, then it is considered binding. The government order was preceded by a veiled threat from finance minister Arun Jaitley. He said, 'Judicial review is the legitimate domain of judiciary but then the Lakshman rekha has to be drawn by all the institutions themselves. Lakshman rekha is very vital.'[48] The government brazenly proposed setting up a secretariat in the supreme court and the high courts to entertain complaints against judges. The chief justice and the collegium were not in agreement as it was perceived to be a threat to the independence of the judiciary. Random complaints can always be used against any judge to pressurise them to take a particular decision or block their upward movement.

With Justice Thakur at the helm, the war continued. Thakur lashed out at the government in court once again: 'The process cannot be allowed to hijack the appointment of judges to high courts. There are 478 vacancies in HCs, which is 44.3% of the total strength of judges. HCs have four million cases pending. The entire system has collapsed.'[49] On 15 August, after the prime minister's speech was broadcast from Red Fort, Thakur said, 'Today we heard our very popular PM's speech for over an hour. I was hoping there will be some reference to the issue of justice ... to appointing judges. However, he did not.'[50]

The government was hiding behind the argument that the memorandum of procedures had not been finalised yet by the supreme court. The government had forgotten that it had agreed that the appointments would continue through the old system till the memorandum was made up. The chief justice's patience had crossed all limits. He threatened to hold the PMO officials in contempt of court for stalling appointments for nine months.[51] On 28 October, Thakur said that the government wanted to lock out the judiciary.[52] The government responded through the media: 'If the government had intended to stall, it would not have appointed 86 new judges to high courts, four to supreme court and 14 Chief justices of HCs and accepted the collegium's recommendation for the transfer of four CJs chief justices and 33 judges from HCs since December last year ... The situation stands like this—the MoP as ordered by the five judges bench, has not been finalised. The government has been appointing according to the old system which is in violation of the constitution bench judgement.'[53] After the rap by the SC, the government did clear ten names for the high courts. But it also rejected for the second time the names of nineteen judges for the Allahabad high court, which was against the constitutional tradition.

The numbers are not important here. What is crucial is the consistently ugly spats between the government and the judiciary during Thakur's tenure. Why did the supreme court say that the government wanted to lock down the judiciary? At least twice, the government flouted tradition and sent back the supreme court's recommendations.

This war was substantially calmer during the terms of Justice Jagdish Singh Khehar and Justice Misra. Justice Khehar, who had been extremely aggressive while striking down the NJAC, was expected to come down hard on the government, but he sobered down considerably as chief justice.

Before Khehar assumed office, the former chief minister of Arunachal Pradesh, Kalikho Pul, committed suicide on 9 August 2016. A suicide note was found in which he alleged that relatives of the supreme court judges had approached him on the judges' behalf, demanding money to settle the sacking of his government in his favour. The content of the letter sullied the reputation of the concerned judges. Pul's wife Dangwimsai Pul knocked on the doors of the supreme court, demanding a CBI inquiry and action against the judges if they were found guilty. Besides the judges, the names of several Congress leaders also figured in the note. Her appeal was converted into a writ petition by Justice Khehar. Her lawyer Dushyant Dave objected strongly: 'We had sought an administrative direction, why was it taken on the judicial side? We want to know the reason behind it. There was a development on Monday evening. A former judge of the supreme court met me on behalf of the CJI. I do not want to say more. I beg your lordships to stay away from this case.'[54] The *Times of India* reported on 1 March 2017 that Dangwimsai Pul had petitioned Vice President Mohammad Hamid Ansari and requested the registration of an FIR and an investigation into allegations of corruption against Chief Justice Khehar and the sitting supreme court judge Dipak Misra.[55] This sinister episode leaves many questions unanswered. Is it just a coincidence that the names of the two future chief justices were found in Kalikho Pul's suicide note? Did this episode in any way impact the functioning of the judiciary? If so, who were the beneficiaries? Ideally, the matter should have been settled fast and furiously. Lurking doubts serve no purpose. But no effort was made to close it quickly.

Thus, the Modi regime has been marked by four incidents involving the judiciary in such a way as to have lowered the prestige of the institution, sullied the claims of independence of the judiciary and raised serious doubts about the intent of the Modi government:

1. A press conference called by the four most senior judges of the collegium.
2. An impeachment motion against Chief Justice Dipak Misra.
3. The chief justice of India, T.S. Thakur, being reduced to tears.
4. The appearance of two contemporary and future chief justices' names in Kalikho Pul's suicide note.

The judiciary is undoubtedly passing through a serious crisis of credibility. The image of the highest court has never been so low. I am constrained to not write about many cases which can be said to demonstrate that the state has become too powerful and politically relevant cases are not judged in the realms of impartiality or within the framework of the law and natural justice. In the corridors of the judiciary, the names of certain judges are openly spoken and their verdicts forecasted before they are pronounced, oftentimes proving true. Yet, no effort has been made by the Modi government to dispel the impression that it is majorly interfering in the justice system.

In the end, I would like to remember what the first home minister of the country, Sardar Patel, had said while introducing the Provincial Constitution Committee report to the Constituent Assembly. He stressed that the committee had paid special attention to the manner of appointing judges because, 'the judiciary should be above suspicion and should be above party influences.'[56] Within the Hindutva fold, Sardar Patel has iconic status. Yet I seriously doubt that his words will have any impact on his adherents in this case.

NINE

Hindutva and the Caucus Race

In the fight between the gladiator and the crown prince, the gladiator was constrained to live in the moment, the prince in the future. The prince had all the time in the world but the gladiator had none—it was a matter of life and death for him as he would have no second chance. The prince could afford to wait, as time was not his enemy. Even if he lost, he was assured of another chance. The gladiator had grown up in uncertainties; insecurities were his playmates. He had fought alone to win, to reach where he was while the prince had lived a pampered existence wrapped up in cotton wool. There were knights to share the prince's burden but the gladiator had only himself to fall back on ... The 2014 elections was the only chance for Modi. For Rahul it was just an interregnum, not the destination. Modi had waited to grasp this moment since eternity and, no matter what came at him, he would not let go. Rahul, the Gandhi, was prodded and urged to prepare. If Modi lost, he would be thrown to the wolves and consigned to the dustbin of history, it would be a full stop for him. For Rahul, this election was only a comma, a semi colon at most, a breather in the long journey of a dynasty.[1]

Ashutosh, *The Crown Prince, the Gladiator and the Hope*

In my book on the 2014 parliamentary elections, this was how I had analysed the battle between the two stalwarts of current Indian politics, Narendra Modi and Rahul Gandhi. Since then, my perception of Modi has not changed. He is still the gladiator who is fighting for his life. For him, every battle is the last—he has to win it in order to live another day. Rahul Gandhi did lose the 2014 elections rather badly, but he was never in a hurry; Modi, on the other hand, has not rested—he has constantly been in election mode. He seems to be a man possessed, full of energy and vitality.

He has not left any stone unturned. He has exhibited no fear—indeed, he has betrayed no emotion. For him, every election is meant to be won, every rival to be vanquished. If Modi is what he is today, the most envied and feared politician, it is because of this ability of his to take every battle to the enemy's camp and then fight to the finish. The gladiatorial instinct is his biggest strength; it is his most dependable armour.

The year 2014 was undoubtedly the pinnacle of Modi's personal glory. Since then, he has taken the BJP to new heights. The BJP, a party which was a fringe player not so long ago, is today ruling in more than twenty states, covering more than two-thirds of the land geographically, while the Congress's hold has shrunk to a few states. Unlike his predecessors, Vajpayee and Advani, he has shown no weakness of any kind, and it is only victory that really matters to him, that defines his destiny and glory. After winning 2014, he moved on to newer territories. Under his leadership, the BJP formed governments in states where it was earlier either a small player or non-existent as a contender—Haryana, Maharashtra, J&K, Assam, Manipur and Tripura. He made sure the BJP recaptured the states of UP, Uttarakhand, Jharkhand and Himachal Pradesh. In Goa, the BJP retained its government despite having fewer seats than the Congress. The BJP won Gujarat despite all odds. In Punjab, it had to suffer because of the people's hatred of the Akali Dal. It lost Karnataka by a whisker.

In hostile lands such as West Bengal and Kerala, the BJP has made fresh inroads, improving its position and emerging as a threat to the well-entrenched parties. In reality, it lost only two assembly elections—Delhi and Bihar—to two bitter rivals, Arvind Kejriwal and Nitish Kumar. Eventually, Kumar surrendered to Modi after his initial belligerence. No other leader in Indian politics had turned his party into a hegemonic entity in such a short span of time.

Before the BJP, it was the Congress that was pervasive. But then, the Congress had been blessed because of its contribution to the freedom struggle. Mahatma Gandhi was the unquestioned leader of pre-Partition India. It was he who turned the Congress's politics into a mass movement. Under his leadership, the Congress reached every nook and corner of India. It became synonymous with India and the torchbearer of the nation. Every ideology and idea found its space within the Congress system. Uniquely, it was both the leader, as well as its own opposition. After Independence, the Congress tried to continue in the same vein. It provided a platform to its most bitter critics—Babasaheb Ambedkar and Syama Prasad Mookerjee were made ministers in the first cabinet formed after Independence. After the demise of Mahatma Gandhi, the Congress was ably led by Pandit Nehru and Sardar Patel. Other parties were too small to challenge it. Despite the inner power struggle and ideological predilections, the Congress's system sustained itself well until 1989, despite a brief interregnum between 1977 and 1980. Then, two ideological streams—the politics of Hindutva and Mandal politics—brought about a sea change in Indian politics and thus began the marginalisation of the Congress. Though it established governments at the centre thereafter—from 1991 to 1996 and from 2004 to 2014—it was not the same Congress that it used to be and became a pale reflection of its glorious past.

It could easily be said that the Ram mandir movement was the most decisive political move in contemporary India. It was not only backed by an ideology, which wanted to alter the basic social fabric of the country, but also backed by an organisation which had millions of motivated foot soldiers. The organisational strength of the RSS is unmatched. The RSS–BJP tried to conflate the Ram mandir movement with the identity of India. Advani writes in his biography, 'By now I was fully convinced that this movement was not only about building a temple in Ayodhya. It was not even merely about reclaiming a holy Hindu site from the onslaught of a bigoted foreign invader in the past. It was equally about reclaiming the true meaning of secularism from the onslaught of pseudo-secularism. It was about reassessing our cultural heritage as the defining source of India's national identity.'[2] The fall of the Babri Masjid on 6 December 1992 was the turning point in this movement. It was not only the most severe attack on the legacy of the freedom struggle but also the most lethal invasion of India's great tradition, which espouses tolerance and peaceful coexistence. Though Advani expressed his anguish on the demolition of the mosque and called it the saddest day of his life, he also did not forget to call it the 'day of Hindu awakening of truly historic import.'[3]

The demolition of the Babri Masjid emboldened the RSS–BJP's further experiments with the Hindutva ideology. It convinced them that Hindutva was widely acceptable. It persuaded them that the BJP could emerge as the main challenger to the Congress system and, in the long run, it could replace them. It encouraged them to believe that if there was a Muslim vote bank, then a Hindu vote bank could also be created and in the near future, the Muslim vote bank could be made irrelevant. Advani was not bold enough to take the experiment to the next level, though he will always be remembered as the Renaissance man for Hindutva.

Ideology has a tendency to be ungrateful, though. It does not tolerate apologists. With the Jinnah episode, Advani became an apologist.[4] On a visit to Pakistan to attend a function organised by the Karachi Council of Foreign Relations, Economic Affairs and Law in Karachi on 5 June 2005, Advani quoted Muhammad Ali Jinnah's speech, delivered in Pakistan's Constituent Assembly on 11 August 1947, in which Jinnah had said, 'You may belong to any religion or caste or creed; that has nothing to do with the business of the State ... you will find that in the course of time Hindus would cease to be Hindus and Muslims would cease to be Muslims, not in the religious sense, because that is the personal faith of each individual, but in the political sense as citizens of the State.'

The RSS's leadership was extremely upset about this as they took this speech to mean that Advani was calling Jinnah secular. Advani's speech created major unrest in the RSS–BJP and the RSS decided to ask him to resign as the president of BJP, which he did. The ideology did away with its most worthy son and there was space for a new leader. In walked Modi, with the legacy of the 2002 Gujarat riots. Modi is Advani's creation, but unlike Advani, he relentlessly pursues the Hindutva ideology without any shame, sorrow or regret, and under his leadership, the ideology has certainly scaled new heights. If Lenin was the creator of the communist state, then Stalin was the consolidator, the empire builder. If, by any stretch of the imagination, Advani were to be compared with Lenin, then Modi would be the Stalin of the Hindutva ideology. 'Stalin had turned himself into the unchallengeable individual locus of state authority. His was a most personal autocracy.'[5] During his regime, Modi too has sculpted himself into the unchallengeable leader within the Hindutva fold. 'Stalin's most original contribution to Marxist philosophy was to insist that the construction of communism relied not only on concrete material conditions, but also on the subjective role of the party in organising, mobilising and transforming society.'[6] I am not sure if Modi has read Stalin or studied the evolution of the communist ideology and the role of the Communist Party in the growth and consolidation of the communist state; but being a quintessential organisation man, he has certainly converted the BJP into a war machine that is ready to fight elections 24/7 and spread its wings in all directions for the construction of a Hindutva state.

DIVIDE TO CONQUER, THEN RULE

Ever since Modi took over the reins of power in the BJP, he has endeavoured to transform the BJP from a cadre-based party to a mass organisation with a clear goal of uprooting opposition governments and installing its own. The slogan of 'Congress-mukt Bharat' is a well thought-out plan. Modi has pursued a six-pronged strategy—mythologise the personal charisma of the leader, make the organisation more muscular, reach out to the neglected sections of Hindu society, camouflage the core ideology in the garb of development, make lethal use of propaganda to discredit the opposition and control the mainstream media. UP is a prime example of this strategy, that seems to be serving the BJP well so far.

In 2014, BJP won seventy-three seats in the state, including the two taken by its ally, Apna Dal. This success was unprecedented, historic and mind-blowing. Yes, the BJP had been a formidable player in UP before—it had formed a majority government in 1991 with Kalyan Singh as the architect of that success; but once the government was dismissed after the demolition of the Babri Masjid, the BJP could not repeat its success due to the rise of the two Mandal parties—the Samajwadi Party (SP) of Mulayam Singh Yadav and the Bahujan Samaj Party (BSP) of Kanshiram and Mayawati. Mulayam Singh Yadav was the unquestioned leader of the Other Backward Classes (OBC) communities and Kanshiram was leading a new revolution of the Dalits in UP. In the next twenty years, the BJP in UP was reduced to an 'upper-caste party'. It had failed to acknowledge the new social realities. The consolidation of the OBC and Dalit communities pushed the BJP into a marginal role. However, Modi knew that if he failed in UP, his fate would be sealed—he would never realise his ambition of becoming the prime minister. He decided to contest the elections from Varanasi and sent his most trusted man, Amit Shah, as the election in-charge of UP. It worked.

To rewrite the same script in 2017 was an uphill task, but again, he did not fail. Belying all naysayers, the BJP romped home with another blockbuster win in UP, winning 312 seats in the UP assembly elections. The most remarkable fact was the jump in its vote share. In the 2012 assembly elections, the BJP had obtained only 15 per cent of the votes, with 47 seats. In 2017, the BJP's vote share touched 39.7 per cent, a phenomenal surge of 24.7 percentage points. Its main contenders, the Samajwadi Party and the BSP, on the other hand, could get only 21.8 per cent and 22.2 per cent respectively. One might argue that the combined vote strength of the Samajwadi Party and the BSP was more than that of the BJP, that if they had fought together, the BJP could not have formed the government. This argument has no substance, though. In 2012, the Samajwadi Party and the BSP contested elections separately, but the BJP was nowhere close to forming the government. A similar story was repeated in the 2007 assembly elections, when the BJP could get only 16.97 per cent votes. These two figures reflect the pathetic condition of the BJP in UP in the pre-Modi era. Yet, thanks to Modi's charisma, the BJP's vote share rose to 42.63 per cent in 2014 and 39.7 per cent in 2017. These figures underline the fact that the BJP's phenomenal rise in UP can only be attributed to Modi and nobody else. Prashant Jha, a senior journalist, deciphered the mystery behind the BJP's stupendous success. He writes, 'They [Modi and Amit Shah] made a strong push for social expansion; they uprooted the upper caste leaders, yet managed them in a way they would not rebel; they began changing the organisational structure; they gave representation and respect to less dominant communities; they leveraged the resentment that existed against the dominant OBC or Dalit groups among those who felt left out; they gave a high number of tickets to OBCs; and they helped the BJP achieve to a larger degree than ever before, Hindu unity across castes.'[7]

So the magnet in 2014 was undoubtedly Modi; but why? Ostensibly, people were upset with Manmohan Singh and were looking for change. Modi was seen as the change. People voted for him en masse. This helped the BJP relocate itself in the mind space of UP voters. In 2017, Modi was not the chief ministerial candidate, but people still believed in him, despite the ruinous demonetisation.[8] The BJP, meanwhile, also worked on its organisation, did some social engineering, identified new leaders, entrusted them with responsibilities and poached locally influential leaders from other parties.

Since the early 1990s, the Mandal politics has also changed. It has created a new privileged class amongst the OBCs, which has garnered all the benefits at the cost of others. The weaker castes have continued to suffer. If the Yadavs were the beneficiary caste among the OBCs due to the partisan politics of the Samajwadi Party, then among the Dalits, the Jatavs emerged as the ruling class. The BJP, led by Amit Shah, smartly exploited the resentment brewing against these two castes. Like the British, the BJP played divide and rule. Sagarika Ghose writes, 'This resulted in most backward castes, non-Yadav OBCs and non-Jatav dalits all clustering with BJP against the three castes—Jatavs, Yadavs and Muslims, represented by BSP, Samajwadi Party and Congress, who were pushed to become only subcaste fronts. Shedding its Brahmin-bania image, BJP created a wider social coalition of poor and backwards [sic]. It gave 119 seats to non-Yadav OBCs such as Rajbhars, Khushwahas and Mauryas. BJP even struck an alliance with the little known Suheldev Bharatiya Samaj Party ... They also gave 69 tickets to non-Jatav dalits, such as Dhobis and Khatiks.'9

UP is still a feudal society where the caste system is very much entrenched in people's psyche. Till the implementation of the Mandal Commission report, the upper castes, particularly Brahmins and Thakurs were dominant. They were the rulers for thousands of years. Other backward castes and Dalits were always on the margins. Mandal politics broke the civilisational hegemony of these two castes. Being in greater numbers helped them assert their presence. The logic of democracy also favoured them majorly.

Mandal politics dramatically altered the nature of democratic expression at the grassroots. Brahmins and Thakurs had to take a backseat, while the OBC and Dalit communities occupied the front row. Mayawati and Mulayam Singh Yadav pampered OBC/Dalit communities during their regimes. The OBCs are 37 per cent of the total electorate of UP whereas Dalits are 20 per cent. The Yadavs form 9 per cent and non-Yadavs 28 per cent of the total population of UP. Among Dalits, the Jatavs—traditionally leatherworkers—are 11 per cent of the electorate and non-Jatavs 9 per cent. With rising consciousness, the dominance of the Yadavs and Jatavs alienated members of other castes within the OBC and Dalit communities. The BJP tried to lure the 28 per cent non-Yadav OBC electorate and the 9 per cent Dalit voters. Meanwhile, Brahmins and Thakurs are approximately 18 per cent (Brahmins 11 per cent and Thakurs 7 per cent) of the electorate. If one adds the 5 per cent Baniya voters, then the upper-caste vote share forms 23 per cent of the UP voters. In electoral politics, this is a good number. What the BJP tried to do is marry these two caste groupings. An amalgamation of the 23 per cent (upper castes) and 37 per cent (the combined strength of OBC and Dalit communities), minus the Yadavs and Jatavs, potentially creates a new vote bank. This could be called the 'Hindu vote bank'. Under the leadership of Modi, the BJP has made an effort to transform itself from an 'upper-caste only' party to a larger conglomeration of the upper castes and the neglected castes of OBCs and Dalits.

This was, of course, easier said than done. It was a mammoth task that needed serious engineering within the organisation. Prashant Jha explains the process: 'To his shock in 2014 he [Amit Shah] discovered that among party office bearers across the state—from Lucknow down to the district level—only 7% were OBCs and 3% were Dalits. This meant that groups which together constituted almost 70% of the population in the state had 10% space in the BJP organisation. The structure was dominated by the Brahmin, Thakur and Banias ... within two years their [OBC and Dalits] share had spiked to 30%. The BJP had engineered a silent almost invisible disruption.'[10]

The BJP traditionally don't go to its ideological enemies, the Muslims, for votes. Muslims constitute 17 per cent of the population in UP. The logic of the BJP's Hindu vote bank is premised on antipathy towards Muslims. To send an unambiguous signal to their voters, the BJP did not give a single ticket to Muslims in the UP assembly elections, like it had done in the parliamentary elections in 2014. Rather, it painted the BSP, Samajwadi Party and Congress as Muslim parties, who only catered to Muslims at the cost of Hindus. The Samajwadi Party and the BSP, in their rush to attract Muslim votes, went out of their way to dole out tickets to Muslims in bulk: 'The BSP gave tickets to 99 Muslim candidates, highest ever by any mainstream party in UP since Independence.'[11] The SP gave tickets to fifty-seven Muslim candidates and the Congress fielded twenty-two. The Samajwadi Party and the Congress had an alliance. Mayawati, meanwhile, committed a political blunder, by admitting noted mafia don Mukhtar Ansari to the party. It was a desperate attempt to appease Muslims. She also merged his party, the Quami Ekta Dal, with the BSP. Several Muslim organisations and clerics openly supported the BSP.

All this provided the BJP with a readymade excuse to divide voters along communal lines. Modi, being an astute politician, hinted not too subtly, that Mayawati and Mulayam Singh Yadav had openly discriminated against Hindus during their regimes. He said, 'If a village gets a graveyard it should get a cremation ground too ... If there is electricity during Holi there should be electricity during Eid too ... If electricity is provided on Ramzan, then it should be provided on Diwali also ... there should be no discrimination.'[12] Nothing is technically wrong with the statement. On the surface, it appears that the prime minister is laying down the ground rules for the administration; but in the given electoral context and against the ideological backdrop, this statement very clearly conveys that non-BJP parties favour Muslims and don't care for Hindus, and that the discrimination is so rampant that it appears even during festivities and funereal rites.

Amit Shah went a step further. He said, '[P]eople of UP should get rid of KASAB ... KA for Congress, SA for Samajwadi Party and B for BSP.'[13] The agenda was clear and the strategy was simple—paint the anti-BJP parties to be anti-national and pro-Pakistan. The reference to Pakistan is invariably aimed at reminding Hindus about the Partition and terrorism, and to identify Muslims as traitors and terrorists. The purpose was to polarise voters over religion—scare Hindus, consolidate votes, marginalise Muslims and win the elections.

In UP, the land of the Ram mandir agitation and a state with a history of communal riots, such polarisation does not require much effort. It becomes easier if the disillusionment on the ground is acute. People were sick and tired of caste politics and rampant corruption in UP; the voters were looking for a change. The BJP succeeded in turning the people's disillusionment against the Samajwadi Party and the BSP into an anti-minority-ism. Engineered episodes such as the Muzaffarnagar riots and the fake exodus of Hindus from Kairana provoked voters to gravitate towards communal voting.[14] The BJP under Modi has mastered this art. Dipankar Gupta's analysis is spot on. He says, 'In the past, conventional wisdom believed that the majority community would be equally divided and hence the trick was to win the minorities to tip the scales. In recent times, and in the most recent elections in India, this formula lies dead in the water. In constituencies with over 25% Muslims voters, the BJP has won 57 seats while the SP–Congress combined and the BSP have captured only 28 and 3 respectively. Therefore, what works instead is majority consolidation, not minority fine-tuning. The fight from now on is not "my minorities versus yours", but "my majority versus yours".'[15]

UP is an example of Modi's appetite for innovation in electoral politics. It also underlines the inner resilience of the ideology. Modi could successfully transform the social base in 2014 and 2017 because the ideology allowed him to tinker with the superstructure of the edifice.

CHOKE OUT THE OTHER

On the other hand, Uttarakhand is a classic example of Modi's ruthlessness in demolishing the opposition. Long before the assembly elections were announced, a plan was scripted to destabilise the Congress government led by Harish Rawat. Under the leadership of senior Congress members Harak Singh Rawat and Vijay Bahuguna, a few MLAs raised the banner of revolt. It was an open secret that this was done at the prompting of the BJP. After a bit of initial hesitation, the governor's report was used to dismiss the elected government. At a time, when the Congress should have been campaigning, announcing welfare schemes and taking populist measures to effectively attract voters, it was embroiled in fighting legal battles in courts and managing its MLAs. The Congress was routed out in Uttarakhand. Out of seventy seats, it could win only eleven whereas BJP bagged fifty-seven—it was the BJP's biggest ever win in the state. Its vote share jumped by 13.5 per cent, from 33 per cent to 46.5 per cent. Rawat contested from two seats and lost both. Most of his cabinet colleagues were also defeated.

COMING FROM BEHIND TO WIN

In Goa and Manipur, too, elections were held at the same time as UP and Uttarakhand. The BJP was not the winner in either of these states.

In Goa, where the BJP led the incumbent government, it could win only thirteen seats, well below the required majority of twenty-one in an assembly of forty. The Congress was the single largest party with seventeen seats. The BJP engineered a midnight coup before the Congress could get its act together. It formed the government by stitching together alliances with the Maharashtrawadi Gomantak Party, Goa Forward Party and various independents. The Congress was shocked. The BJP had managed to snatch victory from the jaws of defeat. Similarly in Manipur, the BJP was way behind the Congress in terms of numbers. It had only twenty-one MLAs against the Congress's twenty-eight, three less than the majority mark. Once again, the BJP moved swiftly. While, the Congress failed to attract the three MLAs it needed to gain majority, the BJP managed more than ten. Ideally, the governor should have invited the single largest party, i.e., the Congress for a consultation to assess if it could prove its majority on the floor of the house. Had the Congress failed to prove the numbers, then the governor would have been well within their rights to invite the BJP. But the governor did not follow the well-established constitutional protocol.

The governors of Goa and Manipur both allowed the BJP to dictate terms to them. The BJP formed governments in both the states. Arun Jaitley, then finance minister, justified the unjustifiable. He said, 'The assembly elections in Goa produced an inconclusive verdict. There was a hung assembly. Obviously in a hung assembly post poll alliance will be formed. The debate between the single largest party lacking majority versus a combination of parties constituting a majority was answered by former President, K.R. Narayan in his communiqué in March 1998 when he invited Sri Atal Bihari Vajpayee to form the government.'[16] But the very same Jaitley took a U-turn when his party did not get a majority in the Karnataka Assembly elections. He said that the single largest party, i.e., the BJP should be called to form the government.

Uttarakhand, Goa and Manipur are examples of political manipulation engineered by the BJP that defied the spirit of the constitution. These instances also show the appetite of the ideology for power-grabbing. This reminds us of the Indira Gandhi era when 'Aaya Ram Gaya Ram (easy come, easy go),' was the norm, when constitutional protocol had no value, when power-grabbing was the only rule.

In certain ways, the Vajpayee government and the United Front government before Modi also tried to follow in the footsteps of Indira Gandhi. Vajpayee sacked the Rashtriya Janata Dal government in Bihar in 1999; in 1998, the Kalyan Singh government in UP was dismissed by I.K. Gujral's United Front government. Yet the Modi era is different. It has openly threatened to make India 'Congress-free', which (as mentioned in the previous chapter) seems to extend to making India opposition-free. It is a dangerous proposition. It is not a routine threat. It is a threat backed by an ideology that promises to make India a Hindu Rashtra. A Hindu Rashtra can be a reality only when every alternate ideology or idea is dead. The Hindu Rashtra—in their opinion, the solution to India's civilisational crisis—can be a reality only when every soul is converted to Hindutva, either by desire or by force.

The state has enormous power. It is the only authority, which has the legitimate power to create an ecosystem that will change the mindset of its citizens and which can force people to accept an ideology. This makes it incumbent upon the ideology of Hindutva to capture the state power by every possible means, to overwhelm every social space, to make available every corner of the country to itself, and either by hook or by crook, to entrench its ideology deep into the psyche of the people. History shows that ideologies do not mind moving in with tanks to capture the space they wish to arrogate to themselves. German National Socialism did it; so did communism. In search of 'living space', Hitler caused the Second World War.[17] For the Communist International, Stalin unhesitatingly moved the Red Army into Eastern Europe. Radical Islam has created havoc the world over.

However, since the world has moved on from the times of Hitler and Stalin and is far more open, integrated and interdependent now, and since India is a functioning democracy, the instruments used by an ideology in India will be quite different—more often than not, democratic tools will be used in ways that may sometimes be sophisticated and sometimes vulgar. In Goa and Manipur, it looked vulgar, though in J&K, when the government with PDP was formed, it was more subtle. Karnataka saw things take a vulgar turn again, but a little differently.

DIFFERENT STROKES FOR DIFFERENT STATES

During the 2018 Karnataka assembly elections, the BJP was confident despite the fact that the Congress's Siddaramaiah government had not fared too badly.

As a chief minister, Siddaramaiah went all out to remain in power. He implemented a number of welfare schemes for the poor, which were quite popular. To drive a wedge into the BJP's Lingayat vote bank, he had gone to the extent of declaring it a separate religion. Lingayatism, though widely regarded as a part of Hindu society, had been demanding a separate identity for centuries. On the day of the counting of votes, the BJP was in a celebratory mood, already distributing sweets in anticipation of capturing another state.

However, by afternoon, the game had changed—neither of the parties had crossed the halfway mark. The BJP emerged as the single largest party, with 104 seats in an assembly of 224. The Congress was the second largest party with 80 seats. The Janata Dal (Secular) (JD[S]) and the BSP together had 38 MLAs. As soon as the Congress realised that it could not form the government, it announced its support for the JD(S) to form the government. This time, it was the BJP that was caught napping. However, the political game took a dramatic turn with the Congress declaration. The BJP cried foul. It now demanded that since it was the single largest party, the governor should call it to explore the possibility of forming a government. This was the same BJP that had followed a different path in Goa and Manipur, where it had opposed the single largest party being invited to form the government.

The Congress and the JD(S) together had 118 MLAs, five more than the majority mark. The BJP had no chance of proving a majority on the floor of the house. Yet this time, Vajubhai Rudabhai Vala, the governor of Karnataka and a long standing member of the BJP, rejected the opposition's demand and invited the BJP to form the government. B.S. Yeddyurappa was sworn in as the chief minister. He was asked by the governor to prove his majority on the floor of the house in two weeks.

The Congress moved fast once again. It filed a petition in the supreme court. The court refused to dismiss the Yeddyurappa government but asked it to prove its majority in forty-eight hours. The BJP was desperate. It resorted to every trick in the book to buy out the MLAs of the Congress and the JD(S). Two MLAs were allegedly abducted by the BJP.[18] Audio clips surfaced on TV channels in which ex-chief minister Yeddyurappa was heard luring Congress MLAs to support his government.[19] Family members of some MLAs were allegedly coerced into pressurising them to defect to the BJP.[20] Apparently, crores of rupees were on offer. The Congress released an audio clip in which the strongman of Karnataka, Gali Janardhana Reddy was allegedly heard promising Congress MLA Basanagouda Daddala that the 'MLA would earn a hundred times what he lost'.[21] The Congress MLAs rejected the offers. The Congress and the JD(S) took their MLAs out of Bengaluru to Hyderabad, putting them up in hotels and guesthouses to safeguard them from being poached by the BJP's money and muscle power. The BJP miserably failed. Yeddyurappa could not prove his majority. He had to resign. H.D. Kumaraswamy became the new chief minister.

This entire episode proves that the ideology that boasted of purity and cleanliness in politics in the early 1990s could throw every constitutional nicety and democratic norm out of the window and employ every trick to install its government. This was politics at its worst, and all to be in power.

KEEPING THE ENEMY CLOSE?

In J&K, the BJP had never been a major player. It had some presence, but only in the Jammu region. However, thanks to Modi's phenomenal popularity, the BJP won twenty-five seats in Jammu in the December 2015 assembly elections. Even then, it drew a blank in the Valley. The PDP managed twenty-eight seats, all in the Valley. The Congress had twelve seats. The Indian National Conference (INC) could get fifteen. It was a hung assembly. Nobody had a majority. Who would form the government, and with whom, was the looming question. To everyone's utter surprise, the two most unlikely parties, the BJP and the PDP, decided to come together and form the government in what Mufti Mohammad Sayeed, who was sworn in as chief minister, called the 'coming together of the North Pole and the South Pole' (also see Chapter 5) and the BJP hailed it as a 'miracle of democracy'.[22]

BJP has always had a hawkish approach to Kashmir. The abolition of Article 370 has been one of the core aims for the BJP since its inception (as discussed in Chapter 5). The PDP has always been considered to be pursuing a 'soft separatist' line. It has demands of self-rule for J&K, reconciliation with Pakistan, engagement with the separatist APHC and scrapping of the Armed Forces (Special Powers) Acts. Pakistani newspaper *Dawn* reports, 'Sayeed says he is a "proud Indian" and believes that Kashmir's future is "safe" with India, but he is the only pro-India politician from Kashmir region who has linked reconciliation with Pakistan, dialogue with the All Parties Hurriyat Conference (APHC) and militant leadership with the region's larger political narrative and engaged New Delhi establishment to acknowledge that peace with Pakistan is the way forward.'[23] The RSS–BJP has never minced words about the PDP. It has always criticised the PDP for flirting with 'anti-India forces'. The hanging of Afzal Guru in February 2013 is a case in point. Guru was one of the accused in the the 2001 terrorist attack on the parliament. The PDP was opposed to his capital punishment and called it a 'travesty of justice', whereas the BJP welcomed the hanging.[24]

At the outset, the BJP's coming together with the PDP might therefore appear strange, a compromise with its ideology, a vulgar opportunism for power. In Indian politics, however, such alliances are not rare. There are many instances in history when sworn political enemies have decided to shake hands to share power and to enjoy the fruits of the government. Karnataka, discussed earlier, is a most recent example. During the election campaign, the Congress and the JD(S) had abused each other, called each other names, but the moment they realised that the BJP might form the government, these two parties decided to be best buddies. Similarly, the PDP and the BJP could not have come together in J&K by any stretch of the imagination—until they did. So it is interesting to ask whether the BJP commited political suicide there. Or was the lust for power overwhelming? Why would the BJP ally with a party whose loyalty to Mother India it finds doubtful?

It has to be understood that the BJP is not simply a political party; it is the product of an ideology. Its political moves can't only be that, especially in a state such as J&K, which has been a serious challenge to the Hindutva ideology. J&K is a Muslim-majority state. It is also a troubled state. As seen in Chapter 5, the RSS–BJP have rejected the mode of its integration into India and its unique demands of a separate constitution and distinct legislature from the beginning. The RSS–BJP therefore have always approached the 'Kashmir problem' with a coloured vision. For them, it is a Muslim space. It is a part of a civilisational war. Like the German National Socialists, the RSS firmly believes in the theory of the internal enemy—in this case, Muslims— being far more dangerous than the external enemy. The RSS is convinced that Muslims can't be trusted, because they have aggressive designs on India. As Golwalkar wrote in *Bunch of Thoughts*:

> Their aggressive strategy has always been twofold. One is direct aggression. In the pre-independence days, Jinnah called it 'Direct Action'. The first blow got them Pakistan. Our leaders who were a party to the creation of Pakistan may try to whitewash the tragedy by saying that it was a brotherly division of the country and so on. But the naked fact remains that an aggressive Muslim state has been carved out of our own motherland. From the day the so-called Pakistan came into being, we in Sangh [sic] have been declaring that it is a clear case of continued Muslim aggression. The Muslim desire, growing ever since they stepped on this land some twelve

> hundred years ago, to convert and enslave the entire country could not bear fruit, in spite of their political domination for several centuries, because the conquering spirit of the nation rose in the form of great and valiant men from time to time who sounded the death-knell of their kingdoms here. But even though their kingdoms lay shattered, their desire for domination did not break up. In the coming of the British they found an opportunity to fulfil their desire. They played their cards shrewdly, some times [sic] creating terror and havoc, and ultimately succeeded in brow-beating our leadership into panicky surrender to their sinful demand of Partition ... their direct aggression, whetted by their success, then turned against Kashmir. There too they met with success, though partial. One third of Kashmir continues to be in their clutches even to this day. Now, Pakistan is trying to gobble up the rest of Kashmir also with the help of powerful pro-Pakistani elements inside Kashmir.[25]

Therefore, the Kashmir issue, from their perspective, is part of a larger Muslim conspiracy, a product of the deep-rooted desire of Muslims to dominate and enslave Hindus.

The problem for the RSS–BJP was that despite their best efforts, they were unable to enter J&K for a long time. For them, the Kashmir Valley was an alien land. To not be an active participant in that war must have been very painful for the ideology. The alliance with the PDP offered them a golden opportunity. As discussed in Chapter 5, during Vajpayee's time, the RSS–BJP did try to join the war via the 'healing touch policy' of Sayeed or through the *'jamhooriyat, kashmiriyat, insaniyat* (democracy, Kashmiri identity, humanism),' rhetoric. Yet, the PDP alliance was the first opportunity where they were getting direct access in the Kashmir government.

The government as an entity is endowed with phenomenal power; it provides unlimited and direct access that can impact people's lives and can alter the power equation between different societal groups. For the BJP, it was the best opportunity to make permanent inroads into the Valley and place their supporters in key positions. It was undoubtedly a risk, but from the long-term perspective, this was a risk worth taking. The alliance continued for three years. In the end, the BJP withdrew support from the Mehbooba Mufti government. But three years is a long time for a government and a political party to draw up a game plan and implement its agenda. Now, only history will tell how well the RSS and BJP will succeed in their game plan.

One thing is certain—Hindutva made a grand entry into the Valley, for which the PDP paid a heavy price. Only the future will tell if the party survives this blow to their crdibility.

If Kashmir was a grand entry, then Assam in 2016 was a grand success. From the ideological point of view, the RSS had been keeping a keen eye on Assam as well. Golwalkar wrote, 'The second front of their aggression is increasing their numbers in strategic areas of our country. After Kashmir, Assam is their next target. They have been systematically flooding Assam, Tripura and the rest of Bengal since long ... the Pakistani Muslims have been infiltrating into Assam for the past fifteen years ... they are entering Assam surreptitiously and the local Muslims are sheltering them. As a result the percentage of Muslims there, which was only 11% in 1950, has now more than doubled. What else is this but a conspiracy to make Assam a Muslim majority province so that it would automatically fall into the lap of Pakistan in the course of time?'[26]

Golwalkar's cry was reflected in the RSS–BJP's campaign against the Bangladeshi Muslims. They have been demanding the identification of such Muslims and their expulsion from India for decades. The local inhabitants of Assam have also echoed this demand. The Asom Gana Parishad (AGP) pioneered this movement and ultimately formed the government in the 1980s. The RSS–BJP had to wait a long while as they could not attract the people of Assam to their cause. They did succeed in 2016. The BJP formed the government together with the AGP and the Bodoland People's Front (BPF).

From an ideological point of view, the victory in Assam was very significant for the RSS–BJP. In Assam, approximately 35 per cent of the population is Muslim. By a rough estimate, for 36 of the assembly seats, Muslims are more than 50 per cent of the constituency's population. If the population of Christians, which is 3.7 per cent, is added to the population of Muslims, then the minorities together comprise 39 per cent of the population. The BJP doesn't expect this group to vote for it. That it still managed to win sixty seats out of the eighty-nine that it contested can only be called an exceptional success, although the BJP's vote share was less than that of the Congress's. It received 29.5 per cent of the votes whereas the Congress got 31 per cent. However, the Congress contested 122 seats, far more than the BJP. The BJP had had only 11.5 per cent of the votes in the 2011 assembly elections; but in 2016, it gained by a massive jump of 18 per cent. In 2014 again, the BJP's share of the votes was only 36.9 per cent. In 2016, its vote share declined again. But then it had contested fewer seats too. However, there is no doubt that the former Congress strongman and number two Congress leader in Tarun Gogoi's cabinet, Himanta Biswa Sarma, played a big role in the BJP's victory—he had switched to the BJP along with 10 Congress MLAs a few months before.

Yet, it is also a fact that the RSS had been working in this region for a long time. 'Senior dedicated RSS cadres have been working in Bodoland and the upper Assam tribal belt for years. About 500 Ekal Vidyalayas was a key contributor and Lok Jagran Manch, also created by Sangh, helped win over intellectuals,' said Rajat Sethi, one of the BJP campaign managers in Assam.[27]

The breakthrough in Assam is also important from another point of view. It offered the BJP a launch pad into the north-eastern states. Christian missionaries are very active in this region and the RSS has always suspected them of being engaged in religious conversion in the name of charity and education. For the RSS, Islam and Christianity both have ulterior motives. In *Bunch of Thoughts*, Golwalkar wrote rather sarcastically, 'So far as Christians are concerned, to a superficial observer they appear not only harmless but as the very embodiment of compassion and love for humanity ... But what is the real and ulterior motive of Christians in pouring crores of rupees in all these activities? ... The various surreptitious and mean tactics they employ for conversion are all too well known.'[28] Golwalkar then specified their real motive. He said, 'Many leading Christian missionaries have often declared unequivocally that their one single aim is to make this country a province of the kingdom of Christ.'[29] So in their worldview, the RSS is fighting to save this country from becoming a kingdom of Christ too.

The north-eastern states, in the BJP's opinion, have been Christianised up to quite an extent; its cadres have been working for a long time to neutralise them. Their job would be easier if they were in the government. Modi and Amit Shah seem ready to go beyond the call of democracy to install either their own government or a friendly government in which they have a major say. Meghalaya is a classic example. Like Goa and Manipur, here also the Congress emerged as the single largest party with twenty-one seats in an assembly of sixty. The BJP won only two seats in the assembly elections held in March 2018, but it again outmanoeuvred the Congress. It assembled all the other regional parties under the NDA and installed an NDA government led by the National People's Party, which had won nineteen seats. Despite only winning two seats, the BJP was the real king. In Tripura, certainly, it had earth-shattering results, which are a testimony to their organisational strength and strategic thinking. The Left Front, which had ruled Tripura for twenty-five years, was reduced to only sixteen seats; the BJP, which had a negligible presence in the state and had not won a single seat in the 2013 elections, won thirty-six seats along with its ally, the Indigenous People's Party. This was certainly a miracle of democracy.

Arunachal Pradesh is another example of the BJP's soaring ambition and the benevolence of its ideology. First, the Congress government was dismissed by the Modi regime, only to be later reinstated by the supreme court. Meanwhile, within three and a half months, forty-three of the forty-four Congress MLAs defected to join the BJP-led NDA. The Congress could only lament that the people's mandate had been for the Congress yet it had been robbed in daylight so that the new dispensation was an 'illegitimate child of the BJP'.[30]

STRAINS OF NERO'S FIDDLE

Meanwhile Gujarat, the original laboratory of Hindutva, has shown glimpses of the limits of the ideology. In 2017, the BJP won there for the sixth time. Yet, for the first time, cracks were showing up in its support base. Despite Modi being the prime minister and Amit Shah the party president—the two most powerful leaders of the country, both belonging to Gujarat—the BJP had to toil hard to get the majority numbers. The Patidar community, which had been instrumental in helping the BJP to dislodge the Congress in the state, had revolted. A young person barely twenty-four years of age, Hardik Patel, led the rebellion.

Modi had been given the reins of power in the state in 2001, an inexperienced but master strategist. Despite the Gujarat riots, he won Gujarat three times in a row, riding the wave of Hindutva. It was because of this success that he started being seen as the future prime minister—a prophecy that finally came true in 2014. However, his successors in the state were not able to carry forward his legacy.

Modi had had the knack to marry Hindutva with dreams of development, in a strategy he proudly called the 'Gujarat model'. Imbued with Hindutva, a section of society trusted Modi, trusted the ideology and did not let his ideological enemy, the Congress, move the BJP from the seat of power. Even so, in the 2017 elections, the BJP was left rattled. There was real danger of it being unseated. Along with Patidars, who were demanding the inclusion of their caste in the OBC list to enjoy the fruits of reservation, Dalits were also upset due to the treatment meted out to them by the keepers of Hindutva. The Una incident (see Chapter 2) infuriated them; they declared war and another young person in his mid-thirties, Jignesh Mevani, emerged as the new icon of Dalits. Rural distress had also increased over the years. Before the assembly elections, experts were already declaring the decline of Hindutva. An astute analyst of the BJP, Nilanjan Mukhopadhyay wrote, 'The BJP would worry with apparently receding Hindutva wave in the wake of economic distress. Moreover, there are signs of caste identity prevailing over religious identity. Alpesh Thakore's decision to align with Congress indicates a social churn but has capacity to fork out old contradictions between the Patidars and OBCs.'[31]

It was not the traditional leadership but rather three young leaders—Hardik Patel, Jignesh Mevani and Alpesh Thakore—who shook the foundation of the RSS–BJP. The BJP, which is known for its use of social media, was forced by locals to run for cover as a social media campaign attacking the claims of development, '*Vikas gando thayo chhe* (development has gone crazy),' became a rage. The BJP tried to counter it with its own campaign, 'Hun chhu vikas, hun chhu Gujarat (I am development, I am Gujarat),' but proved itself to be no match. People did not believe it. Modi had to really bend backwards to win Gujarat. Long before the announcement of elections, he was visiting the state and doing road shows in major cities. Mukhopadhyay wrote, 'Prime Minister Narendra Modi on his fifth visit to the state since September, inaugurated and laid the foundation of a slew of development projects but not without taking pot shots at the Congress.'[32] There were allegations that the Election Commission did not play fair and that by not announcing the election dates along with those of Himachal Pradesh, it helped the BJP to gain some ground. The *Times of India* reported on 25 October 2017, 'Since the poll schedule for Himachal Pradesh was announced on October 12, the Gujarat government has announced projects worth about ₹11,000 crore and about two dozen sops.'[33] And then the alleged sex video of Hardik Patel was released.[34] Clearly the effort was to create a scandal and distract from his political efforts.

By now, the Congress had wisened up. Rahul Gandhi shed his inhibitions and started visiting temples one after the other. So far, the BJP had successfully branded the Congress a 'Muslim party' and encouraged the Hindus to unite and vote out those who appeased Muslims. Now, Rahul Gandhi began to be criticised for falling into the trap of pursuing soft Hindutva. The BJP was definitely unnerved, so much so that they started questioning his credentials as a Hindu. The Congress's temple-hopping was so effective that Modi resorted to accusing former prime minister, Manmohan Singh, of conspiring, at the behest of Pakistan, to make Ahmed Patel the chief minister of Gujarat.

Mild-mannered Manmohan Singh was furious. He demanded an apology from the incumbent prime minister: 'Singh responded strongly to Modi's charge that the meeting at Congress veteran Mani Shankar Aiyar's residence was connected to a statement by a high-ranking former Pakistani army officer calling for the elevation of Ahmed Patel, political secretary to Sonia Gandhi, as the next Gujarat chief minister.'[35] Aiyar put his foot in his mouth and called Modi a 'neech', or lowly, person. The BJP reacted to the statement, and ultimately Aiyar was suspended from the party.

Despite the scare, Modi won Gujarat for the BJP. However, he could only get 99 seats in the assembly of 182, which was the lowest for any winning political party since 1975. The Congress won 77 seats. The BJP improved its vote share marginally from 47.9 per cent to 49.1 per cent. The Congress also increased its vote share from 38.9 per cent to 41.4 per cent. The saving grace for the BJP was the urban voter. In urban constituencies, the BJP was supported by 59.2 per cent of voters. The Congress had the confidence of only 35.5 per cent. A difference of 23.7 percentage points is huge in a democracy. However, in rural areas, the BJP lagged behind: 'Of the 39 urban seats, BJP won 33, Congress just 6; of the 45 "rurban" seats, BJP won 26 and Congress 18. But of the 98 rural seats in the state, BJP won a mere 39, Congress and its allies 55.'[36]

Gujarat undoubtedly set the agenda for the Hindutva ideology. It showed that the Hindu Rashtra is a possibility, provided it is pursued with vigour and supported with a certain degree of charisma. Until Modi assumed charge, the BJP in Gujarat was not very confident. The party was faction-ridden. Modi silenced the voices of dissent and, with an iron hand, brought a sense of discipline to the party. The government was run like a business. He was the leader as well as the CEO of the state. However, as he moved to the centre, cracks came to the fore. Anandiben Patel was not as charismatic and had to be replaced by Vijay Rupani, who also proved to be lacklustre. The BJP did manage to win the 2017 elections, but the message was crystal clear. The ideology can flourish only if there is a strong leader with a focused agenda.

Madhya Pradesh and Chhattisgarh also followed almost the same curve. Uma Bharti was the first choice for chief minister in Madhya Pradesh, while Raman Singh was put in charge in Chhattisgarh. Uma Bharti was aggressive but she was not focused. Ultimately, Shivraj Singh Chouhan was brought in. Now the BJP is about to complete three terms in a row with him in the chair. Raman Singh has been equally effective. Vasundhara Raje Scindia in Rajasthan, B.S. Yeddyurappa in Karnataka and Prem Singh Dhumal in Himachal Pradesh did not have the acumen to consolidate the BJP's gains in those states. So, the BJP had to alternate power with rival parties there.

The 2017 elections in Gujarat have also proved that religion alone cannot be a guarantee of power. Caste identity has the strength to neutralise religious identity. The defeats in Gorakhpur, Phoolpur and Kairana in the UP by-polls just after the historic win in the state are again proof that caste identity can override the gains of religious mobilisation. If Mayawati and Akhilesh Yadav of the Samajwadi Party, representing Dalits and OBCs respectively, decided to join hands and contest elections together, the BJP would be in serious trouble in parliamentary elections scheduled for 2019. Similarly, in Bihar, the combination of two caste leaders, Nitish Kumar and Lalu Prasad Yadav, stalled the march of Hindutva and the BJP faced a humiliating defeat in 2015. Therefore, one can assume that the Mandal forces have the resilience to stop the march of ideology, the making of a Hindu Rashtra. It was for this reason that the RSS–BJP tried very hard to lure a section of the OBCs and Dalits to Hindutva in 2014 and 2017 in UP. It worked partially, but at that time, the Mandal forces were divided. United, they are a great threat to the idea of a Hindu Rashtra.

Assam is a new battleground still. Sarbananda Sonowal has to prove his mettle. Goa could be a case study for him. In Goa, the minorities hold the key. They comprise approximately 35 per cent of the population. The BJP managed to form the government in 2012 as it had the partial support of minorities, especially Christians. In 2017, it lost the battle as it could not retain their goodwill. Manohar Parrikar, as a leader, is cast in the same mould as Modi but he is not blessed with the social demographic, which was a great advantage to his leader in Gujarat. In Gujarat, the minorities are barely 9 per cent of the population.

In this, Assam is very similar to Goa. Minorities constitute 39 per cent of the population. To ignore such a large chunk of the people for an eternity is not possible in electoral politics. Should the Congress and the All India United Democratic Front (AIUDF) decide to shake hands and contest together, the BJP may not enjoy the cakewalk it envisages. The Congress had 31 per cent of votes and AIUDF 13 per cent—together they commanded 44 per cent votes. The BJP and its allies, the AGP and the BPF, on the other hand, had a vote share of 41.5 per cent, which is less than the combined total of its opponents.

A new aspiring class has also emerged in the last two decades. They are the children of the economic boom. They are ambitious and ready to experiment with new ideas. They mostly reside in cities. In 2014, they were besotted by the idea of Modi. Modi lured them into believing that India could be a superpower and Hindutva could be the vehicle for that. The honeymoon continued for a good three years. The BJP's phenomenal success in urban Gujarat is testimony to the fact that it still has not lost hope; but the same cannot be said outside Gujarat. The economy is not in very good health. Rural distress is making an impact for everyone to see. Farmers are on the warpath. A definite fatigue is setting in vis-à-vis Modi and Hindutva.

Modi was successful because he packaged Hindutva as a vehicle for robust economic development, as an idea which was modern in its outlook and which aspired to bring back the glory of the past when India was referred to as vishwa guru (world leader). But once ensconced in power, the new admirers expected that the gladiator would metamorphose into a statesman and Hindutva would be inclusive. Instead, he got busy with power-grabbing.

Ruthlessness became the virtue of Hindutva and regression its only value. But then, why should Modi be blamed? He was simply pursuing the demand of the ideology, which was in a hurry to realise the dream which it dreamt in 1925. The danger is that if the ideology gets too impatient, then the future of democracy in the country will be at stake.

TEN

The Money Trick

I was in Goa, staying in a flat with other AAP members near Miramar beach. We were all there for the 2017 assembly elections. I had been coming here for more than a year. The date was 8 November 2016 and we had heard the prime minister wished to address the nation that evening. It had to be something big. As the clock struck eight, we turned on the television. The prime minister did not disappoint.

DEMONETISATION'S STAKEHOLDERS

Elections were to be held in Goa in February–March of 2017, alongside UP, Uttarakhand, Punjab and Manipur. The BJP, under the leadership of Modi, was on a great high, having won every election since 2014, except in Delhi and Bihar. However, after two-and-a-half years at the centre, people had begun questioning whether Modi had delivered on the promises he had made before 2014. Sceptics believed his popularity was not what it used to be. People were even starting to wonder what his chances were for another term as prime minister.

UP is a crucial state for Modi and the BJP. It is in many ways a microcosm of India, a place that sees the stiffest competition between the two resurgent ideologies—the ideology of the Ram mandir agitation or Hindutva and the ideology evolved out of the Mandal Commission reports. The last two-and-a-half decades have been witness to this fight between Mandir and Mandal adherents, though Hindutva has not been very fortunate in this battle. However, Modi's national rise coincided with the resurgence of Hindutva on a bigger scale. His rise did tilt the balance in favour of Hindutva. With eighty parliamentary seats and a population of more than twenty crore, if the BJP were to sweep UP, then it was easy to assume Modi's march to a second term would be comfortable. Therefore, to prove his critics wrong, it was crucial for the prime minister to win UP. In a way, these state assembly elections were a kind of referendum on his politics, policies and also his personality.

In discussions among party colleagues in the run-up to the elections, we used to say that he would need to come up with something exceptional to stamp his authority in the minds of the people. Therefore, when I heard that he was going to address the nation, we knew Modi's announcement would have a direct bearing on the elections. We had thought it would be big, but we did not imagine that it would be the most shocking since the declaration of emergency by Indira Gandhi on 25 June 1975. As we turned on the TV that evening what unfolded took us by complete shock. Prime Minister Modi changed the lives of more than a billion people—at least for a while—with that one announcement of demonetisation. After extending his Diwali greetings to the citizens, Modi said:

> In the past decades, the spectre of corruption and black money has grown. It has weakened the effort to remove poverty. On the one hand, we are now No. 1 in the rate of economic growth. But on the other hand, we were ranked close to one hundred in the global corruption perceptions ranking two years back. In spite of many steps taken, we have only been able to reach a ranking of seventy-six now. Of course, there is improvement. This shows the extent to which corruption and black money have spread their tentacles.
>
> The evil of corruption has been spread by certain sections of society for their selfish interest. They have ignored the poor and cornered benefits. Some people have misused their office for personal gain. On the other hand, honest people have fought against this evil. Crores of common men and women have lived lives of integrity. We hear about poor auto rickshaw drivers returning gold ornaments left in the vehicles to their rightful owners. We hear about taxi drivers who take pains to locate the owners of cell phones left behind. We hear of vegetable vendors who return excess money given by customers.
>
> There comes a time in the history of a country's development when a need is felt for a strong and decisive step. For years, this country has felt that corruption, black money and terrorism are festering sores, holding us back in the race towards development.

> Terrorism is a frightening threat. So many have lost their lives because of it. But have you ever thought about how these terrorists get their money? Enemies from across the border run their operations using fake currency notes. This has been going on for years. Many times, those using fake five hundred and thousand rupee notes have been caught and many such notes have been seized.[1]

Modi was smart to underline that he was extremely concerned about the growing corruption, that the poor are the main sufferers, and that something big needed to be done to tame this demon. Then he linked it all with the larger goal of economic development. Nationalism walked in via terrorism. He did not name Pakistan but the hint was obvious. Before announcing demonetisation, like a good salesman, he made a pitch, selling dreams—dreams that would not only cure the cancer of the society but also make India great. He addressed the common man and also addressed the core constituency of his ideology. When the stage was set, he declared:

> To break the grip of corruption and black money, we have decided that the five hundred and thousand rupees currency notes presently in use will no longer be legal tender from midnight tonight, that is, 8 November 2016. This means that these notes will not be acceptable for transactions from midnight onwards. The five hundred and thousand rupees notes hoarded by anti-national and anti-social elements will become just worthless pieces of paper. The rights and the interests of honest, hard-working people will be fully protected. Let me assure you that notes of one hundred, fifty, twenty, ten, five, two and one rupee and all coins will remain legal tender and will not be affected.[2]

It was a huge task. Those who criticised him and say that he did not foresee the hardships for the common man are not right. He did in fact caution people.

> In spite of all these efforts there may be temporary hardships to be faced by honest citizens. Experience tells us that ordinary citizens are always ready to make sacrifices and face difficulties for the benefits of the nation. I see that spirit when a poor widow gives up her LPG subsidy, when a retired school teacher contributes his pension to the Swacch Bharat mission, when a poor Adivasi mother sells her goats to build a toilet, when a soldier contributes fifty-seven thousand rupees to make his village clean. I have seen that the

ordinary citizen has the determination to do anything, if it will lead to the country's progress.

So in this fight against corruption, black money, fake notes and terrorism, in this movement for purifying our country, will our people not put up with difficulties for some days? I have full confidence that every citizen will stand up and participate in this 'mahayagna'. My dear countrymen, after the festivity of Diwali, now join the nation and extend your hand in this imandaari ka utsav, this pramanikta ka parv, this celebration of integrity, this festival of credibility.[3]

This speech is a classic example of his genius as a speaker and his unparalleled communication skills. Modi knew that demonetisation would bring hardship and it might backfire, but the packaging of the whole exercise was just brilliant. His biggest talent lies in turning future sufferers into stakeholders and making them feel that they are involved in nation building. He made them owners of the whole exercise. At the same time, by calling it a 'mahayagna', he cleverly gave it a religious colour. The people were left with no excuses, as a complaint would automatically see the speaker bracketed with the defenders of corruption, siding with dishonesty.

THE SUFFERINGS AND THE SAFETY NETS

In the end, when demonetisation failed, the failure had many fathers. Modi was just the originator of the idea, the creator of the big plan. But everyone was an executor, however, and thus everyone failed—why should Modi alone be blamed? This I call the manipulation of minds. No other politician has such talent for it. Yet what unfolded from the morning of 9 November was as unique as the prime minister himself. India had never seen an economic exercise of these proportions. Overnight, hard-earned money had turned into waste paper. The paradox was acute—people had notes in their pockets but they were of no use. People were standing in queues to exchange this denotified paper for usable money, in state after state, city after city, mohalla after mohalla and village after village.

In one stroke, Prime Minister Modi had ensured that approximately 86 per cent of the currency in the markets disappeared. According to the *Times of India*, the existing ₹500 and ₹1,000 currency notes would be accepted until 11 November at government hospitals, pharmacies in government hospitals, railway counters, government buses, airlines, petrol pumps, co-op stores run by the government, milk booths run by state agencies, crematoria and burial grounds. However, one could only withdraw ₹2,000 per day per card from ATMs till 18 November and ₹4,000 per day per card after this. One could withdraw up to ₹10,000 per day and ₹20,000 per week from banks till 24 November. It was also decided that the banned notes could be deposited in banks only up to 31 December.

It was easier said than done. The task was Herculean. The government had not done its homework well or maybe it had rushed into it on bravado alone. It had not considered how the void would be filled if 86 per cent of the circulating currency was withdrawn at once. On the first day itself, serpentine queues were seen all over the country. In Goa, it was painful to see people of all ages standing in queues for hours. The demonetisation measure had been announced on a Tuesday, but the ATMs were to open only on Friday and it was expected that within those two days, the ATMs would be geared to function at their optimum level. Three things had to be done to ensure the entire operation ran smoothly. First, all notes of ₹500 and ₹1,000 were to be removed from the ATMs. Second, notes of lower denominations such as ₹100 had to be stocked. Third, the systems had to be calibrated as, in most of the machines, three-quarters of the cassettes were sized for ₹500 and ₹1,000 currency notes, with only the fourth sized for ₹100. Now the whole system had to be recalibrated for ₹100 and later for the new ₹500 (in a different size) and ₹2,000 notes when they would be introduced. Across the country, 2 lakh ATMs were supposed to be made functional within 2 days; only 1.2 lakh could be made fully operational in fact.

The recalibration was a tricky business. Not just anyone could do it. The job needed specialised training and could only be done by the field staff of the original equipment managers (OEM), who were only two in number with a staff capacity of around 800.

To replenish the cash in two lakh ATMs, eight cash logistics companies were involved, with a workforce of only 40,000 people. Only 8,800 cash vans were available to ferry cash from the banks to the ATMs. There were only six service providers through which banks could place their orders for replenishing the money in their ATMs. Even at peak capacity, on an average day with the normal working hours, only 30,000 to 40,000 ATMs could be stocked.

Another important issue was overlooked. ATMs with ₹500 and ₹1,000 notes could disperse large amounts of cash in a lower volume. Now with every demand, the machine had to cough up five or ten times the number of notes. Before the note ban, a machine could discharge two ₹500 notes to meet a demand for ₹1,000; now the same machine was required to disburse ten notes for that amount. Therefore, the work was multiplied by at least five times. Or one might say that the capacity of the machine was reduced by at least five times. The *Times of India* reported, 'The banks are at present issuing only ₹100 notes to [the cash logistics] firms for supply to ATMs. As a result, the cash capacity of an ATM has gone down from ₹40 lakh to ₹5–10 lakh. "We can't just hire new people, as we are dealing with currency. The volume of currency to be transported has gone up while the amount has gone down. We need more boxes, more trips to each ATMs, more staff, etc. But we have no option but to manage with whatever we have," said an employee of a cash logistics firm.'

It was a kind of war that neither the government nor the common man had been prepared for. On 11 November, when the ATMs started to function once again, there was instantaneous misery. Three deaths were reported due to the note ban, one each in Alappuzha (Kerala), Mumbai and Howrah.[4] Most tragic was the one in Howrah where a woman jumped to her death, when after standing in the ATM queue for a long time, she had to come back without any money. On 12 November, the second day of the ATMs opening, the government realised its folly and announced that for the ATMs to be fully functional would take a minimum of three weeks. Meanwhile, in Delhi alone, the police received 3,343 complaints of violence by 9.00 p.m. of 12 November 2016. Fortunately, none of them were major incidents, but one could see that the social chaos was spreading. It was obvious that a crisis was looming large. It was said that the note ban would cripple terror funding and hawala dealers and put an end to fake currency; instead, it crippled the socio-economic activity of most citizens. The common man was angry, exhausted and traumatised.

It was not just the disappearance of the cash itself that was troubling, but the impact it had on social activities and the economy as a whole. Weddings had to be cancelled as a family could withdraw only ₹20,000 per week, which meant a cash crunch for many traditional celebrations. Private hospitals were refusing patients, as they had no cash. Auto drivers were returning home with their pockets empty. Daily-wage labourers were being refused work and had no option but to sleep on empty stomachs. The mandis, wet markets, were empty. Malls had a deserted look. Usually bustling markets had no buyers. Tourist spots had no tourists. Azadpur Mandi, the largest wholesale market in Asia, witnessed a fall of 40 per cent in sales as no large-denomination transactions were possible. The Taj Mahal, a major tourist destination, saw a considerable drop in the number tourists. 'Shopping malls and markets across the country have reported up to 50 per cent fall in their business in the first weekend after the demonetisation of ₹500 and ₹1,000 notes ... Local market places such as Karol Bagh in Delhi and Crawford Market in Mumbai where transactions are mostly in cash were the hardest hit with footfalls in these markets falling by as much as 70 per cent ... Business in Brigade Road in Bengaluru, which houses several national and international brands such as Arrow, Nike, Puma, Adidas, Soles, Vero Moda and Bling, has slowed down by 70 per cent.'[5]

When there was no money, who would buy even food? One restaurant owner complained, 'There are hardly any customers. Not even half the customers that we usually expect on a weekend.'[6] November was the beginning of the tourist season in Goa, yet when I visited one of the most sought-after beaches, Anjuna, in the second week after demonetisation, I could see only empty chairs and deserted shacks. I was told by their owners that sales were down to 20 per cent. This was the worst season in Goa's history. One day, my friend and I were the only ones in the shack for a good three hours in the evening. The owner was in tears.

THE STORY OF ANKIT VERMA OF FARIDABAD

I got a call from a friend that there was less crowd at this particular branch. So I went there at 8.30 a.m. with five other friends. By then, the crowd had swollen. My father can't leave his job to stand in queue, so I had to go there, abandoning business. And we waited. None of us had any money to buy food so we all stayed hungry, with the hope of laying our hands on some money at the end of the ordeal. At 4.40 p.m., after eight long hours in the queue, the bank authorities said cash was over. The whole day, none of them came out even once to see how we had suffered. What's even worse: they let in people they knew through the back door to withdraw money. And yet they had the audacity to tell us all to go home and come again the day after. We protested and even called the police. But they chased us away. Tired, hurt and dejected, I returned home only to find my younger brother, Ritik (15), down with fever. My mother may have an odd ₹50 or ₹100 note to buy medicine but I have nothing, not even for a packet of biscuits. I don't want to go to the bank again tomorrow, but do I even have an option?'[7]

Ankit's ordeal reflects life just after demonetisation in all the big cities, but life in the suburban areas was no different; in fact, it was worse. Villages were the worst affected as ATMs and banks hardly exist there and cash is the only mode of monetary exchange. Farmers were distraught: 'Agricultural markets in India saw lacklustre trade ... as farmers struggled to cope with scarcity of currency notes. Trade in grains, spices and oilseeds narrowed to a trickle. Hardly any soya bean or maize has been traded in Madhya Pradesh since November 9 ... Similarly, onion and potatoe trade in Hubli and adjoining mandis in Karnataka have stopped since November 11 ... Meanwhile, in Gujarat, cotton and groundnut mandis were closed ... Mandis in Maharashtra like Pandharpur, Rahata, Indapur, Jat, Nashik, Sholapur mandis are closed ...'[8]

The *Times of India* on 13 November captured the mood of the nation very vividly: 'A week, two weeks? A month, two months? How long will it take for normal cash flow to return to the economy? No one has the answer as currency queues at banks get bigger, ATMs remain non-performers and the cash crunch precipitates despair and anger'.

THE FRUIT BORNE

Not everyone was complaining.

Jewellers were happy, for one. As demonetisation was announced, black marketeers rushed to jewellers to buy gold in bulk. This raised such an alarm that the government was forced to announce that if jewellers did not take down the PAN numbers for any transaction, severe action would follow. Local authorities were alerted to keep a close watch on illegal transactions in the gold market.

The black marketeers who dealt in currency were more than happy. Overnight a new market was created where ₹500 and ₹1,000 notes were exchanged for smaller notes. Of course, it was not for free, like at the banks. For the exchange of every note of ₹1,000, ₹300–400 was earned. The value of a ₹1,000 note was now reduced to ₹600–700, depending upon the bargaining capacity of the buyer. The income tax department detected more than ₹100 crore of 'unexplained cash' in the currency conversion black market on the fourth day of demonetisation.[9] The police, paramilitary forces, income tax department and enforcement directorate were all alerted to chase, confiscate and punish illegal cash carried on roads, by rail or by air. Even the Jan Dhan accounts of the poor showed a surge in funds, though many of these accounts had been lying dormant for a long time. In Agra alone, ₹170 crore were deposited since the announcement of demonetisation. This corpus swelled to the tune of ₹21,000 crore within a fortnight of the currency withdrawal. The government was worried.

Soon, the socio-economic crisis turned into a political crisis for the government. The opposition smelled an opportunity to put the prime minster on the mat. Mamata Banerjee thundered, 'This government is anti-people and anti-poor. It has no moral right to continue … I have asked my party MPs to get in touch with all opposition parties, even the CPM and give a befitting reply to this government in parliament.'[10] The opposition was united in its determination to show no mercy. The winter session of the parliament was the ideal platform for it to raise its collective voice. Both the houses witnessed acrimonious exchanges. On 23 November, fifteen big and small parties together registered their protest in front of the Gandhi statue in parliament House and announced a national protest on 28 November. The protests were held in every district headquarter. In a rare show of unity, arch-rivals Samajwadi Party and BSP in UP, CPI (M) and TMC in West Bengal, AIADMK and DMK in Tamil Nadu came together. It was at this time that Nitish Kumar, who had until then been seen as someone who could lead the opposition against the Modi government, distanced himself from the protest and openly supported demonetisation. He later walked out of the opposition camp to join hands with the BJP.

Meanwhile, economic experts were anticipating worse. Credit rating agency Moody's warned that demonetisation would lead to economic disruption, which would result in weaker consumption and the slowing down of economic growth: 'Corporates will see economic activity decline, with lower sales volumes and cash flows. Those directly exposed to retail sales will be most affected.'[11] However, the report also said that in the long run, it would boost tax revenue and fiscal consolidation. Yet the overall picture painted was grim. Senior journalist and noted economist Swaminathan S. Anklesaria Aiyar wrote, '... world-class economists in investment banks are coming up with darker projections. With every day of detailed analysis, the mess looks bigger, and projections get darker. Initial projections of a fall in annual GDP of maybe 0.4% are now increasing to 1–2%. Hence, foreign institutional investors have pulled ₹10,000 crore out of the stock market.'[12] Investment expert Ruchir Sharma was distressed by the government's move too. He wrote, 'It might be more satisfying to punish shady fortunes, but revenge is not a development strategy. Scrapping large bills may destroy some hidden wealth today, but the black economy will start regenerating itself tomorrow in the absence of deeper changes in the culture and institutions that foster it.'[13]

Yet Modi showed no overt signs of nervousness. Neither the ganging up of the opposition nor the socio-economic chaos seemed to affect him. Stridency was his reply to the opposition's chorus. When he was expected to be defensive, Modi picked up the gun and fired at his opponents. He said, 'My government will do everything to protect the honest, but the dishonest have to account for themselves.'[14] He used his most potent weapon, populism. He mockingly said, 'After demonetisation, the poor are enjoying a sound asleep while rich are running from pillar to post to buy sleeping pills.'[15] He confessed that he was aware of the hardships that the people were facing: 'The PM said he saluted citizens for putting up with the inconvenience as those preparing for weddings or tending to ailing relatives found themselves in a bind. "I gave everyone a chance. If you thought it was business as usual, it is not my fault," Modi said. "Earlier, people did not even throw a 25 paise coin into the Ganga but people are now dumping cash."'[16] He declared that if any money that was unaccounted for came to light, he would check accounts from Independence until the present time.[17]

If the opposition had thought that it could turn demonetisation into a political slugfest, Modi took the battle to another level. His genius lay in converting his failure into a collective salvation, invoking the greater good of the people and the nation, making it an ethical battle with a hint of religiosity. The reference to the Ganges is not religious in the literal sense, but it does indirectly connect with the Hindu dharma. In northern India, the Ganges is part of a great culture, a set of everyday traditions and a lifeline. It flows through every soul, it cleanses every sin. It is every Hindu's last wish to meet the great river in their last days. Not simply a river, it is the undying gateway to moksha. In his own style, Modi suggested that he was engaged in a project that no other leader had dared to attempt since Independence, though it was needed to make India great. He said he would stand by demonetisation and was ready to pay any price.

In Goa, on 13 November 2016, while addressing a rally, he unleashed his Brahmastra, making an emotional appeal: 'My brothers and sisters, I was not born for the chair. I left my house, my family, everything for the country. They thought they will pull out my hair and Modi will get angry. Oh, even if you burn Modi alive, Modi is not afraid. I am looting certain people's seventy-year-ill-gotten wealth, they will not leave me alive, they will destroy me.'[18] Modi played martyr with aplomb, ready to sacrifice his life for the betterment of the people. No other leader had played on the psyche of the people so beautifully. Indians might be materialistic in their lives but they look for spirituality in their leaders.

The reason for Mahatma Gandhi's immense popularity was his spiritual self, which the people later discovered in Jayaprakash Narayan in the mid-1970s. Narayan successfully uprooted the powerful Indira Gandhi in 1977. V.P. Singh was the last political leader who laboriously acquired this skill. In the RSS–BJP tradition, Modi is the only one who has successfully transformed himself into a spiritual being for a section of the society that is ready to die for him. Whether we hate him or love him, the truth is that he has marketed himself as a leader who is honestly trying to change the country and who, unlike others, is selfless and devoted to the cause—the image is that of one who is honest and tries hard. It is this ethical capital which proved to be his saviour as this crisis grew.

To add credibility to his intent, on 13 November, Modi had also announced that after 30 December he would take more measures to eradicate black money. He did not ask for forgiveness, but instead asked for people's patience. In Goa, he said at the rally, 'I also feel the pain but bear it till December 30 to straighten things. After that, I am ready to face any punishment meted out by the people in any square.'[19] Meanwhile, his opponents were ready to write his obituary. Even his supporters were sceptical about the outcome. But there was a consensus that demonetisation could be a game changer. Nilanjan Mukhopadhyay, Modi's biographer, wrote, 'As of now, there is no certainty that Modi's gambit will be successful. There, however, is no doubt that politically this step is possibly the biggest game-changer so far in the Modi regime, though it cannot be said whether the game will alter in favour of Prime Minister or against him.'[20]

Still, except for his core constituency, not many were willing to buy Modi's claim that demonetisation was rolled out solely to curb black money. The BJP's own allies, the Shiromani Akali Dal and the Shiv Sena were not convinced. The 'supreme court lauded the intent', but '150 eminent citizens, mostly from the Left, demanded a rollback.'

REGROUP AND RECOVERY

The BJP shrugged off the opposition's reaction as the wailing of those who had lost illegal money and said that they were spreading rumours. In the midst of all their speculations, only one thing could have been said with certainty—that the announcement was well-timed for the UP assembly elections. According to some conjectures, Modi took a gamble to render the opposition parties 'cash-less'. Black money intended to be used in campaigning for the elections was rendered useless. It was alleged that party leaders and friends of Modi and Amit Shah knew of this strategy in advance and they had changed their black currency into white money well ahead of time. By this logic, the BJP was the only party which would have had enough money to spend towards the elections and this would certainly give them an edge.

Some said that this was an attempt to counter the opposition's charge that Modi had failed to fight corruption or nail black money and that his promise of bringing black money stashed in foreign banks back to India and depositing ₹15 lakh in every family's account within a hundred days of forming the government was a jumla (false promise). UP had contributed majorly to his quest to become the prime minster and a loss in that state's assembly elections would send the wrong signal across the country. So Modi, it was said, took a calculated risk to prove the opposition wrong and win back disenchanted voters. Yet nobody actually had a clue and everybody was guessing.

Perhaps Mukhopadhyay was right. He wrote, 'At mid-point of his regime, Modi had little option but to explore new avenues because policies and programmes he pursued since coming to power do not ensure immortality. Most of his predecessors have at least a decision or two that ensure permanence in history. None of Modi's initiative so far matches signatures like that of Jawaharlal Nehru (Five Year Plans and PSUs), Lal Bahadur Shastri (push towards Green Revolution), Indira Gandhi (bank nationalisation and 1971 war), Rajiv Gandhi (communication revolution), PV Narasimha Rao (economic liberalisation), Atal Bihari Vajpayee (Golden Quadrangle) and Manmohan Singh (RTI and rural employment guarantee).'[21]

The stamp of immortality is for historians to debate, but the hard reality was that the crisis was deepening and the BJP was worried. Modi was also concerned. By the end of the first week of demonetisation, he had realised that it might boomerang and the crisis could jeopardise his political career. In addition to utilising his personal charisma and communication skills to soothe the public, he went back to the party and had several meetings with the party leaders. He told them to spread out across the country, help people standing in the queues, serve them water, tea, snacks and food, talk to them and make them understand the reason for such a gigantic task—essentially, tell people that Modi had not done this for himself but for the country and that the Congress could not have done something like this because the Congress itself was a beneficiary of black money. The entire BJP leviathan was yoked to turn the people's attention from personal pain to collective salvation, from individual gain to national pride. The patriotism canard was pushed forward so that people would not complain. On the ground, the RSS–BJP workers spread out to persuade people that those who didn't support demonetisation were not deshbhakts (patriots), that they were supporting dishonesty, that an honest person would bear the pain for the country and not complain, that the entire exercise was for the poor, that it had made the rich uncomfortable because they were dishonest and hence the rich and influential had ganged up to defame Modi. To the Congress's counter-propaganda, Modi said, 'Don't mislead people … I want to ask Congressmen who claim people are facing problems how you turned the entire country into a jail for 19 months by imposing emergency.'[22]

One of Modi's greatest virtues is that he is a master of setting a new agenda, weaving a new narrative and creating a web of believable visions. During the 2014 elections, he succeeded because he sold the country the idea that it needed a powerful leader, a decisive prime minister to make India great again. In the first two-and-a-half years of being in power, he dazzled people with many new utopias. The Swachh Bharat Mission, Make in India, Digital India and Startup India are a few of these. Modi effortlessly moves from one such project to another without being bogged down by the deliverables. Demonetisation was also one such project. But this time, the people were more urgently affected. The opposition went to the people to criticise it, experts disagreed with its feasibility and it was commonly accepted that the execution was messed up. The excuse of suffering for patriotism was a good buffer, but would it be enough to save the day for him and the party? Within a fortnight, Modi offered the country a new gem, a new utopia—to make India a 'cashless' economy. His own radio progamme Mann Ki Baat that aired on 27 November is an excellent example of how effortlessly he walked from one utopian dream to another, from demonetisation to a cashless society. His timing was perfect, his choice of words extraordinary and his ability to sell a magical chimaera was unmatched:

> I knew that people will face new kinds of difficulties in their normal lives … The decision is so big that it would take 50 days for us to emerge out of its impact and move towards normalcy. The whole world is looking at the decision minutely and economists are analysing it. There may be a question mark in the world's mind but India has faith and confidence in its citizens that we will emerge glowing like gold from the fire … despite 'stress of various kinds', 1.3 lakh bank branches, lakhs of bank employees, 1.5 lakh post offices and 1 lakh banking correspondents were putting in long hours on the job considering it a 'yagna of service to the country' … For 70 years, the diseases we are inflicted with … the road to get ourselves rid of those diseases cannot be easy.[23]

Modi's message was simple: What he had done was beyond the ordinary. It was momentous—so big that the whole world was watching. And he had done it to save the country, Mother India, from a dangerous affliction. However, the biggest takeaway was that it was only Modi who could have done this; only he could have taken such a big decision. And after creating that illusion, he moved on to another: 'Our dream is that there should be a cashless society. It is correct that 100% cashless society is never possible. But we can make a start with less-cash-society, then cashless society will not be a far-off destination.'[24]

On 8 November, Modi had made no mention of a cashless society. Once the crisis emanating from demonetisation took a dangerous turn, however, he smartly distracted people from their personal pain to focus on nation building. He conveyed that he knew what he was doing and that there was a method to the madness, implying that he was unveiling his plan in a systematic manner, one phase after another. To convey that he was serious about the whole enterprise, he appealed to the youth in Gandhian style, urging each one to teach at least ten people how to transact without cash, how to use technology, and how to get used to credit cards, online banking and credit exchange. The message was powerful. For the urban middle class, he was a modern man, a visionary, and for the rural poor, he was a saviour who cared for them.

As if to bear witness to Modi's efficacy, the BJP celebrated massive successes in the Maharashtra municipal council and nagar panchayat elections. The BJP won 851 seats against 396 in the previous elections. The Congress and the NCP were second and third with 643 and 638 seats respectively. Both had lost hugely—in 2011, the Congress had won 1,111 seats and the NCP 1,127. The BJP immediately called it a referendum on demonetisation. Similarly, in Gujarat, the BJP swept the local body election. It won 109 of the 134 seats. The BJP used this opportunity to deride the opposition, which had been critical of the note ban. The puzzle, of course, was that if people were as unhappy as they appeared on the surface, why had voters opted for the BJP in both the states? The answer to the mystery lay in Modi's charisma.

There is no denying the fact that the crisis was severe. More than a hundred people died standing in queues.[25] The economy was badly hit. Manmohan Singh, celebrated economist as well as former prime minister, called demonetisation 'organised loot and legalised plunder of the common people'.[26] He had predicted a 2 per cent drop in GDP in the third week of the demonetisation, which was partly realised when data for the April–June 2017 quarter was released: 'Data released by the Central Statistics Office (CSO) on Thursday showed the economy grew 5.7% in April–June; the first quarter of the current fiscal, slower than the previous quarter's 6.1% growth and lower than the 7.9% expansion posted in the first quarter of 2016–17.'[27] According to economists, the lingering effects of demonetisation contributed to this slowdown.[28] The *Times of India* had hinted at the slowdown even on the completion of the first month of demonetisation, with the headline, 'Black Money Antidote Stifles Economy; Demand Shrinks, Jobs Hit, Sentiment Down'.[29] There were clear signs that the real estate and manufacturing sectors and retail businesses would be badly hit, which would lead to widespread job losses.

The manufacturing sector witnessed the sharpest decline. The Nikkei India Manufacturing Purchasing Managers' Index (PMI) dropped to 49.6 per cent in December. The PMI had been 52.3 per cent in the month of November. The decline was the sharpest since 2008 and was reportedly the first contraction in the last twelve months. According to the Centre for Monitoring Indian Economy (CMIE), investment also dipped: 'The data showed 227 new investment proposals worth ₹81,800 crore were announced during this quarter before the demonetisation on November 8. Only 177 investments proposals worth ₹43,700 crore were made between November 9 and December 31.'[30] Core-sector growth also slowed in November to 4.9 per cent, from the 6.6 per cent of the previous month. Bank credit growth dropped to 5.1 per cent. According to the chief economist of the State Bank of India, Soumya Kanti Ghosh, 'credit growth was actually the lowest in over 60 years—since 1954–55—when it was 1.7%.'[31] Value-added tax (VAT) collections, on the other hand, went up by 18.1 per cent in twenty-three states in November and 8.9 per cent in seventeen states in December. Surprisingly, industrial growth rose by 5.7 per cent in November despite fears of cash withdrawal.

In its economic survey on 1 February 2017, the Modi government for the first time admitted that due to demonetisation, the economy might have suffered a 1 per cent GDP loss: '[T]he Survey noted that there had been reports of job losses, decline in farm incomes, and social disruption, especially in the informal, cash-intensive parts of the economy.'[32] The government was still optimistic that in the long run, the note ban would contribute majorly to the economic health of the county.

However, the biggest jolt for the government was the return of 99 per cent of the scrapped currency to the exchequer. According to the RBI report released eight months later, on 30 August 2017, 15.28 lakh crore of the 15.44 lakh crore demonetised were in the Reserve Bank of India.[33] This is to say that 99 per cent of the banned currency was deposited back in the bank. This data raises very serious questions about the tall claims made by the Modi government. The government had expected to earn a windfall of ₹3 lakh crore through demonetisation. If almost all the money was back, that meant that either there had been no black money in the system or the entirety of the black money in circulation had been converted to white money through this process. Instead of the government, the illegal hoarders had benefited. It was only a lose-lose situation for the government. Only ₹16,000 crore proved to be black money, that is, the amount that did not reach the RBI. Interestingly, the RBI ended up spending ₹21,000 crore on reprinting new currency. By this calculation, the government lost ₹5,000 crore in the exercise. Therefore, the pertinent question was what purpose demonetisation had served. On 27 December 2016, at the parade ground in Dehradun, Modi had boasted that demonetisation had destroyed 'terrorism, drug mafia, human trafficking and the underworld' in a trice.[34] I leave it to the reader's judgement how far terrorism, the drug mafia, human trafficking and fake currency have ebbed since then.

However, the RBI data was not released immediately. The public got it only eight months after demonetisation. Meanwhile, the BJP had registered some of the biggest electoral victories in UP and Uttarakhand, proof that people believed in Modi despite the serious disruptions to their social and economic lives.

People endured hardships and voted for the BJP. Overtly, this might seem to defy logic. In a way, historian Richard Overy tried to answer the same question. He unlocked the mystery of how a few regimes succeeded in winning the loyalty of the masses despite causing them severe hardships. While comparing regimes under Joseph Stalin in the Soviet Union and Adolf Hitler in Germany, he writes, 'The powerful appeal of the two systems relied on the extent to which the populations could identify with the central message. In each case, there were important historical circumstances that facilitated willingness to accept distorted versions of the truth. The promises made by the dictatorship were seductively attractive because they reflected aspirations already shared by an important fraction of the population, and easily communicated to the rest. In the Soviet Union, the promise of a revolutionary paradise through redemptive struggle was central to the Bolshevik cause and was used to justify all the sacrifices of the present … for millions of ordinary people struggling to come to terms with the post revolutionary world the distant Utopia provided a subliminal goal in the face of otherwise inexplicable hardships. "It's all very well to build for the future," explained a young factory official to a visiting American journalist. "And we are doing great things. We are building a society that in time will make the civilisation of Western Europe and America seem like barbarism.'"[35]

In case of Hitler's Germany, Overy's thesis is more apt. Germany after the first world war was a defeated nation, a wounded civilisation; the society was badly traumatised. It was looking for a messiah who could give them back their past glory. Hitler promised exactly that. Overy writes, 'The collective psychological trauma of defeat and shame was abruptly reversed in 1933; the more evident it became that Hitler, apparently, could redeem the promises of German political revival, moral renewal and cultural awakening, the more readily the population identified with the dictatorship and the German new age.'[36] As it is evident, Overy does not over emphasise the language of redemption for the success of the Nazi regime. He believes that historical condition also played an important role. The collective desperation of the German people was looking for a process of sublimation. He says, '(P)opular endorsement did not come just in response to the language and propaganda of the regime, but from the insecurities and resentment of those who supported Hitler as the German Messiah even before 1933.'[37]

Overy's study was a long-term project and undertaken many decades after the regimes were actually operational. Modi's regime is recent and continuing. Overy talked about totalitarian systems whereas India is a democracy. It is an open and free society. Therefore, the blind application of the same epithets in the Indian context would not be strictly correct; still, it can't be denied that they offer a window to understanding the phenomenon of Modi's popularity.

Overy suggests that it is the possibility of redemption that created the willingness of people to provide support for the regime, despite hardships. Modi's speeches harness the same idea of redemption. He constantly hammers home the point that India has been suffering from a terminal disease for the last seventy years, and now is the time to redeem the nation. His communication skills, his capacity to create illusions, to weave magic through words and build narratives, gives a sense of purpose to the ordinary life of the person on the streets while his ability to control the media seems to have convinced people who buy into the utopia of his creation. Let us not forget that India did experience a kind of collective trauma, though not to the scale of Germany post World War I, due to the enormity of corruption in the last three years of the Manmohan Singh government.

The success of the Anna Hazare movement and the Aam Aadmi Party winning twenty-eight seats in Delhi in 2013 without any political background was an indicator of the collective desperation. People were extremely unhappy with the Congress led regime. Modi encashed the collective desperation by "promising paradise to the people", during the 2014 elections.[38] His electoral success in 2014 was the result of the communication that he established with the people. People believed he was the redeemer. Modi's subsequent success in most of the assembly elections, even after demonetisation, is testimony to the fact that people trusted him and his promise of a brighter future and a secure society as the product of new and clean politics. However, utopian dreams do not last forever. When the utopia ceases to deliver, when promises fail to connect people's dreams with their reality, then the myth starts unravelling, and that is when a leader, an ideology and the state begin to lose their charisma. Once the data on the logistics and economic repercussions of demonetisation became public, people were faced with the reality—claims were unmasked, the hypnotic spell was broken and the disenchantment with Modi began. In the subsequent assembly elections in Gujarat and Karnataka, Modi's performance was anything but spectacular; in fact, it was less than satisfactory. If the dots from demonetisation to the UP elections could be connected, then there is a lesson for future generations here: Ideology becomes lethal and invincible if it is married to a charismatic personality and can successfully sail through any crisis. Yet even this marriage is fragile if that charismatic personality forgets to deliver on their promises and cannot bring to life the world of make-believe they create. Modi now has to deliver, if the ideology has to sustain its forward movement.

ELEVEN

Hindutva, Media and Propaganda

A cobra used to live in a hole in a mosque. He used to hear the namaaz five times a day. Every day he would carefully listen to the taqreer (speech). One day he thought he too should offer namaaz so that he might go to heaven. The next day, just before namaaz, the poor fellow came out of his hole and started crawling towards the line where those waiting to offer namaaz were standing. When the namaazis saw him, they ran after him with sticks in their hands. The cobra wriggled away as fast as he could with the namaazis chasing him. While escaping, he saw an old Hindu temple. He entered and wrapped himself around the Shivling. When the Hindus saw the cobra wrapped around the Shivling, a crowd gathered; people started praying and offering it milk. The cobra got thinking—Where was I living for so long? I wanted to offer namaaz but they ran after me and threw stones at me. I came in for shelter before Lord Shiva for a few moments and I turned into Sheshnag from a cobra. This is the difference between Islam and Sanatan Dharma. Happy homecoming.

Jay Ho Vaidik Sanatan Dharm Ki
24 July 2018
(Translated from Hindi)

Every year, in the Bahraich district, the Dargah Mela is held in the memory of Syed Salar Masood Ghazi, the maternal nephew of Mehmood Ghaznavi, who lured by the enormous treasure looted by his uncle, was tempted to capture India. Above all he was attracted to the idea of establishing an Islamic State in India after annihilating the kafirs (the non-believers). He was also motivated to make Indian women sex slaves and sell them abroad and collect money. For this purpose he came to India along with troops of about two lakh soldiers and, after defeating many kings in Punjab, reached

UP. He killed Hindus ruthlessly. To behead Hindus, build a minar with their heads, and then, sit on top of that minar while claiming he was the Ghazi, was his favourite thing. In Bahraich he was confronted by an organised army of a very brave king, Raja Suheldev Pasi. Syed Salar Masood Ghazi could not counter his strategic brilliance and indomitable courage, and was killed by him. His troops were defeated by the one-and-a-half-lakh-strong Hindu troops of the Raja. Thus, Raja Suheldev saved India from being converted into an Islamic State. Hindus regained their dignity and grandeur. This battle is counted as one of the fiercest battles in world history. The battle was so ferocious that prisoners of war on both sides were cut into pieces. The end of such a cruel king was not an ordinary victory.

But you will be surprised to know that one can't find a single picture, idol or oil painting of Raja Suheldev Pasi—not only in Bahraich but in the entirety of India. No literature or history book talks about him. 75 per cent Hindus don't even know about him. Only the older generation can confirm that he was as great, brave, intelligent and handsome as Raja Prithviraj Chauhan.

But in contrast to this, the fair held in honour of Syed Salar Masood Ghazi is getting bigger every day. Literature and history about him is safe with the older generation of Muslims. The money offered on his mazaar is growing exponentially. Every day a chaadar is offered at his mazaar. Lohban is burnt, perfume is sprayed and there is a great celebration. In a similar fashion, the mazaar of the commander-in-chief of Syed Salar Masood Ghazi is also ordained the same respect. This mazaar is on the side of the road, near Ghantaghar.

See the difference between the mindset of Hindus and Muslims. Masood Ghazi was a defeated king, killed by Raja Suheldev, and yet Muslims give him so much respect because he killed lakhs of Hindus, to make India an Islamic State, and converted Hindus to Muslims in large numbers. And although he risked his life to save the lives of Hindus and protect India from becoming enslaved by the Mughals, there is no respect for Raja Suheldev … The biggest regret is that even Hindus visit Syed Salar Masood Ghazi's mazaar and make a wish at the dargah.

Tomorrow, the Muslim historians can also claim that there was no king named Raja Suheldev. He was only a figment of the Hindus' imagination.

28 August 2018
(Translated from Hindi)

Just think! Today's Indian Muslim was the coward Hindu of the past. And today's coward Hindu will be the Muslim of tomorrow. Bitter facts:

- Only a few years ago Durga Puja was the main festival of Bengal but today it has been replaced by Muharram. Keep sleeping and cursing Modi.
- History is witness to the fact that Hindus have never helped Hindus, so what can only Modi do?
- What was the reason that Prithviraj Chauhan alone fought Muhammad Ghori? What were the neighbouring Hindu kings doing?
- What was the reason that only Rana Pratap of Mewar fought Akbar? Where were the other kings of India?
- What was the reason that only Shivaji Maharaj of Maharashtra fought Aurangzeb and Afzal Khan? Where were the other Hindu kings?
- When personal jealousies and arrogance among Hindus did not let brave kings come together and fight as one, then what will one Modi do alone? Will all the anti-nationals defeat him too?

Our country has suffered for hundreds and thousands of years because of foreign invasions.

In the past, we Sanatani Hindus were spread all over the world. But today, due to divisions amongst us we are fighting for our own survival, even in India.

This is the last chance. Never ever in the future will a Hinduvadi leader like Modi be born.

3 August 2018
(Translated from Hindi)

Stories like these are freely circulated and spread venom in WhatsApp groups. I accidentally became a member of one such group where these were being circulated with much gusto. Initially, I was not interested in reading even a line and would hit delete the moment some message like this came in, but one day, I read a couple of messages and they held my attention. These messages typically come in bulk and are smartly packaged. Content of this nature is circulated to keep people in the group engaged. Much like in a group of friends, here too jokes are told, inspirational stories posted, cures for various ailments shared, biographies of great nationalistic leaders are repeated, ethical and moral lectures given, life values taught, pictures of Hindu gods and goddesses are sent, 'Good morning' and 'Good night' messages are exchanged, Hindi poetry and cartoons surface ... and in between, such messages pop up.

If one carefully reads the three stories, which I picked out of many, it is easy to comprehend that these have a definite narrative and a well-defined target audience and that the aim is to manipulate a section of the population. These are provocative stories, sprinkled with hate and misinformation. History and mythology form the base of these messages.

MYTH-MAKING

The first story talks about a cobra being ill-treated in the mosque where he is willing to pray to Allah and be a good Muslim, but ultimately it is the Hindu god who saves him. The story ends with a moral that the reader has to decipher: that Hindus are good and Muslims are bad and bloodthirsty. It creates a stereotype, attesting to the difference between the two religions; it conveys that Hindus are so good that they value even the life of a cobra and that the touch of Hindu gods can transform a reptile into an angel. Sheshnag is a mythological character, who Lord Vishnu and his wife Laxmi are often depicted to be resting on. The cobra from the story is transformed in to Sheshnag and now enjoys the company of Ishwar, the Almighty and the Creator of the universe. He is no longer a destroyer. He is now the pedestal of Mother Earth, since Sheshnag in Hindu mythology is credited with holding the earth on his hood.

If the first story manipulates mythology to stigmatise Muslims, then the second one is an attempt to mythologise history. The battle between Raja Suheldev and Syed Salar Masood Ghazi is a historical fact. In 1034, Ghazi was killed on the battlefield. Raja Suheldev defeated his army. It is also true that Ghazi was buried in Bahraich and is a revered figure among both Hindu and Muslim communities there. In fact, there are times when more Hindus visit his mazaar than Muslims. Indeed, it would be wrong to presume that Ghazi was only a Muslim warrior. In his lifetime, he was seen as a warrior-saint. There was a belief that he was blessed with spiritual powers and could cure patients of terminal diseases. He belonged to the great Sufi tradition, which is equally disliked by fanatical Muslims and fundamentalist Hindus. To club Ghazi with other Muslim invaders and then build an anti-Muslim narrative would not be right. It is a distortion of history. It is to poison the minds of Hindus. To project him as a bloodthirsty Muslim zealot who used to revel in killing Hindus and making Hindu women into sex slaves is an attempt to create hatred towards him and, through him, towards Muslims. If he was as bad as Hindutva forces want people to believe, then his mazaar would not have attracted Hindus at all.[1] His memory has survived for almost a thousand years. Do the forces of Hindutva want to suggest that Hindus are so stupid that they continue to worship him for centuries despite knowing about the atrocities he perpetrated upon Hindus? Frankly, this is an attempt to falsify history for political gains.

It is true that Raja Suheldev, the king of Shravasti, was a great warrior, but to say that he has been forgotten by Hindus, that there is no picture, idol or oil painting of him, that there is no literature available on him is a deliberate attempt to mislead people. The fact that WhatsApp messages about him are being circulated is itself proof that he has not been forgotten even after a thousand years. He is certainly not an all-India hero, but he is part of the local folk culture. There is a long folk song called 'Sri Suhel Bavani' composed in his memory, which is recited with great enthusiasm when people meet in and around Bahraich. A big temple for Raja Suheldev also exists. Renowned novelist Amish Tripathi has written a novel around the legend of Suheldev and the Battle of Bahraich.[2] A political party called the Suheldev Bharatiya Samaj Party is also active in UP and has contested elections. Its leader Om Prakash Rajbhar has joined Yogi Adityanath's cabinet. Yet there is such a misinformation campaign; why?

The third composition exposes the design behind such misinformation campaigns. Note the first sentence: 'Today's Indian Muslim was the coward Hindu of the past. And today's coward Hindu will be the Muslim of tomorrow.' It deliberately calls Hindus cowards and is extremely provocative. Then it says that Durga Puja is being replaced by Muharram. Several instances are then recounted to show Hindus have historically not been united in their fight against Muslims. Only then does the narrative reach the main point of how Narendra Modi alone is fighting for the Hindus, and yet the Hindus (like their ancestors) are not helping him fight for their own cause. Finally the message makes an emotional pitch that if Hindus are not united or if they don't support Modi, they won't survive. The intent is to convey that Modi is in the same league as Hindu kings such as Prithviraj Chauhan, Rana Pratap and Shivaji Maharaj, who fought against Greek and Muslim invaders, but like them, Modi is also engaged in a lonely battle. Hindus stand divided once again.

This is a falsification of history. None of the above kings were fighting for the establishment of a Hindu kingdom or for the annihilation of Muslim states. They were kings and like all other kings of the time were out to expand their own kingdoms. To paint the wars they fought as battles between the two religions has no support from history. Yet the misinformation campaign by the Hindutva forces has continued for decades.

It is imperative to question the timing of this rumour that paints Modi as the last chance of survival for Hindus. Two things can safely be surmised here. First, it is an attempt to polarise society along religious lines for the consolidation of Hindus. Second, it is aimed at provoking Hindus to vote for Modi in the 2019 parliamentary elections. The former argument is part of the long-term goal of Hindutva: to construct a Hindu Rashtra, which can only be built if Hindus are united under one banner. This is an ongoing project for the RSS. Whether the RSS's ally is in the government or not, the project continues. However, the second point is more significant. It addresses the immediate cause for this campaign. Modi is no longer as popular as he was in 2014. The opposition parties, that were not united back in 2014, have since realised that they need to work together to fight Modi.

This call for unity of the opposition, produced a certain momentum in the beginning of 2018 and serious doubts were raised about Modi being re-elected in 2019. It is a known fact of Indian politics that when a leader or party is not confident of victory, then it resorts to emotionalism. Modi and the BJP did not ask for votes in the 2014 elections in the name of Hindutva; they did not create a panic that it was the last chance for Hindus; they did not say that this election would be a matter of life and death. Instead, Modi talked about development, the eradication of corruption, robust governance and strong leadership. Yet, this time, as the elections are nearing, talk about Hindu–Muslim rivalry and nationalism is growing. This is an indication that the ruling dispensation is not confident of coming back to power. Hindutva forces know that Modi's loss would be a huge setback for the Hindu Rashtra.

The WhatsApp stories I began this chapter with are not random. Such messages flood social-media platforms almost every day. Facebook, Twitter and WhatsApp are full of such material. They are provocative and explosive, with the potential to create conflict between communities. They target

Hindus, the effort being to convert them into religious zealots and make them ideological warriors. The one-point agenda is to spread hatred towards Islam. For this purpose, stories are concocted, historical facts are distorted, sinister interpretations are trotted out and Hindus are exhorted to stand up and join the battle to save Hinduism. 'Save Hinduism from Islam', is the battle cry. Hindutva is becoming like a modern factory, equipped with the latest technology and information. The idea is to sell the same product—the ideology of Hindutva—using a modern packaging style and smart marketing techniques.

THE RAMAYANA IMPROVISED, AGAIN

Besides the cow protection movement of the 1960s, the Ram mandir movement was the most critical episode in the history of Hindutva. The Babri Masjid was demolished on 6 December 1992, but the temple proposed on the site has not been constructed yet. The land dispute between the two communities, related to the Babri Masjid and the Ram mandir, is still pending before the supreme court as is the work of temple construction. Yet, every day, several stories are circulated regarding the Ram mandir movement. The narrative and the exhortation for Hindus to rise up against Muslims is similar in all. The next story the whole story of the Ram mandir. It details how different Muslim kings and their generals worked against popular Hindu sentiments, destroyed the Ram mandir and built the Babri Masjid in its place. How Hindus fought till the last drop of their blood, and how thousands of Hindus were killed by the Muslim rulers. Mughal kings such as Babar, Humayun and Aurangzeb are portrayed as the main villains. Samajwadi party leader Mulayam Singh Yadav's name has also been added to make the list more contemporary. The story ends with the message that Hindus and their religious places have suffered so much because Hindus are cowards, impotent and not united enough, unlike Muslims. I quote the central message (content is translated from Hindi):

> Lakhs of Ram devotees reached Ayodhya for kar sewa on 6th December and the symbol of Hindu humiliation, Babri Masjid, constructed on the site of Ram janma bhoomi by Babar's general, was destroyed. But due to the extreme disorganisation among Hindus and their impotence, the biggest icon of Hindu religion, Bhagwan Ram is still living in a dilapidated tent.

For the liberation of the janma bhoomi, our ancestors shed their blood like water; today some Hindus shamelessly refers to it as a 'controversial place'. Muslims who have been living with Hindus for centuries have still not forfeited their claim to the janma bhoomi. They don't want to let the temple be constructed so that Hindus continue to be insulted and can be belittled. The community which does not care for the sentiment of its own ilk thinks that Hindus should respect their sentiments. Till date no Muslim organisation has raised its voice for the liberation of the janma bhoomi, never protested nor put pressure on the government. Instead they observe 6 December as a black day. And stupid Hindus believe that the janma bhoomi matter is unsolved because of politicians and courts.

After reading this, Hindus, who don't feel ashamed, should not utter the word 'Ram' in their homes ... and tell their relatives that after their death nobody should chant 'Ram Nam' (as is customarily done in a Hindu funeral procession). The workers of Vishwa Hindu Parishad one day will surely construct the temple after liberating the Ram janma bhoomi. We will establish Ram Rajya after making India indestructible and for this we are ready to sacrifice everything.

This ideological industry, invariably projects Hindus as victims and Muslims as aggressors. It is also repeatedly said that the entire official system is *only* for Muslims and it favours *only* Muslims and finally a day will come when Hindus will be reduced to a minority in their own land and Muslims will rule over them. Read the content below and see how smartly it is woven into a courtroom drama (translated from Hindi):

The judges of the supreme court were shocked to hear sharp questions from actor Anupam Kher. Since 11 May, a five-judge bench was sitting to hear the Triple Talaq matter ...! On the first day of hearing, the court said—'If the triple Talaq matter is related to Islam ... then we won't intervene ...'

Bollywood actor Anupam Kher said bitterly, 'It's okay, My lord, if you don't want to intervene in matters of religion—but in issues like jalikattu, dahi handi, cow slaughter and Ram mandir, which are related to the Hindu religion, you intervene unhesitatingly ...! Don't you think Hindu religion is a religion? Or are you scared of Muslim threats? If you accept Triple Talaq because it is written in the Quran then why don't you accept that Ram was born in Ayodhya, which is written in the Puran? Please tell us, as not only I, but the whole country wants to know! Should it be left to their discretion whether they want to eat beef or not? But they won't eat pork ... because it is against their religion? To not allow women's entry in Shani Shignapur is considered to be an atrocity against women, but to permit or not to permit women's entry in Haji Ali Dargah is the internal matter of their religion? The veil is a social evil but the burqa is part of their religion? Jallikattu indulges in cruelty against animals but the sacrifice of goats on Bakr Eid is related to the dignity of Islam? Dahi-handi is a dangerous game but in the memory of Imam Hussain, the use of swords is a matter of religion? Offering milk to Shiv ji is wastage but offering a chaadar in a mazaar is fulfilling a wish?

'Hum do, humare do, (We are two, we have two),' is family planning … But like worms, they keep producing kids and that is the will of Allah? Saying, India will disintegrate into a thousand parts, is freedom of expression … and not sedition … but saying Vande Mataram, causes danger to Islam? Those who throw stones at soldiers are misguided youth, but in acting in defence, if soldiers take action then they become enemies of human rights? The blast at a dargah leads to the coinage of the term Hindu Terrorism, and those who explode bombs daily have no religion? Look what the dalal media and secular judges have done to our country …. If inequality has to be removed from society, then a sense of equality has to be observed …

The inference is simple for a regular Hindu who is busy with his daily life: that even courts are not neutral and discriminate against Hindus. These stories are mostly in Hindi and their ideal target is the gullible Hindu who has not read history or followed politics too far, or too long. Such content appears as a well-researched piece on a social-media page or in a WhatsApp group message in the form of a website link, and it looks credible. For common folk, mostly reading these articles on their phone, in between other tasks, it is difficult to differentiate between news articles and genuine reports and concocted propaganda pieces. The constant bombardment of such material is hypnotic. Before the person realises, these narratives start to stack up inside their mind. The audience is brainwashed and subconsciously becomes a member of the ideological group. Adolf Hitler, the dictator of Germany, was a master of this tactic. He is probably the best exponent of this art. He said, 'Its (propaganda's) chief function is to convince the masses, whose slowness of understanding needs to be given time in order that they may absorb information; and only constant repetition will finally succeed in imprinting an idea on the memory of the crowd.'[3]

THE POINT OF PROPAGANDA

Hitler started as an ordinary corporal in the army but rose to become the chief of the National Socialist German Workers' Party. By 1933, he had become the chancellor of Germany and the rest is history. Other than his ruthlessness, his genius lay in creating effective propaganda and making dramatic speeches. He used to say, 'It [propaganda] must appeal to the feeling of the public rather than to their reasoning powers.'[4]

The success of propaganda lies in its simplicity. It should avoid being too cerebral. It should also not address too many issues or themes. The matter which has to be impressed upon the minds of the people may be addressed in many forms but the message should always be the same. Hitler writes, 'Every change that is made in the subject of a propagandist message must always emphasise the same conclusion. The leading slogan must of course be illustrated in many ways and from several angles but in the end one must always return to the assertion of the same formula.'[5] Hitler certainly seems to have inspired the Hindutva content producers. They harp on only one theme and that is Hindus are victims in their own country and Muslims are internal enemies—which is very similar to what National Socialist German Workers' Party used to say about Germans being the victims of the conspiracies of Jews.

In the Indian context, the Jews have been replaced by Muslims. The Hindu fanatic is so emboldened that he will imagine conspiracies against Hindus and go to any extent to target Muslims. A classic example is the Facebook page that used to go by the name of Hindutva Varta. In February 2018, this page released a list of 102 inter-faith couples—Hindu women who were involved in a relationship with Muslim men—with the message, 'This is a list of Facebook profiles of those Hindu girls who are either victims of love jihad or in the process of becoming one. Every Hindu lion is requested to track and hunt such boys.'[6] This was an open instigation to violence and the security of such couples was terribly compromised. But this was not the first instance. In the month of November 2017, the same list was published by the Facebook page called Justice for Hindus. The page wrote, 'Hindu girls are converting to Islam because of love jihad. Wake up Hindus otherwise you will lose your homeland, India. Here is a long list of love jihadis with their Facebook ID link.'[7] This page did not overtly incite Hindus to violence but the message was similar: Hindu women were being trapped by Muslim men for ulterior motives and it was up to Hindu men to save them.

Firstly, in a democratic society, who are these strangers to tell grown women and men with whom they should have a relationship? If any woman or her family members sensed trouble of any kind, they would have gone to the law-enforcing agencies. In these cases, there were no such complaints. These Facebook pages have no business interfering in private matters. Secondly, who gave them the permission to disclose the identities of the couples? The disclosure exposed these couples to life-threatening danger. This was a criminal act. Law-enforcing agencies should have taken strict actions against the groups but they ignored it.

Such self-styled Hindutva groups have mushroomed around us since 2014—in digital spaces and also in physical spaces. Countering 'love jihad' is an old campaign of the RSS–BJP. They have been talking about this issue for many years. The chief minister of UP, Yogi Adityanath, tried to make love jihad a focus of his campaign during the by-election for eleven assembly seats in UP, in 2015. Yogi Adityanath was then an MP. He was made chief of the state campaign committee of the BJP.

On social media, the owners of such pages are mostly anonymous. So are the content producers for the WhatsApp groups and other media platforms that spread hateful messages. Nobody knows them, what they look like or what they do in their real lives. Mobile numbers or random pictures are their 'identities'. However, content produced by them travels from one individual to another and from one group to another, reaching millions of people. At the same time, there are senior leaders of the RSS–BJP and other self-professed Hindutva warriors who do not shy away from harping on the same theme openly in public spaces, with their identities proudly signposted. They brazenly produce anti-Muslim content for social media. For every crisis, they blame Muslims and exhort Hindus to seek revenge. There is one gentleman named Prashant P. Umrao. He is very active on Twitter. He is a practising lawyer based in Delhi. He rose to all-India fame after twenty AAP MLAs were disqualified by the Central Election Commission based on his petition, although later all the MLAs were reinstated by the Delhi high court. The matter is still being heard by the Election Commission.

When the Utkal Express met with an accident near Muzaffarnagar, UP, in August 2017, the railways were still investigating the accident when Umrao prematurely jumped to the conclusion that the derailment was a terrorist attack. He tweeted on 19 August 2017, 'Prayers for families who lost their loved ones & injured in #Muzaffarnagar Train accident. Terrorist ploy, Clips of rail-road were removed.'[8] The next day he wrote again, 'It could be an act of terrorism to kill Hindu pilgrims traveling to Haridwar from Puri, Kanpur & Muzaffarnagar accidents similar. Rail Jihad?'[9] Umrao does not use the word 'Muslim', but he is hinting at it with 'Rail Jihad'. It is common knowledge that jihad is related to Islam and in contemporary times used for Islamic terrorism. Here again, Hindus are presented as victims and Muslims are the perpetrators. This man has a history of writing venomous tweets against Muslims. Before Modi became the prime minster, Umrao had written, as reproduced by the Alt News website:[10]

एक एक मियाँ को काटना है। हर मस्जिद तोड़नी है।। बेटा अखिलेश रोक सको तो रोक लो। देशभर के हिंदू वीरों से अनुरोध है चलो मुज़फ़्फ़रनगर।
(Every Muslim has to be butchered. Every mosque has to be demolished, Akhilesh, son, stop us if you can. Hindu warriors, you are requested to go to Muzaffarnagar.)[11]

मुसलमान आधुनिक हथियारों से हिंदुओं का क़त्लेआम कर रहे हैं और सरकार पुलिस उनको रोकने की जगह हिंदुओं को ही दमन कर रही है।
(With modern weapons, Muslims are killing Hindus and, instead of stopping them, the government and the police, are suppressing Hindus)[12]

इमरान मसूद तुम शुरू करोगे और हम ख़त्म करेंगे गोधरा की तरह।फिर चिल्लाते रहना 10 सालों तक गुजरात की तरह।मुज़फ़्फ़रनगर याद है न?
(Imran Masood, you will begin the game but we will end it like Godhra. Then, as in the case of Gujarat, you can cry for ten years. You do remember Muzaffarnagar, don't you?)[13]

Imran Masood is a local politician in western UP. The Godhra and Gujarat riots happened in 2002, killing more than a thousand Muslim citizens. It is alleged that these riots were engineered by Hindutva zealots. Modi was the chief minister of Gujarat at the time. As discussed earlier, Modi's role was investigated by the Special Investigation Team (SIT) appointed by the supreme court. In 2012, based on the SIT report, the lower court gave Modi a clean chit. Zakia Jafri whose husband Ehsan Jafri and 68 others were killed in the Gulbarg Society massacre during the Gujarat riots, 2002, was the original petitioner in this case, challenging the order in the Gujarat high court. The

Gujarat high court upheld the lower court's verdict in October 2017. Zakia Jafri further challenged the high court's clean chit to Modi in the supreme court which has agreed to hear the matter. The tweets mentioned by Umrao are dangerous. The first and third are threatening in nature, while the second tweet again uses the leitmotif of Hindus being victims in their own land.

Anant Kumar Hegde is a member of parliament from Uttara Kannada, Karnataka, and the minister of state for skill development and entrepreneurship at the Centre. It is fascinating to read his tweets:

> Enough is enough, as the world braces to hold #Islam in its horn! Thanks to @realDonaldTrump @PutinRF_Eng & of course @narendramodiji![14]

and

> It is time for #Muslims to decide having either #Peace or rake upon #Moghul ancestry against #Hindu unity towards #newindia #Ayodhya[15]

In a press conference, he said, 'Till the time Islam exists in the world, no one can stop terrorism. If we want to keep a place like Bhatkal peaceful, then we should throw Islam away from this world and we should shut Islam.'[16] It might have shocked some people that Hegde, who used to spit so much venom against a minority community has been made a minister at the centre, but for those who are aware of the nature of the regime, it is not surprising at all.

Hegde is not alone. Senior BJP leader and governor of Tripura, Tathagata Roy, despite holding a constitutional post, is never too bashful to display his anti-Muslim side. On 2 October 2017, he tweeted, 'Multiculturalism in Europe is like "Secularism" in India. It means Muslims will stick to their beliefs and customs. Others will adjust.'[17]

ADMIRED BY THE PRIME MINISTER

There are many who flaunt their jaundiced views on Islam on social media. But what is more horrifying is that the prime minister of the country follows them. Hindutva warriors on social media openly brag that they are followed by the prime minister, with pictures of their meetings splashed on their timelines. Most individuals are not well known or recognisable and have minuscule followings. Alt News published a comprehensive report on this on 7 September 2017: 'As of date Mr Modi has 33.8 million followers and he follows 1779 people. Of the ones he follows, many are government handles, ministers, Heads of States, senior journalists and other such profiles you would expect the Prime Minister of a country to follow. However, a handful of the 1779 are profiles that will make you squirm. Serial abusers, rumor-mongers, misogynists, handles brimming with communal venom ... you will find them all there.'[18] The report goes on to detail specific tweets from such persons:

> @Sinvin43 @BDUTT BarkhaDutt has been a superior prostitute, slept with each n every powerful of India. I have tagged her, for she cant refute[sic].
>
> @RanaAyyub had a great time sleeping with SIT sponsored by @TeestaSetalvad @CedricPrakash just to ensure Blasphemy #RANDI #PappuMeows. Pls[sic] RT
>
> 1 cong leader demands 2 know Modijis CLIENTS when he sold tea. Can he ask a similar question of Soniaji? CLIENTS may be impolite but ...... [sic]
>
> Comparing @RSSorg with that bastard Hamid Ansari? Well only a traitor can do so!
>
> @ArvindKejriwal तेरी माँ की चूत, तू दिल्ली के बहार की नेतागीरी समझेगा भी नहीं, गांड में भरले विधायक को @abpnewshindi @AmitShah @asadowaisi
> (ArvindKejriwal, you motherfucker, you won't understand the politics of places outside Delhi. Shove MLAs in your asshole.)
>
> @tweetfromRaghu TU RESPECT KAREGA BEHNCHO AUKAAD KYA HAI TERI TU RESPECT KAREGA MADAR****
> (You will respect [women], you sisterfucker; you have no guts; you will respect, motherfucker?)
>
> #GodhraAgain The only solution to this problem is to kick out the Muslims to Pakistan
>
> #GodhraAgain #FilthyIslam showing its colors. Kill atleast [sic] 3000 Muslims tomorrow!
>
> हिंदुओं को यदि UP को कश्मीर बनने से रोकना है तो एक बार उसे गुजरात बनाना ही होगा।
> (If Hindus want to stop UP from becoming Kashmir, then it has to be made in to Gujarat once.)

Before expecting Modi to do some James Bondish act, can you pls start boycotting Bangl/Muslim Maids, rickshaw, auto, Kabadiwala, Barber etc?

While the people behind these handles all claim to be proud Hindus and ardent nationalists, the lack of morals in their tweets is notable. They abuse journalists, call Sonia Gandhi names, address Vice President Hamid Ansari in the most disgusting language, use even more unparliamentary language for Delhi Chief Minister Arvind Kejriwal, openly call for the boycott and killing of Muslims and issue threats of repeating the Gujarat riots to teach Muslims a lessons. These are not the kind of persons who should be followed by anyone with allegiance to the constitution of India, but the prime minister does so.

A raging controversy erupted after the murder of Karnataka-based journalist Gauri Lankesh. She was killed by Hindu fanatics who were tutored to believe that the Hindu religion was in danger and she had to be eliminated to save the Hindu dharma. A person called Nikhil Dadhich tweeted (in Hindi), 'One bitch dies a dog's death all the puppies cry in the same tune.'[19] He claimed to be a nationalist. The media discussed the issue and suggested that the prime minister should unfollow such a person, now that it had been brought to his attention; the PM unfortunately did not oblige. The BJP did react, saying that 'he followed Indian opposition leaders, that just because he followed certain people did not mean he agreed with them, and that he had more pressing matters than arguing over whom he followed on Twitter and why.'[20]

The prime minister also follows those who celebrate the killing of Mahatma Gandhi. For such individuals, the killer of Gandhi, Nathuram Godse, is a hero and they believe he did the right thing by assassinating Gandhi. Alt News has reproduced many offensive tweets eulogising Godse and condemning Gandhi. It cites some in a 2 October 2017 article: '"Godse was God sent", "Gandhi should have been hanged", "Godse had valid reasons to shoot Gandhi", "I repeat I am a big Godse fan, so what?" What do the people who posted these tweets have in common? Yes, they all are followed by the honorable Prime Minister of India, Mr. Narendra Modi.'[21] Meanwhile, the prime minister tweeted, 'I bow to beloved Bapu on Gandhi Jayanti. His noble ideals motivate millions across the world.'[22]

Within his own party, the head of the BJP's national IT cell Amit Malviya seemed to justify the use of violence against Gandhi. In response to a tweet with a picture emblazoned 'Why I Killed Gandhi', he wrote, 'Nathuram Godse had his reasons to assassinate M.K. Gandhi. A fair society must hear him out too.' When he was confronted by another Twitter user who said there was no reason that justified assassinating anyone, he responded, 'Actually there have been instances where killings have been deemed to be acceptable … look up case laws …'[23] These tweets were posted on 5 January 2015. By this logic, Pakistani terrorist Ajmal Amir Kasab, who created mayhem on 26/11 in Mumbai, might also have had reasons to do what he and his friends did, but Malviya would certainly not apply this logic to him. Will the BJP and other Hindutva groups accept this position vis-à-vis Pakistani terrorists? I know they will not.

The Hindutva warriors have always hated Gandhi and blamed him for the division of India and the creation of Pakistan. There was a time when Gandhi was not accepted as the Father of the Nation by the RSS–BJP leaders. In fact, Kalyan Singh, the blue-eyed boy of the Ram mandir movement, had gone to the extent of saying in the mid-1990s, that Gandhi could not be the father of the nation and could only be called a great son of India.[24] The name of the RSS had figured prominently in the assassination of Gandhi. The RSS was banned and its second chief, M.S. Golwalkar, was arrested, though he was released later and given a clean chit; yet the suspicions have persisted. In contemporary times, it is difficult to openly condemn Gandhi; but social-media platforms are full of filth spread by fanatical Hindus to malign Gandhi and his legacy. On 27 July 2018, a long poem popped up on my WhatsApp timeline. I am just reproducing four lines:

गांधीज़ी की पाकपरस्ती पर, जब भारत लाचार हुआ
तब जाकर नाथू, बापू वध को मजबूर हुआ।
अगर गोडसे की गोली, उतरी ना होती सीने में,
तो हर हिंदू पढ़ता नमाज़, फिर मक्का और मदीने में।

(When due to Gandhi's favouritism of Pakistan, India became helpless, that's when Nathuram was forced to kill Bapu. If Godse's bullet had not pierced his chest, then every Hindu would have been offering namaz in Mecca and Medina.)

Gandhi was what I would call a good Hindu. He was not a fanatic. He did not aspire to create a Hindu Rashtra; he aspired to create Ramrajya (the kingdom of Ram), which had space for everyone, where every religion was respected and compassion was the underlying thread. Hatred had no place there. Gandhi used to say that 'India's good lay in the unity of heart between Hindus and Muslims ... Three fourth of India can never enjoy freedom if they remain hostile to the remaining one fourth.'[25] However, the proponents of the Hindu Rashtra thrive only on hate. Gandhi was killed not because he was pro-Pakistan; he was killed because he was the biggest obstacle in the path of creating a Hindu Rashtra. He was killed because he did not preach hatred against any religion. He preached love and affection. He preached that to become a devout Hindu, one does not need to hate Islam, kill Muslims, engineer riots, spread lies and assassinate characters or slut-shame Indian women who don't subscribe to one's specific brand of nationalism. It is shameful to see how women journalists of our times like Sagarika Ghose, Barkha Dutt, Rana Ayyub and Swati Chaturvedi, are abused, threatened, intimidated and slut-shamed publicly by those who claim to be true Hindus and Indians.

ARRAIGNING THE FOURTH ESTATE

Rana Ayyub's story is particularly frightening. She is an independent journalist who has written a book about the alleged complicity of Narendra Modi and Amit Shah in the Gujarat riots of 2002. As an undercover reporter, she investigated the case for eight months. She has been openly critical of the Modi regime and the RSS–BJP. But the way she was allegedly treated by the so-called Hindutva brigade is shocking. She wrote in her column in the *New York Times*:

> On April 22, I was alarmed to find a quotation supporting child rapists falsely attributed to me and going viral on Twitter. A parody account of Republic TV, India's leading right-wing television network, had posted the quotation.
>
> I received numerous messages shaming me for supporting child rapists. A Facebook page called Yogi Adityanath Ki Sena, or the Army of Yogi Adityanath, translated the tweet into Hindi and circulated it on social media ....

I tweeted a clarification about the falsehood to no avail: My social media accounts and my phone were inundated with WhatsApp messages urging others to gang-rape me. Various leaders of Mr. Modi's party, who promoted the lie, refused to delete their tweets despite my pointing it out.

The following day, on April 23, another tweet was generated using Photoshop and attributed to me. 'I hate India and Indians,' it said. The online mob asked me to pack my bags and leave for Pakistan, some threatened to tear my clothes ...

In the evening, an activist from the Rashtriya Swayamsevak Sangh, the Hindu nationalist mother ship alerted me to a scurrilous pornographic video being shared on various WhatsApp groups. He had received it from a group with many Bharatiya Janata Party members: a two-minute, 20-second pornographic video of a sex act with my face morphed onto another woman....

A minute later, he shared the video with me ... I saw the first two frames and froze. I wanted to vomit and fought tears ...

Minutes later, my social media timelines and notifications were filled with screenshots of the video. Some commented on how prostitution was my forte. I went into a frenzy blocking them, but they were everywhere, on my Instagram, Facebook and Twitter accounts. Some commenters asked what I charged for sex, others described my body. Many claiming to be nationalist Hindus sent pictures of themselves naked.

I started getting screenshots from friends of a Twitter account created in my name. I was doxxed. A tweet with my name, picture, phone number and address was being circulated. 'I am available,' it said. Someone sent my father a screenshot of the video. He was silent on the phone while I cried. After a while he spoke in a sad, heavy voice. 'I am surprised this did not happen earlier,' he said. 'They want to break you. The choice is yours.' ...

Most of the Twitter handles and Facebook accounts that posted the pornographic video and screenshots identify themselves as fans of Mr. Modi and his party, and argue for turning India into a 'Hindu rashtra' ...

That night the administrator of a Facebook page called Varah Sena wrote, 'See, Rana, what we spread about you; this is what happens when you write lies about Modi and Hindus in India.' ... (The page was deleted after I filed the police complaint.)[26]

Till now, it has not been ascertained who was responsible for slut-shaming Ayyub in such a brazen manner. As somebody who has spent more than two decades in journalism, I can say with some authority that this is a new phenomenon in Indian journalism. The job of a journalist is always dangerous if one happens to be fiercely independent and regularly does stories that catch powerful people on the wrong foot. Pressure is always put on the management and editor to either tone down the story or withdraw it. It happens under every government. Governments by nature have less patience with the free press than is ideal, but the vicious, venomous atmosphere which has unfolded around the media since the beginning of 2013 (when it became apparent that Modi would be the prime ministerial candidate for the BJP and that the BJP would form the government) was hitherto unheard of.

With time, the attacks on those who have been critical of the present regime have increased manifold. Gauri Lankesh's murder shocked the entire nation. Every Left-liberal journalist felt numb. Her murderers have been caught and now it is apparent that she was eliminated as her writing and words were seen by the ultra right-wing as a threat to the Hindu religion. But the matter did not end there. Her murder was used as a tool to terrorise others. After her death, at least four police complaints were filed by journalists saying they had received death threats on social-media platforms. A reporter working for the website the Quint received a message on WhatsApp on 16 September 2017. It was written in Hindi, and said:

> Why was Gauri Lankesh killed?
> Gauri Lankesh was a journalist. She was killed in Bangalore by some Hindutva group. The question that arises is why would any Hindutva element kill a Hindu person.
> Because Gauri used to write against the Modi government. Gauri used to write against RSS and BJP. Gauri was a traitor. She was anti-nationalist and anti-Hindu.
> Now, if anyone in this country dares to write anything against Modiji, RSS or BJP, that person will not be spared. The existence of such persons shall be removed along with the Muslims[27]

Debobrat Ghose, who works with Firstpost; Abhay Kumar from *Asian News International* and Mohammad Ali from the *Hindu* were also threatened multiple times on the phone.

Senior journalists like Rajdeep Sardesai and Ravish Kumar are regularly trolled. Kumar has been bombarded with phone calls and messages issuing death threats for months. His family members have also been targeted. The reason was again the circulation of a fake quote attributed to him, where he supposedly supported the rapists of an 11-year-old girl in a madrasa in Delhi. One Abhishek Tiwari, who claimed to head the Bajrang Dal's student unit in Jaunpur district of UP, sent a video saying, 'I WARN RAVISH IF YOU DEFAME SANATAN DHARM, I WILL KILL YOU. I will chase you to Pakistan and kill you. This is a warning from Bajrang Dal.'[28] Ravish said that he had been getting such threats since April 2018. Despite police complaints, nothing seemed to deter the perpetrators.

VENDETTA AS A POLITICAL TOOL

Even Sushma Swaraj of the BJP was not spared the misogynistic attacks. She is the Minister of External Affairs of the country. She was badly trolled because her ministry had granted a passport to an interfaith couple in Lucknow. The husband was Muslim and the wife a Hindu. When the couple applied for a passport, a passport officer had taunted the man, saying he should convert to Hinduism, while berating the woman for marrying a Muslim. When this incident was reported in the media, the concerned officer was transferred. The Hindutva brigade was enraged. They targeted Swaraj by calling her names. Surprisingly, none of the other BJP leaders came to her defence. Her husband Swaraj Kaushal, a former governor of Mizoram, was the only one who stood by her. When the BJP was severely criticised for its silence, Central ministers Rajnath Singh and Nitin Gadkari finally spoke up in her favour—after a week. If even a powerful leader like Sushma Swaraj is so vulnerable, then imagine the fate of private citizens and journalists!

Are such abuses and threats a basic attribute of the very nature of social media, or are informal campaigns like these designed and orchestrated by someone behind the scenes? One may also ask why so much hate and bitterness is directed against one particular community—Muslims. Is the liberal space shrinking in India with the spread of the right-wing ideology or has the open space always been a myth? The social-media platforms have undoubtedly opened up a Pandora's box that has democratised social intercourse, especially for those who could have never imagined interacting with the rich and the powerful, celebrities and legends, on equal terms. In that, these platforms are truly egalitarian. They allow the marginalised to wander into a new, more connected reality that renders them more visible/

audible, more powerful. They help the disadvantaged feel equally important as the privileged, engaging with them on an equal footing—an unprecedented journey. Since these are new media, they are still evolving. They will take time to settle down, frame their own codes of conduct and define their own rules. Till then, it is intoxicating and overpowering, even chaotic, something that is being exploited by the smart operators.

I refuse to believe that the hate being spewed on social media is an organic construct. It is artificially designed for a purpose. Modi's success lies in his capacity to create an atmosphere of hostility in which he is the slandered and vilified martyr. I don't know if he has read *Mein Kampf* but he seems to have assimilated what Hitler used to say to his followers: 'They must not be afraid of the hostility which their adversaries manifest towards them but they must take it as a necessary condition on which their own right to existence is based.'[29] Modi has been true to every word. He is the one politician within the Hindutva fold (or indeed, anywhere in India) who has been discussed, debated and derided in equal measure. He is both loved and hated, but never ignored—from his first day in office as chief minister to this very day. When he started his campaign as a prime ministerial candidate, he was the centre of political gravity. The whole election seemed to revolve around him. He alone was discussed. He was the hero and he was the villain, and he played both the roles with aplomb. He never minced his words. He used language which had never been used before in Indian political discourse. Abuses and threats were his adrenaline. Even after becoming the prime minister, he did not change.

Modi's one-time counterpart, Barack Obama is a refined and suave person. He was considered an intellectual president. However, the same epithet could not be applied to his election campaign in 2012. He was the first presidential candidate who realised the potential of social media as an instrument of myth-making and aura building. His social-media team created content which was bitter and vitriolic. It had only one goal: to not let Obama's competitors stand a chance. Mitt Romney was the Republican Party candidate. Obama's campaign was so hateful that his wife Ann Romney said, 'It makes you recognise that they are going to do everything they can to destroy Mitt.' She told CBS news, 'I feel like all he's doing is saying, let's kill this guy.' I was told by a member of Modi's campaign team that they followed the example of Obama's campaign.[30]

In the Indian elections of 2014, Rahul Gandhi was Modi's competitor. Modi's campaign team made mincemeat out of Gandhi. He became a caricature. He was projected as a Pappu, someone who had no merit, had no qualification except his dynasty and who would be a disaster as prime minister. The whole campaign was very well choreographed for which social-media platforms were most wonderfully used and exploited. Senior journalist Aakar Patel wrote in his column in *Mint*, 'It is not easy, and I would suggest it is not possible, today in India to put forth a view in the public space that is critical of Modi and not be shouted down. The opposite is true for Congress and especially Rahul and Sonia Gandhi. The Congress is dynastic and arrogant. That is true …. It is difficult to say that the party does not deserve the treatment it is getting in the social media.'[31] At that time, Hiren Joshi, an RSS man and principal secretary to the chief minister of Gujarat, was leading an army of 2,000 volunteers who used to run Modi's campaign on social media.

Hiren Joshi is still with Modi. Now he is part of his core team in the Prime Minister's Office. His job is to monitor social media and traditional media content related to the prime minister, with a team of 200 paid workers, working round the clock. Therefore, it cannot be said that the prime minister is not aware of the content associated with him, which appears in the social media space. It cannot be said that he is not aware that the Twitter handles he follows are spitting venom, issuing death threats and rape threats, and slut-shaming women. If his Twitter handle still follows such creatures and no action is initiated against such accounts, then one can surmise certain reasons for it. It is clear that the very presence of the BJP government at the Centre and Modi being the prime minister have certainly emboldened the fringe elements who subscribe to the Hindutva ideology in its extreme form to be even more brazen and audacious. These elements might have multiplied rapidly since 2014, but even so, it is hard to understand how the government can be a mute spectator to the chaos and anarchy unfolding across social-media platforms—unless the idea is to look the other way.

How else can one explain why no action was taken when the BJP's national IT cell in-charge Amit Malviya circulated a picture of former prime minister Jawaharlal Nehru with his sister Vijaya Lakshmi Pandit and niece Nayantara Sahgal, and linked it with a sex CD purportedly of the young Gujarat leader

Hardik Patel? The very same Malviya circulated a mischievously edited video clip to malign the image of senior journalist Ravish Kumar. Yet he roams free. How can one explain that Anant Kumar Hegde, who is openly posting anti-Islam and anti-Christianity content on social media, is made a minister?

It was not surprising to see the support extended to Mahesh Vikram Hegde, founder of the fake news website Postcard, when he was arrested by the Karnataka police for publishing a fake report that a Jain sage was attacked by a Muslim youth.[32] Union ministers Anant Kumar Hegde and Giriraj Singh, BJP MPs Maheish Girri and Pratap Simha, Karnataka BJP spokesperson S. Prakash and the BJP general secretary of Karnataka C.T. Ravi all jumped to his defence. Union ministers like Kiren Rijiju and Piyush Goyal have been promoting and sharing articles from this website. This only suggests that the content strategy which was devised in the beginning of 2013 is still in use. The only difference is that now it is pursued with more ideological vigour. If before the 2014 elections, the targets were Rahul Gandhi and the Congress, now it is the liberal Left and those who are considered to be enemies of the ideology. If Rahul was proven a Pappu, now the aim is to unsettle, traumatise and disintegrate the spaces for liberal discourse; to malign and discredit all opponents in the eyes of the public and to force them to submit; and to create an ecosystem within which Hindutva can flourish. The idea is to minimise opposition and maximise the support base for the ideology whose ultimate aim is a Hindu Rashtra.

USING THE FOURTH ESTATE

Can this dream of the Hindu Rashtra be achieved without the active support of the mainstream media? In today's India, television channels set the agenda and weave the narrative better than newspapers. What Billy Graham had said about his religious preaching in the 1980s—'Television is the most powerful tool of communication ever devised by man. Each of my prime-time "specials" is now carried by nearly 300 stations across the U.S. and Canada, so that in a single telecast I preach to millions more than Christ did in his lifetime.'[33]—is very relevant in today's India, where more than 400 news channels are blaring news round the clock. Newspapers are still published and purchased zealously, but in terms of reach and potential to set the agenda for the country, they have certainly ceded ground to news channels. The Bofors controversy was probably the last big issue that newspapers pushed to the centre stage. When I started my career in television in the mid-1990s, it was still a toddler and we were jeered at by the newspaper reporters, calling us byte-collecting chicken-heads.

As television moved from the half-hour news capsules on Doordarshan to the 24-hour private news channels, the whole paradigm changed. By 2000, television was the medium in the driving seat and newspapers had to take a back seat in the larger public discourse. To be seen on the prime-time television screen was the cherished dream of every politician and every person of substance. Television had become the prima donna of the news business. As an anchor and editor, I was privileged to engage with the leading politicians and celebrities of the country. It was not like it is today, when many well-regarded politicians avoid appearing on prime-time debates. There was a time when top politicians, including Narendra Modi, Sushma Swaraj, Pramod Mahajan, Arun Jaitley, Yashwant Sinha, Rajnath Singh, Murli Manohar Joshi, Venkaiah Naidu, Jaswant Singh, George Fernandes, Uma Bharti, Ravi Shankar Prasad, Manohar Joshi, Shivraj Patil, P. Chidambaram, Kamal Nath, Digvijaya Singh, Pranab Mukherjee, Arjun Singh, Sheila Dikshit, Sharad Pawar, Mamata Banerjee, Nitish Kumar, Lalu Prasad Yadav, Mulayam Singh Yadav, Sitaram Yechury, Harkishen Singh Surjit, and so on, were more than willing to visit television studios and participate in debates.

The debates were a serious business then. The political actors came well-prepared. Anchoring was also not everyone's cup of tea. This continued, in a slightly diluted form, until Manmohan Singh's tenure, as senior politicians started showing a reluctance to appear on the debate shows and in fact preferred one-on-one interviews. I quit my television career in January 2014. News on television had not reduced itself to a tamasha yet. Nowadays, it is rare to see senior politicians appearing in television debates, discussing the finer points of politics and governance. Instead, parties have a panel of leaders whose key skill is to outshout opponents on the idiot box.

Three prominent trends have emerged since June 2014 in the media. One is that although India never had a tradition of right-wing television channels, there are now several that have become platforms for the propagation of right-wing Hindutva ideology. Muscular nationalism; warmongering; militarism; bashing Islam, Kashmir and Pakistan; and ridiculing and condemning liberal and secular values have become the prime-time favourites. Minor issues related to minority communities have become big talking points and through them, a stereotypical image of Muslims as communal has been established. Every issue is seen through the prism of Hindu-Muslim rivalry. Since 2014, every channel has been giving extra space to RSS activists. Now, RSS leaders are a regular feature on every television debate, whether the issue is relevant to Hindutva or not. This was not the case earlier. Not long ago, they were invited only when the subject was related to the RSS.

Secondly, overt aggression and shouting at others have become the norm. Sober discussion is a thing of the past. Dignity has only a nostalgia value and means nothing more. It's not that heated discussions did not take place earlier, but participants always avoided getting personal and being abusive. Now it is all about attracting eyeballs. The more the shouting, the more heightened the drama, the higher the ratings.

Thirdly, the media had always been watchdogs of the government. Not anymore. Now they have become coy pets of the Central government and ferocious bulldogs for the opposition. Instead of holding the government of the day accountable, they blow the opposition to pieces. Rahul Gandhi and Arvind Kejriwal are their favourite punching bags. Prime Minister Narendra Modi and BJP president Amit Shah are beyond reproach; they are the modern gods who should not be touched or questioned. Whereas earlier the prime minister and top leaders of the party were not spared. In his second stint, Manmohan Singh was hugely criticised and ridiculed as being a weak prime minister. But now one can question Modi only at the risk of losing their job.

Television media is in such a dire state that celebrated editor of yesteryears and rebel BJP leader Arun Shourie likened these channels to North Korean channels which act as mouthpieces of the government.[34] Seasoned journalist and legendary television anchor Karan Thapar wrote, 'These are not good times for the Indian media. Most people I know have formed an irrevocable impression that it's become pusillanimous. Where once newspapers and television channels boasted of challenging and exposing the government, we now flinch from doing so. Worse, when our voices are raised it's against the government's opponents and critics—particularly those who have the gall to question the Prime Minister or the Army Chief—Muslims and Kashmiris, students and Dalits, liberal academics and avant-garde authors. I admit things are worse on television but I'm not the only one to sense that print is also pulling its punches and reining itself in.'[35]

It is ironical that on the eve of the forty-second anniversary of the Emergency in 2018, the Modi government lambasted the Congress and compared Indira Gandhi to Hitler.[36] This at a time when Modi himself is being criticised for being dictatorial and shunning every space for free and critical thinking. Once, I was talking to Sharad Yadav, the seasoned leader of the erstwhile Janata Dal. He characterised the current regime as being worse than the emergency. Leaders of every shade concur with him. Even BJP leaders, MPs and senior Central ministers privately agree. Newspapers were censored during the Emergency; now, barring a few, newspapers are virtually paralysed and do not criticise the government at all.

Digital media is the only space left which has the courage to carry critical stories, expose corruption and scams, and report on the failures of the government. Even such websites are being intimidated with defamation suits. The Wire has been taken to court for publishing a story on how Amit Shah's son Jay Shah's company revenues spiked from a mere ₹50,000 to ₹80 crore in a year. This happened after the company had been running up losses for several years. A prestigious newspaper such as the *Times of India* had to mysteriously pull down a story criticising the Pradhan Mantri Fasal Bima Yojana on 14 September 2017. The Wire reported, 'A story published by the *Times of India*'s Ahmedabad edition about an apparent increase of "300%" in BJP president Amit Shah's assets over the past five years, was removed from the newspaper's website within hours of being published.'[37] While the BJP issued a statement, no explanation was ever given by the newspaper for pulling the plug on this news item.

In the past, the press has been blamed for being anti-Hindu by the right-wing activists and thinkers. I can say from my own experience that the press in India has been more or less free and independent except during the Emergency. Every media institution had its own editorial vision. If there were newspapers and TV channels that had Left-leaning people, then a Right-wing tilt was also the forte of a few. Several editors like Arun Shourie had pronounced sympathy for Hindutva and the RSS. Yet, barring very few exceptions, the treatment of news was not manipulated to suit the interest of a political faction. In his second term (2009–2014), Manmohan Singh faced an extremely hostile media. TV channels were especially scathing. They ran campaigns for days and months on the issue of corruption.

Can the same be done today? No, in fact, the opposite is true. The television news channels also played a role in Modi becoming the prime minister. They seem to have an interest in defending his government. Santosh Desai, the brand guru, writes in the context of the Nirav Modi scandal, 'A ₹11,300-crore scandal broke out last week, and leading English channels immediately scrambled to find a way to protect the government and blame the previous government in a variety of inventive ways. This tactic is hardly a surprise to anyone who has had the misfortune of watching television news regularly. Every time the government faces criticism, the debate gets framed not through the government's actions, but through what the opposition is doing wrong. Even the polls being run are absurdly one-sided. For example, a recent poll by an English news channel in the wake of the Nirav Modi scandal was phrased thus—"Do you support the unsparing nationwide crackdown by the Modi government on bank loot and corruption?"'[38]

There is no doubt that the conduct of some TV channels and their editors and anchors is anything but professional of late. Vishwa Deepak used to work for Zee News. He had worked with prestigious news organisations such as AajTak, the BBC and Deutsche Welle (Germany). He resigned from Zee News after their coverage of the infamous JNU episode around Kanhaiya Kumar. His resignation letter is a moving account of the malaise which has afflicted the fourth estate in India. It is a long letter but I am reproducing a small part of it:

> After May 2014, when Narendra Modi has become the PM, almost every newsroom of the country has been communalized, but here, situations are even more catastrophic. I apologise for using such a heavy word. But I have no other word except this. Why is it that all news is written by adding a 'Modi angle'? Stories are written keeping in mind how it will benefit the agenda of the Modi government. We have seriously started doubting that we are journalists. It feels like we are the spokespersons of the government, or that we are supari killers. Modi is the PM of our country, and is my PM too. But being a journalist, it is difficult to accept so much Modi devotion. My conscience is starting to rebel against me, it seems like I am sick. Behind every story there is an agenda; behind every show there is an effort to call

the Modi government 'great'. Wanting to attack the opposition in every argument. No word other than attack or war is acceptable ....

I can't sleep well these days. I am anxious. Perhaps this is the result of a feeling of guilt. The biggest blot that an individual can have on him is that he is anti-national. However, the question is as journalists, do we have the right to distribute the degree of anti-national? Isn't it the job of the court?

We have tagged many students of JNU as 'anti-national' including Kanhaiya. If among them one gets killed tomorrow, who will take the responsibility? We have not only created an atmosphere for someone's murder and the destruction of a few families but also created a platform to spread riots and cause a civil war. What kind of patriotism is this? What kind of journalism is this?

Are we the BJP or RSS's mouthpieces, for us to do whatever they do? A video which did not even have the slogan of 'Pakistan zindabad' was still aired continuously. How did we blindly believe that these voices which came in the dark were of Kanhaiya or his friends? Instead of 'Bhartiya Court zindabad', they heard Pakistan zindabad and spoilt some people's career, hopes and led their families to destruction.[39]

Umar Khalid, the JNU student who was blamed and jailed along with Kanhaiya Kumar for allegedly raising anti-India and pro-Kashmir slogans on the campus, was attacked with a gun in front of the Constitution Club, hardly a kilometre away from the parliament, on 13 August 2018. This when security was on the highest alert for Independence Day in Delhi, especially in that area. Khalid was pinned down by an assailant who tried to shoot him, but the gun did not fire. His friends pushed the man away. Khalid ran inside to save his life. It was a narrow escape. Later, he blamed the television channels for putting his life at risk by portraying him as an anti-national person. Khalid said, 'It is very difficult for me to say who could be behind the attack, but I want to say one thing—a misinformation campaign has been spread against me in the last two years. Baseless things have been said about me to such an extent in the media, that people have started believing that people like me should be killed.'[40] This incident also hints at the kind of journalism that is pursued by the television channels and anchors who are in a great hurry to pronounce anyone 'anti-national' and a 'traitor' in the court of public opinion, out of their ideological blindness. Had Umar Khalid been killed that day, whose fault would it have been? Who would be to blame?

Two months before this incident, Khalid had approached the Delhi Police with a request for security as he feared a threat to his life. The security was never provided. He also questioned the Delhi Police as to why it had not filed a charge sheet against him (for supposedly raising anti-India slogans) in the last two-and-a-half years, when it was mandatory to file one within ninety days of taking a person into custody. He claimed that he was innocent and that the police had no evidence to prove his guilt. Ironically when the Delhi Police did file the charge sheet in the Patiala House Court, on 14 January 2019, implicating Umar Khalid and Kanhaiya Kumar, it did not take the prior approval of the Delhi government led by Arvind Kejriwal, as was required by law. The court was livid and refused to take cognisance of the sedition case. It said, 'In a charge sheet with such serious allegations, the prosecution has not bothered to file the requisite sanction and as such the charge sheet at this stage is not complete.'[41]

Gauhar Raza, a reputed scientist and well-known Urdu poet and documentary filmmaker was declared an anti-national by Zee News.[42] He recited a poem that was highly critical of the Modi regime, and dedicated it to Kanhaiya Kumar and Rohith Vemula, at the prestigious Shankar-Shad Mushaira. The channel declared it the 'Afzal Premi Gang ka Mushaira'.[43] In one stroke, an institution which had worked as a cultural bridge between India and Pakistan was pulled down, rubbished, declared anti-national and condemned. Indeed, Raza's poem had hinted that blind nationalism which was being pursued around the country would lead to violence and bloodshed. He had said that the country was heading towards becoming Hitler's Nazi Germany: 'German Gas kado se ab tak khoon ki badboo aati hai/andhi watan parasti ham ko us raste le jayegi' (German gas chambers still smell of blood/Blind nationalism will take the country on that path).[44] He goes on: 'Yeh mat bhoolo agli naslen jalta shola hoti hain/ aag kuredoge chingari daman tak to ayegi' (Forget not, the next generation is like a burning ember/If a spark is ignited, fire will burn us all). Adherents of Hindutva might find his poem offensive and distasteful. Yet to call it anti-national and declare Raza a friend of the terrorist Afzal Guru, who was hanged for the attack on parliament, is definitely not journalism. The recitation took place at the fifty-first mushaira. However, due to this controversy, Pakistani poets did not come next year in 2017. Raza complained to the self-regulatory body for news channels, the News Broadcasting Standards Authority (NBSA), which found Zee News guilty, fined it and asked the channel to apologise, which it never did. An institution was killed, meanwhile.

I have no dispute with television as a medium, though it is by nature shrill and absurd. Neil Postman is right when he says, '[T]elevision's conversation promotes incoherence and triviality; that the phrase serious television is a contradiction in terms.'[45] Television does not just produce news; it creates shows, and shows have to be entertaining. To keep the show entertaining, it is imperative to create talking points and generate controversies (even where there are none), but to manufacture news and relentlessly attack only one shade of opinion is not doing justice to the medium. I can understand that in an opinionated climate, it is difficult to be neutral. We have been taught that the slant given to a story or putting a spin on a report involves the art of reading between the lines as well as the hard work of digging out the truth and facing reality. Ideological biases do creep into news presentation but if bias entirely dictates the news, then there is something very wrong with the institution.

HASHTAG HEROISM

In today's world, where Twitter and television have merged to create a bigger impact on the audience, the hashtags used on different TV channels (especially the English ones) offer a curious case study and confirm the concerns raised by Karan Thapar and Santosh Desai. Alt News carried out an interesting exercise of assessing the hashtags used on television during the Gujarat assembly elections. It arrived at the conclusion that NDTV, India Today and CNN News 18 remained more or less neutral in promoting hashtags on their channels but two frontline channels, Times Now and Republic TV, were brazenly anti-Congress and pro-BJP or pro-Modi. Their themes for the hashtags were: attack the Congress, portray the Congress as anti-India, ridicule Rahul Gandhi, attack leaders who have collaborated with the Congress, play the religion card, build up the image of the BJP and Modi, and focus on everything but development. What is most dangerous of these is the deliberate projection of the Congress party as anti-India: 'Rahul Gandhi's jibe on Gujarat model and ease of doing business ratings was reported by Republic TV with the hashtag *#CongSlamsIndiaRise*. One day after the elections were announced,

Republic TV ran the hashtag *#PakHawalaUnderCongress*. Rahul Gandhi's remark saying PM Modi's Gujarat model has failed was debated on Times Now as *#RahulVsIndiaRising*. The unsubstantiated and unverified claim of PM Modi about Pakistan hand in Gujarat elections was reported by *Republic TV* with the hashtag *#PakCongMeeting ... Times Now* was not far behind by digging out a 2013 photograph of Former Finance Minister P. Chidambaram in the same room as Taliban leader Mullah Abdul Zaeef ... with the hashtag *#CongTalibanTango*.'[46] Comparisons between the hashtags used for Rahul and Modi establish the contrast more starkly. Hashtags such as #PappuCensored, #PappuBanaYuvraj, #RahulMughalEmperor, #RahulHinduOrCatholic, #RahulDucks #UPAneDeshBecha, #RahulNeechPolitics were used for Gandhi whereas the hashtags for Modi—#SoldChaiNotNation, #ModiSweepsGujarat, #PMTakesOff, #BJPGujaratBlitzkrieg, #ModiMillionRally, #ModiMalignedIn2017—are self-explanatory.

Another trend, which is pulling down the standard of journalism in this country, is the treatment of Kashmir stories on so-called nationalist television channels. Only one kind of narrative is being run. For such channels, Kashmir is no longer a complex issue. It is simple and straightforward. These channels are openly anti-Kashmir. Local Kashmiris and Kashmiri leaders are anti-nationals and traitors. This line of editorialising has caused deep anger and polarisation in the Valley and outside. Shujat Bukhari, a respected senior journalist based in Srinagar and editor of the daily, *Rising Kashmir*, who was later assassinated had said this about TV channels, 'TV channels became part of a so-called nationalistic agenda ... they have become the drum beaters of a state narrative aimed at criminalising and demonising Kashmiris. They have played a major role in increasing anger in Kashmir.'[47] In fact, the situation became so bad that Dineshwar Sharma, the special representative appointed by the Centre, had to request the home ministry to rein in such channels. 'He [Sharma] has reportedly asked Union Home Minister Rajnath Singh to convene a meeting with certain channels and warn them against spreading "vicious propaganda" on Kashmiris. Four channels are believed to have been singled out for regularly airing exaggerated stories about the Valley, undermining the fragile dialogue initiated by the Centre.'[48]

As a former editor, it is disheartening to hear in the press circles that no editor can survive if they get too adventurous and cross the line drawn by the government. It is discussed in hushed tones that erstwhile editor of the

Hindustan Times, Bobby Ghosh, had to leave because he was running a 'hate-tracker' of killings in the name of religion. It is also said that Siddharth Varadarajan, the founding editor of the Wire, was asked to leave by the board of directors of the *Hindu* for giving disproportionate coverage to anti-Modi articles as an editor, much before the BJP formed the government at the Centre.

Two senior editors—Milind Khandekar and Punya Prasun Bajpai—had to leave the ABP news channel abruptly in August 2018. Another senior anchor Abhisar Sharma known for his anti Modi comments was also asked to leave later by ABP news. This was linked to a recent incident which had left the Modi government embarrassed. On 20 June 2018, a woman in Kanker district, Chhattisgarh, reportedly told the prime minister, in a video conference, that her income had doubled. When the ABP's reporter visited the area and spoke with villagers, this was found to be untrue. This report was broadcast on 6 July. It put the prime minister in an embarrassing position. After this episode, the channel's signals started to get mysteriously disturbed during the flagship show 'Masterstroke' at 9.00 p.m. and ultimately the editor and anchor had to resign.

The Wire, known for being critical of the Modi government, reported on 3 August 2018, 'The Wire has learned that in the run up to these changes at the channel, BJP president Amit Shah told a group of journalists in parliament house last week that he planned to "teach ABP News a lesson".'[49] The matter of their resignation was brought up in the parliament also. The government clarified that it had no role in this entire episode and the channel's falling TRPs might be the reason for the resignations, which defied credulity.

On 11 October 2018, Raghav Bahl, the promoter of news portal the Quint, had his office and residence raided by the Income tax officials. He was accused of tax evasion. Raghav Bahl is one of the most respected media owners and editors. Apparently he invited the government's wrath as he had been very critical of the Modi government.[50]

The resignation of editors can be disturbing; but what is more disturbing is the report published by the Wire that the BJP runs an entire war room in its old national headquarters at 11 Ashoka Road. This story tells of an army of people working day and night, mapping almost every newspaper and television channel in the country. Every prominent journalist is watched by the war room and categorised as being anti-or pro-BJP. A report is sent to higher-ups in the party daily. Secrecy is scrupulously maintained and employees have no idea who or what the information is collated for.[51] Senior leaders of the BJP, when asked, did not offer a logical reason. If there is no good reason, then why is such information gathered, what is its purpose and why it is done so secretly? The next obvious question is, is India turning into a surveillance state? And is the state out to control the thought processes of an entire population by controlling the means of communication and relentless distribution of ideological propaganda.

I can say without any hesitation that the state has already partly succeeded in this. Democracy has been used successfully to reach this point. But this is not the end of the road. This is the beginning. To become a Hindu Rashtra, India has to become an ideological state. Till now, we have only seen a mere glimpse of what that may entail.

Epilogue

Millions of Germans celebrated when Hitler was appointed the chancellor of Germany by President von Hindenburg in 1933. Germany, suffering from the trauma of defeat in the First World War, was sick of political bickering and instability; it was looking for a strong leader who would help the country out of the national suffering. Hitler and his party did not have a majority in parliament, yet his appointment was viewed by many as the turning point in German history. But for a section of society this strong leadership brought about an unpleasant change. Jews, who were approximately 1 per cent of the population, had their lives turned upside down when Hitler became the Chancellor of Germany.

Lucille Eichengreen was a school girl in Hamburg. Like most children she had many friends and a carefree childhood. Her world changed overnight. 'Hitler came to power in January 1933. The children that lived in the same building ... no longer spoke to us. They threw stones at us, they called us names, and that was maybe three months after Hitler came to power, and we could not understand what we had done to deserve this ... And when we asked at home the answer pretty much was, "Oh it's a passing phase, it won't matter, it will normalise." What that actually meant we did not know. But we could not understand the change.'[1] She was not alone.

Eugene Levine used to study in a mixed religion school where, one day, he was taunted by a non-Jewish boy, who was his friend, 'Well, Levine, have you got your ticket to Palestine?' Eugene was shocked. 'But, you see, anti-semitism's always there beneath the surface.'

These incidents are a part of a history that even the Germans don't want to remember any longer. Both the statements, together, hint at a fact that is distasteful, dangerous and apocalyptical. At that point nobody had visualised what lay in store for Jews in the coming days, months and years later—the Holocaust, in which humanity saw the most brutal face ever of any political regime. Lucille's incomprehension at her friends turning into enemies overnight is explained by Eugene who suggested that anti-semitism had always existed in Germany but it was dormant; it waited for a Hitler-like figure to come to power before becoming the monstrosity it did. Laurence Rees agrees with him. He writes, 'Anti-Semitism existed in Germany long before Adolf Hitler, and plenty of other people blamed the Jews, for Germany's defeat in World War 1.'[2]

India is not Germany by any stretch of the imagination and neither could the two historical conditions be the same. Of course, India had its share of trauma as a society when it went to elections in 2014 but it will be unfair to compare this with the Germans' collective desperation after the first World War. Unlike Hitler, Modi was not an appointed prime minister. He was elected by the people of India by legitimate constitutional means. Before the 2014 parliamentary elections he had won three consecutive assembly elections in Gujarat and even his most bitter critic would have to admit that he was hugely popular. In the last thirty years, no other prime minister had won a majority in the lower house of the parliament. Rajiv Gandhi was the last prime minister who had majority numbers in the Loksabha. It is a lesser-known fact of history that Hindenburg who appointed Hitler as chancellor, had refused twice before to appoint him to the post. He had said in November 1932, that a presidential cabinet headed by Hitler would inevitably develop into a party dictatorship with all its consequences, resulting in a worsening of the antagonisms within the German people.[3]

Unlike Hindenburg, Indian president Mr Pranab Mukherjee did not have any choice but to obey the will of the people; and at that time if he had any reservations about the turn of events, he did not share it with anyone. But it is to be noted that a section of the intelligentsia had always viewed Modi as a polarising figure who unabashedly pursued Hindutva and did not hide his views vis-a-vis minorities. His image as a Hindutva icon was one of the major reasons for his success and he did not flinch in exploiting it to the hilt, though he did marry it with the utopia of development and the idea of making India great again. He could succeed only because like in Germany, prejudice against Muslims had been lying dormant in a section of Hindus for long.

To be fair to Modi and the RSS, this prejudice against Muslims existed even before the RSS was formed in 1925. Mahatma Gandhi gave a glimpse of it in his book, *Hind Swaraj,* which was written in 1909. This book is in the form of questions and answers. In the book a reader asks, 'It is said that Hindus and Muslims are bitter enemies. It is said in general that *Miyan aur Mahadev ki nahi banegi* (Muslims and Hindus can't get along). Hindus pray to the God in the east, Muslims pray in the west. Muslims treat Hindus as idol worshipers and hate them. Hindus are idol worshipers, Muslims are idol breakers. Hindus worship cows, Muslims eat them. Hindus are non-violent, Muslims are violent. At every step there are serious differences. How can these be erased and how can Hindustan be one?'[4] Gandhi's detailed response to the question should be the ideal solution to the Hindu-Muslim question in India. He says, 'Religions are different paths to reach the same venue. We can both take two different paths, what is wrong in it? What is the fight?'[5]

It is a historical fact that the RSS, from the day of its inception, has been busy accentuating this prejudice against Muslims in the name of character building, and at a larger level, in the name of nation building. The RSS rebelled against the Gandhian way of thinking vis-a-vis Muslims and the basic nature of Hinduism. It has not changed its opinion on the issue of the Muslim question. Their thinking very clearly questions the loyalty of Muslims to the Indian nation. Even after the departure of Savarkar and Golwalkar, the same ideological stream continues. K.R. Malkani, one of the few well read people within the RSS fold, in my opinion, who was also the editor of the RSS mouthpiece, *Organiser,* writes while quoting Golwalkar, 'The main reason why there is Hindu-Muslim tension in India is that the Indian Muslim is yet to identify fully with India, its people and its culture. Let the Indian Muslim feel and say that this is his country and all these are his people and the problem[of Hindu-Muslim tension] will cease to exist. It is a matter of changing his psychology.'[6]

After Golwalkar, the person who dazzled the Hindutva fold with his intellectual depth and authority was Pt. Deen Dayal Upadhyay, the former president of Bharatiya Jan Sangh (the earlier incarnation of BJP) who died at the relatively young age of 52. He did not majorly differ with Golwalkar on the Muslim question. Like Golwalkar he believed that the loyalty of the Muslims to the nation was suspect and that as a community, Muslims refused to integrate and identify with the national cultural mainstream of the country. He was of the view that Muslims have no option but to accept the Hindu nationality. He says, 'The separatist and anti-national attitude of the Muslim community is the greatest obstruction to Akhand Bharat. The creation of Pakistan is the triumph of this attitude.'[7] But Deen Dayal Upadhyay's position is a little more nuanced than Golwalkar's. Unlike Golwalkar, he did not propose that Muslims either had to live like second-class citizens or had to be driven out of the country. Being a pragmatic politician, he was optimistic that Muslims could be persuaded to join the national cultural mainstream and accept Hindu nationality. He used to say, 'Would any Congressman say that six crore Muslims (the number of Muslims when India was partitioned) should be driven out of India. If not, then (Muslims) will have to be assimilated into the national life of this country. If this country was partitioned by a lack of a feeling of unity, the same feeling of unity can again bring it together. We must strive for this.'[8] On 1 January 1968 he asked Muslims to join the Jan Sangh in great numbers.[9] When Bala Saheb Devras took over the reins of the RSS, he opened the doors of the organisation for Muslims. In 1979, the RSS formally opened its membership to Muslims (and Christians).[10]

Anderson and Damle write, 'The RSS, particularly since the late 1970s, has begun to modify its stance on this issue [admittance of Muslims], engaging in programmes aimed at the cultural assimilation of Muslims, Christians and others who do not practice Hinduism as a religion. Non-Hindus are accepted into shakhas, [the meetings which RSS activists hold every morning where volunteers are given physical and ideological training] there have been Muslims pracharaks; and RSS-affiliated schools enroll a large number of non-Hindus.'[11]

In 2002, in order to reach out to Muslims, a dialogue was initiated with Muslim religious leaders and the Muslim Rashtra Manch (MRM) was formed. One of the top leaders of the RSS, Indresh Kumar was entrusted with the responsibility of furthering this engagement, but most surprisingly, the RSS remained vague about its relationship with the MRM. It never openly accepted it as its affiliate. Despite its paraphernalia, MRM could not cut much ice with the Muslim community. The major reason for it was the RSS's unwillingness to moderate its ideological position on the issue of Muslim participation in the broader framework of Hindu Nationalism. It insists that Muslims change their understanding of Hindu Nationalism and atone for their mistakes committed in the past. It also demands that the issue of their religious identity not be a barrier to accept the cultural icons of Hinduism—Ram, Krishna, and so on—as their ancestors. They would have to accept that they are no different from Hindus except by way of their worship. Virag Pachpore, the co-convener of the MRM writes, 'Muslims in India are [an] integral part of the Indian society and share ancestors, culture and motherland with Hindus. The need is to make them realise this underlying current of unity in diversity.'[12]

I have no hesitation in saying that the RSS's effort is nothing but tokenism, which lacks honesty of purpose. The RSS does not realise that to gain the confidence of Muslims it has to be seen to be changing or moderating its ideological position. If it is still seen to be anti-Muslim then it has no one to blame but its own policies and decisions. The problem with the RSS is that it has failed to understand, that in independent India, two incidents— the demolition of Babri Masjid in 1992 and the 2002 Gujarat riots—have majorly impacted the Muslims' collective psyche, scarred them emotionally, and shaken their belief in the Indian legal system. Modi's identification with Gujarat riots is too overwhelming in the Muslim community.[13] And his rule since 2014 has not helped lessen the burden of history; rather it has created new fissures in their minds, inflicted much deeper emotional wounds and constructed a regime of alienation, helplessness and betrayal. The killing of Akhlaq, Pehlu Khan, Junaid and others by cow vigilantes; the subsequent collaboration of state machinery to save the perpetrators; no urgent and unequivocal condemnation of these incidents from Modi and Bhagwat; felicitation of mob lynching accused and convicted Hindutvavadis by central ministers; provocative statements by BJP/RSS leaders targeting Muslims; sudden closure of abattoirs in UP and other states without any opportunities for alternate ways of livelihood; forced ban on beef in northern and western states by BJP governments at a time when India is the leading beef exporter in the world; the arrest and brutal beatings of Muslim youth in the name of love jihad; insulting and intimidating Muslims who tried to offer namaaz in an open space; regular violations of the symbols of Muslim identity; a nonstop attempt to portray and lampoon them as terrorist and anti-national by the Hindutva Brigade on TV Channels and social media; the Modi government's effort to abrogate instant triple Talaq and through that to build a narrative that the community is regressive, and so on, has built a perception in the community that the Indian state has become anti-Muslim in its ethos and practice. Since 2014, a section of Hindus have rediscovered their Hindutva which if scratched a bit, reveals an anti-Muslim point of view. Flaunting an anti-Muslim attitude is definitely massively on the rise. The stereotyping of Muslims has increased manifold. The present status of Muslims in India, reminds me of Silvia Vesela, a Slovakian Jew, who was held in a temporary camp in 1942, where death was staring her in the face. She said, 'It hurt, it really hurt when I, for example, saw many schoolmates shouting with fists raised, "It serves you right!" Since that time I do not expect anything of people.'[14]

If we dig a bit deeper in history, it is not difficult to find that one of the main reasons for the demand of a separate nation by Indian Muslims before partition was their sense of acute powerlessness. Muslims, historically, have mostly been rulers in the Indian sub-continent, since they arrived on Indian shores. The British rule undoubtedly broke their hegemony but it did not disturb the power balance in the society at the ground level. With the rise of national consciousness and assertion of Hindu intellectuals in the second half of the 19th century the power balance tended to shift away from the Muslims. With Gandhi, a Hindu, emerging as the unchallenged leader of the Congress, eclipsing Mohammad Ali Jinnah, there was despair among the Muslim elite. A sense of being left behind in the race for power ultimately led to the demand for Pakistan and the division of the country. 'The terms of engagement with power for the Ashraf [Upper caste/class Muslims] was not adequate representation according to democratic norms but the parity of Muslims with Hindus based on the erstwhile status of the former as a ruling class. Hamid Dalwai in Muslim Politics in India (1968) remarks that "the idea was to secure a fifty per cent share of power for Muslims. When this attempt failed, the Muslims demanded an independent sovereign state of their own."'[15]

Although the right wing Hindutva proponents accused secular parties of Muslim appeasement, the political position of Muslims did not improve after partition. Their socio-economic condition, in comparison to Hindus and other communities, worsened. However, they continued to be recognised as a religious community whose religious freedom was granted by the constitution. They were free to express themselves as Muslims and practice their religion without fear. The Indian state did not interfere in their religious matters and in the matters related to their Muslim identity. Leading Muslim intellectual, Anwar Alam, writes in his monograph, *Understanding the Process of Radicalisation Amongst Muslims in India,* 'Indian Muslims do suffer from relative deprivation in economic and political spheres but not in religio-cultural spheres ... It is pertinent to note that dominant understanding of Indian secularism among Indian Muslims is the one that expects the Indian state to promote, preserve and protect the Muslim's religious and cultural symbols in the public sphere, which partly explains the absence of any development of large scale trend of radicalisation among them.'[16] This trend continued even after the late 90s, when Jihadi terrorism was globally at its peak. It was remarkable that Jihadi terrorism failed to elicit any major response from the Indian Muslims. This point has to be underlined as this was happening at a time when organisations like Al Qaeda and Islamic State (IS) were attracting Muslim recruits in bulk from across the world, including many European countries. This was also remarkable as India is surrounded by Islamic states like Pakistan and Afghanistan in the North and Bangladesh in the east, where Jihadi terrorists were having a free run and religious fundamentalism had already acquired monstrous proportions. It is also important to note that the militancy in Kashmir too failed to lure Indian Muslims to their cause in the name of Islam. Though the Indian Mujahideen and SIMI (Students' Islamic Movement of India) did try to create havoc after the Gujarat riots, they too were soon neutralised.

However, since Modi took over the reins of the government a paradigm shift has taken place. Muslims have started feeling that the state had now started interfering in matters of their religion and culture. Anwar Alam writes, 'It is the religio-cultural alienation which might strengthen the process of radicalistion among Indian Muslims. The demolition of Babri masjid was a jolt to the faith of the Muslim community. Since 2014 when the present NDA government came into power at the Centre, it has initiated a series of policy measures including the issue of criminalising instant triple talaq and keeping a distance from sharing Muslim/Islamic symbolism in the public domain that deeply concerns the Muslim community: whether they are any longer free to practice their religion freely in this nation.'[17]

During research for this book I met many Muslim intellectuals and leaders. I could sense that there was a definite unease in the Muslim community vis-a-vis the Modi government, guarded by a rather deceptive silence. The present crisis is being perceived as an existential crisis. Therefore a lot of internal churning is going on. It has been acknowledged by the community that the traditional leadership of the Muslim community has let them down. Now, young and educated leaders are taking the lead and trying to organise the community. Older leaders are extremely cautious in articulating their views on issues related to politics, and it has been communicated to all, especially the youth to not get provoked, whatever be the nature of the provocation. Anand Vivek Taneja, Assistant Professor of Anthropology and Religious Studies at the University of Vanderbilt, USA, had been touring areas such as Aligarh, Lucknow, Kolkata, Patna, Hyderabad and so on, across the country for his research on Muslims. During an interview with me, he said, '[The] Muslim community is definitely in a self reflective mood and there is an extraordinary amount of restraint but (the) community also makes a clear distinction that the present problems it is facing is because of the current politics. There is no ill feeling against Hindus per se. Hindus are not seen as religious enemies. The problem is the RSS and Hindutva.' His words were echoed by other Muslim leaders I spoke to. I was told that leaders of secular political parties had been told not to visit them too often as it would provide the RSS-BJP a reason to polarise society along communal lines and help them consolidate Hindu votes.

The 2019 parliamentary elections are undoubtedly being looked at with a lot of curiosity, but it is also understood that even if Modi were to lose the elections the crisis was not going to be over just yet. The threat of Hindutva will continue to loom as it has captured sizeable ground in the last few years. The Muslim community believes that a long-term solution has to be found. Young leaders have been trying to convince their elders that in this hour of crisis, when Muslim identity is severely threatened, there is no scope for fissures in the community, and thus both the sects—Shia and Sunni—have to come together to fight this menace, united. This effort has already borne fruit. Forgetting their religious differences, members of both sects are holding prayers together in mosques.

What has pained the Muslim community the most is the image that has been deliberately foisted on them by the Hindutva forces—that Muslims are not loyal to the country and for them religion is paramount and supersedes their patriotism. Many Muslims tearfully told me that when they had the option to move to Pakistan, they decided to stay back in India and yet their patriotism was being questioned in the name of the national anthem and national song; this was not fair. 'India is our motherland, we are born here and will die here,' many of them reiterated. I was asked why their loyalties were constantly questioned and why they were asked about Jinnah. 'We have nothing to do with him. He was never our icon and will never be.'

There is a realisation in the community that too much emphasis on religion has attracted a bad name for them. Now the effort is to break the stereotype. Anand Vivek Taneja said to me, 'Muslims are engaging themselves with the discourse of constitutionalism instead of making it a religious battle. Their simple demand is that they are citizens of this country and they should be accorded all the privileges which are owed to a citizen.'

But not every Muslim is on the same page, for some their religious identity is most important and they are not willing to dilute it. And that is a real cause of worry for the Muslim leaders. In hushed tones it is being admitted that if this 'repression' continues for long then it will be difficult to restrain youngsters as they are getting restless with every passing day. This is the real danger. One leading Muslim intellectual told me that for the first time he was feeling scared. He said, 'Indian Muslims are not like Arab Muslims. They are Hindu-ised Muslims. In Islam nobody is allowed to pray to anyone other than Allah, but in India, like the Hindus, the Muslims too visit mazaars of Sufi saints, burn lohban and ask for mannat. But if the persecution continues then it can't be ruled out that a few hundred kids may decide to wrap bombs around their waist in the name of Islam.'

Is the RSS aware of this danger? This question is important especially in the light of certain remarks made by RSS chief Mohan Bhagwat, during his three-day stay in Delhi in September 2018, which give the impression that the RSS is either changing or at least trying to in their pursuit of a Hindu Rashtra. Let there be no confusion that the RSS is exclusivist in its ideology, and treats Muslims and Christians as enemies of the Hindu nation. It believes that Indian history is the continuing religious battle between Hindus on one side and Muslims and Christians on the other. However, Mohan Bhagwat's words added a new twist to the whole debate. Bhagwat said that Golwalkar's statement on the internal enemy had a historical context and should be seen as a reaction to the events that unfolded during the Partition, referring to the massive bloodbath and human massacre at that time. He even suggested that Golwalkar's words no longer be considered as representative of the reality today. On the surface it appeared that he was debunking Golwalkar's theory of the internal enemy, which is an integral part of the RSS guru's thesis of Hindutva.

On the first day of his interaction, Bhagwat said something which, if taken as a serious reflection of the RSS way of thinking, dismantles the whole edifice of Hindutva as an ideology. Using the much talked about dictum of Hindu tradition, 'Vasudev Kutumbakam (The entire world is family)' he said, 'The RSS works for the universal brotherhood; unity in diversity is the only foundation of this brotherhood. This idea is Hindutva. And that is why we say ours is a Hindu Rashtra.'[18] He elaborated further, 'A Hindu Rashtra does not mean it has no place for Muslims. The Sangh works towards universal brotherhood and the cardinal principle of this brotherhood is unity in diversity. This thought comes from our culture, which the world calls Hindutva. That's why we call it a Hindu Rashtra.'[19]

Bhagwat's statement comes as a big surprise because, not only Golwalkar but even Savarkar, the original ideologue of Hindutva, treated Muslims as enemies, as has been amply discussed in the previous chapters of this book. Like Mohammad Ali Jinnah, Golwalkar and Savarkar too believed in the two-nation theory that Hindus and Muslims could never live together and had to form two separate nations. The whole structure of Hindutva is based on the enmity towards Islam and hatred towards Muslims. If hate towards Muslims is taken out of Hindutva, then the RSS's ideology falls flat, it loses its oxygen. It no longer has reason to exist. A very senior RSS functionary told me that Bhagwat had uttered these words after a lot of internal debate and in the coming days and years the change in the RSS's attitude towards Muslims would be discernible. The other RSS watchers also vouched for the change. Dilip Deodhar says, '[T]he issue was discussed at the Akhil Bharatiya Prant Pracharak meeting held in July [2018] in Somnath, where pracharaks from across the country had come for the annual brainstorming meet ... the gathering discussed that the philosophy of Hindutva did not mean that Indian society would be devoid of Muslims or other communities and Hindus could not co-exist with them.'[20]

To stretch his argument, Bhagwat had also pressed for another departure in the same speech. Against Savarkar and Golwalkar's theory of 1200 years of religious war with Islam, Bhagwat hinted that things were all right between Hindus and Muslims till 1881, and the situation took a different turn only later. He referred to Muslim reformer Sir Syed Ahmed Khan and said, 'Sir Syed Ahmed Khan's speech in Lahore where he was felicitated by the Arya Samaj after he came back as a barrister, is much talked about these days. In the Arya Pratinidhi Sabha, the presenter said, while introducing Khan, that while many among Hindus had become barristers, Khan was the first one among Muslims, which is why the Arya Samaj had decided to felicitate him. Sir Syed replied by saying that was pained that the Samaj had not thought of him as one of their own. "Are we not the sons of Bharat Mata? In history, what has changed except our way of worship?" he said. So till 1881 we all knew about it, later slowly we lost this understanding. This has to be brought back.'[21]

Then, Bhagwat added, 'We call it Hindu. If you don't want to say this, you can call it Bharatiya. I respect that too.'[22]

If the RSS is actually transforming then the substitution of the word 'Hindu' with 'Bharatiya' is massive. It will be a major turning point in the Sangh's history. But the question is whether it is actually so. No doubt, Bhagwat's speech was immediately lapped up as a major sign of course-correction by the RSS in the context of a fast changing world. If Left-liberals are sceptical then a section of right wing intellectuals are optimistic. Swapan Dasgupta, wrote in his column, 'Depending on how the message is digested by the RSS, BJP and society, India could well be on the cusp of defining an enlightened Hindu consensus.'[23]

But I don't agree with Swapan Dasgupta, and I have my reasons. Ideological organisations like the RSS, which have been banned three times in the past, have immense resilience to survive and an infinite capacity to deceive. There are innumerable examples in history, when ideologies, for their own survival, compromised with their worst enemies. This, in ideological parlance, is called a strategic retreat or tactical adjustment. Hitler and Stalin both indulged themselves with a non-aggression pact in August 1939. The Nazi-Soviet Pact could only be termed as the most unholy alliance ever in world history. Hitler who hated Jews and communists and had vowed to annihilate both was more than willing to accept Stalin's offer of a treaty. Though, both the parties knew that ultimately they would end up fighting each other, they both needed time for that final war. William Shirer made a telling comment—'Stalin, the Führer's mortal enemy, had made this possible.'[24]

The RSS, at present, is suffering from the mortal fear of losing the 2019 parliamentary elections due to the non-performance of the BJP government at the centre and the declining popularity of Modi. In 2014, the middle and upwardly mobile class voted overwhelmingly for Modi, and not for the BJP, because Modi presented himself as the messiah of development. Despite this stupendous victory, the BJP could garner only 31 per cent votes. That was the time when everything was going well for Modi and the Congress was demoralised due to corruption charges against its members.

Now, closer to elections, the Congress is showing signs of aggression. Rahul Gandhi is no longer the 'Pappu' he had been made out to be, Priyanka Gandhi has made an entry into active politics and the opposition parties are more than willing to come together to defeat Modi and, very importantly, there is a definite disappointment and disillusionment among the middle class voters with Modi and the BJP. When an old admirer of Modi like Sadanand Dhume writes, 'Moreover, to put it mildly, Modi's BJP has not exactly lived up to expectations …'[25] or Modi's biographer, Nilanjan Mukhopadhyay says, 'But barely seven months after a stunning victory in Uttar Pradesh which led supporters to claim that 2019 was a "settled affair" and for Omar Abdullah to declare that instead of the next hustings, the opposition must prepare for 2024, the scenario has altered dramatically,' then it is a matter of concern for Modi supporters.[26] It is to be noted that both the writers had written these words in the second half of 2017. Since then a lot of water has flown in the Ganges.

Bhagwat's attempt to portray a moderate image of Hindutva is a well thought out strategy to entice disappointed middle class voters to support the BJP. It is an effort to convey to liberal Hindus who are sympathetic to the BJP that Hindutva is not like Jihadi fundamentalism, the Taliban, the Islamic State or the Muslim Brotherhood of Egypt, who are not open-minded and in whose scheme of things, the voice of dissent has no place and bigotry is the only rule. This is a kind of ideological deception. If the RSS really had changed then it would not have raised the pitch for the construction of Ram mandir in Ayodhya immediately after Bhagwat's outreach programme in Delhi. It was also astonishing as this was the time when the supreme court was hearing the Ram janmabhoomi matter.

For a good four years and a quarter, the Hindutva Brigade did not raise the Ram mandir issue at all. Suddenly, it has remembered that there is a Ram mandir and it has to be constructed. For more than two decades it believed that the judiciary should decide the Babri Masjid/Ram mandir dispute. Now all of a sudden it announces that Hindus can't wait any longer and the Central government should pass a law for the mandir's construction. If the Ram mandir was so important then why did it not put pressure on the Modi government in the first year itself? Why now? It is plain to see that this has been planned to create the kind of communal hysteria which existed in 1992 (which ultimately led to the destruction of the Babri Masjid) across the country. Public meetings in more than 500 districts were organised by the Akhil Bharatiya Sant Samiti backed by the RSS to whip up the frenzy. This clearly shows their real intent.

Only the future will tell if the Hindutva brigade's efforts will bear fruits, but the objective and neutral assessment of Indian politics dictates that Modi along with the RSS has successfully neutralised the import of the Muslim vote bank. Gone are the days when political parties used to flock around Muslim clergies and leaders. Now, no political party has the gumption to talk about Muslim votes. The Congress which had survived on Muslim votes for decades is now out to project itself as a Hindu party. Rahul Gandhi is hopping from one temple to another since the Gujarat assembly elections in 2017, and is out to prove that he is a true janeudhari (wearer of the sacred thread, worn by Brahmin and upper-caste men) Hindu. In Madhya Pradesh assembly elections, where Muslims are only 6.57 per cent of the population, the Congress's manifesto looks more like the BJP's. It has promised to develop Ram Van Gaman Path Yatra, a mythical route that Lord Ram took during his 14-year-exile from Ayodhya in MP. It has promised to build gaushalas (cow sheds) in every village panchayat, along with encouraging the production of cow urine and cow dung cakes for commercial purposes. It has also promised to create a spiritual department and will promote Sanskrit as a language. The Manifesto also talks about making a Maa Narmada Nyas Adhiniyam for the development of religious places, along the holy river Narmada at an estimated cost of Rs 1,100 crore.[27] It is to counter BJP's Narmada Sewa Yatra. Digvijaya Singh, the former chief minister of MP for two terms, had done a parikrama (circumambulation) on foot, around the river Narmada, which is around 3600 km. He took six months to complete the trek.

Rahul Gandhi is projected in MP as a devout follower of Lord Shiva. He kicked off his campaign in August 2018 from Omkareshwar Jyotirlinga Temple, by paying obeisance to Lord Shiva. In between he went to Kailash Mansarovar.[28] Posters depicting him as a Shiva devotee were splashed all over the place. With the RSS–BJP trying to create frenzy for the construction of the Ram mandir, Congress leaders are telling the electorates that it is only the Congress, and its leader Rahul Gandhi, who can build the Ram temple. Congress's star campaigner for Madhya Pradesh, Acharya Pramod Krishnan said, 'Rahul Gandhi is a decent man. If he becomes PM, Ram mandir will be built.'[29] A similar statement was also repeated by the senior Congress leader and former cabinet minister, C.P. Joshi in Rajasthan. He said, 'Rajiv Gandhi unlocked the Babri Masjid premises and allowed religious rites inside the disputed structure. Only a Congress PM can get the temple built.'[30]

The RSS–BJP is finding it difficult to counter the soft-Hinduism of the Congress, so they are questioning Rahul's credibility as a true Hindu. A section of liberal intellectuals and thinkers are also upset with the Congress. Prof Apoorvanand, who has no sympathy for the RSS–BJP, terms Congress's emphasis on being seen as a Hindu party, as an idiotic step. He writes, 'The Congress has stopped talking about secularism which was its special contribution … their leaders are not tired of saying that theirs is a party of good Hindus. Their leaders are writing books on why they are good Hindus and why leaders of the BJP are not good Hindus. So has the debate in the country been reduced to determining the good Hindu and bad Hindu?'[31]

Prof Apoorvanad is not to be faulted. Discourse in India since the demise of Gandhi has been propelled by Left-wing politics, which is influenced by the western concept of secularism, which because of historical reasons, negates religion in the public and political sphere. In the West, the Church and the state had bitter fights for the control of society. In this battle, the state finally won and banished religion to the private space and made it heavily regulated. The Indian reality is different. Due to the organisation of the Hindu society around the rigid caste system, there was always a clear distinction of work between the political and religious leaders. Kings were supposed to rule and priests were to advise. This relationship was purportedly, based on mutual respect, and since this had the sanction of the scriptures therefore rarely was the boundary crossed.

The Left has failed to grasp the true nature of Indian life, which is overwhelmingly dominated by Hinduism. In the Indian context, religion or Dharma, as spelled by Hindu scriptures, is all pervasive. It is omniscient. It is a way of life. Unlike Semitic religions, Hinduism is not defined, neither does it have one book or one God or one way of adherence, worship or prayer. According to the former president of India, S. Radhakrishnan, 'The Hindu attitude to religion is interesting. While fixed intellectual beliefs mark off one religion from another, Hinduism sets itself no such limits. Intellect is subordinated to intuition, dogma to experience, outer expression to inward realisation. Religion is not the acceptance of academic abstraction or celebration of ceremonies but a kind of life or experience of reality.'[32] Radhakrishnan hints that at best Hinduism is vague, and it is this vagueness which is its biggest strength. According to him, Hinduism defies definition and remains open to interpretation. Since its rules change from community to community, and over time, it is not a rigid system of beliefs and rites and is, in fact one that absorbs from other cultures and people.

In his book, *Adi Shankaracharya*, Pavan K. Verma writes, 'Hinduism in comparison to other religions is highly spiritual. It is not materialistic. Life is a pursuit of attainment of Moksha , the ultimate salvation. And the most important concept that the Gita enunciated was that of nishkama karma, of action, without attachment or thought of reward, done without selfish desire in a spirit of surrender …. It is not the body but the soul which is paramount in Hindu religion. In Mahabharata Lord Krishna tells the great warrior Arjuna—"He is never born, and he never dies. He is in eternity: he is for everyone. Never born and eternal, beyond times gone or to come, he does not die when the body dies."'[33]

The problem with the Left thinkers and Hindutvavadis is that both ignore the essence of Hinduism. Left-thinking, in its essence, is anti-religion, and that is why communist states banned religion from people's lives. Hindutva, though certainly not anti-religion, has a bitter fight with the core values of Hinduism. It believes that it is because of the core values of Hinduism that Hindus suffered the domination of other religions for more than 1200 years.

Among modern Indian thinkers and leaders, nobody seems to have a better grasp of Hinduism than Gandhi. Other than the religious and spiritual dimension of Hindu dharma he also mastered the art of how to use it politically to inspire the common man in the streets for bigger projects. His 'experiments with truth' were nothing but a successful experiment with the Hindu ethos. Gandhi says, 'Hinduism tells everyone to worship God according to his own faith or dharma, and so it lives at peace with all the religions.'[34] This goes against the basic premise of Hindutva. Gandhi's Hinduism is not in competition with any other religion. It does not quarrel with other religions and does not fight to impose its idea on another. But Hindutva is in a state of perpetual war with Islam and Christianity. Gandhi's understanding of the Hindu dharma is in direct conflict with Hindutva. What is understood to be the core value of Hinduism by Gandhi and other great seers of the Hindu civilisation, are considered to be the principle reasons for the Hindu dharma's decline for the Hindutvavadis.

Gandhi, while defining the Hindu dharma, rejected dogmas and cherished ethical values as enshrined in the Hindu tradition. For him ethical values were supreme and were the way of life for a Hindu. He says, 'According to my belief, a Hindu is anyone who, born in a Hindu family in India, accepts the Vedas, the Upanishads and the Puranas as holy books; who has faith in the five Yamas [ethical values that guide a Hindu's life]—satya (truth), ahimsa (non-violence) asteya (non-stealing), brahmacharya (chastity) and aprigraha (non-avarice) ... and practices them to the best of his ability ...'[35] These five yamas were listed by sage Patanjali in Yogsutra. Though Sandilya Upanishad lists ten yamas—it adds ksama (forgiveness), dhrti (fortitude), daya (compassion), arjava (sincerity) and mitasara (measured diet)—and other sages and scriptures do add a few more virtues to the list but truth, non-violence, compassion and tolerance are common throughout.

For Gandhi these core values of Hinduism, particularly ahimsa, are cardinal principles, and should not be compromised in any way. In Hindu tradition, ahimsa has been given a very exalted position. 'Ahimsa Parmo Dharma (non-violence is the best religion)' is an often repeated axiom for Hindus. Prabhash Joshi, the legendary editor of *Jansatta*, wrote in his column, 'Ahimsa Parmo Dharma—this essence has emanated from Mahabharata and is a Hindu thought.'[36] Gandhi's use of non-violence as a political tool to fight the repressive colonial force was a unique experiment in world history. His experiments with truth and non-violence mesmerised the whole world. Albert Einstein wrote to Gandhi after the salt satyagraha on 27 September 1931, 'You have shown that we can achieve the ideal even without resorting to violence.'³⁷

But while the whole world admired Gandhi and his non-violence, Hindutva forces abhorred him. Because, in their opinion, the core values of Hinduism—truth, non-violence, tolerance, forgiveness and compassion—are the reasons that Hindus were vanquished and ruled by foreign invaders for more than 1,200 years in history. Savarkar termed these core values 'perverted-virtues'. He writes, 'It was this confused religious thought, the distorted sense of virtues and the blind religious tolerance which culminated in the religious suicide of the Hindus.'³⁸ Savarkar becomes more scathing, 'Naturally the tendency to retaliate in the same fashion even on the religious front to face religious aggression with counter religious offensive—to meet cruelty with supra cruel blows, craft with super craft, violence with extreme violence and to consider this war policy to be highly religious duty of a brave warrior—lay dormant in our national mind … more respectable than (this) truthful conduct was considered the practice of non-violence as the highest form of virtue … which later on hastened our terrible downfall … Manliness and valour came to be condemned as the vilest vices.'³⁹

The RSS agrees with Savarkar. While lamenting the state of affairs in the country Golwalkar says, 'How can a society given to self derision, weakened by all round disruption and dissipation, kicked and humiliated at every point by any and every bully in the world teach the world?'⁴⁰ He obliquely blames Gautam Buddha and Mahatma Gandhi and their philosophy of ahimsa. He does not see virtue in ahimsa and feels that too much stress on ahimsa is the reason for the weakness of Hindu society and the Indian state. Given the stature of Gandhi and his saint-like status in the minds of Indians, he dare not criticise Gandhi publicly but his hints are obvious. He writes, '(T)he thinking in our country during the last few decades has been of looking down upon strength as something sinful and reprehensible. A wrong interpretation of "non-violence" has deprived the national mind of the power of discrimination. We have come to look upon strength as "violence" and to glorify our weakness … A dense cloud of dust is raised in the form of high-sounding words like "peace" and "non-violence" with an assumed air of moral authority only to cover up our imbecility.'⁴¹

Golwalkar goes on to justify violence. He hides behind the holy books—The Ramayana and The Mahabharata. He says that to protect dharma,

Lord Ram and Krishna both had to use violence as the last resort. It is true that even Gandhi had said that if one had to choose between cowardice and violence then the latter would be preferable. But in Hindutva there is no either or. Non-violence is seen with contempt. It is not a coincidence that Hedgewar started the RSS as an organisation from akhaadas (a place where wrestlers practice body building). These akhaadas became a meeting point as well as recruitment grounds for the RSS, and they continue to hold shakhas here every day. In these shakhas, volunteers are trained to use lathis, (wooden clubs), both for defense and attack; the emphasis is more on the physical aspect of the body and less on the evolution of mind. In a way, it can be said that shakhas are producing modern day Hindu warriors. It is also to be remembered that every year on Vijay Dashami (the day, according to Hindu mythology, when Lord Ram defeated Ravan, the king of Lanka), the RSS chief does shashtra puja (worship of arms). Like the RSS, Gandhi also wanted to make India strong. He wrote, 'The Hindus as a body are ... not equipped for fighting. But not having retained their spiritual training, they have forgotten the use of an effective substitute for arms and, not knowing their use nor having an aptitude for them, they have become docile to the point of timidity and cowardice.'[42] In his opinion the loss of spiritualism was the reason for the decline of India as a nation. To regain the old glory India had to attain its spirituality.

It is also worth a mention that on two counts there is a very uncanny resemblance between the Hindutva thought process and Gandhi's wisdom. Firstly, like Hindutvavadis, Gandhi too believed that India is an old civilisation and unlike European thinkers he opined that India was a nation even before the British rule. Secondly, like Hindutvavadis, Gandhi was also a great supporter of cows. He considered cow protection an integral part of Hinduism. When he was asked how he would define himself as a Sanatani Hindu, he went on to cite cow protection as a very important component of his Hindu belief system. For him cow protection was the central feature of Hinduism and was more important than swaraj (freedom).[43] But both the world views refused to meet beyond this point.

Gandhi's approach for the protection of cows underlines the difference between Hinduism, as understood by him, and Hinduism used by the Hindutva brigade to further their own agenda. Gandhi was a humanist and Hindu-Muslim unity was very close to his heart. He knew that Muslims ate beef and that was one of the reasons for the friction between the two communities, but he was dead against the use of violence against Muslims for the protection of cows. He wrote, 'For the protection of cows there is only one solution; with folded hands I should try to convince them (Muslims) that for the sake of the country they should not kill cows. If they are not convinced then I should let cows die because that is beyond me. If I feel extremely concerned about cows then I should sacrifice my life but in no circumstances should (I) kill Muslims. This is religious law and this is what I believe.'[44] Gandhi and Hindutva both talk about Vasudev Kutumbakam but Gandhi's Vasudev Kutumbakam was all encompassing, while Hindutva's actions prove its claim to be a farce. For Gandhi it was a matter of conviction, a matter of universal faith not a political ploy, but for the RSS it is a matter of political strategy, it is politics. Gandhi was aware of Hindutva's larger design and that is why he said, 'If twenty-three crore Hindus (the number of Hindus pre-independence) are not strong enough to defend themselves against seven crore Muslims, either the Hindu religion is false or those who believe in it are cowardly and wicked.'[45]

Gandhi's Hinduism and his understanding of religion were well beyond the boundaries of dogma and negativism. His conviction was based on love whereas Hindutva is defined by hate, which is used as an instrument of political mobilisation to create an artificial construct called the Hindu Rashtra. Baba Saheb Ambedkar had said, 'If Hindu Raj becomes a fact, it will no doubt, be the biggest calamity for this country ... Hindu Raj must be prevented at any cost.'[46]

RSS's Hindutva is at war with Gandhi's Hinduism. There is no denying the fact that the RSS along with the government led by Modi has succeeded in neutralising Muslims during their regime. But the battle is still on. This battle is between Gandhi's Hindus and the Hindutvavadis. The RSS knows that Gandhi's Hindus are the biggest obstacle in its march towards the attainment of a Hindu Rashtra. It is because of this reason that liberal Hindus are incessantly criticised, attacked, humiliated, intimidated, shamed, insulted and physically violated by the so-called warriors of Hindutva. The problem with the RSS is that it knows very well that it can't fight with Gandhi publicly, so it has invented a circuitous route. It attacks Jawaharlal Nehru whom Gandhi anointed his successor. Nehru becomes an easy target since he was in the government.

Nehru had his shortcomings. As a prime minister he did commit mistakes. But one thing which is undeniable about him is that he was the true successor of Gandhi, and never dithered on the issue of Hindu-Muslim unity about which Gandhi had said, 'India's good lay in unity of heart between Hindus and Muslims.'[47] Gandhi went on to say, 'I (therefore) advise every Hindu to place full trust in his Muslim brethren ... it is the highest duty of every Hindu to help Muslim.'[48]

In his book, Rafiq Zakaria quotes Nehru saying in the true Gandhian spirit, 'You are Muslims and I am a Hindu. We may adhere to different religious faiths or even to none, but that does not take away from that cultural inheritance that is yours as well as mine. The past holds us together, why should the present or the future divide us in spirit?'[49] Rafiq Zakaria further writes, 'To him (Nehru) Hinduism represented an amalgam of the best in humanity; he was proud of his Hindu heritage. He was fond of the Ramayana and the Mahabharata.'[50]

The RSS blames Nehru for promoting Muslim communalism for votes in the garb of Muslim appeasement. If Nehru can be faulted for this, then Gandhi should be called the originator of the idea of Muslim appeasement. Because it was Gandhi who openly supported the Khilafat movement in India in 1919 and later on as well, but his endeavour was to unite Hindus and Muslims, bridge the gap between both the communities and to foil the British policy of divide and rule. Nehru, after becoming the prime minister, carried forward Gandhi's legacy. Gandhi is colossal in stature, not just in the minds of Indians but worldwide. He is harder to discredit than Nehru. The RSS–BJP recognises this and has planned its moves accordingly. As is said in the game of chess, to kill the king, first target the knight. Nehru is that knight through which the legacy of Gandhi is being targeted.

The RSS's ideology does not agree with the thesis of Gandhi. It believes that Gandhian thought further weakens Hindu society. To correct the mistakes of history, Gandhi and his memory have to be obliterated. Now that the BJP is in power, occupying a hegemonic position, they will make every effort and try every trick in the book to make this a possibility. They will not leave a single stone unturned to prevail upon the 'other' Hindus, Gandhi's Hindus, the liberal Hindus. History is at a crossroads. At stake is not Gandhi or Nehru but the entire Hindu civilisation, which believes in 'Vasudev Kutumbakam' and 'Ahimsa Parmo Dharma'. In this context the battle in 2019 will be the decisive battle. It will not be fought between political parties but between two Indias—the Hindu India and the Hindutva India.

Endnotes

Introduction

1. The Sachar Committee was formed in 2005 by the then prime minister Manmohan Singh to study the socio-economic status of Muslims in India. The committee was headed by former chief justice of Delhi high court, Rajinder Sachar. The 403-page report was presented to the Lok Sabha on 3 November 2006.
2. Divyesh Singh, 'RSS Calls Sabarimala Verdict Mockery of Religious Leadership', *India Today,* 13 October 2018, https://www.indiatoday.in/india/story/rss-calls-sabarimala-verdict-mockery-of-religious-leadership-1367153-2018-10-13.
3. Milan Kundera, *The Unbearable Lightness of Being*, trans. Michael Henry Heim (Harper & Row, New York, 1984).
4. 'Bulandshahr Violence an Accident, Says UP CM Yogi Adityanath', *Times of India,* 8 December 2018, https://www.google.com/amp/s/m.timesofindia.com/city/lucknow/bulandshahr-violence-an-accident-says-up-cm-yogi-adityanath/amp_articleshow/66994816.cms.
5. 'Bulandshahr Incident a "Political Conspiracy": Adityanath', *Times of India,* https://timesofindia.indiatimes.com/india/bulandshahr-incident-a-political-conspiracy-adityanath/articleshow/67163639.cms.
6. Shastrarth was a great tradition in ancient India of debate between scholars. It was a kind of religious/philosophical contest between philosophers or knowledgeable people. Indian philosopher Shankracharya also participated in shastrarth with seers of other thought processes to establish his superiority over others. His most famous shastrarth was with Pandit Madan Mishra, who, after defeat, became his disciple.

7. Christophe Jaffrelot, 'Hindu Rashtra, De Facto', *Indian Express*, 12 August 2018, https://indianexpress.com/article/opinion/columns/hindu-rashtra-de-facto-bjp-rss-gau-rakshak-mob-lynching-5301083/.
8. Ibid.
9. Ibid.

ONE: Making Sense of Saffronisation

1. Ashutosh, *The Crown Prince, the Gladiator and the Hope: Battle for Change* (HarperCollins, India, 2015).
2. Swayamsevaks are activists who swear by the RSS ideology, i.e., Hindutva, and work for the RSS. Every member of the RSS is called a swayamsevak, whether at the top or the bottom of the organisation.
3. Pracharaks are trained volunteers of the RSS who work full time for the organisation. They form the backbone of the organisation and it is their job to recruit and train people for the RSS and spread their message. They mostly remain unmarried.
4. Ashutosh, *The Crown Prince*.
5. Santosh Desai, 'What Unites Us', *Times of India*, 29 February 2016, https://blogs.timesofindia.indiatimes.com/Citycitybangbang/what-unites-us/.
6. V.D. Savarkar, *Six Glorious Epochs of Indian History*, trans. and ed. S.T. Godbole (Kindle edition). (The print edition is an independent publication with copyrights belonging to Himani Savarkar and internet rights are with Swatantryaveer Savarkar Rashtriya Smarak Trust.)
7. Ibid.
8. M.S. Golwalkar, *Bunch of Thoughts* (Sahitya Sindhu Prakashana, Bangalore, 1996, reprinted 2000).
9. Ibid., 180.
10. Ibid., 181–82.
11. Nathuram Godse, *Why I Assassinated Gandhi* (Farsight Publishers, India, 2014, revised edition).
12. 'Baudhik' refers to intellectual work and 'karyewah' is a secretary or an executive head of a group. Baudhik karyewah is a person in charge of the intellectual cell in the RSS.
13. Vasudha Venugopal, 'Nathuram Godse Never Left RSS, Says His Family', *Economic Times*, https://economictimes.indiatimes.com/news/politics-and-nation/nathuram-godse-never-left-rss-says-his-family/articleshow/54159375.cms.

14. Godse, *Why I Assassinated Gandhi*.
15. Ibid.
16. Rajmohan Gandhi, *Patel: A Life* (Navjivan Trust, India, 2011).
17. Ibid.
18. Des Raj Goel, *Rashtriya Swayamsewak Sangh* (South Asia Books, 1979).
19. 'Top Five Controversial Comments by Yogi Adityanath', *Economic Times*, https://economictimes.indiatimes.com/news/politics-and-nation/top-five-controversial-comments-by-yogi-adityanath/articleshow/57707151.cms.
20. As telecast on NDTV on 7 February 2018.
21. The 'halala' custom practised by some Muslims, dictates that a man cannot remarry his former wife after divorcing her unless the woman first marries another man and consummates that marriage.

TWO: The Politics of Gau Raksha

1. In August–September 2013, clashes took place between Hindus and Muslims in Muzaffarnagar district of Uttar Pradesh, which resulted in sixty-two deaths, including that of forty-two Muslims. More than 50,000 people were displaced and lived in tents for months. Akhilesh Yadav was the chief minister at that time. It was believed that Muzaffarnagar riot was engineered for the political purpose of creating a Hindu–Muslim divide.
2. Purusharth Aradhak, 'Lynching Planned to Stoke Unrest: Intel', *Times of India*, 5 October 2015, https://timesofindia.indiatimes.com/india/Lynching-planned-to-stoke-unrest-Intel/articleshow/49220545.cms.
3. Damini Nath, 'Dadri Incident a Well-planned Conspiracy, Says Report', *Hindu*, 7 October 2015, https://www.thehindu.com/news/national/other-states/dadri-incident-a-wellplanned-conspiracy-says-report/article7731343.ece.
4. Purusharth Aradhak, 'Young, Educated, and Ready to Fight for "Right"', *Times of India*, 2 October 2015, https://timesofindia.indiatimes.com/city/noida/Young-educated-and-ready-to-fight-for-right/articleshow/49189741.cms.
5. Aditi Vatsa, Manish Sahu, 'Dadri Lynching: UP Homeguard Spread Beef Rumour to Instigate Attack on Father and Son, Says Police', *Indian Express*, 4 October 2015, https://indianexpress.com/article/india/india-others/dadri-lynching-up-homeguard-spread-beef-rumour-to-instigate-attack-on-father-and-son-says-police/.

6. Purusharth Aradhak, 'Priest Who Started It All Missing', *Times of India*, 2 October 2015, https://timesofindia.indiatimes.com/city/noida/Priest-who-started-it-all-missing/articleshow/49190063.cms.
7. Poonam Agarwal, 'Dadri Lynching: Strangely, the Temple Priest is Not a Witness', Quint, 25 December 2015, https://www.thequint.com/news/india/dadri-lynching- strangely-the-temple-priest-is-not-a-witness.
8. Ibid.
9. Aradhak, 'Lynching Planned to Stoke Unrest: Intel', *Times of India*.
10. Aman Sharma, Manmohan Rai, 'Cow's Meat in Sample: BJP Leaders Demand Jail for Mohammad Akhlaq's Family', *Economic Times*, 2 June 2016, https://economictimes.indiatimes.com/news/politics-and- nation/cows-meat-in-sample-bjp-leaders-demand-jail-for-mohammad-akhlaqs-family/articleshow/52544356.cms.
11. Pervez Iqbal Siddiqui, '"We are victims turned into accused"', *Times of India*, 28 July 2016, https://timesofindia.indiatimes.com/city/lucknow/We-are-victims-turned-into-accused/articleshow/53424127.cms.
12. Ibid.
13. Pervez Iqbal Siddiqui, 'Meat Not from Akhlaq House: Report', *Times of India*, 2 June 2016, http://epaperbeta.timesofindia.com/Article.aspx?eid=31804&articlexml=Meat-not-from-Akhlaq-house-Report-02062016015009.
14. Aman Sharma, 'Mohd Akhlaq's Family Should Be Sent to Jail: Sangeet Som', *Economic Times*, 2 June 2016, https://economictimes.indiatimes.com/opinion/interviews/mohd-akhlaqs-family-should-be-sent-to-jail-sangeet-som/articleshow/52544491.cms.
15. Purusharth Aradhak, 'Release Accused and Arrest Cow Slaughterers: BJP', *Times of India* (Noida/Ghaziabad Edition), 1 October 2015.
16. Purusharth Aradhak, 'I Should Have Guarded Akhlaq's House: Rana', *Times of India*, 7 October 2015, https://timesofindia.indiatimes.com/india/I-should-have-guarded-Akhlaqs-house-Rana/articleshow/49251104.cms.
17. Sandeep Rai, 'Muslims Kill Cows Because Their Intentions Are Clear—to Hurt the Religious Sentiments of Hindus', *Times of India*, 2 October 2015, https://timesofindia.indiatimes.com/city/noida/Muslims-kill-cows-because-their-intentions-are-clear-to-hurt-the-religious-sentiments-of-Hindus/articleshow/49184996.cms
18. 'Saffron Hawks Stir Communal Pot in Dadri', *Times of India*, 8 October 2015, https://timesofindia.indiatimes.com/city/noida/Saffron-hawks-stir-communal-pot-in-Dadri/articleshow/49265923.cms.

19. 'Beef or Meat: Yogi Adityanath Wants Akhlaq's Kin Booked for Cow Slaughter', *Economic Times*, 1 June 2016, https://archive.siasat.com/news/beef-meat-yogi-adityanath-wants-akhlaqs-kin-booked-cow-slaughter-965432/.
20. 'Case Slapped On Kin Of Dadri Victim', *Times of India*, 16 July 2016, https://www.freepressjournal.in/india/case-slapped-on-kin-of-dadri-victim/889908.
21. S.A. Aiyar, 'The Dadri Effect: Killing Beef-eaters Will Not Win Elections', *Times of India* 19 October 2015, https://timesofindia.indiatimes.com/blogs/Swaminomics/the-dadri-effect-killing-beef-eaters-will-not-win-elections/.
22. Chaitanya Kalbag, 'The Beef With India's Economy: Challenge on Government's Plate', *Economic Times*, 8 October 2015, https://blogs.economictimes.indiatimes.com/the-needles-eye/the-beef-with-the-indian-economy-the-challenge-on-the-governments-plate/.
23. 'Vedas Say Kill Those Who Slaughter Cows: Panchjanya', *Times of India*, 19 October 2015, https://timesofindia.indiatimes.com/india/Vedas-say-kill-those-who-slaughter-cows-Panchjanya/articleshow/49445823.cms.
24. Ibid.
25. Aakar Patel, 'BJP Summoned the Gau Raksha Genie, Now It Must Bottle It', *Times of India*, 2 July 2017, http://www1.epaperbeta.timesofindia.com/Article.aspx?eid=31805&articlexml=AAKARVANI-BJP-summoned-the-gau-raksha-genie-now-02072017012044.
26. Alok K.N. Mishra, '2 Muslims Herding Buffaloes Thrashed, Hanged in Jharkhand', *Times of India*, 19 March 2016, https://timesofindia.indiatimes.com/city/ranchi/2-Muslims-herding-buffaloes-thrashed-hanged-in-Jharkhand/articleshow/51465433.cms.
27. Gayas Eapen, 'Jaisingpur Mourns Pehlu Khan's Death', *Times of India*, 07 April 2017, https://timesofindia.indiatimes.com/city/jind/jaisingpur-mourns-pehlu-khans-death/articleshow/58073901.cms.
28. 'Rajasthan Police Deliberately Weakened Pehlu Khan Lynching Case, Says Independent Report; Family Sees Little Hope for Justice', Firstpost, 26 October 2017, https://www.firstpost.com/india/rajasthan-police-deliberately-weakened-pehlu-khan-lynching-case-says-independent-report-family-sees-little-hope-for-justice-4178381.html.
29. Ibid.
30. Pankaj Doval, 'Antisocials by Night Turn Gau Rakshaks by Day: PM', *Times of India*, 07 August 2016, https://timesofindia.indiatimes.com/Antisocials-by-night-turn-gau-rakshaks-by-day-PM/articleshow/53579893.cms.
31. 'Action Against Cow Slaughter as Per Law: PM', *Times of India*, 30 June 2017, http://epaperbeta.timesofindia.com/Article.aspx? eid=31807&articlexml=Action-against-cow-slaughter-as-per-law-PM- 30062017019040.

32. Bharati Jain, 'Don't Tolerate Cow Vigilantism, Punish Those Who Take Law in Their Hands, Centre Tells States', *Times of India*, 9 August 2016, https://timesofindia. indiatimes.com/india/Dont-tolerate-cow-vigilantism-punish-those-who-take-law-in-their-hands-Centre-tells-states/articleshow/53621585.cms; https://www.pressreader.com/india/the-times-of-india-new-delhi-edition/20160810/281526520444934.
33. Amit Anand Choudhary, 'We Have No Role to Play in Cases of Cow Vigilantism, Centre Tells SC', *Times of India*, 22 July 2017, https://timesofindia.indiatimes.com/india/we-have-no-role-to-play-in-cases-of-cow-vigilantism-centre-tells-supreme-court/articleshow/59704098.cms.
34. 'Entire Kashmir Is Ours; Gaurakshaks Should Work as Per the Law: RSS Chief Mohan Bhagwat', *Economic Times*, 12 October 2016, https://economictimes.indiatimes.com/news/politics-and-nation/entire-kashmir-is-ours-gaurakshaks-should-work-as-per-the-law-rss-chief-mohan-bhagwat/articleshow/54801934.cms.
35. 'RSS Chief: Violence Only Defames Effort of Cow Protectors', *Times of India*, 10 April 2017, https://timesofindia.indiatimes.com/india/rss-chief-calls-for-all-india-ban-on-cow-slaughter/articleshow/58099954.cms.
36. Baiju Kalesh, Krishna Kumar, 'RSS' Seshadri Chari Slams Alwar Incident', *Economic Times*, 10 April 2017, https://economictimes.indiatimes.com/news/politics-and-nation/rss-seshadri-chari-slams-alwar-incident/articleshow/58103369.cms.
37. Narendra Jadhav, *Ambedkar: Awakening India's Social Conscience* (Konark Publishers, New Delhi, 2014).
38. Ibid.
39. Shamsul Islam, *Golwalkar's We or Our Nationhood Defined: A Critique with the Full Text of the Book* (Pharos Media and Publishing, India, 2015, second edition).
40. D.N. Jha, 'How the Story of the Cow in India Is Riddled with Puzzles and Paradoxes', *Indian Express*, 07 October 2015, https://indianexpress.com/article/opinion/columns/elusive-holiness-of-the-cow/.
41. Ibid.
42. Ibid.
43. Jadhav, *Ambedkar*.
44. Jha, 'How the Story of the Cow in India Is Riddled with Puzzles and Paradoxes'.
45. Vaibhav Purandare, 'The Cow and Savarkar: Where the Bovine Is Not Divine but the Framework Is Still Hardline Hindutva', *Times of India,* 9 June

2017, https://timesofindia.indiatimes.com/blogs/toi-edit-page/the-cow-and-savarkar-where-the-bovine-is-not-divine-but-the-framework-is-still-hardline-hindutva/.
46. Samagra Savarkar Vangmaya, ed. Shankar Ramchandra Date, vol. 3 (Samagra Savarkar Vangmaya Prakashan Samiti, Maharashtra Prantik Hindu Sabha, Pune, 1963-65), p. 167.
47. 'What Mahatma Gandhi Said to Those Who Wanted Beef Banned in India', Wire, 1 October 2018, https://thewire.in/politics/what-mahatma-gandhi-said-to-those-who-wanted-beef-banned-in-india.
48. Vikas Pathak, 'Golwalkar Saw Slaughter of Cow as "Mental Slavery"', *Hindu*, 6 November 2015, https://www.thehindu.com/news/national/rss-golwalkar-saw-slaughter-of-cow-as-mental-slavery/article7851746.ece.
49. Ibid.
50. Ibid.
51. Chandana Chakrabarti 'When P.M. Bhargava's Biochemistry Lesson on Beef Threw Golwalkar Into a Fit', Wire, 2 August 2017, https://thewire.in/history/p-m-bhargavas-biochemistry-lesson-beef-threw-golwalkar-fit.
52. Ibid.
53. 'Modi Calls Dadri, Ghulam Ali Row "Saddening, Unfortunate"', *Times of India*, 15 October 2015, https://timesofindia.indiatimes.com/india/Modi-calls-Dadri-Ghulam-Ali-row-saddening-unfortunate/articleshow/49350355.cms.
54. Ramesh Babu, Ravik Bhattacharya, '"Never Favoured Beef Ban": BJP's Balancing Act in Kerala, Bengal', *Economic Times*, 21 January 2016, https://www.hindustantimes.com/india/never-favoured-beef-ban-bjp-s-balancing-act-in-kerala-bengal/story-n9ciJpArbkGGySH7486KPJ.html.
55. 'Mumbai court strikes down ban of consuming beef in Maharashtra', *National* (Abu Dhabi), 6 May 2016, https://www.thenational.ae/world/asia/mumbai-court-strikes-down-ban-of-consuming-beef-in-maharashtra-1.212059.
56. 'Abattoirs Violating NGT Guidelines Won't Be Spared: Yogi Adityanath', DNA, 26 March 2017, https://www.dnaindia.com/india/report-abattoirs-violating-ngt-guidelines-won-t-be-spared-yogi-adityanath-2368484.
57. S.A. Aiyar, 'Mass Closure of Abattoirs Will Hit Muslims, Dalits, Farmers', *Times of India*, 02 April 2017, https://blogs.timesofindia.indiatimes.com/Swaminomics/mass-closure-of-abattoirs-will-hit-muslims-dalits-farmers/.
58. 'Will Hang Cow Killers, Chhattisgarh CM Raman Singh Says', *Times of India*, 1 April 2017, https://timesofindia.indiatimes.com/india/will-hang-cow-killers-chhattisgarh-cm-raman-singh-says/articleshow/57963628.cms.

59. Srinath Raghavan, 'Do Empires Manage Diversity Better Than Nation States?', *Open*, 14 July, 2017, http://www.openthemagazine.com/node?page%3D590=laagwkyoqv& page=191.

THREE: Victimhood No More

1. Sarah Hafeez, '"Am I not a Hindu? Don't I have same Constitution?" asks UP Dalit groom', *Indian Express*, 1 April 2018, https://indianexpress.com/article/india/am-i-not-a-hindu-dont-i-have-same-constitution-asks-uttar-pradesh-dalit-groom-5119019/.
2. Savarna are the upper caste, namely Brahmin, Kshatriya and Vaishya.
3. Badri Narayan, 'How BJP Won Uttar Pradesh', *Mint*, 4 June 2014, https://www.livemint.com/Opinion/tjLK1iWmbHnQv LsnzaIbwK/How-BJP-won-Uttar-Pradesh.html.
4. 'My Birth Is My Fatal Accident: Full Text of Dalit Student Rohith's Suicide Letter', *Indian Express*, 19 January 2016, https://indianexpress.com/article/india/india.news-india/dalit-student-suicide-full-text-of-suicide-letter-hyderabad/.
5. S. Santosh, 'Dalitization of Politics and the Suicide Note of Rohith Vemula', *Seminar*, no. 691 (March 2017), http://www.india-seminar.com/2017/691/691_santhosh_s.htm.
6. Rohith Vemula, 'Online diary of Rohith Vemula: Resist Sangh's Sullying of Ambedkar's Legacy', Daily O, 12 August 2016, https://www.dailyo.in/politics/rohith-vemula-br-ambedkar-caste-system-dalit-politics-sangh-parivar-bjp-university-of-hyderabad-ambedkar-student-association/story/1/12335.html.
7. Ibid.
8. 'The Letter from BJP MP Bandaru Dattatreya Which Led To Rohith's Eviction and Suicide', India Resists, 18 January, 2016, https://indiaresists.com/the-letter-from-bjp-mp-bandaru-dattatreya-which-led-to-rohiths-eviction-and-suicide/
9. Sandhya Ravishankar, 'No University for Dalits', Wire, 21 January 2016, https://thewire.in/society/no-university-for-dalits.
10. 'Writer Ashok Vajpeyi to Return D Litt from Hyderabad University', *Times of India*, 19 January 2016, https://timesofindia.indiatimes.com/india/Writer-Ashok-Vajpeyi-to-return-D-Litt-from-Hyderabad-University/articleshow/50641994.cms.
11. 'After Ahmedabad and Agra Rallies, BJP Feels Dalit Heat: Time for Party to Rethink Poll Strategy', Firstpost, 1 August 2016, https://www.firstpost.com/

politics/after-ahmedabad-and-agra-rallies-bjp-feels-dalit-heat-time-for-party-to-rethink-poll-strategy-2927064.html.; Asees Bhasin, 'Ahmedabad Rally: Dalits Demand Firearms and Permanent Jobs', Quint, 1 August 2016 https://www.thequint.com/news/india/ahmedabad-rally-dalits-demand-firearms-and-permanent-jobs.

12. Darshan Desai, 'At Massive Rally in Ahmedabad, Dalits Pledge Not to Pick Up Gujarat's Carcasses', Scroll.in, 31 July 2016, https://scroll.in/article/812910/at-massive-rally-in-ahmedabad-dalits-pledge-not-to-pick-up-gujarats-carcasses.
13. Ibid.
14. One of the largest communities of India, the Chamars are a scheduled caste with a single generic name. The name 'Chamar' is derived from the Sanskrit charmakar (leather worker). They have traditionally worked with leather, as the name suggests, tanning hides and crafting shoes and bags. They were relegated to living on the outer edges of villages due to the smell of rotting hides from their workshops and the chemicals they used in their home-based workshops.
15. Rana, Udaipur Singh; News18.com, 25 May 2017; https://www.news18.com/news/immersive/politics-of-saharanpur-riots.html.
16. Uday Singh Rana, 'When Caste Killed Community in Saharanpur', News18, 25 May 2017, https://www.news18.com/news/immersive/politics-of-saharanpur-riots.html.
17. Ibid.
18. The Mahars (also known as Maha, Mehar, Taral, Dhegu Megu) are an Indian community, living largely in the state of Maharashtra, where they comprise 12–15 per cent of the population, and neighbouring areas. Most of the Mahar community followed B.R. Ambedkar in converting to Buddhism in the middle of the twentieth century. As of 2017, the Mahar caste has been designated as a scheduled caste in sixteen Indian states.
19. Thomas Crowley, '200 Years of Anti-caste Struggle', *Jacobin*, 25 January 2018, https://jacobinmag.com/2018/01/caste-modi-bjp-hindutva-dalit.
20. Ibid.
21. Chandan Haygunde, 'Dispute over Samadhi at Vadhu Budruk: "Descendant" Wants Construction at Samadhi, Cops Tell Him "Seek Govt Nod"', *Indian Express*, 9 February 2018, https://indianexpress.com/article/cities/pune/dispute-over-samadhi-at-vadhu-budruk-descendant-wants-construction-at-samadhi-cops-tell-him-seek-govt-nod-5355397/.
22. 'Maharashtra Bandh: Removal of Board at Mahar Samadhi Was Trigger for Bhima-Koregaon Clash', Firstpost, 4 January 2018, https://www.firstpost.

com/india/maharashtra-bandh-removal-of-board-at-mahar-samadhi-was-trigger-for-bhima-koregaon-clash-4286677.html.
23. 'Bhima Koregaon Violence: Jignesh Mevani-Umar Khalid Event Denied Permission; 16 FIRs Lodged', *Economic Times*, 4 January 2018, https://economictimes.indiatimes.com/news/politics-and-nation/violence-hits-mumbai-parts-of-maharashtra-as-caste-clash-turns-ugly/articleshow/62337411.cms.
24. 'RSS: Violence a Handiwork of "Breaking India Brigade"', *Times of India*, 4 January 2018, https://timesofindia.indiatimes.com/india/rss-violence-a-handiwork-of-breaking-india-brigade/articleshow/62358989.cms.
25. V.D. Savarkar, *Six Glorious Epochs of Indian History*, trans. and ed. S.T. Godbole (Kindle edition), ch. 1, para. 46.
26. Narendra Jadhav; *Ambedkar Awakening India's Social Conscience* (Konark Publishers, 2014).
27. B.R. Ambedkar, *The Untouchables: Who Were They and Why They Became Untouchables* (Kalpaz Publications, 2017).
28. Jadhav, *Ambedkar*, p. 523.
29. According to Hindu mythology, Brahmins were fashioned from the mouth of Brahma, the Kshatriyas from the arms, Vaishyas from the thighs and Shudras from the feet. Hence the Shudras are also called 'foot-born'.
30. Jadhav, *Ambedkar*, p. 164.
31. Jadhav, *Ambedkar*, p. 163.
32. Savarkar, *Six Glorius Epochs*, ch. 7, para. 392.
33. Ibid.; M.S. Golwalkar, *Bunch of Thoughts* (Sahitya Sindhu Prakashana, Bangalore, 1996, reprinted 2000), p. 353.
34. Rakesh Sinha, *Dalit Question and RSS* (India Policy Foundation, 2014).
35. Ibid.
36. Golwalkar, *Bunch of Thoughts*.
37. Ibid.
38. Shamsul Islam, *Hindutva: Savarkar Unmasked* (Media House Delhi, 2016, 4th edition).
39. Ibid.
40. Jyotirmaya Sharma, *Hindutva: Exploring the Idea of Hindu Nationalism* (Harper Collins, 2015).
41. Ibid.
42. Deshastha Brahmins are a Hindu Brahmin sub-caste mainly from the Indian state of Maharashtra or the northern area of the state of Karnataka. The word 'deshastha' derives from the Sanskrit de☐a (inland, country) and -stha (resident), literally translating to 'residents of the country'. The valleys

of Krishna and Godavari rivers and a part of the Deccan plateau adjacent to the Sahyadri hills were collectively termed desha—the original home of the Deshastha Brahmins. Chitpavan Brahmins or Kokanastha Brahmins (Brahmins native to the Konkan) belong to a Hindu Brahmin community inhabiting the Konkan area, the coastal region of the state of Maharashtra in India. The community came into prominence during the eighteenth century, when the heirs of the peshwa from the Bhat family descended from Balaji Vishwanath, became the de facto rulers of the Maratha empire.

43. Savarkar, *Six Glorious Epochs*, ch.16, para. 1004.
44. B.R. Ambedkar, *Annihilation of Caste: The Annotated Critical Edition* (Navayana Publishing, New Delhi, 2014), p. 214.
45. Abhiram Ghadyalpatil, Shaswati Das, 'Maharashtra Cops Crack Down on "Urban Naxals" in Five States', *Mint*, 29 August 2018, https://www.livemint.com/Politics/83dgRkXPQhrsgfHuFKkgyJ/Maharashtra- cops-crack-down-on-urban-Naxals-in-five-states.html.
46. Mohua Chatterjee, 'Combative BJP Endorses Arrest of "Urban Naxals"', *Times of India*, 9 September 2018, https://timesofindia.indiatimes.com/india/combative-bjp-endorses-arrest-of-urban-naxals/articleshow/65737378.cms.
47. 'Bhima Koregaon Exclusive: "Secret" Official Report Blames Sambhaji Bhide and Milind Ekbote for the Violence', *Times of India*, 1 September 2018, https://www.timesnownews.com/india/article/exclusive-bhima-koregaon-violence-secret-state-documents-pune-police-maharashtra-government-accuse-sambhaji-bhide-milind-ekbote-for-clashes-hindutva/278017.
48. 'भीमा-कोरेगांव हिंसा में 5 लोगों की गिरफ्तारी पर बोलीं अरुंधति रॉय, 'इमरजेंसी की घोषणा होने वाली है (Arundhati Roy Calls the Arrest of Five People in the Bhima-Koregaon Violence a Declaration of Emergency)', NDTV, 28 August, 2018. https://khabar.ndtv.com/news/india/bhima-koregaon-violence-arundhati-roy-calls-it-deceleration-of-emergency-1907675.
49. Nilanjan Mukhopadhyay, 'BJP, Sangh's Dalit Outreach Faces Challenge', *Economic Times*, 22 July 2016, https://blogs.economictimes.indiatimes.com/et-commentary/bjp-sanghs-dalit-outreach-faces-challenge/.
50. In 1923, the legislative council of Bombay passed a resolution and allowed 'untouchables' to use public tanks, wells, schools, courts and dispensaries. In the town of Mahad (in Maharashtra), the Municipality declared that it had no objections if the 'untouchables' used the Chavadar tank. In 1927, the 'untouchables' led by Ambedkar gathered to use the water of the Chavadar tank and as they drank the water they were attacked by upper-caste people.

Twenty were injured. Mahad Satyagraha was the first collective protest of 'untouchables' under the leadership of Ambedkar.
51. Anubhuti Vishnoi, 'The New-age Dalits Are Unapologetic, Unashamed of Their Identity', *Economic Times*, 1 August 2016, https://economictimes.indiatimes.com/news/politics-and-nation/the-new-age-dalits-are-unapologetic-unashamed-of-their-identity/articleshow/53481973.cms.
52. Ibid.
53. Ibid.
54. 'What Is the Furore over the SC/ST Act About?', News Minute, 4 April 2018, https://www.thenewsminute.com/article/explainer-what-furore-over-scst-act-about-79018.
55. Ambedkar, *Annihilation of Caste*, pp. 303–04.

FOUR: Hindutva at War with History

1. Muzamil Jaleel, 'Kathua Chargesheet: In J-K Child Gangrape, Rituals, a Chilling Invite and a Police Cover-up', *Indian Express*, 17 April 2018, https://indianexpress.com/article/india/kathua-chargesheet-in-jk-child-gangrape-rituals-a-chilling-invite-and-a-police-cover-up-5132283/.
2. 'Kathua Minor's Rape-Murder Was Over Cow Slaughter, Say J&K Cops', *Times of India*, 12 April 2018, https://timesofindia.indiatimes.com/city/jammu/kathua-minors-rape-murder-was-over-cow-slaughter-say-jk-cops/articleshow/63724198.cms.
3. 'In Rajasthan, Murder Of A Muslim Man Is Recorded On Camera, Killer Rants About "Love Jihad"', *Outlook*, 7 December 2017, https://www.outlookindia.com/website/story/in-rajasthan-this-man-kills-muslim-on-camera-and-gives-a-reason-for-the-crime-to/305269.
4. 'Rajasthan Man Releases New Hate Video From Jail, Shambhulal Regar New Video From Jail', Nyooz TV, https://www.youtube.com/watch?v=dcz859c6oPc.
5. 'Letter: Sardar Vallabhai Patel to RSS Chief Guru Golwalkar—1948', Kractivist, 8 October 2013, http://www.kractivist.org/letter-sardar-vallabhai-patel-to-rss-chief-guru-golwalkar-1948-godse-mustread/
6. Richard Overy, *The Dictators: Hitler's Germany, Stalin's Russia* (Penguin, London, 2005), p. 635.
7. Ibid., pp. 641–42.
8. William L. Shirer, *The Rise and Fall of the Third Reich: A History of Nazi Germany* (Arrow Books, Great Britain, 1998), p. 167.

9. Ian Kershaw, *Hitler* (Penguin, London, 2009), p. xl.
10. Shamshul Islam, *Golwalkar's We or Our Nationhood Defined: A Critique* (Pharos Media & Publishing, Delhi, 2015), p. 148.
11. Ibid.
12. Adolf Hitler, *Mein Kampf* (A.B.C Publishers, New Delhi, 1968).
13. Ibid., p. 276.
14. Islam, *Golwalkar's We or Our Nationhood Defined*, p. 150.
15. Rajmohan Gandhi, *Revenge and Reconciliation: Understanding South Asian History* (Penguin, Delhi, 2006), p. 226.
16. Islam, *Golwalkar's We or Our Nationhood Defined*, p. 183.
17. Gandhi, *Revenge and Reconciliation*, p. 238.
18. Rajmohan Gandhi, *Mohandas: A True Story of a Man, His People and an Empire* (Penguin, New Delhi, 2006), p. 642.
19. Jyotirmaya Sharma, *Hindutva: Exploring the Idea of Hindu Nationalism* (HarperCollins, New Delhi, 2015).
20. Ibid.
21. Ibid., p. 116.
22. Ibid.
23. Ibid., p. 66.
24. Ibid.; p. 33.
25. Purushottam Agrawal, *Sanskriti: Varchasva aur Pratirodh* (Rajkamal Prakashan, Delhi, 2008).
26. V.D. Savarkar, *Six Glorious Epochs of Indian History*, trans. and ed. S.T. Godbole (Kindle edition), ch. 8, para. 442.
27. Dhananjay Keer, *Veer Savarkar* (Popular Prakashan Ltd., Mumbai, 2012).
28. '"I Won't Say Bharat Mata Ki Jai": Asaduddin Owaisi to Mohan Bhagwat', *Times of India*, 14 March 2016, https://timesofindia.indiatimes.com/india/I-wont-say-Bharat-Mata-Ki-Jai-Asaduddin-Owaisi-to-Mohan-Bhagwat/articleshow/51394628.cms.
29. 'Muslims Mustn't Say "Bharat Mata Ki Ja"': Deoband', *Times of India*, 2 April 2016, http://epaperbeta.timesofindia.com/Article.aspx?eid=31813&articlexml=Muslims-mustnt-say-Bharat-mata-ki-jai-Deoband-02042016001030.
30. Ibid.
31. 'Jamat Backs Fatwa on "Bharat Mata"', *Times of India*, 3 April 2016; https://timesofindia.indiatimes.com/india/Jamat-backs-fatwa-on-Bharat-Mata/articleshow/51666308.cms.
32. Mohammed Wajihuddin, 'Islam Does Not Prohibit Expressing Love for State', *Times of India*, 17 March 2016, https://timesofindia.indiatimes.

com/city/mumbai/Islam-does-not-prohibit-expressing-love-for-state/articleshow/51447876.cms.
33. '"All Indians don't look upon Bharat as their mother"', *Times of India*, 18 March 2016; https://timesofindia.indiatimes.com/india/All-Indians-dont-look-upon-Bharat-as-their-mother/articleshow/51450231.cms.
34. Wajihuddin, 'Islam Does Not Prohibit Expressing Love for State'.
35. The Razakars were a private militia organised by Qasim Rizvi to support the rule of Nizam Mir Osman Ali Khan Siddiqi, Asaf Jah VII, and to resist the integration of the princely state of Hyderabad and Berar into the dominion of India. They also attempted to make the Nizam accede his princely state to Pakistan instead of India.
36. Rajesh Ramachandran, 'Asaduddin Owaisi's Remark: Razakars Don't Say "Bharat Mata Ki Jai"', *Economic Times*, 17 March 2016, https://blogs.economictimes.indiatimes.com/Polibelly/asaduddin-owaisis-remark-razakars-dont-say-bharat-mata-ki-jai/.
37. Pervez Iqbal Siddqui, Sandeep Rai, 'UP Govt Orders Madrassas to Submit Videos of I-Day Events', *Times of India*, 12 August 2017, http://epaperbeta.timesofindia.com/Article.aspx?eid=31804&articlexml=UP-govt-orders-madrassas-to-submit-videos-of-12082017037014.
38. M.S. Golwalkar, *Bunch of Thoughts* (Sahitya Sindhu Prakashana, Bangalore, 1996, reprinted 2000), ch.16.
39. Ibid.
40. Abhinav Garg, Sana Shakil, 'Kanhaiya Was Shaking Like a Coward, Won't Forget: Lawyer', *Times of India*, 18 February 2016, https://timesofindia.indiatimes.com/india/Kanhaiya-was-shaking-like-a-coward-wont-forget-Lawyer/articleshow/51036272.cms.
41. Somreet Bhattacharya, 'Serial Attacker First Felicitated, Now Marches Free at India Gate,' *Times of India*, 20 February 2016, https://timesofindia.indiatimes.com/india/Serial-attacker-first-felicitated-now-marches-free-at-India-Gate/articleshow/51063691.cms.
42. Akshay Deshmane, 'JNU Stir: When Defenders of Civil Rights Turned Attackers at Patiala House Court', *The Economic Times*, 16 February 2016. https://economictimes.indiatimes.com/news/politics-and-nation/jnu-stir-when-defenders-of-civil-rights-turned-attackers-at-patiala-house-court/articleshow/51002252.cms.
43. Rakesh Mohan Chaturvedi, 'Jan Swabhiman Abhiyan: Inspired by JNU stir, BJP to take nationalism debate to masses', 17 February 2016, https://economictimes.indiatimes.com/news/politics-and-nation/jan-swabhiman-

abhiyan-inspired-by-jnu-stir-bjp-to-take-nationalism-debate-to-masses/articleshow/51016558.cms

44. 'JNU Row: Timeline of Lawyers "Unleashing Anarchy" in Court', *Times of India*, 18 February 2016, https://timesofindia.indiatimes.com/india/JNU-row-Timeline-of-lawyers-unleashing-anarchy-in-court/articleshow/51036310.cms.

45. Dhananjay Mahapatra, Abhindav Garg, 'Was Kanhaiya Boxed Inside Courtroom?', *Times of India*, 19 February 2016, https://timesofindia.indiatimes.com/india/Was-Kanhaiya-boxed-inside-courtroom/articleshow/51050597.cms.

46. Ibid.

47. Sana Shakil, Somreet Bhattacharya, 'Cops Fail to Shield Kumar from blows', *Times of India*, 18 February 2016, https://timesofindia.indiatimes.com/city/delhi/Cops-fail-to-shield-Kumar-from-blows/articleshow/51031550.cms.

48. Ravish Tiwari, 'Hyderabad, JNU Incidents Show Unease of Anti-nationals: RSS', *Economic Times*, 12 March 2016, https://economictimes.indiatimes.com/news/politics-and-nation/hyderabad-jnu-incidents-show-unease-of-anti-nationals-rss/articleshow/51365922.cms.

49. 'Clashes at Ramjas College: Journalists Assaulted by Cops on Campus', *Times of India*, 23 February 2017, https://timesofindia.indiatimes.com/city/delhi/journalists-assaulted-by-cops-on-campus/articleshow/57300800.cms.

50. Sanjana Agnihotri, 'From DU Violence to Gurmehar Kaur Debate: All that Happened and Who Said What', *India Today*, 1 March 2017, https://www.indiatoday.in/fyi/story/gurmehar-kaur-abvp-ramjas-college-twitter-who-said-what-sehwag-kejriwal-rijiju-963376-2017-03-01.

51. '"Heartbroken" Gurmehar Kaur Takes on Virender Sehwag, Says "These People Troll You at Expense of Your Father's Death', *Financial Times*, 27 February, 2017, https://www.financialexpress.com/india-news/heartbroken-gurmehar-kaur-takes-on-virender-sehwag-says-these-people-troll-you-at-expense-of-your-fathers-death/568806/.

52. Gurmehar Kaur, *Small Acts of Freedom* (Penguin Random House, New Delhi, 2018).

53. Savarkar, *Six Glorious Epochs of Indian History*.

54. Shamsul Islam, *Indian Freedom Movement and RSS: A Story of Betrayal* (Pharos Media & Publishing Ltd. 2017).

55. Golwalkar, *Bunch of Thoughts*, p. 151.

56. Ibid., p. 138.

57. Ibid., p. 47.

58. Ibid., p. 46.
59. Islam, *Indian Freedom Movement and RSS*.
60. Tathagata Roy, *Syama Prasad Mookerjee: Life and Times* (Penguin Viking, USA, 2018).
61. Golwalkar, *Bunch of Thoughts*.
62. Islam, *Indian Freedom Movement and RSS*.
63. Bipan Chandra, *India's Struggle for Independence: 1857–1947* (Penguin, Delhi, 1989).
64. Ibid., p. 23.
65. Narendra Jadhav, *Ambedkar: Awakening India's Social Conscience* (Konark Publishers, New Delhi, 2014), p. 124.
66. Ibid., p. 144.
67. J.B.P More, *Muslim Identity, Print Culture and the Dravidian Factor in Tamil Nadu* (Orient Blackswan, 2004).
68. Sharma, *Hindutva*, p. 114.

FIVE: The Kashmir Question

1. Rajmohan Gandhi, *Patel: A Life* (Navjivan Publishing House, Ahmedabad, 2013).
2. Sheikh Abdullah, *Flames of the Chinar: An Autobiography of Sheikh Abdullah*, tr. Khushwant Singh (Penguin, India, 1993).
3. Ibid., p. 83.
4. Ibid., p. 86.
5. Gandhi, *Patel*, p. 434.
6. Sheikh, *Flames of the Chinar*, p. 94.
7. Gandhi, *Patel*, p. 443.
8. Abdullah, *Flames of the Chinar*, p. 95.
9. Saeed Naqvi, *Being the Other: The Muslim in India* (Aleph Book Company, India, 2016), pp. 189–91.
10. Ibid., pp. 191–92.
11. Arshi Javaid, 'A Minister's Loose Remark Has Reopened One of the Darkest Chapters of Jammu's History', Scroll.in, 29 May 2016, http://scroll.in/article/808707/a-ministers-loose-remark-has-reopened-one-of-the-darkest-chapters-of-jammus-history.
12. Ibid.
13. Abdullah, *Flames of the Chinar*, p. 97.
14. Ibid., p. 72.

15. Ibid.
16. Shridhar D. Damle, Walter K. Andersen, *The Brotherhood in Saffron: The Rashtriya Swayamsevak Sangh and Hindu Revivalism* (Westview Press, 1988).
17. A.G. Noorani, 'BJP Raj in Kashmir?', *Greater Kashmir*, 23 November 2014; http://www.greaterkashmir.com/news/gk-magazine/bjp-raj-in-kashmir/180931.html.
18. Noorani, 'Dogra Raj in Kashmir', *Frontline*, 24 November 2017; http://www.frontline.in/the-nation/dogra-Raj-in-Kashmir/article9946288.ece.
19. Ibid.
20. Ibid.
21. Tathagata Roy, *Syama Prasad Mookerjee: Life and Times* (Penguin Viking, USA, 2018), p. 289.
22. Ibid., p. 350.
23. Abdullah, *Flames of the Chinar*.
24. Roy, *Syama Prasad Mookerjee*, p. 346.
25. Ibid., pp. 350–51.
26. Ibid., p. 411.
27. 'Modi–Mufti Meet: North, South Poles Unite', *Deccan Chronicle*, 10 January 2016, https://www.deccanchronicle.com/150228/nation-current-affairs/article/modi-mufti-meet-north-south-poles-unite.
28. According to the original constitution of J&K, the head of the government was called the prime minister but on 30 march 1965, the designation was changed to chief minister, like in other states of India, through an amendment brought into the state's constitution; When Mufti Mohammad Sayeed assumed office as the chief minister of J&K he followed what was called the policy of healing touch. He believed that the people of Kashmir were badly wounded and needed to be healed to create an environment of dialogue to find a solution to the Kashmir issue. To win the confidence of the people he disbanded the Special Operation Groups (SOG), removed security barricades, did away with frisking, nocturnal raids, crackdowns and made security forces accountable.
29. 'Poor Turnout at Mufti's Funeral Worries PDP', *The Hindu*, 17 January 2016, http://www.thehindu.com/news/national/other-states/Poor-turnout-at-Mufti-funeral-worries-PDP/article14001925.ece.
30. Hakeem Irfan Rashid, 'Is Mehbooba Mufti Buying Time Before Becoming Jammu & Kashmir's CM to Reset BJP-PDP Equation?', *Economic Times*, 24 January 2016, http://economictimes.indiatimes.com/news/politics-and-nation/is-mehbooba-mufti-buying-time-before-becoming-jammu-kashmirs-cm-to-reset-bjp-pdp-equation/articleshow/50699151.cms.

31. Ibid.
32. Hizbul Mujahideen is a terrorist organization operating in Kashmir. It was formed in 1989, supported and funded by Pakistan. It is an Islamist group, which propagates the merger of Kashmir with Pakistan.
33. Bashaarat Masood, 'Clashing with Forces, Mourners Make Their Way to Funeral', Indian Express, 10 July 2016, http://indianexpress.com/article/india/india-news-india/clashing-with-forces-mourners-make-their-way-to-funeral-2904368.
34. Mir Ehsan, Muzamil Jaleel, 'J&K: 11 Killed, over 200 Hurt as Burhan Wani's Death Sparks Violence, Protests', *Indian Express*, 10 July 2016, http://indianexpress.com/article/india/india-news-india/11-killed-over-200-hurt-as-burhans-death-sparks-violence-protests-2904360.
35. Omar Farooq Khan, 'Now, Pakistan Targets PM Modi Directly, Blames Him for J&K', *Times of India,* 16 July 2016, violencehttps://timesofindia.indiatimes.com/india/Now-Pakistan-targets-PM-Modi-directly-blames-him-for-JK-violence/articleshow/53236211.cms.
36. Hakeem Irfan Rashid,'BurhanWani Incident Shows that Homegrown Militancy is Back After a Prolonged Hiatus', *Economic Times,* 2 August 2016, http://economictimes.indiatimes.com/news/politics-and-nation/burhan-wani-incident-shows-that-homegrown-militancy-is-back-after-a-prolonged-hiatus/articleshow/53242360.cms.
37. Aarti Tikoo Singh, 'Who Was the Real Burhan Wani, "Paper Tiger" or "Indian Agent"?', *Times of India,* 12 July 2016, https://timesofindia.indiatimes.com/india/Who-was-the-real-Burhan-Wani-paper-tiger-or-Indian-agent/articleshow/53163220.cms.
38. Aarti Tikoo Singh, 'J&K IAS Topper Blames Govt for Maiming "Own Citizens"', *Times of India*, 17 July 2016, http://timesofindia.indiatimes.com/city/srinagar/JK-IAS-topper-blames-govt-for-maiming-own-citizens/articleshow/53245959.cms.
39. M. Saleem Pandit, 'No Cops in Four South Kashmir Districts as Protests Rage',. *Times of India,* 23 August 2016, http://timesofindia.indiatimes.com/city/srinagar/No-cops-in-four-South-Kashmir-districts-as-protests-rage/articleshow/53818227.cms.
40. Dileep Padgaonkar, 'Impasse in Kashmir: A Muscular Approach, Coupled with Development, Cannot Resolve the Main Political Problem', *Times of India*, 12 July 2016, http://blogs.timesofindia.indiatimes.com/talking-terms/impasse-in-kashmir-a-muscular-approach-coupled-with-development-cannot-resolve-the-main-political-problem.

41. Between 1989 and 1990 approximately six lakh Kashmiri Pandits migrated from the Kashmir Valley to other parts of India when militant organisations started targeting Kashmiri Hindus. Their houses were burnt down and prominent Hindu citizens were killed. Kashmiri Pandits had been an integral part of Kashmir, though they formed only 65 per cent of the local population. But they used to dominate in the state bureaucracy especially during the time of Raja Hari Singh.
42. Aarti Tikoo Singh, 'Kashmir Conflict on Verge of Merging with IS War: Baig', *Times of India*, 25 August 2016, http://timesofindia.indiatimes.com/india/Kashmir-conflict-on-verge-of-merging-with-IS-war-Baig/articleshow/53852302.cms.
43. Kashmiri culture is known for its Sufi tradition, secular ethos and communal harmony. Its Islamic tradition was never rigid. It is moderate and inclusive. Despite Jinnah's advocacy of Pakistan in the name of Islam, Kashmir did not support Jinnah and his idea of Pakistan; 'Rajnath Singh: Those Who Believe in Kashmiriyat, Insaniyat & Jamhooriyat Welcome for Talks', *Indian Express*, 24 August 2016, https://indianexpress.com/article/india/india-news-india/rajnath-singh-those-who-believe-in-kashmiriyat-insaniyat-jamhooriyat-welcome-for-talks/.
44. Manoj Joshi, 'Uri: Isolating the War Party, and Not Demonising Pakistan is Needed', *Economic Times*, 20 September 2016, http://blogs.economictimes.indiatimes.com/toi-edit-page/uri-isolating-the-war-party-and-not-demonising-pakistan-is-needed.
45. Swapan Dasgupta, 'End of India's Strategic Restraint: Miles to Go', *Daily Pioneer*, 2 October 2016, https://www.dailypioneer.com/2016/columnists/end-of-indias-strategic-restraint-miles-to-go.html.
46. Manash Pratim Bhuyan, 'Army Chiefs Defends Human Shield, Says "Dirty War" Needs "Innovative" Response', Wire, 28 May 2017, https://thewire.in/government/army-chiefs-defends-human-shield-says-dirty-war-needs-innovative-respons.
47. 'Army Chief Bipin Rawat Steps in Political Waters by Commenting on Kashmir's Education System, Faces Backlash', Firstpost, 15 January 2018, https://www.firstpost.com/india/army-chief-bipin-rawat-steps-in-political-waters-by-commenting-on-kashmirs-education-system-faces-backlash-4303317.html.
48. Ibid.
49. 'J-K Govt Withdraws Stone-pelting Cases against 9,730 People, Recommends Amnesty for 4,000', *India Today*, 3 February 2018, https://www.indiatoday.in/india/story/jandampk-govt-okays-withdrawal-of-stone-pelting-cases-against-9730-1161052-2018-02-03.

50. 'Centre Asks Security Forces Not to Launch Operations in J&K during the Holy Month of Ramzan', Press Information Bureau, 16 May 2018, http://pib.nic.in/newsite/PrintRelease.aspx?relid=179358.
51. Hakeem Irfan Rashid, 'Ready for Talks with Right-minded People: Rajnath Singh on J&K Separatists', *Economic Times*, 8 June 2018, https://economictimes.indiatimes.com/news/politics-and-nation/ready-for-talks-with-right-minded-people-rajnath-singh-on-jk-separatists/articleshow/64502465.cms
52. 'After Mehbooba Mufti Experiment, over to Army', *Times of India*, 20 June 2018, https://timesofindia.indiatimes.com/india/after-mehbooba-mufti-experiment-over-to-army/articleshow/64655465.cms.
53. M.S. Golwalkar, *Bunch of Thoughts* (Sahitya Sindhu Prakashana, Bangalore, 1996, reprinted 2000), p. 179

SIX: The Line between Nationalism and Terrorism

1. 'He Confessed to Role in Hyd Blast', *Times of India*, 9 March 2017, http://epaperbeta.timesofindia.com/Article.aspx?eid=31808&articlexml=He-confessed-to-role-in-Hyd-blast-0903201701501.
2. 'The Swami Aseemanand Interviews', *Caravan*, 8 February 2014, https://caravanmagazine.in/reportage/swami-aseemanand-interviews
3. 'He confessed to Role in Hyd Blast', *Times of India*.
4. Supriya Sharma, 'Not Just Rohini Salian, Public Prosecutor in Ajmer Blast Case is Also Unhappy with NIA,' Scroll.in, 14 April 2015, http://scroll.in/article/747397/not-just-Rohini-Salian-public-prosecutor-in-Ajmer-blast-case-is-also-unhappy-with-nia.
5. Also named in reports as Rajendra Choudhury or Rajender Chaudhury.
6. Rahul Tripathi, 'Aseemanand Bail: NIA Brass Scuttled Plans for Appeal in HC', *Indian Express*, 9 April 2017, http://indianexpress.com/article/india/aseemanand-bail-nia-brass-scuttled-plans-for-appeal-in-hc-4605723.
7. Ajoy Ashirwad Mahaprashasta, 'Explainer: Is No One Guilty in the Mecca Masjid Blast?', Wire, 16 April 2018, http://thewire.in/security/mecca-masjid-blasts-case-verdict-explainer
8. Leena Gita Reghunath, 'A Violent End', *Caravan*, 1 March 2017, http://www.caravanmagazine.in/perspectives/sunil-joshi-murder-trial-collapse-weakens-fight-hindu-fundamentalism.

9. Vicky Nanjappam, 'Sunil Joshi: The RSS Leader Who Knew Too Much', Rediff, 9 December 2013, http://www.rediff.com/news/report/sunil-joshi-the-rss-leader-who-knew-too-much/20131209.htm.
10. 'Sunil Joshi Murder Case Probe Says RSS Pracharak Made Sexual Advances on Sadhvi Pragya', *India Today*, 17 August 2014, https://www.indiatoday.in/india/story/rss-sunil-joshi-murder-case-probe-says-pracharak-made-sexual-advances-on-sadhvi-pragya-204376-2014-08-17.
11. Reghunath, 'A Violent End', *Caravan*.
12. 'Malegaon Blast Case: Sadhvi Pragya Singh Thakur, Prasad Purohit to Face Trial for Terrorism', *Mint*, 27 December 2017, http://www.livemint.com/Politics/FiO9Z5xFcox53cdynDOCAO/Malegaon-blast-case-Sadhvi-Pragya-Lt-Col-Prasad-Purohit-to.html.
13. Anupam Dasgupta, '"Abhinav Bharat" Slideshow May Have Helped Nail Purohit', *Mumbai Mirror*, 25 August 2017, http://mumbaimirror.indiatimes.com/mumbai/crime/abhinav-bharat-slideshow-may-have-helped-nail-purohit/articleshow/60216131.cms.
14. Rahul Tripathi, 'Who is Lt Col Purohit? How is He Linked to Malegaon and Other Blast Cases?', *Indian Express*, 22 August 2017, http://indianexpress.com/article/explained/who-is-lt-col-purohit-how-is-he-linked-to-malegaon-other-blast-cases-4807723.
15. Bharti Jain, 'Malegaon Mystery Deepens', *Times of India*, 14 May 2016, http://epaperbeta.timesofindia.com/Article.aspx?eid=31808&articlexml=MALEGAON-MYSTERY-DEEPENS-14052016014021.
16. Anand Patel, 'Exclusive: Col Purohit was Falsely Implicated, UPA Wanted to Hasten Probe, Says Ex-top Military Intelligence Officer', *India Today*, 1 September 2017, http://www.indiatoday.in/india/delhi/story/lieutenant-colonel-shrikant-prasad-purohit-2008-malegaon-blast-case-upa-government-1035602-2017-09-01.
17. Ibid.
18. Deeptiman Tiwary, 'Probe Said Purohit Held "Illegal" Meetings with Radical Hindu Groups', *Indian Express*, 31 August 2017, http://indianexpress.com/article/india/lt-col-prasad-shrikant-purohit-malegaon-blast-probe-said-purohit-held-illegal-meetings-with-radical-hindu-groups-4821363.
19. Deeptiman Tiwary, 'Lt Col Shrikant Prasad Purohit Claims He Kept Army in Loop, Army Blew His Cover', *Indian Express*, 24 August 2017, https://indianexpress.com/article/india/colonel-shrikant-purohit-claims-he-kept-army-in-loop-army-blew-his-cover-4810786/,
20. B. Raman, 'Malegaon Blast of 2008: Need for an Independent Inquiry—Analysis', *Eurasia Review*, 1 July 2012, http://www.eurasiareview.com/01072012-malegaon-blast-of-2008-need-for-an-independent-enquiry-analysis.

21. Sunanda Mehta, 'Since This New Govt Came, I Have Been Told to Go Soft on Accused (Hindu Extremists): Special Public Prosecutor Rohini Salian', *Indian Express*, 25 June 2015, http://indianexpress.com/article/india/india-others/since-this-new-govt-came-i-have-been-told-to-go-soft-on-accused-hindu-extremists-special-public-prosecutor.
22. Sunanda Mehta, Utkarsh Anand, 'Rohini Salian Names NIA Officer Who Told Her to "Go Soft" Against Malegaon Blasts Accused'. *Indian Express*, 13 October 2015; http://indianexpress.com/article/india/india-news-india/rohini-salian-names-nia-officer-who-told-her-to-go-soft/.
23. Sunanda Mehta, 'Since This New Govt Came', *Indian Express*.
24. 'Supreme Court Dismisses Plea against Appointment of Sharad Kumar as Vigilance Commissioner', *Indian Express*, 10 September 2018, http://www.newindianexpress.com/nation/2018/sep/10/supreme-court-dismisses-plea-against-appointment-of-sharad-kumar-as-vigilance-commissioner-1870118.html.
25. 'Samjhauta Express Blast Investigation: Interview with Vikash Narain Rai', Wire, 5 June 2016, http://youtu.be/inOnMFqFAtU.
26. 'RSS Leader Paid for Samjhauta Blast', *Times of India*, 25 January 2011, http://timesofindia.indiatimes.com/india/RSS-leader-paid-for-Samjhauta-blast/articleshow/7357774.cms.
27. Ibid.
28. Shishir Gupta, 'Purohit Plotted to Kill RSS Leader Indresh Kumar: Report', *Indian Express*, 28 January 2011, http://indianexpress.com/article/news-archive/web/purohit-plotted-to-kill-rss-leader-indresh-kumar-report.
29. Manish Kumar, '5 Years Ago, He Spoke of RSS. Now Minister, His Explanation', NDTV, 25 April 2018, http://www.ndtv.com/india-news/as-home-secretary-rk-singh-spoke-of-rss-terror-link-now-power-minister-he-explains-1842275.
30. Ibid.

SEVEN: Matters of Statecraft

1. Ed. Isaac Deutscher, The Age of Permanent Revolution: A Trotsky Anthology (Dell Publishing Co., New York, 1964 and 1970).
2. Rohit Kumar Singh, 'Modi's Conspiracy to Remove Advani from President Race: Lalu Prasad on Babri Verdict', *India Today*, 19 April 2017, https://www.indiatoday.in/india/story/lk-advani-babri-masjid-demolition-verdict-972273-2017-04-19.

3. Advani was opposed to Modi being the prime ministerial candidate of BJP. He did not attend the National Executive meeting held in Goa, where, on 9 June 2013, Modi was appointed the chairman of the campaign committee, the precursor to his appointment as prime ministerial candidate. The very next day, Advani wrote a letter to the party president Rajnath Singh: 'For some time I have been finding it difficult to reconcile to the current functioning of the party or the direction in which it is going. I no longer have the feeling that this is the same idealistic party created by Dr Mookerjee, Pandit Deendayal ji, Vajpayee ji whose sole concern was the country and its people. Most leaders of ours are now concerned just with their personal agendas. I have decided, therefore, to resign from three main fora of the party, namely the national executive, the parliamentary board and the election committee.' He later boycotted the 13 September 2013 meeting of the parliamentary board, which elected Modi as the prime ministerial candidate of the BJP.
4. 'Supreme Court Faults Dropping of Babri Conspiracy Charge Against L.K. Advani', *Times of India*, 7 March 2017, http://timesofindia.indiatimes.com/india/babri-demolition-case-conspiracy-charge-against-l-k-advani-to-return/articleshow/57504211.cms.
5. Ross Colvin, Satarupa Bhattacharjya, 'A "caged parrot" - Supreme Court describes CBI', Reuters, 10 May 2014, https://in.reuters.com/article/cbi-supreme-court-parrot-coal/a-caged-parrot-supreme-court-describes-cbi-idINDEE94901W20130510.
6. Amit Anand Choudhary, 'L.K. Advani, Murli Manohar Joshi Part of Plot to Raze Babri: CBI', *Times of India*, 7 April 2017, http://timesofindia.indiatimes.com/india/l-k-advani-murli-manohar-joshi-part-of-plot-to-raze-babri-masjid-cbi/articleshow/58057059.cms.
7. Ibid.
8. 'Lalu Accuses PM of "Crafting" Advani Trial', *Times of India*, 20 April 2017, http://timesofindia.indiatimes.com/india/lalu-accuses-pm-of-crafting-advani-trial/articleshow/58259986.cms.
9. The Mandal Commission was constituted on 1 January 1979 by the Janata Party government, headed by Morarji Desai. It was mandated to identify socially and educationally backward classes. B.P. Mandal was the chairman of the commission. The commission recommended 27 per cent reservation for other backward castes in government jobs. The report was submitted in 1983 but its recommendation was not acted upon till Prime Minister V.P. Singh, in August 1990, decided to implement its recommendations of 27 per cent reservations in government jobs, which led to widespread protests.

10. The fodder scam is about illegal withdrawal of money from the government treasury for the ostensible purchase and supply of cattle fodder in Bihar. The scam was assessed to be of 950 crore and the then chief minister Laloo Prasad Yadav was one of the accused. He has been convicted in three separate cases by courts and has been jailed. For more details, https://indianexpress.com/article/what-is/what-is-the-fodder-scam-a-look-at-what-all-has-happened-since-1996-4645719/
11. Benami property is a kind of corrupt practice to save tax. Benami implies buying land/property by a person but not in his/her own name but in some other name, so that the transaction is not recorded in the person's name. The Modi government brought a law in 2016 called the Benami Transaction Prohibition Amendment Act 2016, which included a jail sentence for those found guilty.
12. 'Rabri's Cattle-shed Worker Gifted Her Land Worth 31 Lakh: Sushil Modi Lalu, Mishra Appear in Court,' *Times of India,* 7 June 2017, http://epaperbeta.timesofindia.com/Article.aspx?eid=31806&articlexml= Sushil-Modi-Rabris-worker-gifted-her-land-worth-07062017012044.
13. 'I-T Dept Attaches Tej Pratap Yadav's Property under Benami Property Act', *Economics Times,* 27 April 2018, https://economictimes.indiatimes.com/politics/i-t-dept-attaches-tej-pratap-yadavs-property-under-benami-property-act/articleshow/63938690.cms.
14. 'Army Out on Streets, Civil War Likely: Mamata', *Times of India*, 2 December 2016, http://timesofindia.indiatimes.com/india/Army-out-on-streets-civil-war-likely-Mamata/articleshow/55739569.cms.
15. http://naradanews.com
16. Neeraj Chauhan, 'Narada Sting Operation: CBI Files FIR Against 12 Trinamool Leaders for "Criminal Conspiracy"', *Times of India,* 17 April 2017, http://timesofindia.indiatimes.com/india/narada-sting-operation-cbi-files-fir-against-12-trinamool-leaders-for-criminal-conspiracy/articleshow/58227792.cms.
17. 'Not a Big Deal Even if Sudip Took 2-3L for Polls: Mamata', *Times of India*, 4 January 2017, http://timesofindia.indiatimes.com/india/no-big-deal-if-sudip-took-rs-2-3l-for-polls-mamata/articleshow/56322666.cms.
18. Mamata Banerjee (@MamataOfficial), 3 January 2017.
19. 'Not a Big Deal', *Times of India*; 'No Democracy in Bengal Under Mamata: BJP', *Business Standard*, 3 January 2017, http://www.business-standard.com/article/news-ians/no-democracy-in-bengal-under-mamata-bjp-117010301061_1.html.
20. 'Election Commission "Making Mockery Of Law", Says Arvind Kejriwal', NDTV, 7 April 2017, https://www.ndtv.com/video/news/news/election-commission-making-mockery-of-law-says-arvind-kejriwal-453532.

21. 'India Today-Cicero Mood of the Nation Opinion Poll: End of Honeymoon for Modi, Still the Best PM', *India Today,* 2 April 2015, https://www.indiatoday.in/india/north/story/modi-bjp-mood-of-the-nation-kejriwal-rahul-gandhi-246933-2015-04-02.
22. Jaya Menon, 'AIADMK Sees a BJP Conspiracy in IT Raid', *Times of India,* 22 December 2016, http://timesofindia.indiatimes.com/city/chennai/aiadmk-sees-a-bjp-conspiracy-in-i-t-raid/articleshow/56112563.cms,
23. A. Subramani, 'It's a Rocky Road Ahead for Sasikala', *Times of India,* 6 February 2017, http://timesofindia.indiatimes.com/city/chennai/its-a-rocky-road-ahead-for-sasikala/articleshow/56990746.cms.
24. Bharani Vaitheesvaran, V. Prem Shanker, 'Missing Governor in the Middle of Tamil Nadu Political Storm', *Economic Times,* 9 February 2017, https://economictimes.indiatimes.com/news/politics-and-nation/missing-governor-in-the-middle-of-tamil-nadu-political-storm/articleshow/57048242.cms.
25. C.L. Manoj, 'Centre in Strategic Position to Pull Strings in AIADMK Fight', *Economic Times,* 9 February 2017, http://economictimes.indiatimes.com/news/politics-and-nation/centre-in-strategic-position-to-pull-strings-in-aiadmk-fight/articleshow/57048340.cms.
26. 'Why Don't They Raid Amit Shah: Mamata Banerjee on IT Raid in Tamil Nadu Chief Secretary's House', *Economic Times,* 21 December 2016, http://economictimes.indiatimes.com/news/politics-and-nation/why-dont-they-raid-amit-shah-mamata-banerjee-on-it-raid-in-tamil-nadu-chief-secretarys-house/articleshow/56099498.cms.
27. Dhananjay Mahapatra, 'Chidambaram Moves SC for Right to Privacy, Right to Live in Dignity', *Times of India,* 24 February 2018, http://timesofindia.indiatimes.com/india/chidambaram-moves-sc-for-right-to-privacy-right-to-live-in-dignity/articleshow/63050779.cms.
28. 'CBI Raids Chidambaram, Son Karti's Residences in Chennai', *Economic Times,* 17 May 2017, http://economictimes.indiatimes.com/news/politics-and-nation/cbi-raids-chidambaram-son-kartis-residences-in-chennai/articleshow/58692059.cms.
29. Devesh K. Pandey, Nirnimesh Kumar, 'Karti Chidambaram Held in INX Media Bribery Case', *Hindu,* 28 February 2018, updated 1 March 2018, http://www.thehindu.com/news/national/inx-media-case-karti-chidambaram-arrested-in-chennai/article22875605.ece.
30. 'CBI Raids Chidambaram', *Economic Times.*
31. 'Arun Jaitley Dismisses Charge of Vendetta, Backs Agencies Conducting Searches', *Economic Times,* 17 May 2017, http://economictimes.indiatimes.

32. Sanjeev Singh, with PTI, 'Former Union Minister Shankarsinh Vaghela Cries Foul After CBI Raid at his Home', NDTV, 17 June 2015, http://www.ndtv.com/india-news/cbi-case-against-me-is-politics-of-vendetta-says-former-union-minister-shankarsinh-vaghela-772683.
33. Mohan Singh Chaturvedi, 'Don't Link Karnataka Income-Tax Raids with Gujarat Rajya Sabha Polls: FM Arun Jaitley to Congress', *Economic Times*, 3 August 2017, http://economictimes.indiatimes.com/news/politics-and-nation/dont-link-karnataka-it-raids-with-gujarat-rajya-sabha-polls-arun-jaitley-to-congress/articleshow/59878814.cms.
34. Ibid.
35. Sohrabuddin Sheikh was a criminal, who was part of an extortion racket in Gujarat. He was killed on 26 November 2005, allegedly in police custody. Later, his wife Kauser Bi and his friend Tulsi Prajapati were also killed allegedly in a police encounter. It was said that the killing was carried out by the Gujarat Police officials at the behest of their political masters. Amit Shah, the president of the BJP (2014–present), then the minister of state for home affairs, was arrested in 2010. Later, he was given a clean chit by the CBI Court. It is alleged that Sohrabuddin's encounter is linked to the murder of senior BJP leader Haren Pandya.
36. Ajmer Singh, 'Ahmed Patel, Son-in-Law and Son under ED Focus', *Economic Times*, 29 December 2017, http://economictimes.indiatimes.com/news/politics-and-nation/ahmed-patel-son-in-law-and-son-under-ed-focus/articleshow/62288830.cms.
37. 'Toppling Govts with Cash, Muscle is BJP's New Model', *Times of India*, 21 March 2016, http://timesofindia.indiatimes.com/india/Rahul-Gandhi-attacks-BJP-over-Uttarakhand-political-crisis-says-money-and-muscle-being-misused/articleshow/51480021.cms.
38. Vineet Upadhyay, 'Don't Try Any Hanky-panky, Uttarakhand HC Warns Centre', *Times of India,* 8 April 2016, https://timesofindia.indiatimes.com/india/Dont-try-any-hanky-panky-Uttarakhand-HC-warns-Centre/articleshow/51733240.cms.
39. Vineet Upadhyay, 'Modi Govt Left Red-faced as High Court Scraps Central Rule in Uttarakhand', *Times of India*, 22 April 2016, http://timesofindia.indiatimes.com/india/Modi-govt-left-red-faced-as-high-court-scraps-central-rule-in-Uttarakhand/articleshow/51934744.cms.
40. Kautilya Singh, 'My Phones Are Being Tapped, BJP Indulging in Politics of Blackmail: Rawat', *Times of India*, 9 May 2016, http://timesofindia.indiatimes.

com/india/My-phones-being-tapped-BJP-indulging-in-politics-of-blackmail-Harish-Rawat/articleshow/52178790.cms.
41. 'This is the Beginning of "CBI Yug" in Uttarakhand: Harish Rawat', *Economic Times*, 6 May 2016, http://economictimes.indiatimes.com/news/politics-and-nation/this-is-beginning-of-cbi-yug-in-uttarakhand-harish-rawat/articleshow/52138622.cms.
42. 'CBI Summons Harish Rawat in Sting Operation Case', *Times of India*, 24 December 2016, http://timesofindia.indiatimes.com/india/cbi-summons-harish-rawat-in-sting-operation-case/articleshow/56149573.cms.
43. R. Sedhuraman, 'SC Restores Congress Govt in Arunachal Pradesh', *Tribune*, 13 July 2016, http://www.tribuneindia.com/news/nation/sc-restores-congress-govt-in-arunachal-pradesh/265298.html.
44. Hemanshi Dhawan, 'Government's Blackout of 2 TV News Channels Dangerous for Democracy', *Times of India*, 7 November 2016, http://timesofindia.indiatimes.com/india/Governments-blackout-of-two-TV-news-channels-dangerous-for-democracy/articleshow/55282622.cms.
45. 'CBI Says NDTV Caused 48 Crore Loss to ICICI Bank, Searches Prannoy Roys' Homes', *Times of India*, 6 June 2017, http://timesofindia.indiatimes.com/india/cbi-says-ndtv-caused-rs-48-crore-loss-to-icici-bank-searches-prannoy-roys-homes/articleshow/59008723.cms.
46. Ibid.
47. 'Indira Jaising's NGO Barred by MHA from Receiving Foreign Funds for 6 Months', *Indian Express*, 2 June 2016, http://indianexpress.com/article/india/india-news-india/indira-jaising-ngo-licence-suspended-fcra-home-ministry-tax-filings-2829436.
48. 'Gujarat CM, Daughter Linked to Land Scam', *Times of India*, 6 February 2016, http://timesofindia.indiatimes.com/india/Gujarat-CM-daughter-linked-to-land-scam/articleshow/50873644.cms.
49. 'Amit Shah's Son Slaps 100 Crore Defamation Suit on a Website', *Times of India*, 9 October 2017, http://timesofindia.indiatimes.com/india/amit-shahs-son-slaps-rs-100-crore-defamation-suit-on-a-website/articleshow/60994676.cms.
50. 'No Conflict of Interest in Shirdi Industries: Piyush Goyal', *Times of India*, 5 April 2018, https://timesofindia.indiatimes.com/india/no-conflict-of-interest-in-shirdi-industries-piyush-goyal/articleshow/63619488.cms.
51. 'Congress Demands Sacking of Piyush Goyal over Links with Private Firm', *Indian Express,* 4 April 2018, http://indianexpress.com/article/india/congress-ghulam-nabi-azad-modi-jaitley-sacking-piyush-goyal-private-firm-shirdi-5123556.

52. 'Piyush Goyal Sold Pvt Firm at 1000 Times its Value in 2014: Report', Quint, 28 April 2018, http://www.thequint.com/news/india/piyush-goyal-piramal-group-the-wire-report.
53. '"No Wrongdoing": BJP, Piramal Group React to The Wire's Story on Piyush Goyal', Wire, 29 April 2018, https://thewire.in/political-economy/no-wrongdoing-bjp-piramal-group-react-to-the-wires-story-on-piyush-goyal.
54. 'Chhattisgarh PDS Scam: Congress Demands CM Raman Singh's Resignation', *Economic Times*, 4 July 2015, https://economictimes.indiatimes.com/news/politics-and-nation/chhattisgarh-pds-scam-congress-demands-cm-raman-singhs-resignation/articleshow/47937261.cms.
55. 'Congress Rakes up Panama Papers Leak to Corner Chhattisgarh CM's son', Money Control, 8 July 2018, https://www.moneycontrol.com/news/india/congress-rakes-up-panama-papers-leak-to-corner-chhattisgarh-cms-son-2684371.html.
56. According to the *Guardian*, the Panama Papers are an unprecedented leak of 11.5m files from the database of the world's fourth biggest offshore law firm, Mossak Fonseca. The records were obtained from an anonymous source by the German newspaper *Suddeutsche Zeitung*, which shared them with International Consortium of Investigative Journalists (ICIJ). The documents show the myriad ways in which the rich can exploit secretive offshore tax regimes. For further details, see, https://www.theguardian.com/news/2016/apr/03/what-you-need-to-know-about-the-panama-papers.
57. 'Bhosari Land Scam: Activist Moves Court against ACB Report on Eknath Khadse', *Indian Express*, 15 May 2018, https://indianexpress.com/article/cities/pune/bhosari-land-scam-activist-moves-court-against-acb-report-on-eknath-khadse-5176924/.
58. Ibid.
59. Richard Overy, *The Dictators: Hitler's Germany, Stalin's Russia*, W.W. Norton & Company, Reprint edition (January 17, 2006).
60. 'Congress-mukt India Does Not Mean End of Opposition: Amit Shah', *India Today*, 27 May 2018, https://www.indiatoday.in/4-years-of-modi-government/story/congress-mukt-india-does-not-mean-end-of-opposition-amit-shah-1242730-2018-05-27.

EIGHT: Wheels of Justice Squeaking and Squealing

1. Amit Anand Chaudhary, Dhananjay Mahapatra, 'Four Top Judges Revolt against CJI; Supreme Court on Trial', *Times of India*, 13 January 2018,

https://timesofindia.indiatimes.com/india/four-top-judges-revolt-against-cji-supreme-court-on-trial/articleshow/62480926.cms.
2. Ibid.
3. Amit Anand Choudhury, Dhananjay Mahapatra, 'Four Top Judges', *Times of India*.
4. 'People's Confidence in Judiciary Affected, Ball in CJI's Court to Resolve Issues, Says Soli Sorabjee', *Times of India,* 8 May 2018, https://indianexpress.com/article/india/peoples-confidence-in-judiciary-affected-ball-in-cjis-court-to-resolve-issues-says-soli-sorabjee-5168484/.
5. 'One Had to Confront CJI for "Misusing" his Powers: Prashant Bhushan', *Business Standard*, 13 January 2018, http://www.business-standard.com/article/news-ani/one-had-to-confront-cji-for-misusing-his-powers-prashant-bhushan-118011200588_1.html.
6. 'Former CJI RM Lodha: It Must Have Been Last Resort for SC Judges', NewsX, 12 January 2018, https://www.newsx.com/national/former-cji-rm-lodha-it-must-have-been-last-resort-for-sc-judges
7. Prabhash K. Dutta, 'How a Medical Admission Scam Led to Clash between Top Two Judges of Supreme Court', *India Today*, 10 November 2017, updated 11 November 2017, http://www.indiatoday.in/india/story/supreme-court-dipak-misra-j-chelameswar-medical-admission-mci-scam-1083840-2017-11-10.
8. Ibid.
9. Dhananjay Mahapatra, 'Simmering Differences in Supreme Court Had First Erupted over Medical Scam PIL', *Times of India*, 13 January 2018, http://timesofindia.indiatimes.com/india/simmering-differences-in-supreme-court-had-first-erupted-over-medical-scam-pil/articleshow/62480997.cms.
10. Niranjan Takle, 'A Family Breaks Its Silence: Shocking Details Emerge in Death of Judge Presiding over Sohrabuddin Trial', *Caravan*, 20 November 2017, https://caravanmagazine.in/vantage/shocking-details-emerge-in-death-of-judge-presiding-over-sohrabuddin-trial-family-breaks-silence.
11. Ibid.
12. Ibid.
13. Ibid.
14. Amit Anand Choudhary, 'SC Judges Assigned Loya Case Want Another Bench to Hear It', *Times of India*, 17 Jan 2018, https://www.pressreader.com/india/the-times-of-india-mumbai-edition/20180117/282815011653091.
15. Amit Anand Choudhury, Dhananjay Mahapatra, '"Nothing Suspicious" about Loya Death, Petition an Attack on Judiciary, Says SC', *Times of India*, 20 April 2018, http://timesofindia.indiatimes.com/india/nothing-suspicious-about-

loya-death-petition-an-attack-on-judiciary-says-sc/articleshow/63837611. cms.
16. '5 Charges against CJI Dipak Misra in the Congress' Notice of Impeachment', *Hindustan Times,* 20 April 2018, https://www.hindustantimes.com/india-news/charges-against-cji-dipak-misra-in-the-congress-notice-of-impeachment/story-xN6GfyfxR1IsadHAPjb86O.html.
17. '"SC Rift as Big a Threat to Judiciary as Revenge Plea"', *Times of India*, 21 April 2018, http://timesofindia.indiatimes.com/india/sc-rift-as-big-a-threat-to-judiciary-as-revenge-plea/articleshow/63852579.cms.
18. Ibid.
19. Akhilesh Singh, Rumu Banerjee, 'Venkaiah Naidu Rejects Motion to Remove CJI, Congress to Challenge Order in Supreme Court', *Times of India*, 24 April 2018, http://timesofindia.indiatimes.com/india/venkaiah-naidu-rejects-motion-to-remove-cji-congress-to-challenge-order-in-supreme-court/articleshow/63887949.cms.
20. 'Govt Asks SC to Reconsider Justice Joseph's Name, Says His Elevation "Not Appropriate"', *Times of India,* 27 April 2018, https://timesofindia.indiatimes.com/india/govt-asks-sc-to-reconsider-justice-josephs-name-says-his-elevation-not-appropriate/articleshow/63932422.cms.
21. 'Govt's Joseph Step Not Linked to his Uttarakhand Ruling: Ravi Shankar Prasad', *Times of India*, 3 May 2018, http://timesofindia.indiatimes.com/india/govts-joseph-step-not-linked-to-his-uttarakhand-ruling-ravi-shankar-prasad/articleshow/64007807.cms.
22. Anusha Soni, 'Why a Divided Supreme Court Collegium Deferred Decision on Justice KM Joseph's Elevation', DailyO, 3 May 2018, https://www.dailyo.in/variety/supreme-court-collegium-justice-km-joseph-elevation-appointment-of-judges-indu-malhotra-cji-dipak-misra/story/1/23876.html.
23. Amit Anand Choudhary, 'Impeachment of CJI Not a Solution, Says Justice Chelamswar', *Times of India*, 8 April 2018, http://timesofindia.indiatimes.com/india/impeachment-of-cji-not-a-solution-says-chelameswar/articleshow/63661901.cms.
24. Granville Austin, *Working a Democratic Constitution: A History of the Indian Experience* (Oxford University Press, India, 2003).
25. Golak Nath Vs. The State of Punjab was a 1967 Indian supreme court case, in which the court ruled that parliament could not curtail any of the fundamental rights in the constitution.
26. Austin, *Working a Democratic Constitution,* p. 198.
27. Kesavananda Bharati Vs. State of Kerala was a landmark decision case in the history of the Indian supreme court. It was argued between October 1972 and

March 1973. The case is credited with upholding the basic structure of the constitution of India.
28. Austin, *Working a Democratic Constitution,* p. 181.
29. Swapnil Tripathi, 'April 26—Revisiting the Black Day of Indian Judiciary', LiveLaw, 26 April 2018, http://www.livelaw.in/April-26-revisiting-black-day-Indian-judiciary.
30. Austin, *Working a Democratic Constitution.*
31. L.K Advani, *My Country, My Life* (Rupa & Co, India, 2008).
32. In India, 'the Emergency' refers to a twrnty-one-month period from 1975 to 1977 when Prime Minister Indira Gandhi had a state of emergency declared across the country. Officially issued by President Fakhruddin Ali Ahmed under Article 352 of the constitution because of the prevailing "internal disturbance", the Emergency was in effect from 25 June 1975 until its withdrawal on 21 March 1977. The order bestowed upon the prime minister the authority to rule by decree, allowing elections to be suspended and civil liberties to be curbed. For much of the Emergency, most of Gandhi's political opponents were imprisoned and the press was censored. The final decision to impose an emergency was proposed by Indira Gandhi, agreed upon by the president of India, and thereafter ratified by the cabinet and the parliament (from July to August 1975), based on the rationale that there were imminent internal and external threats to the Indian state.
33. Dhananjay Mahapatra, 'Lack of Transparency in Judge Selection Always Gave Govt the 'Delay' Handle', *Times of India,* 7 May 2018.
34. Atul Dev, 'Balancing Act', *Caravan,* 1 June 2017, http://caravanmagazine.in/reportage/chief-justice-khehar-executive-judiciary.
35. 'Ishrat Jehan Case Judge Quits after Transfer to Allahabad HC', *Hindustan Times,* 26 September 2017, https://www.hindustantimes.com/india-news/ishrat-jehan-case-judge-quits-after-transfer-to-allahabad-hc/story-QadGxTrDxileJ4ZkcdOnzN.html.
36. Murli Krishnan, 'Saddest Day for Indian Judiciary; Spineless Collegium Has Succumbed to Executive Caprice, Yatin Oza', Bar & Bench, 26 September 2017, http://barandbench.com/saddest-day-Indian-Judiciary-spineless-Collegium- succumbed-caprice-executive-Yatin-Oza.
37. 'Court Can't Be Third Chamber of Legislature, Says Jaitley', *Economic Times,* 19 October 2015, http://economictimes.indiatimes.com/news/politics-and-nation/court-cant-be-third-chamber-of-legislature-fm-arun-jaitley/articleshow/49440675.cms.
38. Faizan Mustafa, 'Does the Government Want "Parrot Judges"?', *Tribune,* 23 May 2016, http://www.tribuneindia.com/news/comment/does-the-government-want- parrot-judges/240746.html.

39. Ibid.
40. Austin, *Working a Democratic Constitution,* p. 254.
41. Charles S. Maddock, Kazimierz Grzybowski, 'Law and Communist Reality in the Soviet Union', *American Bar Association Journal,* no.55 (October 1969), pp. 938–42.
42. Ibid.
43. Richard Thornburgh, 'The Soviet Union and the Rule of Law', *Foreign Affairs* (Spring 1990), http://www.foreignaffairs.com/articles/russia-fsu/1990-03-01/soviet-union-and-rule-law.
44. Maddock, Grzybowski, 'Law and Communist Reality'.
45. Austin, *Working a Democratic Constitution,* p. 174.
46. Damayanti Datta, 'What Made CJI TS Thakur Cry in Front of PM Modi', *India Today,* 26 April 2016, https://www.indiatoday.in/magazine/cover-story/story/20160509-chief-justice-of-india-tirath-singh-thakur-judicial-system-law-cases-828809-2016-04-27.
47. 'Why is the Govt Sitting over 170 Names: Chief Justice of India TS Thakur', *Times of India,* 25 April 2016, http://timesofindia.indiatimes.com/india/Why-is-the-govt-sitting-over-170-names-Chief-Justice-of-India-TS-Thakur/articleshow/51971729.cms.
48. 'Judiciary Must Set Own Limits: Arun Jaitley', *Economic Times,* 17 May 2016, http://economictimes.indiatimes.com/news/politics-and-nation/judiciary-must-set-own-limits-arun-jaitley/articleshow/52293374.cms.
49. Dhananjay Mahapatra, 'CJI Lashes Out at Government for Stalling Appointment of HC Judges', *Times of India,* 13 August 2016, http://timesofindia.indiatimes.com/india/CJI-lashes-out-at-government-for-stalling-appointment-of-HC-judges/articleshow/53678287.cms.
50. Samanwaya Rautray, 'CJI Thakur Disappointed PM Modi Didn't Mention Appointment on Judges in I-Day Speech', *Economic Times,* 16 August 2016, http://economictimes.indiatimes.com/news/politics-and-nation/cji-thakur-disappointed-pm-modi-didnt-mention-appointment-on-judges-in-i-day-speech/articleshow/53708603.cms.
51. Samanwaya Rautray, 'Supreme Court Threatens To Hold PMO Officials in Contempt', *Economic Times,* 29 October 2016, https://economictimes.indiatimes.com/news/politics-and-nation/supreme-court-threatens-to-hold-pmo-officials-in-contempt/articleshow/55118078.cms.
52. Dhananjay Mahapatra, 'Govt "Stalling" Appointments to "Lock Out" Judiciary: SC', Times of India, 29 October 2016, https://timesofindia.indiatimes.com/india/Govt-stalling-appointments-to-lock-out-judiciary-SC/articleshow/55124375.cms.

53. 'Govt. Blames SC for Judges Vacancies', *Times of India*, 29 October 2016, https://timesofindia.indiatimes.com/india/Govt-blames-SC-for-judges-vacancies/articleshow/55124390.cms.
54. Amit Anand Choudhary, Dhananjay Mahapatra, 'Kalikho Pul's Widow Withdraws Letter after Allegations', *Times of India*, 24 February 2017, http://timesofindia.indiatimes.com/india/kalikho-puls-widow-withdraws-letter-after-allegations/articleshow/57321549.cms.
55. 'Probe CJI for Kalikho Pul's suicide, His Widow Petitions Vice-president Ansari', *Times of India,* 1 March 2017, https://timesofindia.indiatimes.com/india/probe-cji-for-kalikho-puls-suicide-his-widow-petitions-vice-president-ansari/articleshow/57402338.cms.
56. Granville Austin, 'How Was Politics to be Kept Out of the Courts?', Scroll. in, 12 July 2014, http://scroll.in/article/670075/granville-austin-how-was-politics-to-be-kept-out-of-the-courts.

NINE: Hindutva and the Caucus Race

1. Ashutosh, *The Crown Prince, the Gladiator and the Hope: Battle for Change* (HarperCollins, India, 2015), pp. 281–82.
2. L.K Advani, *My Country, My Life* (Rupa & Co, India, 2008), p. 373.
3. Ibid., p. 409.
4. 'Advani and Jinnah', *Economist*, 9 June 2005, https://www.economist.com/asia/2005/06/09/advani-and-jinnah.
5. Robert Service, *Stalin: A Biography* (Pan Books, 2005).
6. Richard Overy, *The Dictators: Hitler's Germany, Stalin's Russia* (Penguin, London, 2005).
7. Prashant Jha, *How The BJP Wins: Inside India's Greatest Election Machine* (Juggernaut, India, 2017).
8. On 8 November 2016, Prime Minister Narendra Modi announced that currency notes of 500 and 1000, in use till then, would no longer be valid legal tender from midnight thereof. These two currency notes made up approximately 86 per cent of the currency in circulation and their withdrawal created mayhem across the country.
9. Sagarika Ghose, 'UP and Away: Narendra Modi's Approach Touches the Poor', *Times of India*, 12 March 2017, http://timesofindia.indiatimes.com/elections/assembly-elections/uttar-pradesh/news/up-and-away-modis-approach-touches-the-poor/articleshow/57602105.cms.
10. Jha, *How The BJP Wins*.

11. Ashish Tripathi, 'Mayawati's Jumbo Jet Could Not Take Off with Dalit–Muslim Formula', *Times of India*, 12 March 2017, http://timesofindia.indiatimes.com/elections/assembly-elections/uttar-pradesh/news/mayawatis-jumbo-jet-couldnt-take-off-with-dalit-muslim-formula/articleshow/57602161.cms.
12. ANI UP (@ANINewsUP), https://twitter.com/ANINewsUP/status/833237614945849349.
13. Kasab was a Pakistani terrorist and a member of the Lashkar-e-Taiba Islamist group, through which he took part in the 2008 Mumbai terrorist attacks in Maharashtra. Kasab was seen on CCTV during his attacks on Chhatrapati Shivaji Terminus along with another recruit, Ismail Khan. Kasab reportedly told the police that they wanted to replicate the Islamabad Marriott hotel attack, and reduce the Taj Hotel to rubble, replicating the 9/11 attacks in India. Kasab was the only attacker captured alive by the police. On 3 May 2010, Kasab was found guilty of eighty offences, including murder, waging war against India and possessing explosives. On 6 May 2010, the same trial court sentenced him to death on four counts and to a life sentence on five counts. Kasab's death sentence was upheld by the Bombay high court on 21 February 2011. The verdict was upheld by the supreme court of India on 29 August 2012. Kasab was hanged on 21 November 2012 at 7:30 a.m. and buried at Yerwada Jail in Pune.
14. 'UP Elections 2017: After "SCAM", BJP Coins "KASAB" Acronym for Congress, SP and BSP', *Times of India*, 22 February 2017, http://timesofindia.indiatimes.com/elections/assembly-elections/uttar-pradesh/news/up-elections-2017-after-scam-bjp-coins-kasab-acronym-for-congress-sp-and-bsp/articleshow/57298758.cms.
15. Senior BJP leader Hukum Singh released a list of 346 Hindu families on 14 June 2016. He said that these Hindu families had been forced to leave Kairana by Muslims and Kairana had become a new Kashmir. This was big news but later he took a U turn and said that the exodus was due to the prevailing law and order situation. It was also found that more than a hundred Muslim families had also migrated. The Kairana issue took on communal colour on the eve of UP assembly elections in 2017. It is said that it helped BJP polarise voters along communal lines.

Localised fights between Hindus and Muslims escalated into riots between August and September 2013 in which 62 people lost their lives and 93 were injured. More than 50,000 people were rendered homeless and lived in relief camps for months. Justice Vishnu Shah Commission blamed members of SP and BJP for the violence. For more details, see, https://www.epw.in/journal/2014/2/reports-states-web-exclusives/fact-finding-report-independent-inquiry.

16. Dipankar Gupta, 'Lesson of 2017: Decisive Leadership Wins Elections', *Times of India*, 12 March 2017, http://timesofindia.indiatimes.com/home/sunday-times/all-that-matters/lesson-of-2017-decisive-leadership-wins-elections/articleshow/57597747.cms.
17. 'Governor Right in Inviting BJP-led Coalition: FM Arun Jaitley', *Economic Times*, 15 March 2017, http://economictimes.indiatimes.com/news/politics-and-nation/congress-didnt-even-submit-a-claim-to-goa-guv-but-complains-too-much-arun-jaitley/articleshow/57630045.cms.
18. Ian Kershaw, *Hitler*, (Penguin, London, 2009).
19. 'Congress MLA Being Kept in Captivity by BJP: Siddaramaiah', *Times of India*, 18 May 2018, https://timesofindia.indiatimes.com/india/congress-mla-being-kept-in-captivity-by-bjp-siddaramaiah/articleshow/64223664.cms.
20. 'Congress's Big Claim: Yeddyurappa Caught Bribing on Tape', *India Today*, 19 May 2018, https://www.indiatoday.in/india/video/congress-big-claim-yeddyurappa-caught-bribing-on-tape-1236773-2018-05-19.
21. T.S. Sudhir, 'Cancelled Flights, Disappearing MLAs, Midnight Escape. How the Karnataka Drama Unfolded after Hours', DailyO, 18 May 2018, https://www.dailyo.in/politics/karnataka-elections-verdict-congress-mla-horsetrading-hotel-taj-krishna-hyderabad-yeddyurappa/story/1/24237.html.
22. 'Karnataka Row: Congress Moves Supreme Court over pro-Tem Speaker Appointment', *Hindu*, 18 May 2018, http://www.thehindu.com/elections/karnataka-2018/live-karnataka-government-formation-bjp-congress-jds-supreme-court-hearing/article23922641.ece.
23. 'India's Ruling Hindu Party Comes to Power in Kashmir Coalition', *Guardian*, 1 March 2015, http://www.theguardian.com/world/2015/mar/01/indias-ruling-hindu-party-comes-to-power-in-kashmir-coalition.
24. Gowhar Geelani, 'PDP–BJP Alliance Could be a "Paradigm Shift" in Kashmir's History', *Dawn*, 27 February 2015, http://www.dawn.com/news/1166271.
25. Mehboob Jeelani, 'PDP: Afzal's Hanging a Travesty of Justice', *Hindu*, 14 February 2016, https://www.thehindu.com/news/national/other-states/pdp-afzals-hanging-a-travesty-of-justice/article8234905.ece
26. M.S. Golwalkar, *Bunch of Thoughts* (Sahitya Sindhu Prakashana, Bangalore, 1996, reprinted 2000), pp. 178–179.
27. Ibid., p. 179.
28. 'Assam Identity Pitch, RSS Work Led to Lotus Bloom', *Times of India*, 20 May 2016, http://timesofindia.indiatimes.com/elections-2016/assam-elections-2016/news/Assam-identity-pitch-RSS-work-led-to-lotus-bloom/articleshow/52352257.cms.

29. Golwakar, Bunch of Thoughts, p. 188.
30. Ibid., p. 189.
31. Ranju Dodum, 'Congress Loses Arunachal as 43 MLAs join BJP Ally', *Hindu*, 16 September 2016, https://www.thehindu.com/news/national/Congress-loses-Arunachal-as-43-MLAs-join-BJP-ally/article14984231.ece.
32. Nilanjan Mukhopadhyay, 'View: No Date, but Gujarat in Middle of Poll Season', *Economic Times*, 23 October 2017, http://economictimes.indiatimes.com/news/politics-and-nation/view-no-date-but-gujarat-in-middle-of-poll-season/articleshow/61177550.cms.
33. Ibid.
34. 'When a State Goes Populist—Rs 11,000 crore in sops for Gujarat since October 12', *Times of India*, 25 October 2017, http://timesofindia.indiatimes.com/india/when-a-state-goes-populist-rs-11000-crore-in-sops-for-gujarat-since-october-12/articleshow/61216805.cms.
35. 'Sex Clip Goes Viral, Hardik Patel Cries Foul', *Times of India*, 14 November 2017, https://timesofindia.indiatimes.com/india/sex-clip-goes-viral-hardik-patel-cries-foul/articleshow/61636240.cms.
36. '"Apologise for Falsehoods and Canards", Manmohan tells PM', *Times of India*, 12 December 2017, http://timesofindia.indiatimes.com/india/apologise-for-falsehoods-and-canards-manmohan-tells-pm/articleshow/62029118.cms.
37. 'Urban Gujarat Stays with BJP, Cong rules in Agri Pockets', *Times of India*, 19 December 2017, http://timesofindia.indiatimes.com/india/urban-gujarat-stays-with-bjp-cong-rules-in-agri-pockets/articleshow/62127237.cms.

TEN: The Money Trick

1. 'PM Modi's Demonetisation Speech on 8 November 2016', Zee News, 8 November 2016, http://zeenews.india.com/economy/pm-modis-demonetisation-speech-on-8-november-2016-read-full-text-2055235.html.
2. Ibid.
3. Ibid.
4. 'India Ctuck in Long Queue as ATMs Play Cash Me If You Can', *Times of India*, 12 November 2016, http://epaperbeta.timesofindia.com/Article.aspx?eid=31805&articlexml=India-stuck-in-long-queue-as-ATMs-play-12112016001024.
5. 'Weekend Sales Crash by Half at Malls and Markets as People Go Cashless', *Economic Times*, 14 November 2016, http://economictimes.indiatimes.com/industry/services/retail/weekend-sales-crash-by-half-at-malls-and-markets-as-people-go-cashless/articleshow/55406143.cms.

6. 'Restaurants Have Just Foods for Thought', *Economic Times*, 14 November 2016, https://retail.economictimes.indiatimes.com/news/food-entertainment/food-services/restaurants-have-just-food-for-thought/55408954.
7. '"After 8 Hours in Queue, My Pocket was Still Empty"', *Times of India*, 13 November 2016, http://timesofindia.indiatimes.com/city/delhi/After-8-hours-in-queue-my-pocket-was-still-empty/articleshow/55395144.cms.
8. Madhvi Sally, 'Currency Drought Leaves Mandis Deserted', *Economic Times*, 16 November 2016, http://economictimes.indiatimes.com/markets/commodities/news/currency-drought-leaves-mandis-deserted/articleshow/55452827.cms.
9. 'IT Department Expands Operations, Detects Rs 100 crore "Excess" Sales, Cash', *Indian Express*, 11 November 2016, https://indianexpress.com/article/india/india-news-india/demonetisation-it-department-expands-operations-detects-rs-100-crore-excess-sales-cash-4370559/.
10. 'Mamata Ready to Join Hands with Left to Fight "Black Government"', *Times of India*, 13 November 2016, http://timesofindia.indiatimes.com/Mamata-ready-to-join-hands-with-Left-to-fight-black-government/articleshow/55393948.cms.
11. 'Note Ban to Badly Disrupt Economic Activity in Short Run: Moody's', *Times of India*, 25 November 2016, http://timesofindia.indiatimes.com/business/india-business/Note-ban-to-badly-disrupt-economy-activity-in-short-run-Moodys/articleshow/55609119.cms.
12. Swaminathan S. Anklesaria Aiyar; 'View: Demonetisation Gives Modi Moral High Ground but Hit the Economy Hard', *Economic Times*, 22 November 2016, http://blogs.economictimes.indiatimes.com/et-commentary/view-demonetisation-gives-narendra-modi-moral-high-ground-but-also-hit-the-economy-hard.
13. Ruchir Sharma, 'Revenge No Development Strategy: Populist Nationalism Cannot Paper over Economic Chaos Unleashed by Demonetisation Drive', *Times of India*, 21 November 2016, http://blogs.timesofindia.indiatimes.com/toi-edit-page/revenge-no-development-strategy-populist-nationalism-cannot-paper-over-economic-chaos-unleashed-by-demonetisation-drive.
14. 'PM Modi Hints at More Steps Next Year to Root out Black Money', *Times of India*, 13 November 2016, http://timesofindia.indiatimes.com/india/PM-Modi-hints-at-more-steps-next-year-to-root-out-black-money/articleshow/55396220.cms.
15. 'Demonetisation: Hardship Necessary; Bear with my Justice which is "Kadak", Like My Chai', *Economic Times*, 15 November 2016, http://economictimes.

indiatimes.com/news/politics-and-nation/my-justice-is-a-little-karak-like-my-chai-pm-narendra-modi/articleshow/55413316.cms.
16. 'PM Modi Hints at More Steps', *Times of India*.
17. Ibid.
18. The brahmastra is a mythical weapon that never misses its target when used and destroys the target completely. It has been mentioned in Hindu scriptures like the Ramayana, the Mahabharata and the Puranas. It is believed to have been created by Lord Brahma, one of the trinity of Hindu religion—Brahma, Vishnu and Mahesh, for upholding Dharma and Satya.
19. 'Demonetisation: Hardship Necessary', *Economic Times*.
20. Bindiya Chari, 'Modi Promises Relief to Citizens after Dec, More Pain for the "Few Corrupt"', *Times of India*, 14 November 2016, http://epaperbeta.timesofindia.com/Article.aspx?eid=31808&articlexml=Modi-promises-relief-to-citizens-after-Dec-more-14112016001017.
21. Nilanjan Mukhopadhyay, 'Modi Harnessing the Sentiments of Masses Against the Rich', *Economic Times*, 15 November 2016; http://blogs.economictimes.indiatimes.com/et-commentary/pm-narendra-modi-harnessing-sentiment-of-masses-against-the-rich.
22. Ibid.
23. 'Demonetisation: Hardship Necessary', *Economic Times*.
24. 'Mann Ki Baat: PM Modi for a Less-Cash Society Towards a Cashless Society', *Economic Times*, 28 November 2016, http://economictimes.indiatimes.com/news/politics-and-nation/mann-ki-baat-pm-modi-urges-people-to-move-towards-less-cash-society/articleshow/55646381.cms.
25. Ibid.
26. Tim Worstall, 'India's Demonetisation Kills 100 People Apparently—This Is Not An Important Number', *Forbes*, 2 December 2016, https://www.forbes.com/sites/timworstall/2016/12/08/indias-demonetisation-kills-100-people-apparently-this-is-not-an-important-number/.
27. Ravish Tiwari, 'GDP Can Decline by 2 Percentage Points, Says Manmohan Singh', *Economic Times*, 25 November 2016, https://economictimes.indiatimes.com/news/politics-and-nation/gdp-can-decline-by-2-percentage-points-says-manmohan-singh/articleshow/55609076.cms.
28. 'GDP Growth at 3-yr Low of 5.7% in Apr-June as GST, DeMonBite', *Times of India*, 1 September 2017, http://epaperbeta.timesofindia.com/Article.aspx?eid=31804&articlexml=GDP-growth-at-3-yr-low-of-57-01092017029009.
29. Ibid.

30. 'Black Money Antidote Stifles Economy; Demand Shrinks, Jobs Hit, Sentiment Down', *Times of India*, 8 December 2016, 'http://timesofindia.indiatimes.com/india/Black-money-antidote-stifles-economy-Demand-shrinks-jobs-hit-sentiment-down/articleshow/55865183.cms.
31. 'Slowdown in New Investments Post Demonetisation: CMIE', *Economic Times*, 3 January 2017, http://economictimes.indiatimes.com/news/economy/finance/slowdown-in-new-investments-post-demonetisation-cmie/articleshow/56302642.cms.
32. Mayur Shetty, 'Bank Credit Growth Slowest in Decades, Demonetisation Effect, say Economists', *Times of India*, 6 January 2017, http://timesofindia.indiatimes.com/business/india-business/bank-credit-growth-slowest-in-decades-demonetisation-effect-say-economists/articleshow/56363740.cms.
33. 'Demonetisation Created Uncertainty: Eco Survey', *Times of India*, 1 February 2017, http://epaperbeta.timesofindia.com/Article.aspx?eid=31805&articlexml=Demonetisation-created-uncertainty-Eco-Survey-01022017014025.
34. '99% of Scrapped Notes Back with Banks, Says RBI Report', *Times of India*, 31 August 2017, https://timesofindia.indiatimes.com/business/india-business/99-of-scrapped-notes-back-with-banks-says-rbi-report/articleshow/60299647.cms.
35. Yogesh Kumar, 'Note Ban Destroyed Terror Funding, Drug Mafia, Human Trafficking: PM Modi', *Times of India*, 28 December 2016, http://timesofindia.indiatimes.com/india/note-ban-destroyed-terror-funding-drug-mafia-human-trafficking-modi/articleshow/56207314.cms.
36. Richard Overy, *The Dictators: Hitler's Germany Stalin's Russia*,(W. W. Norton & Company; Reprint edition, 2006).
37. Ibid.
38. Ibid.
39. Adolf Hitler, *Mein Kampf* (Houghton Mifflin Company, 1998).

ELEVEN: Hindutva, Media and Propaganda

1. Bipin Chand Agarwal, 'Bahraich's Annual Dargah Mela to Begin on June 2', *Times of India*, 28 May 2013, http://timesofindia.indiatimes.com/city/allahabad/Bahraichs-annual-Dargah-Mela-to-begin-on-June-2/articleshow/20300394.cms.
2. The novel is yet to be published.
3. Adolf Hitler, *Mein Kampf* (Houghton Mifflin Company, 1998), p. 163.
4. Ibid., p. 159.

5. Ibid., p.163.
6. 'Hindutva FB Page Publishes List of 100+ Couples in Inter-faith Marriages, Calls for Violence', Alt News, 4 February 2018, https://www.altnews.in/hindutva-fb-page-publishes-list-100-couples-inter-faith-marriages-calls-violence/
7. Ibid.
8. @ipppatel, 19 August 2017, http://twitter.com/ippatel/status/ 898905497188749314.
9. Ibid.
10. Arjun Sidharth, 'Prashant P. Umrao: Unmasking a One-man Hate Factory,' Alt News, 6 February 2018, https://www.altnews.in/prashant-p-umrao-unmasking-one-man-hate-factory/.
11. Ibid.
12. Ibid.
13. Ibid.
14. @AnantkumarH, 5 February 2017, http://twitter.com/anantkumarh/status/828279408259575809.
15. @AnantkumarH, 20 March 2017, http://twitter.com/AnantkumarH/status/844096938786013184.
16. Pratik Sinha, 'Newly Sworn Minister Anantkumar Hegde's Twitter Account Gives a Peek into His Mindset', Alt News, 4 September 2017, http://www.altnews.in/newly-sworn-minister-anantkumar-hegdes-twitter-account-gives-peek-mindset.
17. @tathagata2, 1 October 2017, https://twitter.com/tathagata2/status/914667387114291200.
18. Sam Jawed, 'Hall of Shame—Serial Abusers, Sexist Bigots, Rumour Mongers Followed by PM Modi on Twitter', 7 September 2017, https://www.altnews.in/hall-shame-serial-abusers-sexist-bigots-rumour-mongers-followed-pm-modi-twitter/.
19. Jeffrey Gettleman, 'India's Modi Criticized for Following Twitter Feed Tied to Nasty Post', *The New York Times*, 8 September 2017, http://www.nytimes.com/2017/09/08/world/asia/india-modi-twitter.html.
20. Ibid.
21. 'What Do These Nathuram Godse Fans Have in Common? They Are All Followed by PM Modi on Twitter', Alt News, 2 October 2017, http://www.altnews.in/godse-fans-common-followed-pm-Modi.
22. @narendramodi, 2 October 2017, https://twitter.com/timesofindia/status/914678568575225856.

23. 'What Do These Nathuram Godse Fans Have in Common?', Alt News.
24. 'The Lost Legacy of Mahatma Gandhi', BBC News, 28 January 1998, http://news.bbc.co.uk/2/hi/51468.stm.
25. M.K. Gandhi, *Hindu Dharma* (Orient Paperbacks, 1991), p. 53.
26. Rana Ayyub, 'In India, Journalists Face Slut-Shaming and Rape Threats', *New York Times*, 22 May 2018, http://www.nytimes.com/2018/05/22/opinion/india-journalists-slut-shaming-rape.html.
27. Abhishek Dey, 'Journalists in Delhi-NCR Receive Identical Messages Threatening Them With Gauri Lankesh's Fate', Scroll.in, 28 September 2017, http://scroll.in/article/851462/journalists-in-delhi-ncr-receive-identical-messages-threatening-them-with-gauri-lankeshs-fate.
28. Shreyashi Roya, 'Ravish Kumar Threatened by Trolls over Fake Quote on Rape Case', Quint, 26 June 2018, http://www.thequint.com/news/india/ravish-kumar-death-threats-fake-news.
29. Adolf Hitler, *Mein Kampf* (Houghton Mifflin Company, 1998), p. 294.
30. Shushannah Walshe, 'Ann Romney Believes Obama Strategy Is "Kill Romney"', ABC News, https://abcnews.go.com/blogs/politics/2012/07/ann-romney-believes-obama-strategy-is-kill-romney/.
31. Aakar Patel, 'Are You a "Pappu" for Propaganda Doctors?', *Mint*, 8 November 2013, http://www.livemint.com/Leisure/fgP5yTgA1jCDji7VTmJj6M/Are-you-a-pappu-for-propaganda-doctors.html.
32. Soumya Roa, 'Arrest of Postcard News Co-founder Shines a Light on India's "Fake News" Problem', Scroll.in, 30 March 2018, https://scroll.in/article/873872/arrest-of-postcard-news-co-founder-shines-a-light-on-indias-fake-news-problem.
33. Neil Postman, *Amusing Ourselves to Death: Public Discourse in the Age of Show Business* (Penguin, 1985), p. 118.
34. Meghnad Bose, 'Tale of Two Republics: Why Shourie Compared Our Media to N Korea's', Quint, 9 June 2017, https://www.thequint.com/news/india/tale-of-two-republics-arun-shourie-indian-media-north-korea.
35. Karan Thapar, 'Stooping to Cover', *Indian Express*, 21 February 2018, http://indianexpress.com/article/opinion/columns/stooping-to-cover-narendra-modi-interview-indian-media-journalism-5071858.
36. 'Arun Jaitley Compares Indira Gandhi to Hitler, PM Modi Backs Him', *Times of India*, 26 June 2018, https://timesofindia.indiatimes.com/india/arun-jaitley-compares-indira-gandhi-to-hitler-pm-modi-backs-him/articleshow/64739693.cms.

37. 'Reliance-Run Websites, Times Now and New Indian Express Take Down Story on Amit Shah', *Wire*, 22 June 2018, http://thewire.in/media/amit-shah-bank-demonetisation-news18-new-indian-express.
38. Santosh Desai, 'The Limits of Propaganda?', *Times of India*, 19 February 2018, http://blogs.timesofindia.indiatimes.com/Citycitybangbang/the-limits-of-propaganda.
39. '"It Feels Like We Are Govt Spokespersons": Full Text of Zee News Staffer Vishwa Deepak's Resignation Letter', *First Post*, 22 February 2016, http://www.firstpost.com/india/it-feels-like-we-are-govt-spokespersons-full-text-of-zee-news-staffer-vishwa-deepaks-resignation-letter-2637666.html.
40. Aranya Shankar, Mahender Singh Manral, 'JNU's Umar Khalid Has Narrow Escape, Assailant's Gun Jams', *Indian Express*, 14 August 2018, http://indianexpress.com/article/india/umar-khalid-shot-constitution-club-of-india-delhi-unhurt-5304467.
41. 'Sedition Case: Court Cites Lack of Approval, Pulls up Police over JNU Chargesheet' *Indian Express,* 20 January 2019, https://indianexpress.com/article/cities/delhi/sedition-case-court-cites-lack-of-approval-pulls-up-police-over-jnu-chargesheet-5546652/.
42. Gauhar Raza, 'Gained in Translation: They Called Me "Anti-national"', *Indian Express,* 17 September 2017, https://indianexpress.com/article/opinion/columns/they-called-me-anti-national-afzal-premi-gang-rohith-vemula-kanhaiya-kumar-muslim-jihadi-gauhar-raza-zee-news-afzal-premi-gang-rohith-vemula-kanhaiya-kumar-4846949/.
43. Ibid.
44. Rohit Vats, 'Indo-Pak Poetry in the Times of Paranoid Patriotism', *Hindustan Times,* 7 March 2016, https://www.hindustantimes.com/art-and-culture/indo-pak-poetry-in-the-times-of-paranoid-patriotism/story-xO7Ycy6teJq7Wv6r9vsLNM.html.
45. Neil Postman, *Amusing Ourselves to Death*.
46. Sam Jawed, 'Media Bias in Gujarat Elections: An Analysis of Hasgtags Used by TV Channels', Alt News, 14 December 2017, http://www.altnews.in/media-bias-gujarat-elections-analysis-hashtags-used-tv-channels.
47. Rayan Naqash, '"It Sells to Bash Kashmiris": How National TV Channels Have Deepened Resentment in the Valley,' Scroll.in, 19 January 2018, https://scroll.in/article/865181/it-sells-to-bash-kashmiris-how-national-tv-channels-have-deepened-resentment-in-the-valley
48. Ibid.

49. 'High-Profile Exits, Diktats on Modi at ABP News Revive Fears of Media Censorship', Wire, 3 August 2018, https://thewire.in/media/abhisar-sharma-abp-news-punya-prasun-bajpai-amit-shah-media-censorship.
50. 'Tax Raids on Quint Founder Raghav Bahl's Noida Home, Office', *Hindustan Times*, 11 October 2018, https://www.hindustantimes.com/india-news/media-baron-raghav-bahl-s-premises-raided-by-i-t-dept-over-alleged-tax-evasion/story-dZe2igWwqdTss8AIFOEtUO.html.
51. Ishita Mishra, 'Pro-BJP or Anti-BJP: Inside the Modi-Shah Media Tracking "War Rooms"', Wire, 11 Augsut 2018, https://thewire.in/politics/narendra-modi-amit-shah-bjp-india-media.

Epilogue

1. Laurence Rees, *The Holocaust: A New History* (Penguin, 2017).
2. Laurence Rees, *Auschwitz: The Nazis & The Final Solution* (BBC Books, 2005).
3. Rees, *The Holocaust*.
4. M.K. Gandhi, *Hind Swaraj*, tr. Amritlal Thakoredas Nanavati (Navjivan Prakashan Mandir, 2006).
5. Ibid., p. 32.
6. Walter K. Anderson & Shridhar D. Damle, *The RSS: A View to the Inside* (Penguin Viking, India, 2018).
7. *Pt Deen Dayal Upadhyaya: A Profile*, ed. Sudhakar Raje (Deen Dayal Research Institute, India, 1992).
8. Ibid., pp. 183–84.
9. *Deen Dayal Upadhyaya: Sampoorna Vangmaya, Khand 14*, ed. Dr Mahesh Chandra Sharma (Prabhat Prakashan, 2016), p. 201.
10. Anderson, Damle, *The RSS*, p. 95.
11. Ibid., p. 109.
12. Ibid.
13. Revati Laul, *The Anatomy of Hate* (Context, India, 2018).
14. Rees, *The Holocaust*.
15. Khalid Anis Ansari, 'It's Not Just Religion, It's Also Caste', *Indian Express*, 29 March 2018, https://indianexpress.com/article/opinion/columns/hindu-muslims-the-minority-space-caste-system-in-india-5115108/.
16. Anwar Alam, 'Understanding the Process of Radicalisation Amongst Muslims in India', *Monograph*, http://www.ppf.org.in/wp-content/uploads/2018/12/Understanding-the-process-1-12-18.pdf.

17. Ibid.
18. 'Hindu Rashtra Doesn't Mean No Place for Muslims in India: Mohan Bhagwat', *Economic Times,* 18 September 2018, https://m.economictimes.com/news/politics-and-nation/hindu-rashtra-doesnt-mean-no-place-for-muslims-in-india-mohan-bhagwat/videoshow/65862578.cms).
19. Ibid.
20. Krishna Kumar, 'Bhagwat's Statement on Golwalkar After Much Thought: Deodhar', *Economic Times,* 21 September 2018, https://economictimes.indiatimes.com/news/politics-and-nation/bhagwats-statement-on-golwalkar-after-much-thought-deodhar/articleshow/65894558.cms.
21. 'Hindu Rashtra Doesn't Mean No Place for Muslims in India: Mohan Bhagwat', *Economic Times.*
22. Ibid.
23. Swapan Dasgupta, 'We May Be on the Cusp of an Enlightened Hindu Consensus', *Times of India,* 23 September 2018, https://timesofindia.indiatimes.com/blogs/right-and-wrong/we-may-be-on-the-cusp-of-an-enlightened-hindu-consensus/.
24. William L. Shirer, *The Rise And Fall of the Third Reich* (Arrow Books, 1998), p. 528.
25. Sadanand Dhume, 'Is India Turning Religious?', *Times of India,* 21 October 2017, https://timesofindia.indiatimes.com/blogs/toi-edit-page/is-india-turning-religious-missteps-by-modi-may-not-be-enough-for-congress-to-return-to-power/.
26. Nilanjan Mukhopadhyay, 'From Being the Only Option to Being the Best Bet, Decline in Narendra Modi's Following Is Bad News for BJP', Firstpost, 9 October 2017, http://www.Firstpost.com/politics/from-being-the-only-alternative-to-a-best-decline-in-Narendra-Modi's-following-is-bad—news-for-bjp-4122699.html.
27. 'MP Polls: BJP Manifesto, Like Cong's, Has cow, Narmada Reference', *Outlook,* 17 November 2018, https://www.outlookindia.com/newsscroll/mppollbjpcongmanifestos/1423595.
28. Every year thousands of devotees make a pilgrimage to this place, which is situated on a peak of 6638 metres in the Kailash range. According to Hindu mythology, Lord Shiva sits at the Kailash mountain in meditation with his wife Parvati, and it is believed that a parikrama around Kailash Parvat, which is 52 km, on foot and a holy dip in the Mansarovar lake, brings good fortune.
29. 'TNN, Cong Tries to Steal BJP's Thunder, Says Only Its PM Can Build Temple', *Times of India,* 23 November 2018, https://timesofindia.indiatimes.

com/india/congress-tries-to-steal-bjps-thunder-says-only-its-pm-can-build-temple/articleshow/66758424.cms?utm_source=twitter.com&utm_medium=social&utm_campaign=TOIDesktop.
30. Ibid.
31. 'क्या इस देश में अब बहस सिर्फ़ अच्छे हिंदू और बुरे हिंदू के बीच रह गई है?', Wire, 17 November 2018, http://thewirehindi.com/63366/politics-congress-bjp-hindu-muslim-seculariosm/.
32. S. Radhakrishnan, *The Hindu View of Life* (Harper Element, 2012).
33. Pavan K. Varma, *Adi Shankaracharya: Hinduism's Greatest Thinker* (Tranquebar Press, 2018), p. 71.
34. M.K. Gandhi, *Hindu Dharma* (Orient Paperbacks, 1991).
35. Ibid.
36. Prabhash Joshi, *Hindu Hone ka Dharma* (Rajkamal Prakashan, India, 2003).
37. Jayadev Jana, 'Gandhi and Einstein', *Statesman*, 19 June 2017, https://www.google.co.in/amp/s/www.thestatesman.com/opinion/gandhi-and-einstein-1497905436.html/amp.
38. V.D. Savarkar, *Six Glorious Epochs of Indian History*, trans. and ed. S.T. Godbole, chap. 8.
39. Ibid., p. 645.
40. M.S. Golwalkar, *Bunch of Thoughts* (Sahitya Sindhu Prakashana, Bangalore, 1996, reprinted 2000).
41. Ibid.
42. Gandhi, *Hindu Dharma*.
43. Ibid., p. 19.
44. *Gandhiji*, tr. Amritlal Thakoredas Nanavati (Hind Swaraj, Navjivan Prakashan Mandir, 2006), p. 33.
45. Gandhi, *Hindu Dharma*, p.53.
46. Subhash Gatade, 'Ambedkar against Hindu Rashtra', Sabrang, 8 December 2015, https://www.sabrangindia.in/article/ambedkar-against-hindu-rashtra.
47. Gandhi, *Hindu Dharma*, p. 53.
48. Ibid. pp. 54–55.
49. Rafiq Zakaria, *Indian Muslims: Where They Have Gone Wrong?* (Popular Prakashan & Bhartiya Vidya Bhavan, 2004), pp. 126–27.
50. Ibid.

Acknowledgements

Many moons ago French philosopher René Descartes said, 'I think therefore I am.' In the post-truth era it is important to think to live. My book is an attempt to think. It is an attempt to live.

Before Narendra Modi became the prime minister, I was so sure of his ascendency to power that I planned to write a book about his regime. And therefore I laboriously collected and collated information and data about his life and times from then on. I had an inkling of things to come. I had discussed how things may unfold with a few friends and I was not too off the mark.

In the initial three years of the Modi regime it was impossible to have a critical discussion about him. His supporters were not willing to listen to even a word against him. His critics seemed to have already made up their minds about him; it was difficult to extract their true feelings. In such a polarised ecosystem, it was hard to understand what the two sides were thinking. Initially, while conducting interviews during my research for this book, to my surprise, I discovered that many people changed their opinions as soon as they realised that it was going to be reproduced in a book. So much so that sometimes the change in opinions was rather dramatic. Therefore, barring a few, I decided to not tell people on the outset that it was for a book. It is partly for this reason that I have not revealed the identities of the people I have spoken to. However, all the quotes are genuine and have been honestly reproduced, though I admit few of the quotes might not be verbatim as I was writing them from memory.

I must also admit that I have neither been enamoured of Modi as a politician, nor attracted to Hindutva as an ideology. I have always been a critic. Yet, I did try to keep my biases on the back burner to the fullest of my cognitive ability.

While writing the book I benefited through my interactions with many eminent politicians, academicians, journalists and others. They were kind enough to lend me not just their ear but also their time. I would like to especially mention a few. Pavan K. Varma was more than kind to read a few chapters. His suggestions were extremely valuable. Ashutosh Varshney took time out of his busy schedule to speak to me and go through a few chapters. His advice helped me add certain nuances. I met Shekhar Gupta a few times. He was very patient. His experiences as a journalist helped me fine-tune many points. I really hounded Shashi Tharoor and despite his busy schedule, and shuttling between Kerala and Delhi he graciously made time for me, though this was also the time he was finishing his own book, *The Paradoxical Prime Minister*. I have always been in awe of Prem Shankar Jha for his knowledge of Indian politics. The passionate discussions with him were enlightening. I really pushed Rajdeep Sardesai, my ex-boss, to read four chapters. He was extremely candid with his observations. Raghav Bahl is amongst the most brilliant political minds in India. He had initially supported Modi hoping he would bring change. His insight into politics and economics was greatly enriching. Pratap Bhanu Mehta is one of the foremost thinkers of our time. Talking to him gave me the confidence that I was on the right track. My generation grew up reading Saeed Naqvi. His open-heartedness and eloquence is unmatched. He most warmly treated me to lunch and helped me understand the psyche of the 'new normal' in India. Prabhu Chawla is one of the most informed journalists in Delhi. Nobody knows more about the games in the corridors of power than him. My interactions with him cleared many doubts about the government and the Sangh Parivar. I am always fascinated by the insight that senior journalist Nilanjan Mukhopadhyay brings to his columns. His observations helped me refine my understanding of the relationship between the Modi government and the top leadership of the RSS. Shahid Siddiqui is like a friend though he is much older. Talking to him on the issues of minorities was very informative. Anwar Alam, a globetrotter and friend for thirty years and counting—his experiences in the Arab World and my discussions with him that went on for hours, opened new vistas for my own understanding of minorities in India. And last but not the least, my dear friend Nagendra Sharma who has always been most brutal with his opinions, was not only forthcoming with his views on my manuscript but also made certain suggestions which made my writing better. Thank you is too small a word to express my gratitude to them all.

I must also express my gratitude to my many friends in the RSS and the BJP, who hold senior positions and spoke to me most candidly, sharing their knowledge about the inner workings in the organisation and the government. These were strictly off the record and not to be quoted and their identities were not to be revealed. These conversations helped me correct my perceptions, rejig my opinions, clear doubts and reshape arguments. I wish I could name them, but then I am constrained by my promise. Thank you, friends.

To Karthika V.K., a friend and editor I owe many thanks. Like all writers, I too am possessive about every word I write and fought for every word changed and deleted. For all the discussions, hand-holding and patience, thank you. I would like to extend my gratitude to Sangamitra Biswas at Westland and Manidipa Mandal for their exacting editing that has provided the book its shape.

In 2015, I wrote *The Crown Prince, The Gladiator and The Hope: Battle for Change*. I started the book as a journalist and ended it as a political activist. When I started writing this book, my third, I was a political activist and by the time I finished it I was a journalist once again. Life has come full circle. In this extraordinary journey, I would like to thank my family, friends and well-wishers for their support and love.

I could not end without a special thanks to Maneesha, my life partner and friend who is always the first reader and editor of my English writings. She painstakingly not only points out mistakes but also helps polish the language. Without her discipline, this book would not have been completed. I also sincerely want to thank all my friends, colleagues and family members who always put up with my eccentricities. And last but not the least I want to fondly acknowledge Billo, the newest member in my family who invariably sits in my lap when I sit down to write, and Mogu and Chhotu for their unconditional love.

www.ingramcontent.com/pod-product-compliance
Lightning Source LLC
LaVergne TN
LVHW010308070526
838199LV00065B/5481